Social and Cultural Lives of Immune Systems

Social and Cultural Lives of Immune Systems introduces a provocative new hypothesis in medico-social theory – the theory that immunity and disease are in part socially constituted, and that immune systems function not just as biological entities but also as symbolic concepts charged with political significance. Bridging elements of psychology, sociology, body theory, immunology, and medical anthropology, twelve papers from leading international scholars explicate some of the health-hazards of emotional and social pressure, whilst analyzing the semiotic and social responses to immunity and to imagery associated with it. Is it possible, as some experts now claim, that the terminology of immunity, dependent upon the defense of the self from invasion by an alien other, has entered modern consciousness to a point where it serves as a metaphor and indicator of wider political realities? If one's social status affects one's immune competence, can health interventions avoid taking poverty and discrimination into account? Can immunological rhetoric genuinely be shown to affect operations as diverse as military action, crime policy, and international food distribution? If this is the case, what conclusions can be drawn from the fact that tactics of disclosure, emotional openness, and inclusion are clinically proven to boost immunity, whereas division, denial, and containment – apparently modeled on the activities of immune cells – ironically raise susceptibility to disease?

Social and Cultural Lives of Immune Systems features contributions from David Napier, Emily Martin, Daniel E. Moerman, and others alongside critical data from trauma-writing interventions in the US and New Zealand, European drug trials, US clinical practice, and global fieldwork on stress, status, and cultural capital. Possibly the first cultural analysis of embodiment to give close attention to immune function, and certainly one of the first studies of immunology, disease, and healing to look seriously at concepts of the social self, it offers a comprehensive framework for future study in an exciting new area.

James M. Wilce Jr is Associate Professor of Anthropology at Northern Arizona University. He specializes in sociocultural perspectives on language, illness, and healing, and is author of *Eloquence in Trouble: Poetics and Politics of Complaint in Rural Bangladesh* (1998).

Theory and Practice in Medical Anthropology and
International Health
A series edited by Susan M. DiGiacomo
University of Massachusetts, Amherst

Social and Cultural Lives of Immune Systems

Edited by James M. Wilce Jr

Routledge
Taylor & Francis Group

LONDON AND NEW YORK

First published 2003
by Routledge
11 New Fetter Lane, London EC4P 4EE

Simultaneously published in the USA and Canada
by Routledge
29 West 35th Street, New York, NY 10001

Routledge is an imprint of the Taylor & Francis Group

Typeset in Times by
Florence Production Ltd, Stoodleigh, Devon
Printed and bound in Great Britain by
The Cromwell Press, Trowbridge, Wiltshire

British Library Cataloguing in Publication Data
A catalogue record for this book is available from the
British Library

Library of Congress Cataloging in Publication Data
Social and cultural lives of immune systems / edited by
  James M. Wilce, Jnr.
      p. cm. – (Theory and practice in medical anthropology
  and international health)
  Includes bibliographical references and index.
    1. Medical anthropology.   2. Immune system.   3. Culture –
  semiotic models.   4. Body, Human – Social aspects.   5. Body,
  Human – Symbolic aspects.   I. Wilce, James MacLynn, 1953– .
  II. Series.
  GN296.S613 2003
  306.4'61 – dc21   2002031935

ISBN 0–415–31004–0 (hbk)
ISBN 0–415–31005–9 (pbk)

Contents

Illustrations

Figures

Plates

Tables

Contributors

James M. Wilce Jr is Associate Professor of Anthropology at Northern Arizona University.

Roger J. Booth is Professor of Molecular Medicine and Pathology at The University of Auckland.

Richard Cone is Adjunct Professor of Biology at Johns Hopkins University.

Kathryn P. Davison works with Tonic Capital, 594 Broadway, Suite 309, New York 10012.

Seamus A. Decker is Visiting Lecturer in Anthropology at Yale University.

Barry G. England is Professor of Pathology, University of Michigan Hospitals, Ann Arbor.

Mark V. Flinn is Professor of Anthropology at University of Missouri, Columbia.

Laurence J. Kirmayer is Professor and Director of the Division of Social and Transcultural Psychiatry at McGill University.

Margot Lyon is Senior Lecturer in Anthropology at The Australian National University.

Samuel J. Mann is Associate Attending Physician and Associate Professor of Clinical Medicine at the Weil Medical College of Cornell University.

Emily Martin is Professor of Anthropology at New York University.

Thomas W. McDade is Assistant Professor of Anthropology at Northwestern University.

Daniel E. Moerman is Professor of Anthropology at the University of Michigan, Dearborn.

David Napier is Professor and Dana Faculty Fellow in Anthropology and Art at Middlebury College.

James W. Pennebaker is Professor of Psychology, University of Texas, Austin.

Laurie J. Price is Associate Professor and Chair of Anthropology at California State University, Hayward.

Carol M. Worthman is Professor and Chair of Anthropology at Emory University.

Acknowledgements

The chapters in this book are selected and revised from papers presented at panels (sharing their title with this book) at the 1997 meetings of the Society for Medical Anthropology (Seattle, March) and the American Anthropological Association (AAA; Washington, DC, November). The panels brought together psychologists, anthropologists, and immunologists interested in the relation of culture and social organization to notions of, and actual workings of, immune systems. Volume contributors Napier and Kirmayer offered comments on the AAA papers that were exceedingly helpful in moving the volume onward.

In a broad sense the ideas arose out of an accident – the fact that the editor encountered James Pennebaker's work during his graduate studies in anthropology at UCLA, a hotbed of interest in psychoneuroimmunology (PNI). In addition to Pennebaker, I received encouragement to bring about this sort of interdisciplinary rapprochement from contributor Daniel Moerman, who also convened the roundtable, "Placebo and Nocebo Effects: Developing a Research Agenda," sponsored by the Program in Alternative Medicine of the NIH, in Bethesda, December 1996 at which I was a rather passive participant. My work at the intersection of culture and PNI has also been encouraged over the years by my colleagues in Arizona – Heidi Wayment and Steven Barger at NAU, and Steve Hoffman at ASU. In the years since the 1997 panels that gave rise to these papers, our series editor Susan DiGiacomo has given constant support, for which we are all grateful.

A version of Daniel Moerman's chapter appeared in *Medical Anthropology Quarterly* (*14*(1), 2000). We are grateful to the American Anthropological Association for permission to include it here.

A version of Cone and Martin's chapter appeared in *The Visible Woman*, edited by Paula Treichler and Constance Penley. We are grateful to NYU Press for permission to reprint this revision here.

Finally, Julene Knox at Routledge has rallied the resources of the press and guided the book into paper. Thank you, Julene.

Chapter 1

Introduction

Social and cultural lives of immune systems in a semiotic universe

James M. Wilce Jr

Human immune systems evolve and function in social contexts. Cultures formulate varying representations of immunity and health, and such cultural concepts might well have feedback effects on immune function. Thus "immune systems" have social and cultural lives. To say this is simply to remind ourselves that human immune systems are human. Like all aspects of our bodies, our immune systems are embedded in sociocultural life, and this book's contributors illustrate that claim in rich and varied ways. They face squarely the paradox evoked by the title: to label something a "system" is to attribute to it a large degree of autonomy, but this autonomy, according to these essays, is a chimera.[1] These authors reassert the social ontology, the social and cultural lives, of immune systems. Not only this; they challenge the autonomy of the psyche in "psychoneuroimmunology." Thus, for example, most of our contributors reflect on local forms of "stress" – or simply "cortisol response"[2] – and "social support" (McDade, this volume), forms whose significance is always relative to local sociocultural realities.

Thus, taken together, these chapters reinsert immune systems and psyches in their social and cultural contexts. Why is this necessary? Health scientists admit, without controversy, that epidemics are social events; but, beyond the recognition of infection's social context, when have culture, society, and immune systems appeared, intertwined, within the pages of a single book? This volume brings together disciplines that are barely on speaking terms. It does so by bringing together authors from disciplines – anthropology, psychology, immunology, and psychiatry – whose practitioners usually ignore one another. This coming together was face-to-face before it was in cover-to-cover (book) form. It results from two panels in 1997 – one at the spring meetings of the Society for Medical Anthropology in Seattle, the other at the fall meetings of the American Anthropological Association.

This book not only brings authors together across disciplines; it also reorganizes previous cross-disciplinary dialogues that were differently hyphenated, as Lyon notes in her chapter. So, for example, biological-anthropologists[3] have studied variability in immune-related markers across different populations, but seldom attended to cultural themes; and rarely have sociocultural anthropologists paid much attention to biological measures. Recently, when culture theorists have engaged the topic of immunology, it has often been to subject it to a kind of deconstructionist discourse analysis – very useful, but not the same as engaging it on its own terms, as the anthropological contributors have done here.[4] Kirmayer and Pennebaker, on the other hand, are among the few psychiatrists and health-psychologists – and Booth is among the few immunologists – who are grappling with the fundamentally comparative social and cultural issues that occupy anthropologists.

Social and Cultural Lives of Immune Systems builds bridges, and the disciplinary divides it spans are sometimes thorny. Bridge-building takes courage and hard work. No true dialogue – least of all ours – represents unanimity. Still, each of these chapters engages common themes and uses disciplinary concepts and terms perhaps unfamiliar to the audiences for which each of us usually writes. We are, that is, learning each other's languages. The results are heartening. Two contributors – immunologist Cone and anthropologist Martin co-author a chapter that is itself a dialogue between their two disciplines. They find, of all things, the political economy of global food distribution to be a common interest. Such are the fruits of dialogue across disciplines with very different epistemological traditions. Such dialogue finds different manifestations in each of the book's four parts. In this introduction I offer my semiotic perspectives on the dialogue and its results.

Part I

Part I opens up some of the theoretical issues that arise in trying to bring anthropology into a close encounter with psychoneuroimmunology (PNI). Both fields struggle to find a model for relating bodies, illness, health, emotions, and sociocultural contexts – and particularly one that avoids Cartesian dualism.

Among contributors are some long-time collaborators. Pennebaker, Booth, and Davison have in the past collaborated in research in New Zealand and the US. Pennebaker's chapter summarizes a lifetime of work, work that provided the original impetus for this volume (see the editor's introduction to Pennebaker's chapter). Pennebaker describes *Homo sapiens* as one of many species curious about its environment; but our species is uniquely occupied with forming coherent *narratives* in and about that potentially chaotic environment – about war, divorce, or job loss, for instance. Pennebaker amasses a wealth of evidence that the human body suffers from active suppression of distressing memories of trauma and finds relief – mediated by immune functions – when that distress is put in words. But not just any words seem to help survivors of trauma; what helps is to develop, over time, a coherent narrative version of the traumatizing event (Brison 1999).

In contrast with Mann's, Pennebaker's model does not involve the Freudian unconscious. Pennebaker's writing interventions aim to help research subjects to find narrative organization for traumas of which they are already aware. However, among his studies of trauma and their health effects, one in particular pursued the role of early traumas in major illness later in life (Pennebaker and Susman 1988). Those illnesses included high blood pressure and cancer. The traumas were previously undisclosed rather than unconscious; however, their discovery of the ill-effects of very old traumas (from childhood in some cases) on adult health and immune function finds echoes in chapters herein by Mann, Decker *et al.*, and Flinn and England.

Pennebaker found that those who put traumatic experience into words derive benefits measured in clinical and laboratory (immunological) terms. The question is whether those benefits are cross-culturally variable, and indeed whether human biologies are variable, as Lock has proposed (1998).[5] Pennebaker points to evidence of the universality of the benefit derived by those who "put their stress into words." Booth and Davison find that the distribution of benefits is unequal and, in part, culturally determined. Pennebaker, Booth, and Davison share much in common; they employ similar immunological and linguistic measures (in the analysis of narratives). But, in Booth and Davison's small study of "writing stress" carried out among three ethnic groups of medical students in New Zealand – Caucasians, Polynesians, and Asians – the benefits of "writing stress" patterned according to ethnicity. Indeed, Wilce and Price argue that we must expect such benefits to vary cross-culturally. Their argument hinges on concepts of metaphor and embodiment. They propose that the notion of putting stress into words is a metaphor, one that "works" – as in Pennebaker's empirical observations – where it is shared. This is but one example of the embodiment of culture (a theme of Kirmayer's chapter as well). But Wilce and Price provide ethnographic evidence that the peoples of the world might embody differing cultural metaphors. Although new PNI research would be needed to test their hypothesis, the logic of such embodiment leads them to expect socially variable immune responses to disease, responses reflecting variable cultural metaphors. Lyon, the final contributor to this section, challenges psycho-neuroimmunology to incorporate deeper, i.e. more social and hermeneutical, visions of emotion.

Wilce and Price – like other contributors to this volume (particularly Napier and Kirmayer) reflect the tendency of North American anthropology to embrace "culture" – most often defined in terms of shared meanings and values – as a key explanatory term. Culture, in North American "cultural anthropology," is about meaning[6] contributor Moerman proposes, for example, to replace talk of "placebo effects" with "meaning effects" (this volume; Moerman and Jonas 2002). Culture in this anthropological tradition consists of notions, including "popular notions of the self" (Wilce and Price). By contrast, "social anthropology" – best represented in universities in the UK and Australia (where Lyon teaches) – places a greater emphasis on social structure. Despite this difference, both anthropological traditions have noted global diversity in conceptions of the self (Carrithers, Lukes, and Collins 1985; Harris 1989; Heelas and Lock 1981).

The problem of the self is relevant enough to immunological discourse to merit special attention here. In all of her writings, including her contribution herein, social anthropologist Margot Lyon examines how such fundamentally social phenomena as the co-presence of bodies affects bodily functions (including breathing, Lyon 1994). She shares with many cultural anthropologists a skepticism toward reading individualistic notions of self into this book's focal phenomenon, psychoneuroimmunology. "The conventional rhetoric of immunology has tended to place emphasis on understanding how immune function is ultimately concerned with the determination of 'self' as opposed to 'not self,'" even as most anthropologists work to deconstruct this metaphor.[7] Among this book's multiple audiences, immunologists and psychologists might find any anthropological deconstruction of "the self" – and particularly the self/nonself distinction favored by Burnet (1959) and followers – less familiar than its relative acceptance by Booth and Davison (this volume),[8] though even among immunologists doubts about the utility of this self/nonself metaphor are increasing (Tauber 2000). Our readers may perceive some real differences in the perspectives of those two chapters, for example. Yet we exaggerate tension between the two positions if we make them into straw men. In fact both are exceedingly nuanced. Tauber (1995) explores how deeply the metaphor – or theory – of the "immune self"[9] pervades immunology as it emerged after Darwin starting with the work of nineteenth-century Russian zoologist and pioneering immunologist Elie Metchnikoff. The immune self metaphor flowered in the writings of Frank M. Burnet (1959). As depicted by Tauber, this immune self is so dynamic, so dialectically related to its environment, that we would be hard put to accuse immunologists of reifying this "self" or projecting a Western notion of a tightly bounded or individuated self onto the immune system. Perhaps "the immune self" is a reification of this dynamic relationship; but cultural anthropologists representing the discourse on this immune self might in fact tend to reify what can be a very nuanced conceptualization of self–other dynamics in immunology. Nor should we speak of a single, simple (even "deconstructionist") anthropological approach to selfhood.[10] This volume – chapters by Lyon and Kirmayer in particular – go well beyond such oversimplified representations of academic others, again opening the domain to a true dialogue.

Lyon prioritizes social over cognitive and symbolic analyses, while other chapters (e.g. Pennebaker, Mann) explore imaginal cognitive processes as social products in themselves (e.g. Wilce and Price, Napier, and Kirmayer). This reflects, in part, the differences between social and cultural anthropology. But, rather than highlight such divides, I would propose a higher-level theory of communication, signification, meaning, or metaphor – more precisely, a semiotic theory – that might transcend our differences. Semiotics, the study of signs and their physical vehicles (Peirce 1931–1958; Hoffmeyer

1996; Sebeok 1991), offers a unique perspective on all sorts of relations – among signs, among living things, or (to mention a more specific example) between living things like sunflowers and the sun.[11] Perhaps only by way of analogy with the form of semiosis or sign-making most familiar to us (i.e. human language-use), we can call sign relations "relations of meaning." But the study of "meaning" need not entail the study of "symbols" – those particular signs (embodied in various material vehicles such as audible language, visible art, etc.) that human groups use, quite arbitrarily, to represent whatever they are felt to designate. "Symbols" represent one semiotic phenomenon, one that is irrelevant to large swaths of the universe we inhabit, despite its relevance to human language. The social, interpersonal, and interbodily relations that Lyon claims as relevant to emotion and PNI are semiotic processes in that they involve the exchange of signs. The particular socioemotional processes she explores – conditioning, habit, mimesis, and emotional contagion – do not involve conscious exchange of linguistic symbols. But they are no less semiotic. Mimesis – a kind of "iconicity" (signification by resemblance of the sign and the object)[12] – and emotional contagion work through exchanges of signs. These exchanges are tacit but essential to the processes Lyon describes.

A semiotic perspective on Booth and Davison's chapter is particularly useful. In situating immune function within broader human and social contexts, Booth and Davison invoke a concept that Booth proposed a decade ago – the model of teleological coherence or harmony of purpose. This model reflects an engagement with European biosemiotics, the study of sign systems found in all life forms, whether cell-level biochemical exchange or the scent-marking, calls, and cries of animals (Uexküll 1907 and Uexküll 1993). We must understand teleological coherence on semiotic terms. That is, if, as Booth has long argued, psychoneural and immune systems share common goals (coherence, harmony of purpose) in "maintaining a self-identity" (Booth and Ashbridge 1993: 11),[13] there must be communication – and thus a semiotic system that is at least partially shared – across systems within a person or other organism (especially psychoneural and immune systems), communication that facilitates identity-maintenance.[14]

To open up this issue of semiosis or communication within the organism has the advantage of establishing for use a common metalanguage – a way of describing languages or codes – which we can use to make higher level links. That is, once we join Nobel laureate immunologist N. K. Jerne (1985) in speaking of the "language" or communicative code of the immune system itself, and between immunological entities and mind, we will find it easier to accommodate interpersonal communication in language or other sorts of systems in a social model of psychoimmune function.[15] If we envision immune systems as well as persons and societies all functioning in a semiotic world, we might more easily grasp what narrative might have to do with health and immunocompetence in Pennebaker's findings. Booth and Davison have made this easier by invoking the major histocompatibility complex (MHC) molecules as a key example of their harmony-of-purpose model. These MHC molecules,[16] whose task it is to carry antigens to T lymphocytes, are sign vehicles. The semiotic term "vehicle" takes on a semi-literal sense in the role MHC molecules play in binding processed antigens and presenting them to the T-cells.

We are arguing that microbiological material carries significance. And that significance can be not only intraorganismic but social. These very sign vehicles can carry significance *between* animals, humans included. Mate selection in several species seems influenced by odor preferences, and MHC molecules are a key part of what animals smell and respond to. MHC-based mate selection preferences generally lead to pairs with dissimilar MHC – evidently an advantage. Granted animal "scents," by contrast with our "sense," may seem a "primitive" level of social semiosis.[17] The important point here, however, is that social and cultural lives *always* entail exchanges of signs, and those signs are always packaged in material forms. The sound waves that bear spoken language are physical signs, as are MHC molecules. Biomaterials constituting immune systems – entities like immunoglobulins measured by McDade (this volume) and the interleukins measured by Flinn and England (this volume) – play complex roles in social lives of humans and other animals. Put differently, many sign-vehicles that help maintain self-identity – which Booth and Davison stress as a key function of the immune system – have significant functions in social cohesion or attunement as well.

Let us turn the relationship around. We have started from the microsigns of biomaterial and argued for their social significance. Looking at the relationship from the other end, social life entails exchanging signs. And those signs, in turn, create other signs.[18] Complementarity between MHC/HLA molecules can evidently facilitate sexual attraction; in this case, the simple conjunction of two sets of MHC, two low-level signs, is interpreted in terms of a more abstract sign, something like "eligible partner." At the level of our complex but nonetheless familiar lives, in intimate relationships the exchange of relatively simple signs – say, the exchange of angry words (none of which would necessarily mean much on its own) in a marital argument signal something new. Little signs – separate words, coming together in a context (situational and grammatical) – thus form a higher-level, more abstract sign, "relationship troubles." For all its abstractness, such a sign nonetheless has a very concrete, embodied set of immunological outcomes (Kiecolt-Glaser *et al.* 1987). These relations among signs – and particularly, meta-signs like "x is a stressful sign" – are, in human beings, always mediated by cultures. In fact, cultures are grand sign systems, conventions guiding the exchange and interpretation of signs of all sorts, from sneezing to laying on of hands.[19]

The significance of this semiotic perspective holds across a diversity of perspectives and unites them. If, with Lyon, we are inclined to look at

behavior and social structure as key determinants of the relations that constitute PNI, then we look beyond cultural values and images to more implicit
connections between agents, emotions, and immunocompetence, like "emotional contagion." This term (Hatfield, Cacioppo, and Rapson 1994)
encompasses widely described findings of exquisite (but largely unconscious)
synchrony between persons as they interact with each other (Russell *et al.*
1980). Interactants exchange signs of many kinds – visible, audible, and
perhaps others – that enable such synchrony. What potentiates synchrony is
a rapid and subliminal exchange of cues, signs, or signals. But synchrony
itself becomes a sign of being "in tune" (Wilce in press), which can in turn
be a sign of "social safety and comfort." The consequences of such emotions
– healthy and even transformative (Napier, this volume) or unhealthy in
immunological and clinical outcomes – are thus signs, too, with material
aspects, e.g. levels of salivary cortisol.

Part II

Part II, "PNI in the wild" offers healthy doses of theory but also the sorts of
data necessary to demonstrate the viability of rethinking psychoneuroimmunology in the context of cultural diversity. Anthropologists often work
in settings where few psychologists have ventured – hence the section's title
– but rarely do they combine lab work with such fieldwork. The teams of
authors represented in Part II are exceptions. The collaboration between
Pennebaker, Booth, and Davison is paralleled by that between the three
lead authors of the chapters constituting Part II – Flinn, Decker, and McDade.
And so this is a very coherent trio of chapters. Taking stress-hormonal and
immunological measures during social-anthropological fieldwork is quite
without parallel. The contributors to Part II find variation in current status
and in childhood stress correlated with variability of subjects' immune
function, shedding light on how different forms of status might or might not
buffer stress.

Just what sort of status is most relevant to immune function, presumably
mediating the impact of stress, is a question to which Decker *et al.* and
McDade present different answers. McDade's findings in Samoa – linking
higher SES with greater resiliency in, or resistance to, the stresses associated
with bereavement and the challenge of financing *faalavelave* ceremonies –
resonate with our intuitions about the relatively easy life of those with greater
wealth. Decker *et al.* cite evidence for either an inverse relationship (in others'
studies that found higher SES correlating with higher "stress," or at least
higher salivary cortisol levels) or – in their own study – a lack of any association between SES and salivary cortisol.[20] This raises issues about what
"stress" actually is, issues on which Napier's chapter reflects in detail. But
chapters in Part II also raise important issues about the workings of human
societies, the role of culture, and the means by which sociocultural realities

affect immune function. They build their models on ample empirical evidence regarding social structure, but empiricism alone cannot account for their evidence. Their models, which supplement SES data with evidence of social actors' *perception* of others and of shared ideals (Dressler and Bindon 2000), and their recursive perception of others' perceptions of them, account for interpersonal variability in stress response better than any model that attempted to correlate stress more directly with social structure or SES.

These chapters thus demonstrate the key role cultures play in mediating the perception of stress and coping with it. They contribute, therefore, to a view of human PNI responses as, in part, cultural products. And they lend themselves to the sort of multilayered semiotic framework that, I argue, best reveals the unity of our work. Signs of childhood distress persist into adulthood. At that point, the sort of status that matters most, at least in Decker's findings, is the manifesting of signs of living according to the shared values of a local moral community. Both the emotions "stored up" from childhood and the adult patterns of action assigned different values in local moral universes are signs in local semiotic worlds and affect cortisol levels as independent variables, apart from signs of wealth and economic status.

Part III

Part II represents traditional anthropological fieldwork, if by traditional we mean fieldwork in small-scale or face-to-face societies, work characterized by intensive observation in a small community.[21] Anthropology tries to make the so-called exotic more familiar. Part II tells First World readers that stress is very much at home among the Dominican Bwa Mawego and Samoans. But the other side of its agenda, more in focus in Part III, is to exoticize the familiar – to uncover the workings of culture among people close to "home" (home to author and many readers) and demonstrate that it is not only Others who "have culture." Anthropologists with this agenda have at times turned for inspiration to Freud, whose *Civilization and Its Discontents* is evoked in the title of Part III. Part III points to the workings of culture among partici-pants in clinical drug trials in Europe (Moerman) and in the political economies that affect food distribution and patterns of allergy in complex societies around the world (Cone and Martin). First, however, it argues that any adequate model of PNI and stress must follow Freud's gaze into the unconscious. Part III opens with a chapter highlighting the lessons offered to PNI by the study and treatment of hypertension.

At first glance, a chapter on hypertension seems somewhat out of place in a volume on immune systems in sociocultural perspective. However, Mann writes from decades of experience combining cardiology with psycho-analysis to offer recommendations for the field of psychoneuroimmunology. Mann's psychoanalytically-informed clinical studies of chronic high blood pressure cases offer unique grounds for his argument that PNI needs to take unconscious stress much more seriously than it has to date. Mann shares with Pennebaker and Booth and Davison some of the perspectives common in health psychology, while challenging others. They believe that what eats us from the inside – to give concreteness to the metaphoric notion of damaging stress that pervades popular and academic understandings in the US – needs resolving through verbal expression. And they both rely on measures of personality and coping style used widely by health psychologists. Some people cope with stress by repressing it. Pennebaker (this volume) has investigated the role of this "repressive coping style" – in which a given participant's writing about a self-selected traumatic event evinces little or no traumatic emotion (and the person receives little or no benefit from the intervention).

In anthropology – and psychology, for that matter – psychoanalytic approaches have gone in (e.g. Devereaux 1967) and out (e.g. Kleinman and Becker 1998) of fashion. However, most anthropologists recognize various levels of awareness, and the largely unconscious nature of human motivation (Giddens 1979). Such a recognition is important to the critique of rationalism in the western tradition that Freud began and anthropology has continued. It underlies the practice theory[22] on which Decker *et al.* draw (this volume) as well as the theory of embodiment pursued by various contributors, particularly Lyon. A recognition of the long-term effects of childhood trauma, likewise, underlies the chapters by Flinn and England and Decker *et al.*

Mann's chapter raises questions about repressive coping style but also about ethnicity and class. Why do African-Americans experience relatively high rates of hypertension? This question has also occupied anthropologists like Dressler (1996). Mann's model of essential hypertension foregrounds the role of long-term unconscious trauma. This thread runs throughout Mann's argument, whether or not he is addressing the differential interethnic distribution of disease; but he applies a psychoanalytic model to the racial gap in rates of hypertension as well, attributing high rates among black Americans to childhood trauma. There are other ways to understand the higher rates of hypertension among African-Americans, such as anthropologist William Dressler's model, which highlights the inability of many African-Americans to achieve the material and social desiderata stipulated in widely shared cultural models of success. That is, they cannot achieve cultural consonance, and this failure is itself a major source of stress (Dressler and Bindon 2000; see also Decker *et al.*, this volume, and McDade, this volume). Further, even though black children may, in fact, be more likely to suffer child abuse than are other children, it is crucial to keep in mind the larger sociocultural context in which the abuse would occur. For instance, Socha *et al.* (1995) argue that it is precisely *distressed* parents in distressed communities (including African-American communities) who lean toward punitive and coercive means of control or discipline at home. They argue, in fact, that such disciplinary styles have constituted a survival mechanism for such communities.

The particular studies surveyed by Mann grab our attention. Why are bus drivers in California's Bay Area who suffer from hypertension *less* likely than their counterparts with normal BP to report high stress (Winkelby, Ragland, and Syme 1988)? These bus drivers – hypertensive or not – may well be predominantly African-American (Kaponda 2001). Mann cites evidence that "African-Americans who had hypertension were *less* likely to report being victims of discrimination than those with a normal blood pressure (Krieger and Sidney 1996)."[23] How shall we interpret this finding? One possibility is that Krieger and Sidney's research subjects who reported being victims also resisted discrimination and thus tended to avoid chronic victimization. From the perspective of health psychology, "assertive" verbal action, in this case naming (recognizing) and resisting discrimination, brings health benefits whenever it functions like the verbal "assertion" of one's feelings about trauma (Pennebaker, this volume). By contrast, one of the clearest conclusions of Pennebaker's many investigations is that those who are constantly aware of, and may "complain" about, the stressors in their lives derive no health benefit (e.g. in lower BP). So, neither repressive copers nor individuals with high scores for "Negative Affect" (those who are "excessively" aware of distress) experience health benefits from their complaining or repressing. Winkelby's hypertensive bus drivers and the African-Americans who *reported* less discrimination (Krieger and Sidney 1996) might be those who would also score high in repressive coping style.

The previous paragraph differs little from the standard PNI literature. We must go further. Whatever we say about the individual health costs or benefits of one style of coping or another, we are on unavoidably *political* ground. To explore that ground befits an inquiry into the social and cultural lives of immune systems. The stakes in studies like Krieger and Sidney's spill out beyond psychology theory to enter the sociopolitical realm. In fact, Krieger and Sidney frame their own conclusions in terms of the damaging effects of discrimination.[24] When they report the costs of discrimination and the possible health benefits of resistance, they do so with a recognition of their own engagement in a political field of action. From the vantage point of this book, a complete social account of health – from the epidemiology of hypertension to the social lives of immune systems – must include an account of the politics of health and of PNI. Even if some contributors tentatively accept the apparent individualism of the health psychology model of stress, coping, and disclosure, the chapters as a whole contribute to a holistic and reflective sociopolitical awareness of the context of health, immune function, and the discourse of PNI.

Moerman's chapter raises the crucial question of placebo effects in relation to culture. He explores fascinating cross-national differences in placebo-controlled trials of remedies for hypertension, Generalized Anxiety Disorder, and ulcer disease. Although we lack the evidence we would need to confirm the bacterial causation of all ulcers, and thus to confirm a PNI-based explanation of "spontaneous remission" or cure by placebo, Moerman at least raises the possibility that cultural differences mediate PNI effects. Such an interpretation fits his evidence. Moerman's chapter exemplifies a culturalist approach in anthropology. For Moerman, culture is neither a "space" in which all members of a population move about, nor a frame shared equally by all who may claim participation in it. This is apparent in his representation of a study involving Chinese-Americans (Phillips, Ruth, and Wagner 1993), whose American world is not the heartland of Chinese culture per se, and amongst whom there are wide differences in degrees of identification with "traditional Chinese culture." Yet, after admitting the significance of intra-cultural variation, Moerman still asserts the explanatory power of culture per se. Why should the placebo effect vary so much from nation to nation in randomized controlled trials of medicines for ulcers, etc.? Moerman proposes that cultures, as systems of meaning, make the difference.

The final chapter in this section, Cone and Martin's, links an anthropological analysis of the social distribution of allergies and the global circulation of food to an immunologist's account of how allergies (with their strong auto-immune dimensions) are caused and prevented. The political-economic contexts affect immune function in individuals and whole populations as they are affected by food and its international distribution; thus the political is even more clearly topical in Cone and Martin's chapter than in Mann's. And the political economy of food distribution is bound up with the question of variation in human patterns of adaptation – biological but also cultural – in a particularly interesting way. It is not that the culture concept plays a major role in Cone and Martin's chapter; they do not speak of "local cultures."[25] But global capitalism is a (recent) cultural invention, and most anthropologists consign to the realm of culture the production, distribution, preparation, and consumption of food. We can infer from Cone and Martin's account that such food systems, until now quite local, have co-evolved with local populations and immune systems that also seem to vary from place to place (or food-culture to food-culture). In fact, food sciences and human biology – or at least those practitioners whom the corporate giants of the global food industry have employed to legitimize their growing influence – might have underplayed the degree to which human adaptation is local. Individuals and local populations might be so adapted to the particulars of local foods that the increasing homogenization of food cultures through globalization of food distribution and consumption[26] destabilizes immune function. And, since even recent models (Tauber 2000) see the immune functions as a coherent, homeostatic system, such destabilization is dangerous. Here we have immune systems participating actively in a sociocultural life in which they adapt, face challenges, and try to re-adapt. And this sociocultural life –

the life-context in which food is produced and consumed – is, once again, unavoidably political.

Part IV

The chapters by Napier and Kirmayer cap the book with "Critical Retrospectives."[27] Napier asks how we can understand the contexts of immune function without grappling with human experience in its own terms. It is in richly variable human subjectivities that we see the stamp of cultural systems of meaning, and the roots of the emotional processes that must lie at the heart of an adequate theory of PNI. In invoking the category of "experience," Napier raises the issue of epistemology lurking at the edges of other contributors' discourse. How can scientists of different disciplines find common ways of knowing the context of immune function – or, in terms more familiar to social scientists, knowing the context of human life, health, and illness? How to reconcile bench science with fieldwork, experimentation with experience, the nomothetic with the idiographic? To the extent that this book answers the question, it does so in many voices. The contributors lead us to encounter body and society in new ways, resisting dualisms not only of mind and body or of biology and psychology – this much has been common in psychoneuroimmunological theory – but of individual and group, biology and sociology, body and culture.

The interplay of body and culture is a central theme for Kirmayer. Recognizing embodiment as a complex phenomenon comprised at least of phenomenological, biological, and political dimensions, Kirmayer finds this volume contributing to three (trans-)disciplinary languages necessary to address embodiment. Those are psychophysiology, sociophysiology, and an ethnography of those discursive practices whose power helps constitute shared notions of immune systems. Psychophysiology – the domain of expertise underlying chapters by Pennebaker, Mann, Moerman, and Booth and Davison – is a sourcebook for many of the other chapters and the target of critique in a few. The three chapters constituting Part II (by lead authors Flinn, Decker, and McDade) break new ground toward what Kirmayer calls a sociophysiology of the responsiveness of bodies (and immune systems) to various forms of social status and stress. Discursive practices – from naming new immunological entities (Cambrosio and Keating 1992) to artistic renderings of "lower" immune entities as "drudges" in women's shoes – are political-and-semiotic acts. Contributor Emily Martin (1994) is a pioneer in the kind of critical analysis that deconstructs the signs – linguistic and graphic – used in the science of immunology, signs that help reproduce structures of social and economic power. Chapters herein by Cone and Martin, Napier, and Wilce and Price explore the manifestations of power – the power of images, meta-images, or of consumer capitalism as a rapidly spreading global system – not only in popular discourses *about* immune systems but in various forms of embodiment.

Together with our readers, who will answer these essays in their own ways – medical practitioners, immunologists, social scientists, and others – we hope to move the interdisciplinary dialogue forward. This volume represents a start.

Notes

1 We are reminded that the concept of immune entities functioning together, and the term "immune system," are both recent (as Booth and Davison mention, this volume). And, for a deconstructionist history of "the immune system" as a discourse category co-invented (at least in popular consciousness) by mass media, see Martin 1994.

2 Stress might indeed be a black box. To avoid the problem of defining such a term, Flinn (this volume) operationalizes it in biochemical terms as "the cortisol response." Black box or not, however, the term *stress* or *setres* has a life of its own, not only in American public culture but, as an English loanword in Javanese, in Indonesia (see Wilce and Price, this volume). Public circulation of signs (including keywords) pertaining to immunology is one dimension of the socio-cultural lives of immune systems.

3 Admittedly the term usually appears without hyphens.

4 Deconstructionist perspectives on immunology – including important work by Haraway (1993) and volume-contributor Martin (1994) – are acknowledged by Lyon (this volume).

5 Lock supports this claim with evidence of the profound variability of the experience of menopause in Japan and the West.

6 I am by no means claiming to adequately represent contemporary North American anthropologists, many of whom draw their theory from the UK and continental Europe and whose work on embodiment leads them away from intellectualist, cognitivist, or notional definitions of culture.

7 Wilce (1998) reviews the anthropological literature that problematizes a bounded self.

8 Cone and Martin (this volume) also devote a great amount of attention to the "immune self" and its need to distinguish self from nonself, though Martin's deconstructionist aims on those boundaries surface in her other writing.

9 Recently (2000), Tauber has reflected on the growing shift in immunology *away from* the metaphor of the immune self.

10 "The anthropological position" regarding cross-cultural variability in "the self" defies characterization, since it ranges from the deconstructionist to the relativist to the universalist. For a nuanced view by two psychoanalytically trained anthropologists, see Spiro 1993 and Hollan 1992.

11 The sunflower example is Peirce's (1931–1958: I.274). Sunflowers become representamens (like signs, but lacking a mental element per se) by passing on to their offspring a certain way of orienting themselves toward the sun. The sun is the orienting object here. For further discussion, see http://suo.ieee.org/ontology/msg03069.html

12 This definition of icon, and my semiotic perspective in general, reflects the parlance of American philosopher Charles Peirce more than any other source of semiotic theory.

13 If we prefer Jerne's (1985) scientific deconstruction of "the immune self," we are still left with a need to maintain homeostasis (Tauber 2000).

14 Jerne's model of immune function, which renders unnecessary the metaphor of the immune self, relies rather on a vision of "intricately balanced feedback loops" whose "perturbation" "would trigger immune responsiveness" (Tauber 2000: 243).

15 This is not to say that the linguistic metaphor fits this object (the workings of the immune system) very well. Language simply becomes the default example of semiosis to humans who rely on it so much, and thus a useful starting point if it is not taken as a perfect analogy.

16 In human biology MHC molecules are called HLA loci.

17 And humans do not often like thinking of themselves being influenced by smells in the way animals are.

18 In Charles Peirce's semiotics, the relationship between a sign and an object entails a new sign, an interpretant. For a sunflower to face the sun and in some sense reflect it causes it to be a sort of interpretant of the sun. To the extent that reading this sentence results in a concept in your mind, it is an interpretant – not an interpretation but a kind of metasign or countersign – of the original sentence.

19 This discussion should not be taken to imply that stimuli are only stressful to people when filtered through higher level conceptual signs. Noise and shouting are probably somewhat stressful outside the context of something interpretable as an "argument," in the absence of any angry intent. What I am arguing is that, especially when we are talking about culture, signs consistently beget other signs, and that some stress can come from an interpretation of events that is likely to have the force of a judgment by a reference group. Marital arguments can spawn just such signs – fears of the significance of the event to the couple and to others. And Part II is filled with evidence that perceptions of one's own conduct and status, and guesses about others' perceptions, do affect empirically measurable levels of stress.

20 The particular socioemotional processes Lyon explores in particular for their potential utility in rethinking PNI – conditioning, habit, mimesis, and emotional contagion – could help model the link described in Part II (especially Decker *et al.*) between interpersonally variable levels of social approval and PNI-relevant measures including cortisol and EBV antibody titers.

21 In fact even McDade's work, represented in that section, is broader – spanning 14 villages in Samoa – than Flinn's or Decker's.

22 Practice theory (Giddens 1979, Bourdieu 1977) tries to transcend the older sociological understandings that social structure somehow pre-exists and predetermines social action, positing instead a dialectic between agency and structure.

23 The emphasis is mine.

24 On this point, see my editor's note in Mann's chapter.

25 They do situate food in the context of cultural meanings. See their note 10.

26 Clearly homogenization is only one dimension of globalization, typically crosscut by unique local patterns of cultural hybridity (Inda and Rosaldo 2002).

27 These capstone chapters arise out of comments which these two contributors prepared as discussants at the 1997 American Anthropological Association panel.

References

Booth, R. J. and Ashbridge, K. R. (1993). A fresh look at the relationship between the psyche and immune system: teleological coherence and harmony of purpose. *Advances, The Journal of Mind-Body Health, 9*(2), 4–23.

Bourdieu, P. (1977 [1972]). *Outline of a theory of practice* (R. Nice, trans., vol. 16). Cambridge: Cambridge University Press.

Brison, S. J. (1999). Trauma narratives and the remaking of the self. In M. Bal, J. Crew, and L. Spitzer (eds), *Acts of memory: cultural recall in the present* (pp. 39–54). Hanover, NH: University Press of New England/Dartmouth College.

Burnet, F. M. (1959). *The clonal selection theory of acquired immunity*. Nashville: Vanderbilt University Press.

Cambrosio, A. and Keating, P. (1992). A matter of FACSP: constituting novel entities in immunoogy. *Medical Anthropology Quarterly*, 6(4), 362–384.

Carrithers, M., Lukes, S., and Collins, S. (eds) (1985). *The category of the person*. Cambridge: Cambridge University Press.

Devereaux, G. (1967). *From anxiety to method in the behavioral sciences*. The Hague: Mouton.

Dressler, W. W. (1996). Hypertension in the African American community: social, cultural, and psychological factors. [Review] [52 refs]. *Seminars in Nephrology*, 16(2), 71–82.

—— and Bindon, J. R. (2000). The health consequences of cultural consonance: cultural dimensions of lifestyle, social support, and arterial blood pressure in an African American community. *American Anthropologist*, 102(2), 244–260.

Giddens, A. (1979). *Central problems in social theory: action, structure and contradiction in social analysis*. Berkeley and Los Angeles: University of California Press.

Haraway, D. (1993). The biopolitics of postmodern bodies: determinations of self in immune system discourse. In S. Lindenbaum and M. Lock (eds), *Knowledge, power, and practice: the anthropology of medicine and everyday life* (pp. 364–410). Berkeley: University of California Press.

Harris, G. G. (1989). Concepts of individual, self, and person in description and analysis. *American Anthropologist*, 91(3), 599–612.

Hatfield, E., Cacioppo, J. T., and Rapson, R. L. (1994). *Emotional contagion*. Cambridge: Cambridge University Press.

Heelas, P. and Lock, A. (eds) (1981). *Indigenous psychologies: the anthropology of the self*. London/New York: Academic Press.

Hoffmeyer, J. (1996). *Signs of meaning in the universe* (B. J. Haveland, trans.). Bloomington: Indiana University Press.

Hollan, D. (1992). Cross-cultural differences in the self. *Journal of Anthropological Research*, 48(4), 283–300.

Inda, J. X. and Rosaldo, R. (eds) (2002). *The anthropology of globalization: a reader*. Malden/Oxford: Blackwell Publishers.

Jerne, N. K. (1985). The generative grammar of the immune system. *Bioscience Reports*, 5(6), 439–451.

Kaponda. (May 29, 2001). 20,000 gone: Stop the exodus. *Poor magazine online*. http://www.poormagazine.com/index.cfm?L1=news&category=37&story=341

Kiecolt-Glaser, J. K., Fisher, L. D., Ogrocki, P., Stout, J. C., Speicher, C. E., and Glaser, R. (1987). Marital quality, marital disruption, and immune function. *Psychosomatic Medicine*, 49(1), 13–34.

Kleinman, A., and Becker, A. E. (1998). "Sociosomatics": The contributions of anthropology to psychosomatic medicine. *Psychosomatic Medicine*, 60(4), 389–393.

Krieger, N. and Sidney, S. (1996). Racial discrimination and blood pressure: the CARDIA study of young black and white adults. *American Journal of Public Health*, *86*(10), 1370–1378.

Lock, M. (1998). Menopause: lessons from anthropology. *Psychosomatic Medicine*, *60*(4) (Special Issue: Cross-Cultural Research)), 410–419.

Lyon, M. L. (1994). Emotion as mediator of somatic and social processes: the example of respiration. In W. Wentworth and J. Ryan (eds), *Social perspectives on emotion* (vol. 2, pp. 83–108). Greenwich, CT: JAI Press.

Martin, E. (1994). *Flexible bodies: the role of immunity in American culture from the days of polio to the age of AIDS*. Boston: Beacon.

Moerman, D. E. and Jonas, W. B. (2002). Deconstructing the placebo effect and finding the meaning response. *Annals of Internal Medicine*, *136*(6), 471–476.

Peirce, C. S. (1931–1958). *Collected papers of Charles Sanders Peirce*. Cambridge, MA: Belknap (Harvard University).

Pennebaker, J. W. and Susman, J. R. (1988). Disclosure of traumas and psychosomatic processes. *Social Science and Medicine*, *26*(3), 327–332.

Phillips, D. P., Ruth, T. E., and Wagner, L. M. (1993). Psychology and survival. *Lancet*, *342*(8880), 1142–1145.

Russell, M. J., Switz, G. M., and Thompson, K. (1980). Olfactory influences on the human menstrual cycle. *Pharmacology, Biochemistry and Behavior*, *13*(5), 737–738.

Sebeok, T. (1991). *A sign is just a sign*. Bloomington: Indiana University Press.

Socha, T. J., Sanchez-Hughes, J., Bromley, J., and Kelly, B. (1995). Invisible parents and children: exploring African American parent–child communication. In T. J. Socha and G. H. Stamp (eds), *Parents, children, and communication: frontiers of theory and research* (pp. 127–145). Mahwah, NJ: Lawrence Erlbaum.

Spiro, M. (1993). Is the Western conception of the self "peculiar" within the context of the world cultures? *Ethos*, *21*(2), 107–153.

Tauber, A. I. (1995). *The immune self: theory or metaphor?* Cambridge and New York: Cambridge University Press.

—— (2000). Moving beyond the immune self? *Seminars in Immunology*, *12*(3), 241–248.

Uexküll, J. von (1907). *Umwelt und Innenwelt der Tiere*. Berlin: J. Springer.

Uexküll, T. von, Geigges, W., and Herrmann, J. M. (1993). The principle of teleological coherence and harmony of purpose exists at every level of integration in the hierarchy of living systems. *Advances, The Journal of Mind-Body Health*, *9*(3), 50–63.

Wilce, J. M. (1998). *Eloquence in trouble: the poetics and politics of complaint in rural Bangladesh*. New York: Oxford University Press.

Wilce, J. M. (in press). To "speak beautifully" in Bangladesh: subjectivity as *pāgalāmi*. In J. Jenkins and R. Barrett (eds), *The edge of experience: culture, subjectivity, and schizophrenia*. New York: Cambridge University Press.

Winkelby, M. A., Ragland, D. R., and Syme, S. L. (1988). Self-reported stressors and hypertension: evidence of an inverse association. *American Journal of Epidemiology*, *127*(1), 124–134.

Part I

Theoretical perspectives

Chapter 2: Editor's note

Throughout his career, James Pennebaker has led an exciting program of research combining health and social psychology, text analysis, and theoretical models of great interest to anthropologists, clinicians, and medical researchers. This chapter is an extremely eloquent, lucid summary of that lifetime's work. Here Pennebaker explains well-replicated findings of health and immunological benefits following the disclosure of traumatic events.

In many ways the impetus for this whole volume comes from a lecture Pennebaker presented at UCLA in 1990, while I was a graduate student there, exploring anthropological models to link the domains of language, emotion, and health. Among Pennebaker's collaborators are Booth and Davison (this volume). The questions Pennebaker's writings raise for anthropology are addressed by Wilce and Price (this volume). The placement of Pennebaker's essay in the volume indicates the importance of his life's work to our joint project.

Telling stories

The health benefits of disclosure

James W. Pennebaker[1]

Although it is not fashionable in anthropology these days to suggest that there are universals, I would like to suggest that the act of translating upsetting experiences into words is associated with better physical and mental health in virtually all societies. Let me explain my thinking on this.

A large number of mammalian species, including humans, occasionally work at deceiving others outside their troup or living unit. To the outsiders, individuals attempt to appear stronger or weaker, healthier or sicker than they really are. Within human groups, people deceive not only outgroup members but ingroup members as well – spouses, children, village leaders. In truth, it is beyond my expertise to know if people in all human cultures behave counter to the established rules in their society and, if they do, they occasionally keep their actions secret. Similarly, I cannot attest to whether all human cultures have words such as "lie," "deceive," "trick," "shame," or "guilt" in their vocabularies. Whatever the final judgement as to the universality of deception, our data would suggest that, to the extent that individuals must actively conceal important information from others in their social network, the act of concealment should be stressful.[2]

A second universal that is relevant to my thesis is that all human groups use language and, with it, create and tell stories. Further, the purpose of narratives is to structure people's experiences and to find meaning in complex, unpredictable events.

I come to this essay not as an expert in culture but as a psychologist who was initially interested in the use of writing as a way to affect people's health. Through a series of experiments, my colleagues and I discovered that when people put their emotional upheavals into words, their physical and mental health improved markedly. Further, the act of constructing stories appeared to be a natural human process that helped individuals to understand their experiences and themselves. This work started over a decade ago when, as part of a laboratory experiment, I asked students to write about their deepest thoughts and feelings about traumatic experiences. Much more happened than just their writing about traumatic experiences, however. The writing exercise often changed their lives. There was something remarkable about their expressing themselves in words.

The basic technique we used was straightforward. Students were brought into the laboratory and were told that they would be participating in a study wherein they would write about an assigned topic for four consecutive days for 15 minutes each day. They were assured that their writing would be anonymous and that they would not receive any feedback on it. As far as they knew, the purpose of the project was to learn more about writing and psychology. The only rule about the writing assignment was that once they began writing, they were to continue to do so without stopping without regard to spelling, grammar, or sentence structure. Participants were then randomly assigned to either an experimental group or a control group.

Those who, by a flip of the coin, ended up in the experimental group were asked to spend each session writing about one or more traumatic experiences in their lives. In the words of the experimenter:

> For the next four days, I would like for you to write about your very deepest thoughts and feelings about the most traumatic experience of your entire life. In your writing, I'd like you to really let go and explore your very deepest emotions and thoughts. You might tie your topic to your relationships with others, including parents, lovers, friends, or relatives, to your past, your present, or your future, or to who you have been, who you would like to be, or who you are now. You may write about the same general issues or experiences on all days of writing or on different traumas each day. All of your writing will be completely confidential.

Those who were assigned to the control condition were asked to write about non-emotional topics for 15 minutes on all four days of the study. Examples of their assigned writing topics included describing the laboratory room in which they were seated or their own living room. One group, then, was encouraged to delve into their emotions and the other was to describe objects and events dispassionately.

The first writing study that Sandra Beall and I conducted yielded astounding results (Pennebaker and Beall 1986). Most striking was that beginning college students immediately took to the task of writing. Those in the experimental condition averaged writing 340 words during each 15-minute session. Although many cried, the vast majority reported that they found the writing to be extremely valuable and meaningful. Indeed, 98 percent of the experimental participants said that, if given the choice, they would participate in the study again. Most surprising to us was the nature of the writing itself. The students, who tended to come from upper-middle class backgrounds, described a painful array of tragic and depressing stories. Rape, family violence, suicide attempts, drug problems, and other horrors were common topics. Indeed, approximately half of the people wrote about experiences that any clinician would agree was truly traumatic.

Even the ways the participants wrote was remarkable. The same students who would turn in sloppy, poorly constructed, appallingly spelled term papers or essay exams would write eloquently about their own personal tragedies. When given the opportunity in the study, the participants intuitively knew how to put together their life experiences into remarkably coherent narratives with few spelling or grammatical errors.

What made this first experiment so compelling for us, however, was not just the narratives themselves. Rather, we were primarily interested in how the writing exercise influenced physical health. During the school year, we followed the students' illness visits to the university health center in the months before and after the experiment. To our amazement and delight, we discovered that those who had written about their thoughts and feelings drastically reduced their doctor visit rates after the study compared to our control participants who had written about trivial topics. Confronting traumatic experiences had a salutary effect on physical health.

Over the last decade, more than two dozen studies from multiple laboratories around the world have confirmed and extended the basic findings. Some of the general results include:

- Writing benefits a variety of groups of individuals beyond undergraduate college students. Positive health and behavioral effects have been found with maximum security prisoners, medical students, community-based samples of distressed crime victims, arthritis and chronic pain sufferers, men laid off from their jobs, and women who have recently given birth to their first child. These effects have been found in all social classes and major racial/ethnic groups in the United States, and in samples in Mexico City, New Zealand, Japan, French-speaking Belgium, and the Netherlands.[3]
- Writing influences more than just physician visits. Four different laboratories report that writing produces positive effects on blood markers of immune function. Other studies indicate that writing is associated with lower pain and medication use among sufferers of arthritis and asthma, and, in a sample of students taking professional-level exams, such as the Graduate Record Exam, lower levels of depression. Additional experiments have demonstrated that writing is linked to higher grades in college and faster times to getting new jobs among senior-level engineers who have been laid off from their jobs.[4]
- Despite the clear health and behavioral effects, writing about traumatic experiences tends to make people feel more unhappy and distressed in the hours after writing. These emotions, in many ways, can be viewed as appropriate to the topics the individuals are confronting. When questionnaires are administered to participants at least two weeks after the studies, however, experimental volunteers report being as happy or happier than controls. Interestingly, among highly distressed samples,

such as the unemployed engineers, writing about losing their jobs produced immediate improvements in moods compared to controls. Emotional state after writing depends on how participants are feeling prior to writing: the better they feel before writing, the worse they feel afterwards and vice versa.[5]

- Although most experiments have focused primarily on writing, a few studies have compared writing with talking into a tape recorder. Overall, writing and talking have produced comparable effects. Additional experiments by Edward Murray and his colleagues at the University of Miami suggest that writing about traumatic experiences brings about comparable changes to talking to a psychotherapist – at least among a psychologically healthy sample.[6]

- There are no strong indications that some personality types benefit more from writing than others. A recent analysis of several writing studies by Joshua Smyth (1998) suggests that men may benefit somewhat more than women. This effect, however, still must be tested in future studies. Although traditional measures of neuroticism, depression-proneness, and extraversion are unrelated to the benefits of writing, a recent experiment by Alan Christensen and Timothy Smith indicates that individuals who are particularly hostile and suspicious benefited more from writing than people who were low in these traits (Christenson and Smith 1993).

- The effects of the writing are not related to having an audience or presuming one does. In most studies, participants turn in their writing samples with the understanding that only the experimenters will examine what they have written. Other experiments, however, have allowed participants to keep their writing samples or, in one masters' thesis by Jeanne Czajka (1987), students wrote on a child's magic pad where their writing was erased as soon as they lifted the plastic sheet on the writing tablet.

- Although the original studies required participants to write on four consecutive days for 15 minutes each day, later studies have varied the number of sessions from one to five days and from 15 minutes to 30 minutes each session. The summary project by Smyth hints that the longer time the study lasts, the better (Smyth 1998). Again, this effect needs to be examined experimentally.

- A variety of writing topics produce comparable health benefits. Although the earlier studies asked volunteers to write about traumas, more recent experiments have had new students write about their thoughts and feelings about coming to college or, in the case of the unemployed engineers, about the experience of getting laid off (Spera et al. 1994). Most impressive is a recent study by Melanie Greenberg and her colleagues at the State University of New York at Stony Brook wherein previously traumatized students were asked to write about an imaginary trauma rather than something they had experienced directly (Greenberg et al. 1997).

Their results indicated that writing about someone else's trauma as though they had lived through it produced health benefits comparable to a separate group who wrote about their own traumas. What is critical in all of these studies, however, is that people are encouraged to explore their emotions and thoughts no matter what the content might be.

Why does writing or talking about emotional experiences influence health? This has been the central question that has guided our research over the last several years. Three general research directions have provided a number of answers.

One possibility is that by writing about emotional experiences, people simply become more health conscious and change their behaviors accordingly. Very little evidence supports this. As indicated by the Smyth review, most experiments find that after writing about emotional topics, participants continue to smoke, exercise, diet, and socialize in ways similar to those in the control conditions (Smyth 1998). The one exception may be alcohol intake. In two studies with non-imprisoned adults, people who wrote about emotional topics later reported a drop in the amount of alcohol they were drinking each day. This pattern has not held up for college students.

A second possible explanation for the value of writing is that it allows people to express themselves. If the driving process is self-expression, one could argue that both verbal and nonverbal forms of expression would provide comparable benefits. Dance, music, and art therapists, for example, assume that the expression of emotion through nonverbal means is therapeutic. It should be noted, however, that traditional research on catharsis or the venting of emotions has failed to support the clinical value of emotional expression in the absence of cognitive processing.[7] In our own lab, we have attempted to determine the degree to which language is necessary for physical and mental health improvement. A recent experiment by Anne Krantz and me sought to learn if the disclosure of a trauma through dance or bodily movement would bring about health improvements in ways comparable to writing (Krantz and Pennebaker, cited in Pennebaker, 1997). In the study, students were asked to express a traumatic experience using bodily movement, to express an experience using movement and then write about it, or to exercise in a prescribed manner for three days, ten minutes per day. Whereas the two movement expression groups reported that they felt happier and mentally healthier in the months after the study, only the movement plus write group evidenced significant improvements in physical health and grade point average. The mere expression of a trauma is not sufficient to bring about long-term physiological changes. Health gains appear to require translating experiences into language.

A third broad explanation for the effects of writing is that the act of converting emotions and images into words changes the way the person organizes and thinks about the trauma. Further, part of the distress caused by the trauma lies not just in the events but in the person's emotional reactions to them. By integrating thoughts and feelings, then, the person can more easily construct a coherent narrative of the experience. Once formed, the event can now be summarized, stored, and forgotten more efficiently. Tests of this general idea are still in progress. However, preliminary findings are encouraging.

One of our first systematic approaches to understanding the potential cognitive benefits of writing was to examine the essays themselves. Independent raters initially compared the writing samples of people whose health subsequently improved after the experiment with those whose health remained unchanged. Essays from those who improved were judged to be more self-reflective, emotionally open, and thoughtful. Not being content with clinical evaluations, we decided to subject the essays to computer text analyses to learn if language use could predict improvements in health among people who had written about emotional topics.

Unbeknownst to me at the time this decision was made, no standard computer programs existed that specifically measured emotional and cognitive categories of word usage. Conceptually, such a program was very easy to write. Practically, Martha Francis and I spent over three years doing it. The result was a computer program called LIWC (Linguistic Inquiry and Word Count) that analyzed essays in text format (Pennebaker, Francis and Booth 2001). LIWC was developed by having groups of judges evaluate the degree to which over 2,000 words or word stems were related to each of several dozen categories. Although there are now over 70 word categories in the most recent version of the LIWC program, only four were of primary interest to us. Two of the categories were emotion dimensions and the other two were cognitive. The emotion categories included negative emotion words (e.g. sad, angry) and positive emotion words (e.g. happy, laugh). The two cognitive categories, causal and insight words, were intended to capture the degree to which participants were actively thinking in their writing. The causal words (e.g. because, reason) were included because they implied people were attempting to put together causes and reasons for the events and emotions that they were describing. The insight words (e.g. understand, realize) reflected the degree to which individuals were specifically referring to cognitive processes associated with thinking. For each essay that a person wrote, we were able to quickly compute the percentage of total words that these and other linguistic categories represented.

The beauty of the LIWC program is that it allowed us to go back to previous writing studies and link word usage among individuals in the experimental conditions with various health and behavioral outcomes. To date, the most extensive re-analysis of data concerns six writing studies: two studies involving college students writing about traumas where blood immune measures were collected, two studies where first year college students wrote about their deepest thoughts and feelings about coming to college, one study of maximum security prisoners in a state penitentiary, and one study using professionals who had unexpectedly been laid off from their jobs after over 20 years of employment (Richards *et al.* 2000).

Analyzing the use of negative and positive emotion words, Tracy Mayne, Martha Francis, and I uncovered two important findings (Pennebaker *et al.* 1997). First, the more that people used positive emotion words, the more their health improved. Negative emotion word use also predicted health changes but in an unexpected way. Individuals who used a moderate number of negative emotions in their writing about upsetting topics evidenced the greatest drops in physician visits in the months after writing. That is, those people who used a very high rate of negative emotion words and those who used very few were the most likely to have continuing health problems after participating in the study. In many ways, these findings are consistent with other literatures. Individuals who tend to use very few negative emotion words are undoubtedly most likely to be characterized as repressive copers – people whom Dan Weinberger, Gary Schwartz, and Richard Davidson have defined as less able to identify and label their emotional states (Weinberger *et al.* 1979). Those who overuse negative emotion words may well be the classic high neurotic or, as Watson and Clark call them, high Negative Affect individuals (Watson and Clark 1984). These individuals are people who ponder their negative emotions in exhaustive detail and who may simply be in a recursive loop of complaining without attaining closure. Indeed, this may be exacerbated by the inability of these individuals to develop a story or narrative.

Although the findings concerning emotion word use were intriguing, they paled in comparison to the robust results surrounding the cognitive word categories. Remember that in our studies, people wrote for three to five days, 15–30 minutes per day. As they wrote, they gradually changed what they said and how they said it. The LIWC analyses showed strong and consistent effects for changes in insight and causal words over the course of writing. Specifically, people whose health improved, who got higher grades, and who found jobs after writing went from using relatively few causal and insight words to using a high rate of them by the last day of writing. In reading the essays of people who showed this pattern of language use, it became apparent that they were constructing a story over time. Building a narrative, then, seemed to be critical in reaching understanding. Interestingly, those people who started the study with a coherent story that explained some past experience did not benefit from writing.[8]

These findings are consistent with current views on narrative and psychotherapy in suggesting that it is critical for the client to confront their anxieties and problems by creating a story to explain and understand past and current life concerns. The story can be in the form of an autobiography or even a third person narrative. Interestingly, our data indicate that merely having a story may not be sufficient to assure good health. A story that may have been constructed when the person was young or in the midst of a trauma may be insufficient later in life when new information is discovered or broader perspectives are adopted. In our studies, as in narrative therapies, then, the act of constructing the stories is associated with mental and physical health improvement. A constructed story, then, is a type of knowledge that helps to organize the emotional effects of an experience as well as the experience itself.

Within the psychological literature, there is a broadly accepted belief that humans – and perhaps most organisms with at least a moderately complex nervous system – seek to understand the worlds around them. If we feel pain or hear a strange noise, we try to learn the cause of it. Once we understand how and why an event has occurred, we are more prepared to deal with it should it happen again. By definition, then, we will be far more motivated to learn about events that have unwanted or, on the contrary, very desired consequences than about common or predictable events that don't affect us. Similarly, events with large and significant personal consequences will be examined to a greater degree than relatively superficial events.[9]

Over the course of a normal day, we are constantly surveying and analyzing our worlds. The person in the car behind us honks his horn while we sit at a red light. Automatically, we ask questions such as, "Is the person honking at me?" "Is the light green?" "Do I know this person?" As soon as we come to some understanding as to the meaning of the horn honk, we adjust our behavior (we go if the light is green, wave if it is a friend) or return to our private world if the honk was not relevant to us. As soon as this brief episode is over, we will probably put it out of our mind forever.

Whereas the search for the meaning of a honking horn is a brief, relatively automatic process, major life events are far more difficult to comprehend. If our lover leaves us, a close friend dies, or we face a significant career setback, we generally mull the event over in our mind trying to understand the causes and consequences of it. To complicate matters, a major life event usually consists of many events and experiences. If our lover has gone, it will affect our relationships with others, our finances, how we view ourselves, and even our daily eating, sleeping, talking, and sexual habits. In trying to understand this experience, we will naturally attempt to ask ourselves why this happened and how we can cope with it. To the degree that the event is unresolved, we will think, dream, obsess, and talk about it for days, weeks, or years.

Exactly what constitutes meaning or understanding is far less clear. Philosophers, psychologists, poets, and novelists have noted that a single event can have completely different meaning for different individuals. Following the death of a very close friend, some may find meaning in religion ("God has a plan"), others in understanding the cause of the death ("he smoked, what can you expect?"), yet others in exploring the implications for their own lives ("he would have wanted me to change my life"). Simple analyses relying on a single causal explanation may be useful in explaining some aspects of the death but will probably not be helpful in all aspects. We may have a straight-forward explanation on why the friend died, but we still must deal with a change in our friendship network, our daily routine of talking with our friend, etc. The beauty of a narrative is that it allows us to tie all of the changes in our life into a broad comprehensive story. That is, in the same story we can talk both about the cause of the event and its many implications. Much as in any story, there can be overarching themes, plots, and subplots – many of them arranged logically and/or hierarchically. Through this process, then, the many facets of the presumed single event are organized into a more coherent whole.

Drawing on research on conversation and language, Leslie Clark points out that conveying a story to another person requires that the speech act be coherent (Clark 1993). Linguistic coherence subsumes several characteristics, including structure, use of causal explanation, repetition of themes, and an appreciation of the listener's perspective. Referring to the work of Labov and Fanshel (1977), Clark emphasizes that conversations virtually demand the conveying of stories or narratives which require an ordered sequence of events.[10]

Once a complex event is put into a story format, it is simplified. The mind doesn't need to work as hard to bring structure and meaning to it. As the story is told over and over again, it becomes shorter with some of the finer detail gradually leveled. The information that is recalled in the story is that which is congruent with the story. Whereas the data (or raw experience) was initially used to create the story, once the story is fixed in the person's mind only story-relevant data is conjured up. Further, as time passes, we have the tendency to fill in gaps in our story to make the story more cohesive and complete. The net effect of constructing a good narrative is that our recol-lection of emotional events is efficient – in that we have a relatively short, compact story – and undoubtedly biased.

A common example can be seen in talking to people who have recently undergone a divorce. In the first weeks following the separation, individuals often talk (or, in our studies, write) about the many facets of the breakup. Often the accounts are long-winded, inconsistent, yet highly emotional. Over time, however, the explanations become simpler, even simplistic, such as "the reason our marriage fell apart was because he was a self-centered philanderer." With such one-dimensional summations of the end of their relationship, individuals overlook the nuances – both positive and negative – of the marriage.[11]

Ironically, then, good narratives can be beneficial in making our complex experiences more simple and understandable but, at the same time, they distort our recollection of them. Translating distress into language ultimately allows us to forget or, perhaps a better phrase, move beyond the experience. As an indirect test of this, Michael Crow and I studied how people thought and talked about the Persian Gulf War during the time it was ongoing and in the months following its completion (discussed in Pennebaker 1997). Once a week, over 200 students in each of several classes were asked how many times in the previous 24 hours they had talked, thought, and heard about the war. We also asked the participants how worried, upset, and angry they were about the war during each questionnaire administration.

Approximately two and a half years later, we were able to track down 76 students who had completed the majority of the war questionnaires. At the beginning of the follow-up telephone interview, we asked people to tell us about the war and then we asked them a series of objective questions about it (e.g. who were we fighting, who was their leader, on what day did the war start). Among those people who were most upset about the war, the more they talked about it during the war, the poorer their memory about it two and a half years later. Our sense is that they constructed a coherent narrative about the event and, once the war was over, they were easily able to move beyond it. By the time we interviewed them, they simply couldn't recall much about the war since they had had no reason to rehearse or relive the experience. It was a story that had resolved itself in the distant past.

In many ways, the war project was more titillating than definitive. We don't know how or why they talked about the war. We suspect that those who were most emotional about it were expressing their concerns and fears as well as mulling over the daily reports through the media. They may not have been focusing on the facts of the war at all – which is what we tested them on over two years later. However, the fact that these same people had the greatest difficulty in remembering who their own country was fighting in the first place suggests that the act of talking may have been instrumental in putting the war behind them. Because of these findings, we are now beginning to explore how people naturally talk about emotional events in the real world. In the future, we hope to be able to tie naturally-occurring discussions about distressing experiences to our long-term memories of them.[12]

One basic question in our research concerns why people tell or write stories. By extension, why do authors write novels, poems, and other forms of literature? As our work suggests, authors are not merely trying to vent their emotions or let off steam. Although we have never systematically studied professional writers, we suspect that they are often attempting to understand their own lives and emotions.

At this point, we are just beginning to determine the linguistic features of good narratives. By "good," of course, we mean stories that are associated with improved physical health. That some of the features of trauma writing by inexperienced writers overlaps with word patterns of the best selling fiction books is promising. Unfortunately, we are not yet in the position of proclaiming that writing literary stories is good for one's health.[13] The art of story telling, however, includes many of the basic ingredients of writing about personal traumas. Although an author may never have been a merchant in Venice or photographed bridges in Iowa, many of the core emotions and experiences inherent in fiction deal with the life conflicts. Creating stories to explain these personal conflicts and emotions helps the narrator to organize and move past them.

Notes

1 Correspondence should be addressed to James W. Pennebaker, Department of Psychology, Mezes Hall, University of Texas, Austin, TX 78712 (e-mail: Pennebaker@psy.utexas.edu). Preparation of this paper was aided by a grant from the National Institutes of Health (MH52391).
2 *Ed. The hypothesis that other violations of norms besides lying are stressful in themselves is central to Dressler's model of stress and culture (2000). For the possibility that promising is unthinkable and lying not stressful in at least one culture, see Rosaldo 1982.*
3 Within the United States, the disclosure paradigm has benefited senior professionals with advanced degrees at rates comparable to maximum security prisoners with sixth grade educations, see Spera *et al.* 1994: 722–733 and Richards *et al.* 2000.

Among college students, we have not found differences as a function of the students' ethnicity or native language. The disclosure paradigm has produced consistently positive results among French-speaking Belgians (Rimé 1995), Spanish-speaking residents of Mexico City (Dominguez *et al.* 1995), multiple samples of adults and students in the Netherlands (Schoutrop *et al.* 1996), English-speaking New Zealand medical students (Petrie *et al.* 1995: 787–792), and in a college student sample in Kyoto, Japan (Masao Yogo, Doshisha University, unpublished data).

There is some evidence that writing may not always work by itself in samples that may have disordered cognitive processing or relatively severe depression. For instance, a recent large-scale study in the Netherlands on recently bereaved older adults failed to find benefits of writing, see Stroebe and Stroebe 1996. Similarly, in a study conducted in Israel among a group of 14 post-traumatic stress disorder (PTSD) patients, the half assigned to write and orally expand about their traumas seemed to get worse compared to controls. The authors suggest that writing may not benefit PTSD patients in the absence of cognitive and/or coping skills training (Gidron *et al.* 1996). Further, severe cases of PTSD may be associated with the inability to cognitively organize traumatic experiences despite the continuous ruminating and emotional responses to thoughts of the precipitating traumas.

Ed. Very few studies of writing about trauma have treated ethnicity as a separate, independent variable. Despite the significance of the cross-national survey in this note (above), most of the populations Pennebaker mentions are European, or European in origin, and speak Indo-European languages. This might well indicate a large degree of cultural homogeneity among them, at least regarding the modernist value of psychologizing expressivity (Kusserow 1999; Wilce and Price this volume).

An alternative interpretation of the Gidron et al. *study is to recognize that the Israeli sample includes Sephardic Jews whose orientation is not European, and that Hebrew (presumably the primary language of all participants) is not an Indo-European language, and that it is at least as much this cultural difference as the fact that the patients suffered PTSD that caused writing to be less effective. Silove* et al. *found disclosure unhelpful to Cambodian trauma survivors as well (1995).*

In regard to the findings of Stroebe et al. *in the Netherlands, given the difference between (normal) bereavement and clinical depression, and given Pennebaker's finding that writing does facilitate "adaptive bereavement" (Pennebaker* et al. *1997), it is possible that cross-national variation in the efficacy of writing trauma exists even between European populations. See, in this volume, Moerman's chapter.*

4 Writing or talking about emotional experiences relative to writing about superficial control topics has been found to be associated with significant drops in physician visits from before to after writing among relatively healthy samples: Pennebaker and Beall 1986; Greenberg *et al.* 1996: 588–602; Pennebaker *et al.* 1990. Recent studies with individuals suffering from chronic arthritis show that emotional writing reduces symptoms of pain and results in less medication use (e.g. Kelley *et al.* 1997; Smyth *et al.* 1999). Indeed, Smyth *et al.* report that emotional writing among outpatients with chronic asthma and arthritis are assessed as healthier in the months following the writing than those who write about control topics.

Writing and/or talking about emotional topics has also been found to influence immune function in beneficial ways, including t-helper cell growth using a blastogenesis procedure with the mitogen PHA (Pennebaker *et al.* 1988: 239–245), antibody response to Epstein-Barr virus (Esterling *et al.* 1994: 130–140), and antibody response to hepatitis B vaccinations (Petrie *et al.* 1995).

Behavioral changes have also been found. Students who write about emotional topics evidence improvements in grades in the months following the study (Cameron and Nicholls 1998; Pennebaker and Francis 1996). Senior professionals who have been laid off from their jobs get new jobs more quickly after writing (Spera *et al.* 1994). Consistent with the direct health measures, university staff members who write about emotional topics are subsequently absent from their work at lower rates than controls (Pennebaker and Francis 1996). Interestingly, relatively few reliable changes emerge using self-reports of health-related behaviors. That is, after writing, experimental participants do not exercise more or smoke less (Pennebaker 1993a). The one exception is that the study with laid-off professionals found that writing reduced self-reported alcohol intake.

5 For a general summary of mood and health effects, see Pennebaker 1997.

6 Most studies comparing writing alone (e.g. Esterling *et al.* 1994) versus talking either into a tape recorder or to a therapist find comparable biological, mood, and cognitive effects, see Donnelly and Murray 1991, and Murray *et al.* 1989. Talking and writing about emotional experiences are both superior to writing about superficial topics.

7 Most claims concerning the effectiveness of nonverbal therapies have not been tested experimentally. Note that the term catharsis has changed significantly from Breuer and Freud's description of the talking cure. Their original use of catharsis was a method whereby the patient verbally described her or his emotions and thoughts surrounding anxiety-laden topics. More recently, the term has come to mean the venting of emotions without cognitive processing. Multiple studies on venting (or abreaction) have failed to demonstrate that it is an effective technique to reduce emotional arousal. Indeed, most studies indicate that venting increases emotional experience. See W. A. Lewis, and A. M. Bucher, "Anger, catharsis, the reformulated frustration-aggression hypothesis, and health consequences," *Psychotherapy, 29* (1992): 385–392.

8 For current views on narrative and psychotherapy, see the following sources: Mahoney 1995, Meichenbaum and Fong 1993 and Gergen and Gergen 1988.

9 That individuals attempt to understand their worlds is explicitly or implicitly acknowledged by virtually all schools of thought within psychology. Although Freud argued that people often distorted or repressed negative experiences, the mere fact that they sought psychoanalysis suggested that oftentimes people wanted and needed to understand themselves. Gestalt psychologists were more explicit in stating that a basic need was to attain closure. Even at the perceptual level, organisms are motivated to see a complete circle even if part of the circle is erased or obscured, see Kohler 1947. More recently, cognitive psychologists and therapists indicate that monkeys and humans actively seek to understand the causes of unexpected events and emotions, e.g. Kelley 1967. See also Beck 1976. Even radical behaviorists suggest that individuals seek understanding – even though it may be a futile and naive urge (Skinner 1971).

   Ed. Whereas the striving for insight might indeed be universal, indigenous therapies around the world are often not oriented to insight. The persistence of these indigenous therapeutic modalities is enough to raise questions about whether insight therapies are universally and exclusively valid modalities. See Prince 1980.

10 *Ed. The role of cognition in creating coherence and structuring cognition is well accepted. However, anthropologists also point to the cross-cultural variation in what constitutes a coherent narrative. Variation of a structural sort in what passes for coherent narratives in two cultures is profound enough to affect reciprocal ability of hearers or readers of the others' (translated) stories to remember them accurately (Kintsch 1978). The salience of "circular" or non-linear narrative forms in Javanese literary traditions lead the editor to predict its importance in future studies of Javanese personal trauma narratives (see Becker 1979 and Wilce and Price, this volume).*

11 *Ed. Social factors in this evolution are probably as significant as are psychological factors. Among the former are the decreasing toleration shown over time by members of one's social network for the processing of grief (Pennebaker 1993b), and the role of repetition and of the audience in shaping the "text" of a narrative over time.*

12 Talking about an event can be examined on the cultural level as well as individual. Entire societies, for example, may collectively "forget" important events (e.g. the Korean War or Persian Gulf War) and remember and/or repeatedly commemorate others (e.g. World War II). The processes surrounding collective memories of large-scale experiences are discussed in Pennebaker, Paez, and Rimé 1997.

13 *Ed. But see the remarkable finding of Greenberg and her colleagues (1996) – cited earlier – that even writing fictional or imaginary traumas has benefits.*

References

Beck, A. T. (1976). *Cognitive therapy and emotional disorders*. New York: International Universities Press.

Becker, A. L. (1979). Text-building, epistemology, and aesthetics in Javanese shadow theatre. In A. L. Becker and A. Yengoyan (eds), *The imagination of reality* (pp. 211–243). Norwood, NJ: Ablex.

Cameron, L., and Nicholls, G. (1998). Expression of stressful experiences through writing: effects of a self-regulation manipulation for pessimists and optimists. *Health Psychology, 17*(1), 84–92.

Christensen, A. J., and Smith, T. W. (1993). Cynical hostility and cardiovascular reactivity during self-disclosure. *Psychosomatic Medicine, 55*(1), 193–202.

Clark, L. F. (1993). Stress and the cognitive-conversational benefits of social interaction. *Journal of Social and Clinical Psychology, 12*(1), 25–55.

Czajka, J. A. (1987). *Behavioral inhibition and short term physiological responses.* Dallas, TX: Southern Methodist University.

Dominguez, B., Valderrama, P., Meza, M., Perez, S., Silva, A., Martinez, G., Mendez, V., and Olvera, Y. (1995). The roles of emotional reversal and disclosure in clinical practice. In J. W. Pennebaker (ed.), *Emotion, disclosure, and health.* Washington, DC: American Psychological Association.

Donnelly, D. A. and Murray, E. J. (1991). Cognitive and emotional changes in written essays and therapy interviews. *Journal of Social and Clinical Psychology, 10*(3), 334–350.

Dressler, W. W. and Bindon, J. R. (2000). The health consequences of cultural consonance: cultural dimensions of lifestyle, social support, and arterial blood pressure in an African American community. *American Anthropologist, 102*(2), 244–260.

Esterling, B. A., Antoni, M. H., Fletcher, M. A., Margulies, S., and Schneiderman, N. (1994). Emotional disclosure through writing or speaking modulates latent Epstein-Barr virus antibody titers. *Journal of Consulting and Clinical Psychology, 62*(1), 130–140.

Gergen, K. J. and Gergen, M. M. (1988). Narrative and the self as relationship. In L. Berkowitz (ed.), *Advances in experimental social psychology* (vol. 21, pp. 17–56). New York: Academic.

Gidron, Y., Peri, T., Connolly, J. F., and Shalev, A. Y. (1996). Written disclosure in posttraumatic stress disorder: is it beneficial for the patient? *Journal of Nervous and Mental Disease, 184*(8), 505–507.

Greenberg, M. A., Stone, A., and Wortman, C. B. (1996). Health and psychological effects of emotional disclosure: A test of the inhibition–confrontation approach. *Journal of Personality and Social Psychology, 71*(3), 588–602.

Kelley, H. H. (1967). Attribution theory in social psychology. In D. Levine (ed.), *Nebraska symposium on motivation* (pp. 192–238). Lincoln, NE: University of NE Press.

Kelley, J. E., Lumley, M. A., and Leisen, J. C. C. (1997). Health effects of emotional disclosure in rheumatoid arthritis patients. *Health Psychology, 16*(4), 331–340.

Kintsch, W. (1978). Comprehension and memory of text. In W. K. Estes (ed.), *Handbook of learning and cognitive processes: linguistic functions in cognitive theory* (vol. 6, pp. 57–86). Hillsdale, NJ: Erlbaum.

Kohler, W. (1947). *Gestalt psychology.* New York: Liveright.

Kusserow, A. S. (1999). De-homogenizing American individualism: socializing hard and soft individualism in Manhattan and Queens. *Ethos, 27*(2), 210–234.

Labov, W. and Fanshel, D. (1977). *Therapeutic discourse: psychotherapy as conversation.* New York: Academic Press.

Mahoney, M. J. (ed.). (1995). *Cognitive and constructive psychotherapies: theory, research, and practice.* New York: Springer Publishing.

Meichenbaum, D. and Fong, G. T. (1993). How individuals control their own minds: a constructive narrative perspective. In D. M. Wegner and J. W. Pennebaker (eds), *Handbook of mental control* (pp. 473–490). Englewood Cliffs, NJ: Prentice Hall.

Murray, E. J., Lamnin, A. D., and Carver, C. S. (1989). Emotional expression in written essays and psychotherapy. *Journal of Social and Clinical Psychology, 8*(4), 414–429.

Pennebaker, J. W. (1993a). Putting stress into words: health, linguistic, and therapeutic implications. *Behaviour Research and Therapy, 31*(6), 539–548.

——— (1993b). Social mechanisms of constraint. In D. M. Wegner and J. W.
Pennebaker (eds), *Handbook of mental control* (pp. 200–219). Englewood Cliffs,
NJ: Prentice Hall.

——— (1997). *Opening up: the healing powers of emotional expression.* New York:
Guilford.

——— and Beall, S. K. (1986). Confronting a traumatic event: toward an understanding of inhibition and disease. *Abnormal Psychology, 95*(3), 274–281.

——— and Booth, R. J. (2001) *Linguistic inquiry and word count (LIWC): a computer
text analysis program* (LIWC 2001). Mahwah, NJ: Erlbaum Publishers.

———, Colder, M., and Sharp, L. K. (1990). Accelerating the coping process. *Journal
of Personality and Social Psychology, 58*(3), 528–537.

——— and Francis, M. E. (1996). Cognitive, emotional, and language processes in
disclosure. *Cognition and Emotion, 10*(6), 601–626.

———, Kiecolt-Glaser, J., and Glaser, R. (1988). Disclosure of traumas and immune
function: Health implications for psychotherapy. *Journal of Consulting and
Clinical Psychology, 56*(2), 239–245.

———, Mayne, T. J., and Francis, M. E. (1997). Linguistic predictors of adaptive
bereavement. *Journal of Personality and Social Psychology, 72*(4), 863–871.

———, Paez, D., and Rimé, B. (eds) (1997). *Collective memories of political events:
social psychological perspectives.* Mahwah, NJ: Erlbaum Publishers.

Petrie, K. J., Booth, R. J., Pennebaker, J. W., Davison, K. P., and Thomas, M. G.
(1995). Disclosure of trauma and immune response to a hepatitis B vaccination
program. *Journal of Consulting and Clinical Psychology, 63*(5), 787–792.

Prince, R. (1980). Variations in psychotherapeutic procedures. In H. C. Triandis and
J. G. Draguns (eds), *Handbook of cross-cultural psychology* (vol. 6, pp. 291–349).

Richards, J. M., Beal, W. E., Seagal, J. D., and Pennebaker, J. W. (2000). Effects of
disclosure of traumatic events on illness behavior among psychiatric prison
inmates. *Journal of Abnormal Psychology, 109*(1), 156–160.

Rimé, B. (1995). Mental rumination, social sharing, and the recovery from emotional
exposure. In J. W. Pennebaker (ed.), *Emotion, disclosure, and health.* Washington,
DC: American Psychological Association.

Rosaldo, M. (1982). The things we do with words: Ilongot speech acts and speech
act theory in philosophy. *Language in Society, 11*(2), 203–237.

Schoutrop, M. J. A., Borsschot, J., and Everaerd, W. (1996). The effects of writing
assignments on reprocessing traumatic events: three experimental studies. Paper
presented at The (Non) Expression of Emotions and Health and Disease
Conference, Tilburg, The Netherlands.

Silove, D., Chang, R., and Manicavasagar, V. (1995). Impact of recounting trauma
stories on the emotional state of Cambodian refugees. *Psychiatric Services, 46*(12),
1287–1288.

Skinner, B. F. (1971). *Beyond freedom and dignity.* New York: Knopf.

Smyth, J. M. (1998). Written emotional expression: effect sizes, outcome types, and
moderating variables. *Journal of Counseling and Clinical Psychology, 66*(1),
174–184.

Smyth, J. M., Stone, A. A., Hurewitz, A., and Kaell, A. (1999). Effects of writing
about stressful experiences on symptom reduction in patients with asthma or

rheumatoid arthritis: a randomised trial. *Journal of the American Medical Association 281*(14), 1304–1309.

Spera, S. P., Buhrfeind, E. D., and Pennebaker, J. W. (1994). Expressive writing and coping with job loss. *Academy of Management Journal, 37*(3), 722–733.

Stroebe, M. and Stroebe, W. (1996). Writing assignments and grief. Paper presented at The (Non) Expression of Emotions and Health and Disease Conference, Tilburg, The Netherlands.

Watson, D. and Clark, L. A. (1984). Negative affectivity: the disposition to experience aversive emotional states. *Psychological Bulletin, 96*, 465–490.

Weinberger, D. A., Schwartz, G. E., and Davidson, R. J. (1979). Low anxious, high anxious, and repressive coping styles: psychometric patterns and behavioral and physiological responses to stress. *Journal of Abnormal Psychology, 58*, 369–380.

Chapter 3: Editor's note

Booth and Davison, building on their collaboration with Pennebaker (this volume), report here on a study that gives preliminary support to the hypothesis that culture matters in several ways in relation to immune systems. First, they remind us that, whatever else it might be, the idea of the immune system is one that has spread through popular culture enough that popular notions of one's own vitality and health are today often expressed in terms of perceived immune function (which might or might not have any relation to measurable immune function). But, most importantly, Booth and Davison found that, when asked to write about the most upsetting experience of their lives, the linguistic markers most closely associated with circulating lymphocyte changes are exactly the ones that differ most clearly among three groups of students – Caucasians, Polynesians, and Asians. The door is open for ethnographic investigation of such populations in New Zealand, i.e. studies that would inquire into areas of overlap and non-overlap in social networks and forms of cultural production. This study opens up the topic of interethnic variability; further studies that would test hypotheses about social and cultural (or perhaps biological) origins of that variability would be extremely welcome.

In situating immune function within broader human and social contexts, Booth and Davison invoke a concept proposed a decade ago by Booth (Booth and Ashbridge 1993a) – the model of teleological coherence or harmony of purpose. This model boldly links the immune self (Tauber 1995) and the psychological self and reflects European roots in the philosophical biology of Varela and Maturana and the biosemiotics of Jakob and Thure von Uexküll. Whereas science has felt it necessary to reduce complexity to ever smaller units of analysis in order to understand processes via their parts, Booth and Davison work against reductionism (see Booth and Ashbridge 1993b).

This chapter thus reflects an interactionist model of PNI that traces its roots some decades back. Those roots are in ethology and biosemiotics, the study of sign systems found in all life forms (from biochemical exchanges like the comparison of MHC "scent" involved in odor preference and mate selection described below to bird song). The von Uexkülls' work takes animal behavior as its starting point and the sociality of biological functions it describes is the sociality of groups of animals. In this model, "organism and environment form an inseparable unit of interdependent subject and object" (von Uexküll et al. 1993). The teleological coherence and harmony of purpose of which Booth and Davison speak must be recognized as a fundamentally semiotic phenomenon rooted in the convergence of the codes used at various levels of the life of a person (or other creature) and group. Communication is involved at cellular, mental, and interpersonal levels, and it requires at least some level of sharing of semiotic systems or codes.[1] And yet the sort of communication entailed here must not be reduced to "information exchange." "The term 'information exchange' is misleading because 'what results from communication is not shared information but the emergence of new qualities on the part of both communicating partners" (von Uexküll et al. 1993: 58f). Among the "qualities" emergent in such interchange that are of particular relevance to this chapter and the whole book are emotions as social forms (Lyon, this volume) and their relation to immune function and health.

Thus, this chapter and the past research on which it builds (including Pennebaker's work) represent particularly strong contributions to a complexly semiotic approach to psychoneuroimmunology taking into account communication within the self as well as that pinnacle of cultural achievement, human linguistic communication.

Chapter 3

Relating to our worlds in a psychobiological context

The impact of disclosure on self-generation and immunity

Roger J. Booth[2] *and Kathryn P. Davison*[3]

Introduction

The notion of an *immune system* initially arose within western medicine as a concept of an internal physiological system that protects or defends our bodies against a potentially hostile (pathogenic) environment. Its appearance during the late nineteenth and early twentieth centuries coincided with the development of the germ theory of disease, and much of modern immunological language and research is still based on a metaphor that assumes powerful warlike, hierarchical, autonomous activity. A broader view however, is emerging from interdisciplinary studies of the relationship between immunological and psychological or sociocultural behavior. It conceives of the immune system as an integrative, cognitive system that discriminates between *self* and *non-self* and continually maintains a coherent relationship between *self* and *context* (compare Cone and Martin, this volume). In this chapter we explore how *meaning* in a psychosociocultural context might relate to the *self* that immunologists describe. Interviews in a medical school indicate that the immune system of medical science differs from that perceived as operating in daily lives of individuals, including medical students. Individuals generally attribute feelings of vigor and vitality to a well-functioning immune system, and feelings of fatigue to poor immune function. These findings have implications for social and medical understanding of immunity. Further, the way we relate to our worlds in a psychosocial context may have an impact to how our immune system relates to its world and how immune self/non-self distinction is maintained. Emotional expression through writing can alter the psychosocial milieu and health of an individual. We explore how this might affect immune functioning and whether cultural background may play a part in this.

Immune symbolism

One of the defining aspects of western medicine of the late nineteenth century was the development of the germ theory of disease. The concept of "immunity" as the capacity to be protected from succumbing to an infectious illness following an initial exposure had been appreciated and utilized for many centuries. Yet it was not until the turn of the twentieth century that it began to acquire the symbolism with which it is characterized today. With the identification of an increasing number of pathogenic microorganisms intimately associated with infectious diseases, came the notion of human life existing within a potentially hostile microbial environment. The immune system came to be seen as the means by which living animals defended themselves against such external hostility and protected the body against pathogenic incursions.

As anatomical and physiological components were identified as functioning within the immune process, the language of immunology developed, drawing heavily on the language of war. Indeed, much of modern immunological language and research is still steeped in siege mentality, based on a metaphor that assumes powerful military, hierarchical, autonomous activity of a defensive system within the physical body of an individual. Indeed, as we will explore later, the popular conception of the immune system at the dawn of the millennium in our society is as the system that not only protects against infection and disease, but as the system that actually keeps people healthy.

Recognition and response within the immune system

In order for the immune system to operate against foreign invasion, it must have a means of recognizing that which is considered to be foreign. The fundamental process of immunology therefore becomes one of "self" versus "non-self" distinction. Further, in distinguishing between self and non-self the system must have the ability to respond aggressively towards, and repel, the foreign threat while maintaining benign tolerance towards all that is legitimately part of self. Over the last 50 years, the cellular and molecular biological nature of the immune recognition process and the self/non-self distinguishing capability has been elucidated. Biologically, the immune system of today centers around the behavior of a class of cells called *lymphocytes*, which have the ability to recognize and respond to complex molecular shapes. These shapes are called *antigens* and the structures by which lymphocytes recognize them are called *receptors*. For example, *antibodies* are a form of receptor used by the immune system to recognize and respond to antigens in a particular way.

The cells and molecules of our bodies can also behave as antigens, as can be demonstrated by transferring them to another person in a graft and observing graft rejection. This means that the context in which shapes are recognized by the immune system is important and therefore, the lymphocyte network within our immune systems must be *tolerant* towards our own antigens so as not to destroy ourselves through *autoimmunity*. The modern understanding of immune system behavior includes a variety of contextual features that govern immune recognition and response. These include the previous history of the immune system in the individual and the molecular and cell surface milieu in which lymphocytes get to meet the antigens.

Conceptions of the immune system

As summarized above, the defense model of immunity has generally driven immunological research during this century. With increased understanding of the physiology and molecular mechanics of the immune system, together with the successes of immunization as a medical intervention, has come an increased popular perception of the importance of a "well-functioning immune system" in human health. Because of this, we sought to discover whether the "popular" view of the immune system is at all related to that of medical science. This was done in the course of three research studies using volunteers from within the University of Auckland Faculty of Medical and Health Sciences (mostly medical students). On multiple occasions they completed a symptom inventory, the profile of mood states (POMS) questionnaire, and the following question to assess their perception of their immune status: *"Please mark on the line below what you think to be the state of your immune system today."*

There were no significant relationships between perceived immune status and the age and the sex of the subjects but there were strong correlations between perceived immune status and mood variables (Petrie *et al.* 1999). As well as a total mood disturbance score, the POMS questionnaire produces six mood factors: Tension, Depression-dejection, Anger, Vigor, Fatigue, and Confusion. All the mood factors correlated with perceived immune status, with the strongest associations being between Vigor and Fatigue (negatively). There was also a significant negative correlation between perceived immune status and symptom score. Further, when the subjects were categorized according to cultural background (Caucasian – 83 subjects, Polynesian – 13 subjects, Asian (predominantly Chinese and Indian) – 30 subjects) there were significant differences in perceived immune status ($F(2,475) = 4.99, p < 0.01$), with Polynesians scoring highest and Asian cultural groups the lowest.

These findings indicate not only that the social construction of the immune system centers on efficient defense, protection, and maintenance of health, but also that popular views of immune system activity relate most strongly to feelings of vigor and fatigue. In other words, a "neo-Darwinian" (or perhaps more accurately "Spencerian") "survival of the fittest" notion about immune system function predominates in western culture. Feelings of vitality are associated with a well-functioning immune system while feelings of lethargy or fatigue are considered to be indicative of inadequate immune system activity. In this discourse, illness is viewed as a "deviant" state related to the effectiveness of immune function such that depressed or defective immunity is correspondingly associated with poor health. Such notions accord well with the considerable popularity of "natural health" remedies as methods for "boosting" immunity, thereby giving medical legitimization to the quest for something to make one feel more vigorous and therefore more healthy.[4]

Expanded models of immunity

Much of modern immunological thinking and research still tends to treat immune behavior in a linear fashion in which the system, armed and awaiting challenge, responds to potentially threatening antigens by producing effectors to neutralize, inactivate or destroy the invader. Nevertheless, with the recognition that the system is not autonomous but is intimately intertwined with endocrine and nervous system activities, alternative immune metaphors are emerging in which the system is viewed as interacting with the organism's environment rather than simply protecting against it. For example, Blalock (Blalock 1984; Blalock and Smith 1985) has suggested that as a system involved in molecular shape recognition linked to the nervous system, the immune system is in essence a molecular sense organ, providing a living individual with information about the microscopic topological environment in a manner akin to the way the visual system provides information about the visual environment.

Further refinements emphasize the fact that an immune system operates within an individual continuously generating itself in the context of an ever-changing environment, and thus being in part a reflection and product *of* that environment. In this way, the immune system can be seen as being involved in self-determining processes in concert with other systems associated with self-determination, such as the nervous system. With this approach, it comes as no surprise that the immune system and the nervous system have a large network of physiological interactions with one another; it is expected if the immune system is to operate and maintain a coherent self/non-self relationship throughout life.

Harmony of purpose – the teleological coherence model

The relatively fledgling discipline of psychoneuroimmunology (PNI) is delving into the relationships between psychological, neuroendocrine, and immune behavior, although much of its research continues to employ defense system metaphors of immunity and to explain relationships in terms of cellular and molecular protection mechanisms. One of us (Roger J. Booth) has proposed a model that seeks to go beyond a purely biophysical construction of the immune system and to link its self-generative and self/non-self-distinguishing characteristics to psychological, social, and cultural processes (Booth and Ashbridge 1993a). This model suggests that the immune system, engaged in a broader process of self-determination, shares with the neurological and psychological domains the common goal of establishing and maintaining self-identity. Further, the nature of the relationships is governed by the requirement for coherent coordination among all these self-defining aspects of an individual.

This means that the framework in which immune recognition occurs cannot be considered only as the antigenic or receptor-related, molecular context, but as all the domains of life in which the individual defines him or herself in relation to the environment. In this way, the meaning of events surrounding an *antigenic stimulus* may condition the features (nature, specificity, magnitude, duration, etc.) of any immune response observed. Conversely, the behavior of the immune system towards self and non-self antigens can influence self and relational perceptions within psychosociocultural domains. We experience this in a transient way when we contract a cold or flu for example and see the world and our relationship to it differently. Physiologically these effects can be explained through mechanisms of hormonal cross talk between the *traditional* immune system and the nervous system, but such explanations tell us little about the events in the context of coherent psychobiological self-generation and maintenance.

Some implications of harmony of purpose

One important implication of this model is that the sort of immune behavior observed at different developmental stages of an individual's life will differ but all will be appropriate to, and coherent with, necessities of that stage. Moreover parallels should be observable. For example, there are broad parallels between psychosocial and immunological patterns of behavior during different developmental stages of life. The neonatal period is a time of nascent self/non-self boundary formation and development of a diverse repertoire of response patterns.[5] During the adult years the potentials of established boundaries and response patterns are explored and refined, while the years of old age can be seen as a time more of introspection, accommodation, involution, and disintegration of self boundaries.[6] This analysis contrasts with the current tendency to consider immune activity as something that builds to reach a pinnacle in early adult life and then gradually diminishes or decays.

Another intriguing finding in accord with a harmony of purpose model concerns the multiple functions of certain vital immune components called Major Histocompatibility Complex (MHC) molecules (in humans the main ones are called HLA). The MHC molecules are fundamental antigen-presenting structures of the immune system and are intimately involved in determining whether tissue grafts from one person to another are accepted or rejected.

It is perhaps not surprising therefore that these same MHC molecules are important in an aspect of the limbic system also intimately involved in self-identity – the olfactory system. Soluble MHC molecules are excreted in urine and other body fluids carrying a profile of volatile specific compounds that influence both body odors and body odor preferences (Eggert *et al.* 1998; Pearse Pratt *et al.* 1998; Schellinck *et al.* 1997; Wedekind and Furi 1997; Wobst *et al.* 1998). Thus, the MHC not only plays a key role in the immune system self/non-self recognition, but contributes as well to non-immunological functions associated with self-identity. In fact MHC mediates not only immune functioning in relation to stress (Dreau *et al.* 1999) but functions that are social as well as biological, such as mate choice (Jordan and Bruford 1998).

Self-expression and health

Reconstructing our understanding of immune behavior in terms of harmony of purpose means that we begin to see immunity not so much as defense, but more in terms of coherent self-expression. We might then ask such questions as, does the meaning of events in a psychosociocultural context have implications for the meaning of self in an immunological context? If we alter the meaning of potent events in our lives (by emotional expression for example) is immune activity also affected? To what extent does our cultural background influence the manner in which immunity is affected by emotional disclosure? We make sense of the events in our lives through the narratives we construct to weave those events meaningfully into the web of our existence. How much do those narratives affect our physical selves?

If we think back to childhood and the kinds of family stories that perhaps grandparents or proud old aunts or uncles told us, we immediately get that sense of heritage that goes along with a shared history. We know that we come from the same "stock" because somehow the sharing of stories binds us together. This notion is of course not limited to those who are blood relatives; sharing stories constitutes the heart of psychotherapy. Troubled individuals pay someone to listen to their stories with an expert balance of compassion and disinterest that helps them construct for themselves the nature of their problem, the obstacles they face, and the kind of life that represents cure, or sanity. Over the course of the process, the client's individuation becomes a shared "stock," a self-understanding that has evolved from the kinds of stories that they confide in the therapist. The difference between the kinds of stories that families might tell and the kind that one tells to the psychotherapist is striking: one is a public tale, the other intensely private. But they share the central features of identities shaped and developed through stories. They are both stories that affect our emotions, our construction of who we are, our sense of self.[7]

Furthermore, various investigations are indicating that a coherent sense of self is healing in nature, both psychologically and physically. Investigations into these kinds of stories have been pioneered by James Pennebaker. Initially, in doing some polygraph consulting work for the FBI, he noticed that many interrogated suspects reported overwhelming relief upon confession, regardless of the consequences. The tension of holding back the lie in the face of questioning was apparently agonizing for many of them. Intrigued by this phenomenon, Pennebaker began to wonder whether embarrassing or upsetting details of the personal histories of all people might carry some burden as well. Are there detrimental effects of holding back such secrets? And perhaps more importantly, what would be the impact of letting them out? As discussed in his chapter, Pennebaker has investigated these questions extensively by devising what might be termed a laboratory-based confessional approach. In this research method, subjects are asked to write anonymously and confidentially about highly traumatic or upsetting issues in their lives, usually for around 20 minutes on each of four consecutive days. This group of subjects is urged to explore their deepest thoughts and feelings in their writing each day. An important thing to bear in mind here is that the writing topics are self-selected. A control group is asked to write for comparable periods in a very descriptive, non-emotional way, about relatively mundane topics.

Evaluating self-expression

Numerous studies using this approach have demonstrated salutary effects on the emotional writing group relative to the control group – fewer illness-related doctor visits (Berry and Pennebaker 1993), reduced sympathetic nervous system activity (Pennebaker *et al.* 1987), changes in immune markers (Booth *et al.* 1997; Esterling *et al.* 1990; Pennebaker *et al.* 1988; Petrie, Booth, and Pennebaker, 1998; Petrie *et al.* 1995), lower absentee rates (Francis and Pennebaker 1992), and even faster times to re-employment in a sample of laid-off executives (Spera *et al.* 1994). In each case, subjects in the emotional writing group were encouraged to really let go and tell the story of their experience. Although powerful, this intervention is not a panacea because even though the emotional writing groups as a whole show improved health markers, not everyone who writes about an upsetting experience gets better. Are there ways of telling a story that are more healing than others? What identifiable markers are there?

To address this issue, Pennebaker and Francis (1996) developed a computerized linguistic analysis program known as *LIWC* – "Linguistic Inquiry and Word Count." The LIWC program contains an internal dictionary and categorizing structure that includes about 60 different dimensions. Some are obvious concerns of psychology such as negative emotion, positive emotion, self-discrepancy, insight, and self-references. Others are less obvious topics that show up in a lot of writings: time, space, money, and religion. LIWC also produces summaries of what could be called the linguistic profile of each writing sample: unique word use, words that are more than six letters long, words per sentence, overall word count, etc. These dimensions have also proven to be psychologically valuable in some instances. Each word (or word stem) encountered by LIWC that is contained in its dictionary is counted as an incidence in one or more of its dimensions. For instance, the word "loveliest" is counted as positive emotion and positive feeling, and is registered as a word of more than six letters. A writing sample that is processed by LIWC, then, results in an output that says what percentage of word use is positive emotion, what percentage is insight-related etc., and how many words were in the essay, as well as the percentage of words captured by LIWC's dictionary.

Is it possible to predict therapeutic writing styles by just looking at word usage? This issue of the relationship between word use and meaning is an old and thorny one. Psycholinguists note the difference between surface and deep structures in language. Sometimes the two go together. For instance, I say, "turn left at the next light." In that case, what I say and what I mean are really the same: they are referents about intention, sequence, and space. On the other hand, I could quote my mother: "Eat something, really, is that all the breakfast you're going to have?" The surface structure of this phrase suggests questions about nutrition, while its deep structure translates to something like, "I love you, and I want every detail of your life to reflect that concern."

Self-expression and culture

Methods of handling emotions and manners of expression differ among different cultures. Emotional disclosure through writing and its salutary effects have been developed and explored almost exclusively within a Caucasian American context. The question therefore arises as to whether all cultural groups can benefit from this form of self-expression. To begin investigating this, we used LIWC analysis to compare the emotional disclosure writings of groups of medical students from three different cultural backgrounds. We sought to determine whether there were significant differences in the way people from different cultural backgrounds wrote about traumatic or upsetting topics. Our dataset for this analysis consisted of the writing done as part of four separate studies of the effects of emotional disclosure and immune function at the University of Auckland School of Medicine in New Zealand.

New Zealand is a country poised uniquely amidst a variety of Asian and Pacific cultures; but its citizens are overwhelmingly of European extraction. As a result, the University of Auckland is an interesting meeting ground of foreign-born students and natives who are studying to be doctors at the University of Auckland School of Medicine. We divided the students into three broad categories according to their cultural backgrounds: Caucasians – 63 subjects, Polynesians (comprising indigenous Maori or Pacific Islanders who have grown up in New Zealand) – 9 subjects, and Asians (mostly of Indian and Chinese extraction) – 20 subjects.

All these students had participated in research in which they had been asked to write for 20 minutes on each of four consecutive days about the most upsetting experience of their lives. We asked two questions of the data. First, given these vastly different cultural origins, would their style of expression in these three groupings vary in any consistent way? Second, when given freedom of topic selection, what kinds of domains of concern are reflected in writing? We reasoned that in a very general way, the linguistic markers accessible through LIWC analysis might reflect the differences for example in values observed between Caucasians – with their individualist emphasis, and Polynesians – who embrace a more collective value system (compare Samoans (McDade, this volume)).

Specifically, we predicted that Caucasians would use language that was more self-oriented, and so they would use words like "I," "me," "my," etc. to a greater degree than their Polynesian and Asian counterparts. Similarly, we expected higher use of social referents in the Polynesian accounts – "others," "family," "home," etc., reflecting their more communal orientation. As shown in Figure 3.1, the use of self-references is virtually absent from the Polynesians' writings compared to those of the other two ethnic groups. And by contrast in the social dimensions, the Caucasians' use is markedly lower across all three domains (social, family, and others).

In four different research studies, healthy medical student volunteers were asked to write about the most upsetting events in their lives for 20 minutes each day for four days in an anonymous and confidential environment. Writings were analysed using the LIWC computer program that counts the frequency of words in a variety of categories. Figure 3.1 shows the major word use

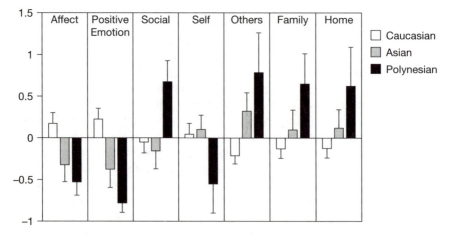

Figure 3.1 Word use analysis of emotional writing.

categories in which there were significant differences ($p < 0.05$) among three cultural groups (total subjects: 63 Caucasian; 20 Asian; 9 Polynesian).

Second, we considered that the accounts of the Caucasians would contain more emotionality. Emotional expression, by Western accounts, is considered to be valuable, honest, even therapeutic. Certainly catharsis lies at the heart of psychoanalytic therapeutic models (Wilce and Price, this volume). By contrast, in the Asian cultures, extreme displays of emotion are undesirable, showing a lack of self-control that results in dishonor to the individual's social group – usually the family. To disgrace one's family through such intemperance is anathema by many Asian societies' standards. Correspondingly Figure 3.1 shows that the use of emotional language by Caucasians differs dramatically from that of the other two groups.

Thus, there are significant differences among cultural groups in the manner of writing about traumatic or upsetting events even though they were all members of the same group of medical students. Because our previous studies revealed differential effects on immune variables of emotional as compared with descriptive expression, it is germane to ask whether emotional expression in different cultural groups might elicit correspondingly different immune changes. As a preliminary exploration of this question, we assessed whether there were any significant associations between changes in immune markers (circulating lymphocyte numbers) following emotional writing and LIWC categories of word use. The results show that the LIWC word categories that associate significantly with circulating lymphocyte changes are "self," "positive feelings," "anger," "friends," "community," "time," and "religion." Intriguingly, these categories are also among those that differentiate most strongly among the three cultural groups. The number of subjects is too small to conduct any further meaningful analysis subdividing by ethnic group; nevertheless these results indicate that the possibility of differential immune effects of emotional disclosure governed by cultural background warrants further investigation.

Conclusions

These social and cultural perspectives on self-expression shed valuable light on the way our surroundings embody us. Even instruments, such as LIWC analysis, that are psychologically quite crude, reflect the distinct way that heritage shapes both the focus and style of our most private expressions. Although the numbers of subjects in each group is not equal (63 Caucasians, 20 Asians, and 9 Polynesians) and there are few in the Polynesian category, the differences in writing styles among these three groups reveal some intriguing differences both in style and content worthy of a more systematic investigation. Moreover, the preliminary analysis of immune data suggests the possibility that the beneficial immune and health effects of emotional disclosure through writing could well be significantly modulated by social and cultural factors. In sum, these findings suggest that emotional writing practices may have different effects for different cultural groups, in terms of health outcomes.

Finally, the overriding metaphor of the immune system is still deeply rooted in defense against a threatening outside (non-self) world. What is becoming clear is that as people re-invent themselves by integrating traumatic issues through emotional disclosure, their immune self/non-self processes are also modulated. Perhaps it is time we realized that the immune system is more than a defense system but rather, a participant in how we generate ourselves. Perhaps it is time for a discourse in which we consider the immune system less of a soldier and more of a gardener, and more as a neighborhood watch and less as a posse.

Notes

1   " 'Communication' presupposes a modulation or tuning-in of one's own codes to the codes of the partners" (von Uexküll et al. 1993).
2   Department of Molecular Medicine and Pathology, Faculty of Medical and Health Sciences, The University of Auckland, Private Bag 92019, Auckland, New Zealand.
3   Tonic Capital, 594 Broadway, Suite 309, New York 10012.
4   Ed. Emily Martin has described the discourse on immune function in similar terms, namely, as reproducing Spencerian notions of the survival of the fittest (1993; compare her chapter in this volume).
5   Ed. Kurtz (1992) argues for true cross-cultural variability in self-formation processes such that the "self"-boundaries formed in childhood might (e.g. in Hindu India) include the whole family.
6   Ed. Lamb finds this pattern in old age to be inverted in West Bengal, India, where aging women are thought to become "more self-contained" (2000: 13). This illustrates the profound cultural variability in concepts of the self.
7   Ed. Admittedly, the act of telling private stories to a therapist is not only specific to Western psychological modernity but is also class-specific (Wilce and Price, and Kirmayer, this volume; cf. Kirmayer 1987).

References

Berry, D. S. and Pennebaker, J. W. (1993). Nonverbal and verbal emotional expression and health. *Psychotherapy and Psychosomatics*, *59*(1), 11–19.
Blalock, J. E. (1984). The immune system as a sensory organ. *Journal of Immunology*, *132*(3), 1067–1070.
—— and Smith, E. M. (1985). The immune system: our mobile brain? *Immunology Today*, 6, 115–142.
Booth, R. J. and Ashbridge, K. R. (1993a). A fresh look at the relationship between the psyche and immune system: teleological coherence and harmony of purpose. *Advances, The Journal of Mind-Body Health*, *9*(2), 4–23.
—— and —— (1993b). The limits of reductionism. *Advances, The Journal of Mind-Body Health*, *9*(3), 65–67.

——, Petrie, K. J., and Pennebaker, J. W. (1997). Changes in circulating lymphocyte numbers following emotional disclosure: evidence of buffering. *Stress Medicine*, *13*(1), 23–29.

Dreau, D., Sonnenfeld, G., Fowler, N., Morton, D. S., and Lyte, M. (1999). Effects of social conflict on immune responses and *E. coli* growth within closed chambers in mice. *Physiology and Behavior*, *67*(1), 133–140.

Eggert, F., Muller Ruchholtz, W., and Ferstl, R. (1998). Olfactory cues associated with the major histocompatibility complex. *Genetica*, *104*(3), 191–197.

Esterling, B. A., Antoni, M. H., Kumar, M., and Schneiderman, N. (1990). Emotional repression, stress disclosure responses, and Epstein-Barr viral capsid antigen titers. *Psychosomatic Medicine*, *52*(4), 397–410.

Francis, M. E. and Pennebaker, J. W. (1992). Putting stress into words: the impact of writing on physiological absentee and self-reported emotional well-being measures. *American Journal of Health Promotion*, *6*(4), 280–288.

Jordan, W. C. and Bruford, M. W. (1998). New perspectives on mate choice and the MHC. *Heredity*, *81*(3), 239–245.

Kirmayer, L. J. (1987). Languages of suffering and healing: alexithymia as a social and cultural process. *Transcultural Psychiatric Research Review*, *24*(2), 119–136.

Kurtz, S. N. (1992). *All the mothers are one: Hindu India and the cultural reshaping of psychoanalysis*. New York: Columbia University Press.

Lamb, S. (2000). *White saris and sweet mangoes: aging, gender, and body in north India*. Berkeley: University of California Press.

Martin, E. (1993). Histories of immune systems. *Culture, Medicine, and Psychiatry*, *17*(1), 67–76.

Pearse Pratt, R., Schellinck, H., Brown, R., Singh, P. B., and Roser, B. (1998). Soluble MHC antigens and olfactory recognition of genetic individuality: the mechanism. *Genetica*, *104*(3), 223–230.

Pennebaker, J. W. and Francis, M. E. (1996). Cognitive, emotional, and language processes in disclosure. *Cognition and Emotion*, *10*(6), 601–626.

——, Hughes, C. F., and O'Heeron, R. C. (1987). The psychophysiology of confession: linking inhibitory and psychosomatic processes. *Journal of Personality and Social Psychology*, *52*(4), 781–793.

——, Kiecolt-Glaser, J., and Glaser, R. (1988). Disclosure of traumas and immune function: health implications for psychotherapy. *Journal of Consulting and Clinical Psychology*, *56*(2), 239–245.

Petrie, K. J., Booth, R. J., and Pennebaker, J. W. (1998). The immunological effects of thought suppression. *Journal of Personality and Social Psychology*, *75*(5), 1264–1272.

——, ——, Elder, H., and Cameron, L. D. (1999). Psychological influences on the perception of immune function. *Psychological Medicine*, *29*(2), 391–397.

——, ——, Pennebaker, J. W., Davison, K. P., and Thomas, M. G. (1995). Disclosure of trauma and immune response to a Hepatitis B vaccination program. *Journal of Consulting and Clinical Psychology*, *63*(5), 787–792.

Schellinck, H. M., Slotnick, B. M., and Brown, R. E. (1997). Odors of individuality originating from the major histocompatibility complex are masked by diet cues in the urine of rats. *Animal Learning and Behavior*, *25*(2), 193–199.

Spera, S. P., Buhrfeind, E. D., and Pennebaker, J. W. (1994). Expressive writing and coping with job loss. *Academy of Management Journal*, *37*(3), 722–733.

Tauber, A. I. (1995). *The immune self: theory or metaphor?* Cambridge and New York: Cambridge University Press.

Uexküll, T. von, Geigges, W., and Herrmann, J. M. (1993). The principle of teleological coherence and harmony of purpose exists at every level of integration in the hierarchy of living systems. *Advances, The Journal of Mind-Body Health, 9*(3), 50–63.

Wedekind, C., and Furi, S. (1997). Body odour preferences in men and women: do they aim for specific MHC combinations or simply heterozygosity? *Proceedings of the Royal Society of London Series B: Biological Sciences, 264*(1387), 1471–1479.

Wobst, B., Zavazava, N., Luszyk, D., Lange, K., Ussat, S., Eggert, F., Ferstl, R., and Muller Ruchholtz, W. (1998). Molecular forms of soluble HLA in body fluids: potential determinants of body odor cues. *Genetica, 104*(3), 275–283.

Chapter 4: Editor's note

Wilce and Price draw on their own ethnographic experience in Bangladesh and Ecuador, and provide interpretations of other sociocultural systems to argue for a profound relativity not only of concepts of immune systems but of bodies and physiologies themselves. In this regard they echo the theme of "local biologies" explored by Margaret Lock (1998). Wilce and Price share with Booth and Davison, and Cone and Martin, a particular concern for the problem of self and other. Their chapter engages Westerners' beliefs – expressed in popular culture and sustained by findings such as Pennebaker's (this volume) – that by some act of imagination, some form of self-expression, they can enhance or preserve their own health. Price and Wilce attempt to place such hopes in a cross-cultural comparative context, thus raising questions about their absolute validity. At the same time, they explore possibilities for a humane or clinically applied cultural psychoimmunology.

Metaphors our bodyminds live by

James M. Wilce Jr and Laurie J. Price

> The body social and the body personal always exist in a mutually consti-
> tutive relationship.
>
> (Comaroff 1985: 8)

> Though military metaphors [for immunologic "defense" processes] may
> govern our thinking from the moment we stop reflecting about them and
> return to our work, this does not, in itself, mean that they are either more
> accurate or more natural than any of the alternatives; it only means that
> culturally we have embraced, and, ultimately, embodied them.
>
> (Napier 1996: 335f).

Culture, images, and imagination

Imagine a very sick person. Imagine her under the care of someone who helps
her relax by suggesting she envision herself lying on a sunny beach. Picture
another person suggesting that she imagine her T-cells killing, doing battle
with, or just gobbling up bad cells – germs or cancer cells. We might even
overhear such a guide telling the patient that if she does so, it will help her
body to fight off her illness. Now imagine a woman in a less clinical setting,
say, a self-help workshop centered on intensive personal journaling. The
workshop leaders tell the woman there is evidence suggesting physical health
benefits come to those who break through inner blocks and move beyond
silent rumination on loss, stress, or trauma, by bringing themselves to write
their most intimate feelings about the event.

Many readers will be able to envision such scenarios; some will have
participated in similar ones. So, if we now propose to define "cultures," in
part, as aids to the imagination, you might accept this as true in several senses.
Sharing a particular culture means shared familiarity with a set of scenarios
like those described above. It also means that participants in such events bring
to them – and/or achieve within them – the imagination that the claims of
caregivers and experts (e.g. about images and their therapeutic effects) make
sense. Science involves the imagination, and the hard science and popular
science invoked in the first paragraph involve plenty. But all science is

cultural activity. It feeds upon and nourishes cultural images. Even textbooks in immunology draw upon images of such obviously sociocultural phenomena as class stratification, nation-states, and war (Martin 1994). And science produces images that enter the popular imagination. In the last several decades, through a trickling down of immunological research, the American public has come to imagine a range of diverse elements – the skin, IgA, and CD-4s – as a single system, the "immune system."

Cultures are not only aids to the imagination. We live by what we imagine; this must include our metaphors (Lakoff and Johnson 1980; Kirmayer, this volume). In this chapter we make the even stronger claim that cultures help to shape actual bodies, partly by means of widely held models, images, and metaphors. Kirmayer has argued (1992) that metaphor not only arises out of embodied experience but, conversely, becomes embodied. Thus he calls for an investigation of "the psychophysiology of metaphor" (336). Much earlier, Moerman (1979) sought in metaphor at least a partial explanation for the efficacy of symbolic healing: "The construction of healing symbols *is* healing." This shaping potential of signs (images, metaphors, symbols) involves culturally particular multistory, reflexive, metalevel phenomena – e.g. feelings about feelings (metasentiment, meta-emotion; Gottman *et al.* 1996), and images of how images work. Imagine we "knew" that guided imagery had high curative efficacy with cancer and had reduced this "finding" to the relaxing effect of the image, which in turn was due to its association with sources of reassurance.[1] This is to say that the image "relaxes" people in part because of a meta-imagination of the efficacy of images and symbols (Lévi-Strauss 1963), the assurance that certain images or imaginative acts carried therapeutic benefit. We propound just such a model of culture-as-multistory/metalevel phenomenon, and thus explain cultures' roles in mobilizing immune response and healing. To do so, we draw on ethnographic as well as experimental evidence.

This book's claim that immune systems have cultural and social lives is an inference from other sorts of evidence, too. No one who accepts the notion of the immune system denies that the life of such systems is embedded in the life of human populations. At one level, our claim that human immune systems (and psychoimmune systems) exist in relation to the empirical and symbolic life of societies is founded on the most fundamental insights of epidemiology – that health and disease have social contexts.[2] The relationship is not one-way but mutual. We see the impact of immunity on social organization when we consider the disorder and cultural turmoil caused by depopulating plagues, including those brought on by colonial contact. On the other hand, the effects of subsistence and housing patterns on social networks and thus on patterns of disease and immunity are well known to epidemiologists. Physiological sociology (Barchas 1976) and anthropological field studies (Part II, this volume) have given us evidence that key immune mediators in the endocrine system may reflect social status and social experience.[3] But human neuroimmunological process must be mediated by psychology and, therefore, by factors like culture that shape individual psychology.[4] Measurable impacts of ideology and other dimensions of cultural life on immune function are less well studied than the more purely sociological factors – like the correlation between high stress and low socio-economic status – in human endocrinology (Part II, this volume).

Popular notions of the self and its boundaries are not only specific to cultures, to political economies, and to the sorts of immune science generated therein (Martin 1994; Cone and Martin, this volume). It is significant that immunology as a science has, until recently, depended on the self/non-self distinction (Booth and Davison, Cone and Martin, this volume), while "socialization (for Samoans, and others) erodes a sense of subjective self" (McDade, this volume) and the assertion of boundaries between that self and one's family is often frowned upon. These constructions of self, emotion, and expressivity might also be nonarbitrarily related to measurable processes in particular bodies in particular social formations. That entails a pressing research agenda, one foreshadowed by Frankenberg's (1986) call for a re-visioning of sickness as cultural performance (see Lock 1993: 142).[5] We would suggest a reconsideration of *health and healing*, too, as performances of cultural potentialities. Culture – social experience and expectations as well as beliefs, images, metaphors, and meta-images – is embodied (Csordas 1990, Farnell 1996).

Our discussion to this point assumes that cultures have some degree of integration. We assume that members of social groups define themselves by a common orientation of their actions to a culture, a semi-shared, semi-integrated system of values and ideas. Moreover, evidence points to the importance, to those social actors, of feeling themselves to be in consonance with dominant cultural values and norms (Decker *et al.*, this volume). Dressler *et al.* (1998) have found evidence of a correlation between feeling, on the one hand, that one is achieving a successful lifestyle as it is defined locally, and one's physical and mental health on the other. "When the individual is continuously checking his or her own cultural consonance and finds it wanting, it is likely to be a frustrating and depressing circumstance. This is a process that is also expressed somatically" (Dressler *et al.* 1998: 440). The groups Dressler studies live with a definition of a successful life(style) that include not only material manifestations – ownership of consumer items – but also associated behaviors. Wilce (2000) is preparing to investigate the hypothesis that living in consonance with widely shared cultural expectations as to what symbolic behaviors are healthiest, or enhance immune function, is also of benefit to the individual by itself. Dissonance has its costs.

Metaphor, minds, and bodies

When Johnson (1987) and Lakoff and Kövecses (1987) say that we live by certain metaphors of the body, they mean that cultural metaphors *reflect* innate biological, embodied experiences. Conversely, some psychoneuroimmunologists – including those who have encouraged guided imagery to fight cancer (Hall and O'Grady 1991) – go beyond this to hypothesize that images *change* somatic processes.[6] We propose a revision of even that model, adding the proviso that culturally variable images of body and healing are variably embodied within and across societies.[7] What we are proposing is "local biologies" (Lock 1998). Pennebaker and his colleagues (e.g. Pennebaker *et al.* 1989) have conducted perhaps the only experimental comparison of the physiological effects of two contrasting ideologies, crystallized in two proverbs (p. 58). Still, their work does not consider ethnocultural diversity (but, for an exception, see the chapter by Pennebaker's collaborators Booth and Davison in this volume).

The body is a rich metaphor for society (Scheper-Hughes and Lock 1987). Body metaphors – including those whose surface structure refers to individual somatic process – conventionally and most relevantly point to social processes. Cognitive linguists and anthropologists have carried out a large proportion of the studies of cultural metaphor to date (Lakoff and Johnson 1980). However, embodiment theorists who are not so wed to cognitivist models have contributed to the area as well (Farnell 1996; Lyon, this volume). We do not need to posit a conscious cognitive processing of cultural symbols through ritual, etc. in order to imagine that cultural metaphors are both enacted and enfleshed in individuals' bodies. It may be more accurate to picture actors doing with their bodies things that make sense in metaphoric ways because of a shared bodily group of action, cognition, and culture (Csordas 1990). Metaphor thus becomes an analytic tool – a way for anthropologists to talk about iconicity between bodily process or action on the one hand and cultural values on the other – rather than a trope to accurately represent the consciousness of actors.

Writing about trauma has a therapeutic efficacy that has been well demonstrated. Pennebaker and others (Pennebaker *et al.* 1989; Esterling *et al.* 1994; Petrie *et al.* 1995) have studied the benefits of writing (in private journal entries) about traumatic experience. Such interventions, and their effects, enact particular cultural metaphors that researchers have not made explicit as such. Writing exercises, and the conclusions drawn from them, reflect a widespread vision Westerners have of how language (written or spoken) communicates – a vision focusing on referentiality and neutrality that we can sum up with "the conduit metaphor."[8] The title of a Pennebaker article, "Putting stress into words," metaphorically takes stress as a fluid-like thing that can be put in words as container-like things.

Words achieve many things, including performing and reshaping selves and social realities, as Booth and Davison imply (this volume). Yet Western folk and philosophical images of language tend to reduce its function to reference to pre-existing objects, including emotions metaphorized as (fluid) things. This imagination of communication also separates message form from message function, treating form as a neutral, non-obstructing conduit through

which semantic notions flow unaffected (Reddy 1993). The metaphor repro-
duced in studies of trauma-writing by Pennebaker (this volume) and
colleagues (Booth and Davison, this volume) is that of bodies as containers
and emotions as fluids to be poured out into neutrally referring words before
their pressures damage the container. We view language differently. Words
are not neutral conduits for objectifiable fluid-like feelings. Rather, words and
gestures perform quite magically; the performative (as opposed to merely
referential or reflective) power of language is certainly central to ritual of all
sorts, including healing ritual (Tambiah 1979). It is precisely the performative power of words and other human signifying acts to unite bodies and
cultural images that must be studied in an investigation of PNI-relevant
therapeutic interventions across cultures.

Psychoneuroimmunology, or PNI, has taken for granted a universal,
preconceptual, precultural human body[9] that responds in predictable ways to
the "same" emotions, meta-emotions, and behaviors. Such behaviors include
reprocessing trauma by writing it, or participating in a guided imagery intervention for cancer patients – one centering on military images of the immune
system. By contrast, we propose that sociocultural contexts that discourage
verbalizing of trauma or paying any attention at all to cancer (even through
"positive" imagery) might engender local psychoimmunologies for which
such acts have a neutral or even negative impact on immune function.[10]

"Healthy" expressive "release" of negative affect: a cultural metaphor in comparative perspective

Lakoff and Johnson (1980) pioneered a useful example of an approach to
culturally particular images and metaphors – though their work generally fails
to draw on actual occurrences in natural discourse. They explored in some
detail the "body as container" metaphor common in European languages.
Lakoff and Kövecses (1987) link this master metaphor with specific English
metaphors for anger. The idioms "bursting with anger" and "barely contain-
able rage" evoke the container metaphor, while indirectly supporting notions
that it is better to "let it out" in a controlled way. Lakoff and Kövecses claim
that the association of anger with metaphors of contained heat *reflects*
embodied experience and is thus likely to prove universal at least in outline
(ibid.: 220f). Given a model that holds idioms to be part of an integrated
semantic network (Good 1977), we could take it as a working hypothesis that
anyone who experiences anger as threatening them with "bursting" might
experience, along with anger, another tension over the risk such anger posed
to their "container."[11] We can also hypothesize that those who "live" such
metaphors might feel the release of tension and anger to be health-inducing.

We are not arguing that Americans share conscious notions linking
catharsis with *immune function* per se, though that might be true (Martin
1994). Rather, we are asserting two things: first, we claim that broader images

that implicitly link a "contained" emotion with risk, and expression with health are culturally salient. Second, we point to the likelihood that such tropes are themselves embodied in a process whereby cultural signs (metaphors, idioms, images) somehow join with physiology (Moerman 1979; Dow 1986; Csordas 1988, 1990; Csordas and Kleinman 1990; Kirmayer 1992; and cf. Barchas 1976, Lyon 1993).

Re-evaluation Counseling (RC, also called "Co-counseling") is a popular movement in the US based on the conviction that emotional discharge is essential for psychological and social well being. Founded in the 1960s, RC is now practiced by many thousands of North Americans (including co-author Price), and has organizations in many other locales around the world. After a multi-week training program, people learn how to be both counselor and counselee. They exchange roles on a regular basis, typically halfway through a given session.[12] In RC theory, when people have distressing experiences, they need to discharge the distress with the attention of another individual, someone who is listening carefully and supportively, but not "telling them what to do." "Discharge" is signaled externally when the person being counseled begins to cry or sob, tremble with cold perspiration, laugh loudly, shout, talk in a fully engaged way, or move around vigorously.[13] RC offers a cultural model that explicitly mandates expression of emotions, and periodic catharsis, a model endorsed by at least a portion of the general population in North America.

Anthropologists argue that such cultural models need to be seen in broad, global, comparative perspective. Theoretical links between local models of self and emotion on the one hand and social structure on the other, were made by Michelle Rosaldo (1984). Arguing that "cultural idioms provide the images in terms of which our subjectivities are formed, and . . . these idioms themselves are socially ordered and constrained," Rosaldo left us a strong form of the social constructionist argument in relation to metaphors of emotion and containment or control. She proposed that the expression of anger is viewed as destructive in "brideservice" or hunter-gatherer societies, whereas in "more complex, tribal . . . 'bridewealth' groups . . . 'anger' held within may work to other people's harm in hidden, witchlike ways."[14] Extending this, it seems clear that in the postindustrial West – and perhaps in classical Greece, given Aristotle's vision of catharsis – it is the one with "unresolved" or "repressed" anger and grief who feels at risk. This anthropology of self must be taken into consideration in any account of PNI – specifically, any account of how writing about trauma might enhance immune function – that presumes to cover the diversity of human societies.

Metaphors and images that involve the activity of immune systems are a subset of metaphors for the body and emotion that have been well studied (Scheper-Hughes and Lock 1987; Desjarlais 1992). We focus on a particular metaphor that seems to have power over our conceptions and even our physiologies (Pennebaker et al. 1989): "Rid the body/container of dangerous repressed emotion" (Lakoff and Kövecses 1987). It exemplifies the subset of cultural models that link body and emotion vis-à-vis health and immunity, and on another implicit meta-image, namely, that active, assertive imaging can engender positive emotions and bodily states (Kiecolt-Glaser *et al*. 1985). Both involve something like "catharsis,"[15] an ancient notion in the West (Scheff 1979) with new manifestations in popular health and immune metaphors.

Hall and O'Grady, reviewing experimental psychosocial interventions designed to enhance immunocompetence, mention a general benefit from relaxation or simply from the relaxation dimension of a guided imagery exercise, a benefit measurable in several clinical populations. The content of the imagery also counts for something.[16] Some images may have "noxious" effects on some participants; but this is true, more generally, of psychological interventions in conditions like cancer – they run the risk of burdening the patient with a sense of responsibility for a condition that is in fact a cultural metaphor for that which is out of control (Balshem 1991).[17] Hall and O'Grady cite such potential noxious consequences as the induction of a sense of burdensome responsibility for the disease or healing (cf. Sontag 1978). Particular individuals may resist particular images, recoiling at the aggressiveness of imagining "the self's" cells killing "other" cells.[18] One Catholic priest in a study of the effects of imagery in cancer treatment substituted a weed-pulling image for it (Hall and O'Grady 1991). The potential for people to generate any such images arises in the post-1970s' sociocultural environment in which the notion of an "immune *system*" per se has gelled and has captured the popular imagination (Martin 1994). Moreover, the potential for embodying the very images that immune sciences present us (as they trickle down through *National Geographic* and *Time* (Haraway 1993; Martin 1994) – including the commonly militaristic ones – is real (Napier 1996: 335f).

The body and emotions provide ample subjects and objects for culture-specific troping or image-building, as the ethnographic cases discussed below make clear. Such tropes or images are often invented and propagated through public discourse. Whatever else they might be, scientific discussions of "emotions" are also discourses, and thus cultural products. The experience of an emotion is not precultural, not ultimately separable from cultural discourses about it, including social evaluations of the emotion (Roseman *et al.* 1995). And the *expression* of emotion cannot be understood apart from the histories of response to it – predictable and therefore expected verbal and gestural responses to equally stereotyped verbal and nonverbal expressions. Such a social model of embodied experience leads us to a reinterpretation of Pennebaker's findings.

An anthropological interpretation of Pennebaker's findings

The Pennebaker studies stand out for examining the extent to which proverbialized models of body and emotion are enacted or embodied by Americans' very physiology.[19] Physiological reflexes of culturally shared idioms are uncovered in Pennebaker's studies of the effects of verbal disclosure of traumatic events and feelings (Pennebaker *et al.* 1989). They began their theory-building process where a cognitive anthropologist might have begun – by making explicit two proverbs that might cohere with, or even inform, their experimental subjects' embodied responses to disclosing trauma – "Let sleeping dogs lie" versus "Confession is good for the soul [and body!]." To incorporate cultural material such as these proverbs is exemplary.[20] Such a cultural self-consciousness is missing from the PNI literature and from hard immunology despite its saturation with culturally and sociopolitically significant metaphors (as Martin has shown, 1994).

Pennebaker *et al.* cite the two proverbs simply as tropes to contextualize their findings. But as anthropologists, we are interested not only in their experiment and the proverbs but in the relation of such proverbs to the expectations and even the physiology of their subjects. The proverbs themselves might help to construct the phenomenal worlds of those who choose whether or not to write emotionally about a trauma, and who then do, or do not, experience a benefit from the writing. Or, in a different model, we might see the proverbs, the conduit metaphor, and the experience of healing as mutually implied in the ways that culture is embodied (Csordas 1990).

In any case, the two proverbs are not equal, and understanding this point is crucial to achieving a clearer vision of the relationship of immune function to culture. Although Pennebaker, Barger, and Tiebout's research subjects were all Jewish Holocaust survivors living in Dallas, and thus could be said to share a great deal of cultural commonality, they did not all respond to the invitation to write their most intimate thoughts and feelings about their experience. Those who wrote most emotionally – following what the authors (not the subjects themselves) called the "confession is good for the soul" prescription – experienced health benefits. Those who followed the "let sleeping dogs lie" proverb experienced slightly *poorer* health in the months following the intervention than in the previous months. Both proverbs were culturally available to the participants. Again, we have adapted Dressler's model of cultural consonance, predicting that those who feel themselves in consonance with cultural norms guiding one's coping with trauma will do better, in part, simply because of the perceived consonance. But if a population "believes" two contradictory proverbs, how can this "consonance" model help explain Pennebaker *et al.*'s experimental outcome? The answer lies in the fact that cultural models are not flat but hierarchical. Folk systems of classification, for instance, consist of superordinate and subordinate taxa. We can posit a hierarchical relationship between the two proverbs, i.e. the dominance of the "confession is good for the soul model" among Jewish-Americans (or, more narrowly, Holocaust survivors). If so, then any behaviors that actors experience as "confession" of their thoughts and feelings about trauma would be consonant with this value, would "feel right," and thus – following

Dressler's findings in a different culture (Dressler *et al.* 1998) – result in reduced stress and improved health.

There is, in fact, much evidence that emotional "confession" is valued over silence in many Ashkenazi (Eastern European-derived) Jewish communities. Even oral confession before a rabbi, acting like a priest, is not unknown in the history of European hasidim (Albert 1973). Myerhoff's ethnographic study of elderly Ashkenazic Jews in a group home in Los Angeles documents the practice of testifying in group sessions to losses and griefs. These sessions constitute an ongoing and shared mourning process, which Myerhoff calls "narrating the self" – a valued activity in this residential community (1979). Kidorf (1963) finds a strong congruence between Freud's model of positive mourning and Jewish belief and practice. In stark contrast to Javanese dicta on the subject (Siegel 1986), Judaism affirms rites of mourning that are verbally and somatically expressive (Goldberg 1981–82).

Now research is needed to test the hypothesis we propose here – that it is not disclosure of upsetting feelings that is universally beneficial to a person's immune system regardless of cultural values, but achieving the sense that one is behaving in consonance with dominant values. There are, at present, no published studies of any cross-cultural or interethnic investigations of the physiological effects of "writing trauma." Thus the remainder of this chapter draws on ethnographic field accounts to underscore the likelihood that the peoples of the world embody divergent metaphors, including some that link (local strategies for managing) trauma with health outcomes. We admit that, at least in relation to hard immunological data, the assertion of this "likelihood" is quite hypothetical, but we urge that studies be carried out to move this from theory to test.[21]

The anthropologist armed with studies like Pennebaker's can be misled by a false sense of familiarity as he or she stumbles across evidently familiar idioms of the body as container used in Asia and Latin America, for instance. When we sense that some opening lines of other cultural scripts overlap our own scripts we presume that their conclusions will also be the same. Not so, except perhaps in the first case study below, which presents some of the roots of the implicit cultural notions which underlie the science of health psychology.

This chapter now turns to six case studies, stories about stories. They describe the role of expression of an emotional or unemotional sort (such as venting, narrating distressing events, or telling the story of an illness that nearly cost a life) in relation to healing. Implicit or explicit in local stories are health-relevant models of bodies, emotion, and society. The point of this set of stories is the point of all anthropology, whose path to holism or adequacy of explanation has traditionally been through comparing disparate cultures – to show how a model that might seem quite natural to me is only one, arbitrary, culturally-specific model.

Disharmony, distress, and coping: Western and Asian models

Literary sources of Western meta-imagery of coping

If our readers share a sense that it is a good thing to cry or to tell one's woes, the notion might well be traced back to *Poetics*, in which Aristotle meta-imagines enacted images of tragedy exercising a purifying or cathartic effect on the audience. Scheff (1979) links Aristotle's reflections on drama with psychotherapeutic theories of "emotion work." The historiography of more recent Western cultural theories of emotional imagery and the meta-image of therapeutic re-experience or expression must include the work of Shakespeare. Some psychological anthropologists regard him as a source of insight into "universal" human nature and emotions. More likely, his work resonates with us because he helped to reproduce or re-present fundamental Western cultural themes. Consider Shakespeare's Thirtieth Sonnet:

> When to the sessions of sweet silent thought
> I summon up remembrance of things past,
> I sigh the lack of many a thing I sought
> And with old woes new wail my dear time's waste:
> Then can I drown an eye, unused to flow
> For precious friends hid in death's dateless night,
> And weep afresh love's long-since-cancell'd woe,
> And moan the expense of many a vanisht sight:
> *Then can I grieve* at grievances foregone,
> And heavily from woe to woe *tell* o'er
> *The sad account* of fore-bemoaned moan,
> Which I new pay as if not paid before.
> But if the while I think on thee, dear friend
> All losses are restored, and sorrows end.
>   (1938: 1228, emphasis added)

The sonnet embraces the need to "grieve at grievances" – and not forego or repress grieving – and "heavily from woe to woe tell o'er the sad account of fore-bemoaned moans." We find the same metasentiment in *Macbeth* (IV, iii).

Macduff is finally told the truth about the murder of his wife and children. Malcolm, standing by, says:

> Merciful heaven! –
> What, man! ne'er pull your hat upon your brows;
> *Give sorrow words*: the grief that does not speak
> Whispers the o'er -fraught heart, and bids it break.
>   (1938: 879, emphasis added)

Shakespeare inherited – but, more saliently, passed on to countless Western audiences – a cultural meta-image of cathartic disclosure of images and feelings too awful to bear within. His poems and his dramatic characters counsel verbal disclosure – giving sorrow words.[22] The images of interiority (one's insides as the seat of feeling), of hearts that can break unless relieved of emotion objects/fluids over-filling them, and of narrative as catharsis/therapy, come down to us as powerful cultural affirmations. Shakespeare leaves most of the responsibility for coping with the sufferer himself. As much as these metasentiments stir us, we must recognize that they are not universal. That is made clear by contrasting metasentiments from other traditions.

Coping with cancer: a Japanese oncology manual

Consider Japanese oncologists, whose writings invoke idioms of conflict and support in describing gentle disclosure of cancer diagnoses. We Western readers might skip to the end of the script and presume that the Japanese idiom parallels American oncology's experiments with guided imagery in which patients may be left alone with their imaginations, but not left without guidance – may in fact be encouraged to use aggressive images. American cancer patients are told to relax, *turn inward*, and draw on and enhance inner strength by envisioning their good cells defeating the invading cancer cells (Hall and O'Grady 1991). In contrast, the Japanese oncologists' *Manual of Terminal Care for Cancer Patients* guides physicians thus: "[I]nform your patients you are a co-fighter in this process . . . [Say,] 'Probably, *we* have a long term fight.'" A later "lesson" suggests, "Another example of demonstrating empathy and being a 'co-fighter' is to touch the abdominal area, perhaps thus indicating a visceral core, and ask 'how is the *common* enemy?' . . . or [suggest] '*We* deal with the enemy with deliberateness'" (cited by Good *et al.* 1994: 859, emphasis added; and see Good *et al.* 1993). While American researchers recognize the therapeutic value of social support, a great gap separates those Japanese meta-images of joint social effort from the individualistic metaphors governing the American metacommunicative practice of guided imagery. Pronouns help mark the contrast – Japanese physicians are told to say "we" to convey a subtly *different* military metaphor suggesting *common* engagement in the struggle against cancer.

Costs and benefits of withholding words in South Asia

The Bangladeshi use of the metaphor "holding something in your abdomen" invites our attention for its deceptive appearance to Westerners. A very situated example arises from a moot, country "court," or conflict-resolution meeting that Wilce attended and recorded during his Bangladeshi fieldwork (Wilce 1996). As I (Wilce) listened to negotiations that followed a violent confrontation needing redress in my field village, I sensed the tensions were still palpable and violence was still possible. At one point, my curiosity was piqued when my friend Jalu Miah gave his testimony and the mediators of the confrontation responded: they framed his revelation as something that had emerged from his abdomen! What Jalu revealed was that he had been threatened with a gun. My mind quite naturally – and mistakenly – heard his testimony and the mediator's reframing thereof in terms of cathartic disclosure of his personal trauma. My misimpression arose, in particular, from the question one of the mediators asked Jalu: "How could you have held the word of testimony in your *peṭ* (abdomen) so long?" But the South Asian ethnotheory implicit therein metaphorically casts the abdomen as a repository for secrets. Thus the chairman chides the aggrieved Jalu for his tardiness in speaking. But the Bangladeshi body metaphor is *not* a parallel to our own ethnotheory of emotion which makes the body a dangerous place to store anger or grief as reified emotion-things. Rather, the mediator upbraided Jalu for impeding the "physiological processes" of the body politic by withholding his testimony until that point. At least from the perspective of those mediating the dispute, for Jalu to hold in his *peṭ* information needed to "disentangle" a problem (Watson-Gegeo and White 1992) was a social offense; Jalu had been part of the social problem rather than contributing to its social resolution.[23]

This metaphor is not isolated. Locally, it appears in Bengali literature, where women are sometimes characterized as being *unable* to store secrets in their *peṭ*.[24] We find a parallel even more relevant to the consideration of emotion and its storability – though it comes from the western side of South Asia – in idioms used by women who have spoken with Veena Das about being victims of torture and rape during communal violence in the Punjab. Do they tell the stories again and again in an attempt to cleanse themselves by disclosing or verbally "refining" their traumatic experience? Quite the contrary. Das says the women consider memories of rape a kind of "poisonous knowledge" – memories that dare not be retraced – "[N]one of the metaphors used to describe the self that had become the repository of poisonous knowledge emphasized the need to give expression to this hidden knowledge" (1996: 84). Rather, these women keep the pain and its story inside their abdomens, hiding the stories as babies are hidden in the womb. The "repression" hardly suggests agency at all, let alone virtue. The Punjabi metaphor suggests both. Agency is suggested in two senses, first in terms of the women's choice and visceral struggle to hold things inside. Then, according to Das the abdomen is also made to represent a uniquely female bodily power – the ability to transform a germ into something safe or even good, something such as occurs in pregnancy (1996: 85). The perspective distilled in the metaphor of these Punjabi women contrasts starkly with post-Freudian (but pre-Foucaldian) Western sensibilities about repression.[25]

When we compare South Asian abdomen metaphors with Western metaphors that involve similar "hiding" of words "inside," we see differences

Plate 4.1 The Bangladeshi girl above is protected from the harm of *nazar* (the evil eye) not by words but by a beauty mark intentionally applied off-center so as to divert *nazar*.

in the "text," "upshot," or ideological shading of the metaphors. The value polarities are switched when we move from Western tropes of "getting it all out" to the Punjabi women's hope to keep it "in" and transform "it."[26] Even when disclosing was valorized as it was in the country court discourse recorded by Wilce, it was for the sake of the health of the body politic, not Jalu's body. Admittedly, we lack even ethnographic evidence as to whether the physiological and immunological processes of these women reflect their sense of the positively transformative potential of holding secrets, or whether they would at least feel themselves to be at risk if they brought their secrets out of their abdomens.

Evidence of that sort comes from ethnographic work in Indonesia.

Setres, *abdomens, and sorcery in Indonesia*

Berman's fieldwork in Java (1998) shows how men and women exercise careful control, especially when speaking Javanese, over how they express emotion. Javanese use the term, *setres*, borrowed from English (stress), to designate a phenomenon so dreadful that it is able to kill, at least in the case of very young children. Parents are, obviously, motivated to protect their children from this threat. Thus, Javanese and Americans share the word

Plate 4.2 Maintaining a bright face despite one's inner state helps guard against threats
such as sorcery in Indonesia (according to Wikan 1990).

Photo courtesy of Laine Berman.

"stress," a belief that it can damage one's health, and a concern to manage it.
There the similarity ends. Where at least middle class Americans (see
Kusserow 1999) encourage their children, as Shakespeare wrote, to "give sorrow words," Javanese parents work hard to desensitize children to sudden
changes. That is, instead of training them to be aware of and express feelings,
they train them early to maintain poise and equanimity, to rise above emotional lability (Berman 1998).

For decades, anthropologists concerned with culture's role in relation to illness and health have described "culture-bound syndromes" (Simons and
Hughes 1985), a concept useful in theorizing American and Indonesian illness
patterns. Most so-called culture-bound syndromes – like *amok* and *latah* –
presented in the literature lend themselves to psychological or behavioral
rather than somatic interpretation. Exceptional accounts include anorexia
nervosa in the US (Swartz 1985) and Balinese "pregnancy with stones."
Wikan (1990) describes the Balinese syndrome involving a bloating of the
abdomen with very hard lumps. It is understood to be caused by sorcery and
can lead to death. Key to understanding it, however, is a set of images we
could consider metaphoric if they weren't so real to the Balinese. The first
is a body-ideal-image in which a flat stomach represents discipline and
self-control, linchpins of a Balinese value system. The bloated stomach, by

contrast, is the very image of failure to live up to Balinese ideals of hard work and self-denial (Wikan 1990: 258). It is feared, not only because of those moral-aesthetic connotations, but also because of its interpretability as a sign of a sorcerer's attack. That is, the abdomen becomes the site in which Balinese might involuntarily be made to embody status-conflict and social tensions as they boil over in that curse called "pregnancy with stones." Wikan writes:

> If, as Hahn and Kleinman [1983] assert, the mindful body [Scheper-Hughes and Lock 1987] responds to its biopsychosocial environment in terms of cultural expectations and beliefs that facilitate or impede nocebo [noxious beliefs] and placebo effects, then pregnancy with stones might be seen as peculiarly Balinese: a culturally constructed expression of particular fears and despairs. It embodies basic Balinese concepts of beauty, morality, and interpersonal evil. The physical embodiments of fears work, to quote Hahn and Kleinman, to retard "integrated bio-psychical processes, demoralizing, *reducing immunological competence and physiological activation*" ... Conversely, contact with a *balian* [traditional healer] might activate hope, and with it, the person's internal therapeutic system.
>
> (Wikan 1990: 258f, emphasis added)

Wikan's evidence that bodies take on local shapes reflecting local emotions points to the link between physiological (and (psycho)immune) processes and societies that we are claiming is mediated by cultural metaphors.

Expressing anger and getting ill in the Andes

In Ecuador, once again we encounter a deceptively familiar model of emotions (especially anger) and bodies. Ecuadorean concepts of the body are characterized by a container model in which the body holds emotions such as sadness, anger, anxiety; these emotions are seen to have a variety of effects on social and biological well being (Stevenson 1977; Tousignant 1984; Bastien 1985; Hess 1994; Larme and Leatherman 2003; Price 2003). Especially in the Sierra (highlands), many cultural rules restrict the circumstances in which it is acceptable and safe to let emotions out, and in what forms. These norms prescribe different modes and occasions of expression for men and women. Although indigenous Andean groups have many distinctive illness beliefs and practices, both Mestizo and Indian cultures believe in the power of various emotions to cause illness (Stevenson 1977; Tousignant 1984; Crandon-Malamud 1991; Warren *et al.* 1994). Andean societies are characterized by fairly well developed concepts of how emotions act and move around inside the body, and their impact on important organs like the heart and brain.[27] Bastien has termed the Andean Indian model "hydraulic" because emotions are seen as resembling liquids in their patterns of action and perceived effects. For instance, in the common folk illness *pena*, sorrow and frustration collect in the heart (viewed as porous) and make it swell (Tousignant 1984). An informant of Price's reported in the summer of 1997 that her father-in-law had died the previous year. She described him as having extreme *iras* (irritation, anger) for almost a year. The simple fact that he felt angry was not seen as his major problem, however. His major risk factor was that he expressed these irritations so frequently. Thus the angers rose to his brain and finally killed him. This sometimes fatal malady is called *colerin* (Stevenson 1977). Consistent with a hydraulic image, blood is seen as rising to the brain with more and more anger over time and then, in serious cases, exploding.

Men in the highlands sometimes curse, or express anger or sadness aloud, especially when they have been drinking. But this is often done in a fairly private setting, and in a general way that avoids direct attacks on particular persons: i.e. a general venting at God for tragedies and misfortunes. Price heard this type of verbal performance on more than one occasion, living in a remote Indian village in central Ecuador. Men staggered home on weekend nights, obviously drunk, but not too drunk to hold forth toward the sky with an elaborate monologue of disappointment and frustration about their lives. They usually did this solo rather than in groups, except during fiestas. Women are not provided with this alcohol-based outlet in Ecuador (Price 1992; Larme and Leatherman 2003). They are expected to remain mostly sober and take care of their children, and the men when they drink too much.

Wakes are a culturally elaborated form of grieving in the highland Andes. But after the wake, participants are expected to – and generally do – behave more calmly. In one case documented by Price in a poor Quito neighborhood, the mother of a young girl who died in a fall was criticized by a neighbor and her *comadre* (godmother of her child) for crying too much and too long (months) after the child's death (Price 1992).

Generally, highland Ecuadoreans – not unlike Balinese – strive to control the expression of their feelings. In this cultural algebra of emotions, control of the external expression of anger or sadness is equated with achieving internal control. There is relatively little acting out. Ecuadoreans see this control as important for health and continuing survival, and unrestrained emotional expression is viewed as a negative and dangerous event. It is important to note that this impact is measured in relation to the community and its constituent social relationships as much as in relation to individual well being. Hence, except for men who are drunk, extreme or prolonged emotional catharsis is rarely an acceptable option. However, a diverse set of traditional healing resources (e.g. healers of fright, herbal teas for anger) is available to help people manage feelings that threaten to overwhelm them. Additionally, informal (and relatively non-cathartic or unemotional) narrative provides an outlet for the indirect expression of feelings: stories permit people to connect with events again, without risking harm (Price 1987).

Andean cultural settings mandate control of emotional expression for the individual's own good. Thus, it is unlikely that unrestrained emotional expression would strengthen the immune system. Most highland Ecuadoreans would view cathartic self-disclosure as putting them at risk, in addition to being socially disapproved outside of a few well-defined situations. This culturally based appraisal would likely nullify benefits that might accrue from a direct positive link between emotional catharsis and the biochemical body and its immunocompetence.

The sick who do not speak: an Aboriginal Australian community

One could hardly ask for a cultural model that contrasts more with our "knowledge" that emotional self-disclosure is healing than the Balinese or even the Ecuadorean, but perhaps the strongest contrast is with an Aboriginal model. The Aboriginal Australian community ("mob") of the Darwin fringe (Sansom 1982) sustains, through discursive practices, a conception of the relationship between illness and health in which narrative plays a key role. This will be familiar to Pennebaker's research subjects. Sansom does not discuss Aboriginal notions of the causes or antecedents of serious illness. Rather, he focuses on the power of the recovered sick body to speak a social message, and on the social nature of the interventions that save the sick person. The ongoing results of illness episodes are profoundly social. The recovered patient bears in his or her body signs that seem in part socially constructed in order to draw attention to the markers themselves, in part to draw attention to another person. This person is the one who nursed him or her back to health and thereby gains all rights to narrate the crisis and its resolution. Anyone ignorant of the original event who happens to notice and ask about the recovered person's recurring signs is told that the one who suffered the original illness cannot be its narrator. Narrative rights have passed to the friend or relative (the "mate") who intervened to save him in those critical days. In this sense the dramas of sickness and healing whose origins we might locate in the psyche are located by these Aboriginals in bodies that point to social relationships.

Note that, in Sansom's ethnographic account, stress is not mentioned, but distress is quite in focus. In the Aboriginal case, this distress is caused by illness, not emotional events like those written by Pennebaker et al.'s research subjects. I am not claiming that the Darwin fringe Aboriginal community does not experience psychological stress over, say, the death of a loved one. Western psychological models of stress are not, however, apparent in what community members told Sansom about illness and recovery. It is true that this neglect of themes relevant to Americans of expert or lay status might simply be an accident of focus – of what Sansom did, and did not, want to know or write. I think not. At the very least Sansom's description of the relation of Aboriginal words to sickness and to sociality serves as a trope, an epitome, the epitome of a non-psychologizing model of healing.

Toward a general model of narrative mediation between illness, health, and sociocultural context

Kleinman (1973) has long argued for a "sociosomatic" perspective to supplement that represented in the term "psychosomatic," which represents a dominant model in Western thought (see the journal *Psychosomatic Medicine*).[28] To term a medical belief system "sociosomatic" is to represent a cultural model of the triadic relation of body, mind, and society that differs from the psychosomatic model, one that sees the body as acting as a repository of social troubles. To these two, I add "somatosocial," to represent a model that accords the body first priority as a sign and determiner even of the social realm. Given the power of such terms to neatly capture bigger concepts, it seems useful here to offer them by way of summing up the models discussed above. Given the centrality of notions of "stress" to PNI, and the centrality in this chapter of semiotic expressions (images, narratives) to coping strategies, we will briefly survey how these terms can sum up models of body, mind, and society but also the relation of that triad to stress and expressiveness. The first element in any of these terms represents the dominant factor in that model, and the absent member of the triad represents what is relatively neglected. For example, the term "psychosomatic" reflects the dominance in the modern West of psychologistic individualism (Kusserow 1999) and the relative neglect of the social in our model of illness and healing.

The "psychosomatic" model, dominant in the US, reifies stress as a thing that can be "put into words." It takes stress as a risk to emotional and physical health unless the background "story" and concomitant emotions are verbally objectified (Hanks 1996), and believes that such objectification is therapeutic, especially in the case of narrative disclosure by private individuals on paper (Pennebaker 1993). The psychosomatic model can be schematized as follows:

> psychosocial stress --→ illness → cathartic narration of the personal experience --→ healing

Note that in this and later schematics, the broken arrows represent (what is conceived as) the natural course of things, while the solid arrow represents a culturally approved strategy to intervene in, alter, or cope with this natural course.

The second, "sociosomatic," model reflects at least some aspects of Ecuadorean thought. Ecuadorean men and women blame some deaths on *colerin*, which is thought to result not just from anger but frequent venting of anger. Let us assume that such expressions reflect interpersonal or social tensions. Yet, the body that must be protected in this model is the body politic, the community. Hence, venting is proscribed unless it is redirected, e.g.

during a drinking bout, toward the sky or God. Here is a schematic representation of an Ecuadorean sociosomatic model:

social conflict --> "evil words" --> illness → drunken venting →
less anger --> no *colerin* death[29]

Balinese models, according to Wikan (1990), are also sociosomatic. The body is vulnerable to the anger of others via sorcery. Sorcery is often thought to be provoked by even the hint of any expression of anger, the letting slip of one's guard that stifles one's expression of sadness or anger. Curative or preventive measures do not involve "expressing one's feelings" at all. They require an inner exertion of will to think and feel differently and to forget the cause of anger or grief.[30] I will take the risk of abbreviating this Balinese coping strategy as sociosomatic "suppression."

social conflict --> expressive slip --> illness (e.g. pregnancy with
stones) → suppression of bad feeling (with social help in the
form of friends and traditional healers) --> healing

The final permutation, which we might call a "sociosemiotic" model of healing-and-its-representation, is represented by Sansom's (1982) Aboriginal Australian community. The Darwin fringe Aboriginal model represents a "somatosocial" conception of the relationship between illness, narrative, and society. The body, rather than the modernist or Freudian psyche, is not only the focus of concern in this community's illness events but also becomes the prompt for narrative expression of the distress, the occasion for strengthening social bonds. Thus, the Aboriginal model can be schematized as follows:

illness → friend's intervention --> *partial* healing leaving noticeable
bodily signs → public narratives of illness and intervention *by the
patient's "mate"*

We have shown how four societies owe allegiance to different models of illness and signs (though we might lump some of them together as "sociosomatic" (Kleinman and Becker 1998). A taxonomy like this would be still more useful if it were an explanatory model like Rosaldo's (see the earlier discussion of her attempt to correlate a taxonomy of cultural models of the self and emotion with kinship systems – brideservice and bridewealth). That is, a more useful taxonomy would relate the Darwin fringe Aboriginal community's model of sickness and speech to the putative fact that it is a "brideservice society." Similarly, it would explain Americans' tendency to locate "witchlike effects of feelings" inside their experiencer, and the Balinese tendency to locate feelings' effects in someone else in the society – in a victim – by appeal to relevant structural features of those societies as well.

Conclusion

Anthropology can enhance understandings of immune function to the extent that it convinces various publics of the relevance of ethnography along with other forms of research. Together, the several forms of research we have drawn on help us envision a cultural psychoimmunology. They illuminate how variable are cultural models of self, illness, healing, and immunological function. They point to possible embodiments of these divergent metaphors. We have argued for a deep cultural consonance, a model that joins two seemingly incomparable sorts of findings. It joins ethnographic accounts of cultural metaphors and verbal images that bodyminds "live by" on the one hand, with experimental evidence from the US that indicates that interventions can teach patients a therapeutic embodiment of images (even of the conduit metaphor). Further research to find measurable immunological reflections of culturally constructed metaphors of body and emotion is a project worth pursuing. Although such research remains to be done, we have put forward a hypothesis that reflects and moves beyond the experimental evidence of Pennebaker and colleagues, and the set of ethnographic case studies we reviewed. That hypothesis is that acts (e.g. writing, disclosing, or hiding words in one's abdomen) that are felt to be consonant with dominant values of one's culture are stress-reducing and thus beneficial.

This hypothesis is a step toward a cultural immunology. A cultural model of (psycho)immunology helps correct imbalances and could thus be part of clinical interventions aimed at enhancing hope.[31] Such a model responds critically to the metaphorical linking (in the self-help literature, for instance) of cancer (or illness in general) with personal failure (Sontag 1978; DiGiacomo 1992; Martin 1993), a link that reproduces Western individualism and reifies agency to the point of blaming the victim for disease.[32] Yet, even critical medical anthropology has the opportunity to build, *with hope*, a sort of multistory edifice on its own partly phenomenological roots. The first "story to be built" is to demonstrate links between body, mind, society, and political economy and healing in cultural specific ways, without collapsing one into another (body into society, etc.; Cone and Martin, this volume). But a second story can be added to this building; a critical anthropology can also be clinically relevant in shaping therapeutic practice, e.g. guiding the training of physicians who are faced with choices about metaphorizing cancer, AIDS, or the common cold. The dilemma for such an applied/critical anthropology becomes that of supporting patients' hopes while avoiding an uncritical reproduction of the *hope in technology* which defines US oncology's "discourse on hope" (Good *et al.* 1990). A PNI that takes cultural variability seriously could not succumb so to a highly particular cultural model (hope in technology).[33] It is a matter of recognizing the sense in which self-healing is both resistance to and a reflection of other technologies of the self and health.[34]

Thus, as DiGiacomo argues, we must strive for the Goldilocks touch *vis-à-vis* meaning, eschewing the dual risk of too little or too much interpretation. To avoid the problem of the meaning of illness altogether – as Sontag and traditional biomedicine call us to do – would be as mistaken as overinvesting the often random experiences of disease with either psychological or socio-political meanings. How can we bring theory and practice to bear in a way that supports patients' hopes and struggles for meaning while somehow avoiding the reproduction of the American ideology of hyperagency that would blame illness on a patient's (improperly handled) feelings (DiGiacomo 1992)? We have argued that cultural metaphors pertaining to PNI or to immune-enhancement are embodied. Because of the possibility that writings like ours (or Bernie Siegel's (DiGiacomo 1992)) come to be part of the cultural and clinical horizon in which illness is experienced, we must search for the "just right" sort of semiotic in a cultural re-visioning of embodiment in PNI. And our search must include the urgent implementation of research agendas designed to test hypotheses related to the variability of psychoimmune processes in relation to culture.

Notes

1 At least in regards to hypertension and conscious stressors, the relaxation hypothesis has not been upheld (Mann, this volume) but it might still be upheld in PNI research (Hall and O'Grady 1991).
2 Several chapters in this volume, such as Cone and Martin's, offer sophisticated visions of the links between human beings, their social organization, and their environment.
3 The same has been well documented for animals.
4 Sudhir Kakar argues for a revision of psychoanalytic theorization of self and society that would

> begin with the idea that the inner space occupied by what is commonly called the 'self'. . . not only contains mental representations of one's bodily life and of primary relationships within the family but also holds mental representations of one's group and its culture, that is, the group's configuration of beliefs about [persons], nature, and social relations.
>
> (1996: 188)

Such a model would leave room for internalization of metaphors of health and healing, and feelings toward key conveyors of those metaphors.
5 By sickness we of course include *pena*, discussed below under "Expressing anger and getting ill in the Andes."
6 If, as Lock (1993) and others have argued, sickness (particularly, but not exclusively, culture-bound syndromes) is a "cultural performance," all the more can that be said of healing and, specifically, of self-therapy through imagery that is guided along culturally-freighted metaphorical paths.
    As I interpret Mark Johnson in *The Body in the Mind* (1987), he acknowledges both possible directions of causal influence in the relationship between embodiment and metaphor. He acknowledges both the constitutive (even somatically

constitutive?) and creative role of the imagination (166ff) and the body as only the ground of imagination (the book's subtitle is "The bodily basis of meaning, imagination, and reason").

For a treatment of deixis – indexical reference – in socially constituted space that attempts to bridge Johnson's phenomenological grounding of spatial perception in the body with a Whorfian affirmation of the role of linguistic structure in constituting the embodied social sense of space, see Hanks 1990.

7 It is important to recognize intracultural variation from the outset of research into the "cultural psychoneuroimmunology" of disclosure proposed in this chapter. Though this is old hat to psychologists, anthropologists have sometimes portrayed cultures as monoliths sharing a single model of, say, persons in need of catharsis.

8 Farnell points out that, whereas speakers of Indo-European languages make gestures that metaphorically reproduce the conduit metaphor, others make gestures that do not so objectify feelings, thoughts, or semiosis (Farnell 1996).

9 For a critique of this sort of embodiment theory, see Farnell 1996.

10 None of this should cause anthropologists to pay any *less* attention to the implications for social control (or the political dimensions) of ideologies which either limit or encourage cathartic expression. (For two very different approaches to that theme, see Lewis 1975 and Briggs 1992.) The more one emphasizes self-agency or the conditionability (Ader and Cohen 1991) or individual control of immune processes, the less one tends to stress the political distribution of stressors and toxins, or the inherent limits imposed by one's genotype on the way psychology might influence immunocompetence. (For an attempt to balance the two, see Martin, this volume). Victim-blaming seems a real risk in the PNI vision (cf. Sontag 1977–78). This argument is made eloquently by DiGiacomo (1992).

11 Blumhagen's (1982) finding that Anglo veterans in the US define high blood pressure as "Hyper-Tension" (i.e. the buildup of tension, worry, anxiety, pressure) supports this view. See Mann, this volume.

12 The founder, Harvey Jackins, writes: "The natural emotional tone of a human being is zestful enjoyment of life. The natural relationship between any two human beings is loving affection, communication and co-operation." (1973:2)

13 According to the RC model, people can only work through distress and get back to rational (i.e. "emotional open or loving" state of being) through this kind of supported emotional discharge, but some cultures make it more difficult to do this than others. Jackins points out that in North American society, someone who seeks attention for discharge is very often rebuffed with admonitions such as: "Don't cry," "Be a big boy," "Get a grip on yourself," "Don't freak out now" (1973). With time, undischarged distress leads to compulsive feeling patterns, and behaviors. In the RC training course completed by Price, these compulsions were represented as "tapes" that play out irrationally, in circumstances where they do not apply. Jackins writes: "In our present state of civilization, the bulk of early distress experiences of any child result exactly from the dramatized distress recordings of adults, which the adult received from earlier generations when they were children" (1975: 6). From the perspective of RC, wars, exploitation, prejudice all proceed from this pattern of undischarged distress, i.e. "Nothing prevents communication, agreement, and co-operation between any humans except distress patterns" (Jackins 1975: 7).

14 Lindstrom's study of Tannese conflict discourse (often called "disentangling" in the Pacific, (Watson-Gegeo and White 1992)) provides an example. One disputant blamed an elder for a death of a child, which was one of the topics of the disentangling meeting. "[H]e . . . claimed that a number of people had heard [the elder . . .] say that the child 'must die' . . . [Thus] the cause of [the child's] . . .

death was a grandfatherly curse" (Lindstrom 1992: 119) – words perhaps uttered idly but seen to work in "witchlike ways." Tanna (Vanuatu) is a bigman society in which men wishing to marry exchange a sister with a male partner, making him their brother-in-law.

15 As the use of this term with strong medical meanings (used exclusively by Hippocrates and colleagues to denote the cleansing of the bowels) by Aristotle in his *Poetics* shows, the joining of emotional and health dimensions under a concept of expulsion-cleansing is ancient. See Scheff 1979.

It should be noted that venting or catharsis is not Pennebaker's own explana-tory category (see his critical comments on catharsis as venting-without-insight in his chapter, this volume). What we claim is that a cleansing or expulsion model, held consciously or unconsciously, underlies not only the writing of Pennebaker's subjects but its effects on their physiologies. Pennebaker 1989 argues that cogni-tive reorganization of trauma rather than pure venting or catharsis explains the immune and health benefits of the disclosure of trauma by his research subjects in their journal entries under his supervision.

A model which seeks to incorporate Pennebaker's own theoretical under-standing of what goes on in his experimental subjects with folk models should look to the process of Weberian rationalization. Let us assume that Weber and others are correct in claiming that all cultures, and the post-Calvinistic capitalist West in particular, undergo rationalization in which magic and passion are subsumed under the increasing dominance of rational practices from bookkeeping (Weber 1958) to talking *about* emotion rather than performing it (Urban 1996: 175f). Let us then imagine that conformity to such valued practices generates less psychobiological stress than resistance (see Decker's contribution to this volume). Given these two assumptions – quite apart from any putative universalist bio-logical explanation of the benefits of "thinking for expressing" (see Slobin 1996; such thinking seems modular, different from other modes) – we should investi-gate the hypothesis that conformity to "rationalization" in the form of writing one's troubles is "good [for the body] to think."

16 "Cancer patients apply the principle [used successfully by athletes for decades] by creating a mental image that culminates in the destruction of their cancer. Because of the widely held belief that immunocompetence is related to the progression of neoplastic disease, many patients create an image that includes natural killer (NK) cells and cytotoxic T cells erod-ing the tumor" (Hall and O'Grady 1991: 1069). In their own trial, which had but one man in it after two months, they found his "circulating levels of thymosin $\alpha 1$ which has been reported to stimulate lymphocyte differentia-tion . . . and total number of circulating lymphocytes increased over this period when the imagery was being carried out [and declined when the man stopped doing it]. Alone, the immunologic measures would be meaningless. However, the data (including the oncologist's report of "metastatic bone disease demonstrating overall improvement") are in support of the conclu-sions of Simonton and Achterberg (regarding physiological reflexes of guided imagery; Achterberg 1984). In a "larger and more comprehensive" trial (Gruber *et al.* 1988) "subjects were instructed to formulate an image that they would feel comfortable with, although this usually involved imagining the immune system being involved in the eradication of the cancer. Patients were encouraged to formulate their own images in order to maximize their participation in this experimental protocol. Participation as well as a degree

of responsibility have been found to be important factors in inducing a general sense of wellbeing."

(Hall and O'Grady 1991: 1070)

17 Hall and O'Grady mention that, "for certain individuals, a strong belief that one's emotional outlook or behavior can reduce the spread of disease can . . . result in the opposite outcome [due to the anxiety provoked by the belief and its locating of agency in ego]" (ibid.: 1076).

18 That imageries such as "the body at war" pervade not only scientific discussion but also media representations and popular thought is made abundantly clear by Martin (1994) and Haraway (1993).

Achterberg writes, "Recent studies showing a relationship between imagery and disease, and specific immune functions are cited to support the role of imagery in health. The data suggest that each image has a biochemical, neuroanatomic component and that imagery can influence and is influenced by activities at the cellular level" (1984: 1). "Cancer can be conceived of as an immune disorder" since it involves a breakdown in the white blood cells' tendency to attack abnormal cells like tumors (ibid.: 6). "An instrument was developed, the Imagery of Cancer ['Image-CA'] . . . which assesses symbology about . . . the cancer, its treatment, and any inherent ability to overcome it i.e. immunological properties)" (ibid.: 7). Images for white blood cells labeled positive in Achterberg's study (those with positive outcomes) were "traditional heroes from history . . . white knights, vikings, and religious figures. Negative symbols for the white blood cells were snowflakes, clouds, or similar weak and amorphous objects" (ibid.: 8). "[S]ignificant correlations were found between both number and activity of white blood cells and the imagery" in healthy subjects. Scores on the Image-CA predicted the status of disease "with 93 percent accuracy for those in total remission, and 100 percent for those who had died or had rapid deterioration at the two-month follow-up" (ibid.: 7).

It should be noted that the content of the imagery used in the Achterberg study was chosen by each patient without consultation, but also that both the images used and the values assigned to them by researchers (or case outcome, or patient's somatic processes – it matters not) reflect the content of shared myths and values (cf. Haraway 1993; Martin 1994).

19 Despite the call for further research by Moerman (1979), the work of Lex (1979) on the neurobiology of trance, and that of Desjarlais on Sherpa understandings of body-mind healing processes (1992), there is a great lack of evidence for specifically physiological reflexes of particular symbols, images, or metaphors.

20 Note that our cultural-embodiment interpretation of Pennebaker's findings is not that of Pennebaker or even, necessarily, of his colleagues.

21 Immunological evidence of variability in cultural response to trauma is needed. But we already have firm clinical evidence that Southeast Asians suffering post-traumatic stress found telling their stories did not lessen their distress (Silove *et al.* 1995).

22 Note how similar is the title of a recent article by Pennebaker: "Putting Stress into Words." John Harvey dedicates his study of grief (2000) entitled *Give Sorrow Words* to Shakespeare.

23 An abdomen metaphor seems to be reflected in the demand of one younger man *vis-à-vis* an elder trying to shut down debate in a Tannese disentangling meeting documented by Lindstrom "[B]rother-in-law has closed the debate and sat down . . . so that people stop talking . . . [but I say] Let people *spill everything out*" (Lindstrom 1992: 114, emphasis added).

24 An example is found in a passage from *Parash Pathar* (Touch Stone or Philosopher's Stone), a short story by Parasuram: *"ekhan sudhu tạr grihini Giribala-ke jānāben, kintu meyeder peṭe kathā thāke nā"* Now he would inform only his wife Giribala, however women cannot keep a secret (citation, transliteration, and translation by Clint Seely: personal communication, 1997).

25 Foucault rejected Freud's theory that Western discursive structures *repressed* sexuality, arguing instead that those structures result in an "incitement to discourse." Popular discourse in the West has ingested Freud's insights, but not Foucault's. Foucault's *History of Sexuality* (1990) proposes a type of investigation that is all too rare, and toward which this book contributes – an investigation of physiological reflexes of culture (or history) itself. Few indeed are the bench scientists taking inspiration from Foucault, or Foucaldians doing bench science. Yet he himself asked whether

> the analysis of sexuality necessarily [must] imply the elision of the body, anatomy, the biological, the functional? To this question, I think we can reply in the negative. In any case, the purpose of the present study is in fact to show how deployments of power are directly connected to the body – to bodies, functions, physiological processes, sensations, and pleasures; far from the body having to be effaced, what is needed is to make it visible through an analysis in which the biological and the historical are not consecutive to one another, as in the evolutionism of the first sociologists, but are bound together in an increasingly complex fashion in accordance with the development of the modern technologies of power that take life as their objective. Hence I do not envision a "history of mentalities" that would take account of bodies only through the manner in which they have been perceived and given meaning and value; but a "history of bodies" and the manner in which what is most material and most vital in them has been invested.
>
> (1990: 151–152)

What Foucault proposed, in our understanding, was an investigation of the embodiment of culture – one which would parallel the case studies in this chapter but add to them physiological measures, including measures of immunocompetence.

26 See also the excerpt from *Parash Pathar* in note 24. Interpreting the passage from the story in light of larger Bengali gender discourses, the ability to hold words inside and keep a secret is valued and the inability is part of what makes women inferior beings.

27 This sets them apart from many cultures that tend to emphasize causes and consequences of illness with minimal attention to in-the-body "process" (Glick 1967).

28 In particular, see the special issue of *Psychosomatic Medicine* edited by Kleinman, and the guest-editor's essay (Kleinman and Becker 1998).

29 Tannese (from Vanuatu; Lindstrom 1992) share a very similar model. Tannese social actors blame some deaths on evil words uttered in the thick of social conflict though not necessarily "intended" as curses ("intentionality" being problematic in Oceanic models of discourse, as Lindstrom points out). If someone becomes sick or dies, competing "statements" may be made invoking divergent island "disciplines" (such as "sex, medicine, and kinship," (Lindstrom 1992: 118)), statements issued in "disentangling" meetings designed to sort out conflict. Such meetings may break down and come, instead, to epitomize conflict as a sort of illness in the social body (a metaphor made explicit in similar meetings in Bangladesh (Wilce 1996)):

social conflict --> "evil words" --> illness or death --> competing narratives of blame → social health or social "illness" as the competing "statements" are either "disentangled" or unresolved.

30 Forgetting trauma requires work and "technologies of forgetting" (Wilce 2002). For a case study of forgetting in Southeast Asia that demonstrates its always political context, see Goodfellow 1999.

31 On hope, see Lyon's discussion of conditioning (this volume), and see Good *et al.* (1990).

32 Notions of "the mindful body" (Scheper-Hughes and Lock 1987) that purport to critique biomedicine – through a recognition not only of explicit metaphors surrounding disease and healing but through a claim that bodies speak – reproduce not only western ideologies but American biomedicine's hegemony, according to DiGiacomo (1992). DiGiacomo and Wikan critique western folk notions allied with psychoneuroimmunology from perspectives gained in Catalonia and Bali (and, in DiGiacomo's case, in encountering oncological practice as a patient, and being on the receiving end of metaphors for cancer).

33 This hope, at the heart of US biomedicine, becomes an example of what Byron Good calls a (very culturally particular) soteriology (1994).

34 In this regard, see Kleinman's (1992) conclusion that illness and the narratives people generate out of it may exemplify "resistance," but that resistance models cease to be useful when they cause us to lose sight of real personal suffering and the random meaninglessness with which it often confronts us. In this, DiGiacomo (1992) concurs.

References

Achterberg, J. (1984). Imagery and medicine: psychophysiological speculations. *Journal of Mental Imagery*, *8*, 1–4.

Ader, R. and Cohen, N. (1991). The influence of conditioning on immune responses. In R. Ader and D. L. Felten, and N. Cohen (eds), *Psychoneuroimmunology* (2nd edn, pp. 653–670). San Diego: Academic Press.

Albert, A. R. (1973). Confession in the circle of R. Nachman of Braslav. *Bulletin of the Institute of Jewish Studies*, *1*, 65–96.

Balshem, M. (1991). Cancer, control, and causality: talking about cancer in a working-class community. *American Ethnologist*, *18*(1), 152–172.

Barchas, P. (1976). Physiological sociology: interface of sociological and biological processes. *Annual Review of Sociology*, *2*, 299–333.

Bastien, J. W. (1985). Quollahuaya-Andean body concepts: A topographical-hydraulic model of physiology. *American Anthropologist*, *87*(3), 595–611.

Berman, L. (1998). *Speaking through the silence: narratives, social conventions, and power in Java*. New York: Oxford University Press.

Blumhagen, D. (1982). The meaning of hypertension. In N. J. Chrisman and T. W. Maretzki (eds), *Clinically applied anthropology* (pp. 297–323). Dordrecht and Boston: D. Reidel.

Briggs, C. (1992). "Since I am a woman, I will chastise my relatives": gender, reported speech, and the (re)production of social relations in Warao ritual wailing. *American Ethnologist*, *19*(2), 337–361.

Comaroff, J. (1985). *Body of power, spirit of resistance*. Chicago: University of Chicago.

Crandon-Malamud, L. (1991). *From the fat of our souls: social change, political process, and medical pluralism in Bolivia.* Berkeley: University of California Press.

Csordas, T. (1988). Elements of charismatic persuasion and healing. *Medical Anthropology Quarterly, 2*(2), 121–142.

—— (1990 [1988]). Stirling Award Essay: Embodiment as a paradigm for anthropology. *Ethos, 18*(1), 5–47.

—— and Arthur Kleinman (1990). The therapeutic process. In T. M. Johnson and C. F. Sargent (eds), *Medical anthropology: contemporary theory and method.* New York: Praeger.

Das, V. (1996). Language and the body: transactions in the construction of pain. *Daedalus, 125*(1), 67–91.

Delvecchio-Good, M. J., Good, B., Schaffer, C., and Lind, S. E. (1990). American oncology and the discourse on hope. *Culture, Medicine, and Psychiatry, 14*(1), 59–79.

Desjarlais, R. R. (1992). *Body and emotion: the aesthetics of illness and healing in the Nepal Himalayas.* Philadelphia: University of Pennsylvania Press.

DiGiacomo, S. M. (1992). Metaphor as illness: postmodern dilemmas in the representation of body, mind and disorder. *Medical Anthropology, 14*(1), 109–137.

Dow, J. (1986). Universal aspects of symbolic healing: a theoretical synthesis. *American Anthropologist, 87*(1), 56–69.

Dressler, W. W., Balieiro, M. C., and Dos Santos, J. E. (1998). Culture, socio-economic status, and physical and mental health in Brazil. *Medical Anthropology Quarterly, 12*(4), 424–446.

Esterling, B. A., Antoni, M. H., Fletcher, M. A., Margulies, S., and Schneiderman, N. (1994). Emotional disclosure through writing or speaking modulates latent Epstein-Barr virus antibody titers. *Journal of Consulting and Clinical Psychology, 62*(1), 130–140.

Farnell, B. (1996). Metaphors we move by. *Visual Anthropology, 8*(2–4), 311–335.

Foucault, M. (1990 [1978]). *The history of sexuality: an introduction* (R. Hurley trans., vol. 1). New York: Vintage.

Frankenberg, R. (1986). Sickness as cultural performance: Drama, trajectory, and pilgrimage root metaphors and the making of disease social. *International Journal of Health Services, 16*(4), 603–626.

Glick, L. B. (1967). Medicine as an ethnographic category: the Gimi of the New Guinea highlands. *Ethnology, 6*(1), 31–56.

Goldberg, H. S. (1981–1982). Funeral and bereavement rituals of Kota Indians and Orthodox Jews. *Omega: Journal of Death and Dying, 12*(2), 117–128.

Good, B. (1977). The heart of what's the matter: the semantics of illness in Iran. *Culture, Medicine, and Psychiatry, 1*(1), 25–58.

—— (1994). *Medicine, rationality, and experience: an anthropological perspective.* Cambridge: Cambridge University Press.

Good, M.-J. D., Good, B., Schaffer. C., and Lind, S. E. (1990). American oncology and the discourse on hope. *Culture, Medicine, and Psychiatry, 14*(1), 59–79.

——, Hunt, L., Munakata, T., and Koybayashi, Y. (1993). A Comparative analysis of the culture of biomedicine: disclosure and consequences for treatment in the practice of oncology. In P. Conrad and E. B. Gallagher (eds), *Health and health care in developing countries: sociological perspectives* (pp. 180–211). Philadelphia: Temple University Press.

——, Munakata, T., Koybayashi, Y., Mattingly, C., and Good, B. J. (1994). Oncology and narrative time. *Social Science and Medicine*, *38*(6), 855–862.

Goodfellow, R. (1999). Sing Wis Ya Wis: What is past is past? Forgetting what it is to remember the Indonesian killings of 1965–66. Paper presented at the Conference, "Remembering and forgetting: the political and social aftermath of intense conflict in Eastern Asia and Northern Europe," Lund, Sweden, 15–17 April.

Gottman, J. M., Katz, L. F., and Hooven, C. (1996). Parental meta-emotion philosophy and the emotional life of families: theoretical models and preliminary data. *Journal of Family Psychology*, *10*(3), 243–268.

Gruber, B. L., Hall, N., Hersh, S. P., and Dubois, P. (1988). Immune system and psychologic changes in metastatic cancer patients while using ritualized relaxation and guided imagery: a pilot study. *Scandinavian Journal of Behavioural Therapy*, *17*, 25–46.

Hahn, R., and Kleinman, A. (1983). Belief as pathogen, belief as medicine. *Medical Anthropology Quarterly*, *14*(4), 16–19.

Hall, N. R. S. and O'Grady, M. P. (1991). Psychosocial interventions and immune function. In R. Ader, D. L. Felten, and N. Cohen (eds), *Psychoneuroimmunology* (2nd edn). San Diego: Academic Press.

Hanks, W. F. (1990). *Referential practice: language and lived space among the Maya.* Chicago: University of Chicago.

—— (1996). *Language and communicative practices* (vol. 1). Boulder: Westview.

Haraway, D. (1993). The biopolitics of postmodern bodies: determinations of self in immune system discourse. In S. Lindenbaum and M. Lock (eds), *Knowledge, power, and practice: the anthropology of medicine and everyday life* (pp. 364–410). Berkeley: University of California Press.

Harvey, J. H. (2000). *Give sorrow words: perspectives on loss and trauma.* Philadelphia: Brunner/Mazel.

Hess, C. G. (1994). Enfermedad y moralidad en los Andes Ecuatorianos. In P. Warren, C. Hess, and E. Ferraro (eds), *Salud y antropologia.* Quito, Ecuador: Ediciones Abya-Yala.

Jackins, H. (1973). *The human situation.* Seattle: Rational Island.

—— (1975). *Guidebook to re-evaluation counseling.* Seattle: Rational Island.

Johnson, M. (1987). *The body in the mind.* Chicago: University of Chicago Press.

Kakar, S. (1996). *The colors of violence: cultural identities, religion and conflict.* Chicago and London: University of Chicago Press.

Kidorf, I. W. (1963). Jewish tradition and Freudian theory of mourning. *Journal of Religion and Health*, *2*, 248–252.

Kiecolt-Glaser, J. K., Glaser, R., Williger, D., Sout, J., Messick, G., Sheppard, S., Ricker, D., Romisher, S. C., Briner, W., Bonnell, G., and Donnerberg, R. (1985). Psychosocial enhancement of immunocompetence in a geriatric population. *Health Psychology*, *4*(1), 25–41.

Kirmayer, L. J. (1992). The body's insistence on meaning: metaphor as presentation and representation in illness experience. *Medical Anthropology Quarterly*, *6*(4), 323–346.

Kleinman, A. (1973). Medicine's symbolic reality. *Inquiry*, *16*(2), 206.

—— (1992). Pain and resistance. In M. J. Delvecchio Good, P. Brodwin, B. J. Good, and A. Kleinman (eds), *Pain as human experience* (pp. 169–197). Berkeley: University of California Press.

—— and Becker, A. E. (1998). "Sociosomatics": the contributions of anthropology to psychosomatic medicine. *Psychosomatic Medicine, 60*(4), 389–393.

Kusserow, A. S. (1999). De-homogenizing American individualism: socializing hard and soft individualism in Manhattan and Queens. *Ethos, 27*(2), 210–234.

Lakoff, G. and Johnson, M. (1980). *Metaphors we live by.* Chicago: University of Chicago Press.

Lakoff, G. and Kövecses, Z. (1987). The cognitive model of anger inherent in American English. In D. Holland and N. Quinn (eds), *Cultural models in language and thought* (pp. 195–221). Cambridge: Cambridge University Press.

Larme, A. C. and Leatherman, T. L. (2003). Why "Sobreparto": women's work, health, and reproduction in two districts in southern Peru. In J. D. Koss-Chiono, T. Leatherman, and C. Greenway (eds), *Medical pluralism in the Andes.* New York: Routledge.

Lévi-Strauss, C. (1963). The effectiveness of symbols. *Structural anthropology* (pp. 186–205). New York: Basic Books.

Lewis, I. M. (1975). *Ecstatic religion: an anthropological study of spirit possession and shamanism.* Harmondsworth: Penguin.

Lex, B. (1979). The neurobiology of ritual trance. In C. D. L. Eugene G. d'Aquili, Jr and John McManus. (eds), *The spectrum of ritual: a biogenetic structural analysis.* New York: Columbia University.

Lindstrom, L. (1992). Context contests: debatable truth statements on Tanna (Vanuatu). In A. Duranti and C. Goodwin (eds), *Rethinking context: language as an interactive phenomenon* (vol. 11, pp. 101–124). Cambridge: Cambridge University Press.

Lock, M. (1993). Cultivating the body: anthropology and epistemologies of bodily practice and knowledge. *Annual Review of Anthropology, 22,* 133–155.

—— (1998). Menopause: lessons from anthropology. *Psychosomatic Medicine, 60*(4) (Special Issue: Cross-Cultural Research), 410–419.

Lyon, M. (1993). Psychoneuroimmunology: the problem of the situatedness of illness and the conceptualization of healing. *Culture, Medicine, and Psychiatry, 17*(1), 77–97.

—— (1994) Emotion as mediator of somatic and social processes: the example of respiration. In W. Wentworth and J. Ryan (eds) *Social perspective on emotion* (Vol. 2, pp. 83–108). Greenwich, CT: JAI Press.

Martin, E. (1993). Histories of immune systems. *Culture, Medicine, and Psychiatry, 17*(1), 67–76.

—— (1994). *Flexible bodies: the role of immunity in American culture from the days of polio to the age of AIDS.* Boston: Beacon.

Moerman, D. E. (1979). Anthropology of symbolic healing. *Current Anthropology, 20,* 59–80.

Myerhoff, B. G. (1979). *Number our days.* New York: Dutton.

Napier, A. D. (1996). Unnatural selection: social models of the microbial world. In S. A. Plotkin and B. Fantini (eds), *Vaccinia, vaccination, vaccinology: Jenner, Pasteur and their successors* (pp. 335–340). Paris: Elsevier.

Pennebaker, J. W. (1989). Confession, inhibition, and disease. *Advances in Experimental Social Psychology, 22,* 211–244.

—— (1993). Putting stress into words: health, linguistic, and therapeutic implications. *Behaviour Research and Therapy, 31*(6), 539–548.

——, Barger, S. D., and Tiebout, J. (1989). Disclosure of traumas and health among Holocaust survivors. *Psychosomatic Medicine*, *51*(5), 577–589.

Petrie, K. J., Booth, R. J., Pennebaker, J. W., Davison, K. P., and Thomas, M. G. (1995). Disclosure of trauma and immune response to a hepatitis B vaccination program. *Journal of Consulting and Clinical Psychology*, *63*(5), 787–792.

Price, L. (1987). Ecuadorian illness stories: cultural knowledge in natural discourse. In D. Holland and N. Quinn (eds), *Cultural models in language and thought* (pp. 313–342). Cambridge: Cambridge University Press.

—— (1992). Metalogue on coping with illness: cases from Ecuador. *Qualitative Health Research*, *2*(2), 135–158.

—— (2003). Illness management, social alliance, and cultural identity in Quito, Ecuador. In J. D. Koss-Chiono, T. Leatherman, and C. Greenway (eds), *Medical pluralism in the Andes*. (pp. 209–233). New York: Routledge.

Reddy, M. (1993). The conduit metaphor: a case of frame conflict in our language about language. In A. Ortony (ed.), *Metaphor and thought* (pp. 164–201). Cambridge: Cambridge University Press.

Rosaldo, M. Z. (1984). Towards an anthropology of self and feeling. In R. A. Shweder and R. A. LeVine (eds), *Culture theory: essays on mind, self, and emotion* (pp. 137–157). Cambridge: Cambridge University Press.

Roseman, I. J., Dhawan, N., Rettek, S. I., Naid, R. K., and Thapa, K. (1995). Cultural differences and cross-cultural similarities in appraisals and emotional responses. *Journal of Cross-Cultural Psychology*, *26*(1), 23–48.

Sansom, B. (1982). The sick who do not speak. In D. J. Parkin (ed.), *Semantic anthropology* (vol. 22, pp. 183–196). London: Academic Press.

Scheff, T. J. (1979). *Catharsis in healing, ritual, and drama*. Berkeley: University of California Press.

Scheper-Hughes, N. and Lock, M. (1987). The mindful body: a prolegomenon to future work in medical anthropology. *Medical Anthropology Quarterly*, *1*(1), 6–41.

Shakespeare, W. (1938). Sonnet 30. In Oxford University Press (ed.), *The works of William Shakespeare gathered in one volume* (p. 1228). New York: Oxford University Press.

Siegel, J. T. (1986). *Solo and the new order: language and hierarchy in an Indonesian city*. Princeton: Princeton University Press.

Silove, D., Chang, R., and Manicavasagar, V. (1995). Impact of recounting trauma stories on the emotional state of Cambodian refugees. *Psychiatric Services*, *46*(12), 1287–1288.

Simons, R. C. and Hughes, C. (eds). (1985). *Culture-bound syndromes: folk illnesses of psychiatric and anthropological interest*. Dordrecht: D. Reidel.

Slobin, D. I. (1996). From "thought and language" to "thinking for speaking". In J. Gumperz and S. Levinson (eds), *Rethinking linguistic relativity* (pp. 70–96). Cambridge: Cambridge University Press.

Sontag, S. (1978). *Illness as metaphor*. New York: Farrar, Strauss, Giroux.

Stevenson, I. N. (1977). Colerina: reactions to emotional stress in the Peruvian Andes. *Social Science and Medicine*, *11*(5), 303–307.

Swartz, L. (1985). Anorexia nervosa as a culture-bound syndrome. *Social Science and Medicine*, *20*(7), 725–730.

Tambiah, S. J. (1979). A performative approach to ritual. *Proceedings of the British Academy*, *65*, 113–169.

Tousignant, M. (1984). "Pena" in the Ecuadorian sierra: a psycho-anthropological analysis of sadness. *Culture, Medicine and Psychiatry, 8*(4), 181–198.

von Uexküll, T., Geigges, W. and Herrmann, J. M. (1993). The principle of teleological coherence and harmony of purpose exists at every level of integration in the hierarchy of living systems. *Advances in Mind-Body Medicine, 9*(3), 50–63.

Urban, G. (1996). *Metaphysical community: the interplay of the senses and the intellect.* Austin: University of Texas Press.

Watson-Gegeo, K. and White, G. M. (eds). (1992). *Disentangling: the discourse of interpersonal conflict in Pacific Island societies.* Stanford: Stanford University Press.

Weber, M. (1958 [1920–1921]). *The protestant ethic and the spirit of capitalism* (T. Parsons, trans.). New York: Charles Scribner.

Wikan, U. (1990). *Managing turbulent hearts: a Balinese formula for living.* Chicago: University of Chicago.

Wilce, J. M. (1996). Reduplication and reciprocity in imagining community: the play of tropes in a rural Bangladeshi moot. *Journal of Linguistic Anthropology, 6(2)*, 188–222.

—— (2000). Culture, health and immunity in narrating stress. RO1 Proposal submitted to the National Institutes of Health.

—— (2002). Genres of memory and the memory of genres: "forgetting" lament in Bangladesh. *Comparative Studies in Society and History, 44*(1), 159–185.

Chapter 5: Editor's note

Lyon's chapter asserts the importance of an understanding of the social ontology of emotion: that the nature of human emotion cannot be viewed as an autonomous phenomenon; rather that it needs to be seen as thoroughly embedded in the social in order to enable an understanding of how social and bodily processes are intertwined. For Lyon, the lack of a social theory of emotion becomes especially apparent in a field such as PNI which attempts to encompass social, psychological, and immunological variables in a unified model. PNI tends to cobble these together without theorizing their interaction in a way that would facilitate the understanding of their integration. The reductionist nature of much of the PNI literature prompts her to reach toward better theories of sociosomatic processes that she sees arising from a broader theory of emotion. Whereas several of the other contributions to this volume take a culturalist perspective, assigning cultural symbols and values a key mediating role in PNI processes, Lyon places greater emphasis on the primacy of social structure and social processes. From her perspective, a cognitivist, intellectualist, or "belief-centered" notion of culture simply reintroduces Cartesian mind–body dualism. Lyon asserts that human immune systems must indeed have social lives, and that these social dimensions must be seen to be mediated by emotional processes. In order to illustrate her points, she takes up four concepts that attempt in partial ways to articulate the interpenetration of bodily and social processes, i.e. conditioning, habit, mimesis, and emotional contagion. She thus sees the social context as more fundamental than mediating signs (including metaphors) and values. This places her chapter in an interesting dialogue with that by Wilce and Price. Both chapters share an interest in theorizing how social life is embodied. Lyon brings to this endeavor a range of works including classical sources such as American pragmatists William James and George Herbert Mead, and French sociologist Marcel Mauss, as well as more contemporary writers. She draws also on her own rich work on embodiment in relation to socioemotional processes (Lyon 1993, 1994, 1995). Like Mann (this volume), Lyon concerns herself with processes that proceed "of their own accord," "outside of normal awareness." But, more than any other contributor to this volume, Lyon would also re-insert a notion of human agency into the discourse on PNI, and seeks to reveal dimensions of agency in each of the four socioemotional processes she describes. As the dialogue between the social and immunological sciences matures, the relevance of her perspective on such processes to particular dimensions of PNI should become an active area of investigation. Lyon's chapter proposes answers to the question of how we can keep the "psycho" in psychoneuroimmunology from "absorbing" a theory of action, i.e. of the socially situated acts of human agents. Her questions, and the extensions she proposes to the "bridging concepts" she takes up here, make Lyon one of the foremost social scientists contributing to rethinking PNI.

"Immune" to emotion

The relative absence of emotion in PNI, and its centrality to everything else

Margot Lyon

> [Mind body problems] are not to be overcome by restricting the scope of explanation, by banishing ontology, but by coming to grips with the complexity of being.
>
> (Engelhardt 1973: 166)

Introduction: reframing

This chapter seeks to reframe the "locus" of immune function, to see it as emergent in the wider context of ongoing social and bodily relations. The proposal for the American Anthropological Association panel for which this contribution was originally drafted suggested a "dialogue between critical anthropology and a phenomenological PNI [psychoneuroimmunology]." My aim here is to enter this dialogue through examining how the complex phenomena glossed under the term immune function might be seen as implicate within social processes – processes in which the body is also inevitably engaged. In what ways can one represent the ongoing processes through which social life "becomes" and simultaneously "is" bodily life? In what ways can one theorize the interrelationship between these two sorts of phenomena, without committing the error of reducing one to the other, nor collapsing the distinction between them? Such a reframing requires a shift in perspectives not only toward the notion of immune functioning but also toward the conceptualization of the place of the body in social life.

Below, following a general introduction, I will examine briefly a series of concepts in science and social science that address, in differing ways, the axis of relationship between bodily and social worlds. Included are the concepts of *conditioning* and *habit*, as well as *mimesis* and *emotional contagion*. I will argue that social-emotional processes are fundamental to understanding the operation of each of these, and more centrally that an examination of the role of emotion is required for the conceptualization of the interrelationship between social and bodily domains within them. An adequate conception of emotion is crucial in any understanding of the dialectic between social and bodily life, and therefore ultimately in understanding issues related to the social origins of health and illness.

PNI, social science and the "hyphenation" of disparate domains

I commence with a brief discussion of the field of PNI. The aim here is not pure critique; rather it is to use dilemmas within the models used by PNI, as well as those used in the social sciences, to reflect more generally on problems in the conceptualization of the interrelationship of social and bodily domains.

Advances made in the field of immunology on a number of fronts in the 1970s and early 1980s seemed to require a broad new perspective on immune function and its relationship to psychological and social domains. Early research in PNI was, to some degree, an outgrowth of research on stress that was itself interdisciplinary. Yet, the scope of immunological research by the 1980s had expanded sufficiently that many scientists argued that it now constituted a new area (Pelletier and Herzing 1988: 31). Earlier research in immunology that had been confined to the elucidation of specific recognition structures – for example, antibody-antigen formation – soon expanded to include knowledge of the operation of a range of specialist cells such as cytotoxic ("killer") cells, "helper" cells, and immunoglobulin-producing cells (Langman 1989: 37). More importantly, the discovery of increasingly complex pathways of communication between neural, endocrine, and immune systems was seen to introduce the possibility of new ways to bridge the growing body of experimental and clinical data and earlier neurophysiological research. Broader models that could offer a more dispersed understanding of immune function and its mediatory role between body and behavior seemed to be required. A new interdisciplinary enterprise, psychoneuroimmunology (PNI), eventually came into being, promising new research agendas that would move beyond the narrower conceptions of the immune system as autonomous and self regulating. Instead it would offer models for the interconnection of bodily systems and psychosocial factors in health and illness. Declaring its roots in "neuroscience, immunology, ethology, psychology, neurology, anatomy, psychiatry, epidemiology, and endocrinology" (Locke *et al.* 1985: xi), PNI presented the possibility of a far broader approach to understanding the development of disease and illness. Immune processes could now be seen "as an integrated part of the organism's psychobiological adaptation to its environment" (Ader 1981: xxi). Here, at least theoretically, was the grand promise of an integrated scientific examination of how thought, feeling, and action are implicated in immune function, and thus in health and disease.

But how were these interrelationships across domains to be modeled, given that the dilemmas of dualism permeate the sciences and social sciences equally? How was the linking of body and behavior to be understood and represented in a way that went beyond the measurement of simple correlations between phenomena in the two domains? This is to pose the fundamental question of the situatedness of sickness, health, and healing – a question that constitutes a main axis of tension in the social scientific study of illness and also in psychoneuroimmunology (Lyon 1993). Within PNI, the focus is typically on the specific mechanisms of communication between immune, endocrine, and nervous systems. There is little attempt in the PNI literature to deal with questions of social *action* or *agency*, even though lip service is given to action through such terms as behavior and psychosocial factors[1] These factors, however, are simply subsumed within the category of central nervous system functioning or seen as an extension of it, through psychological categories such as mind or psyche. The term psycho in the compound word psycho-neuro-immunology *absorbs* action by converting it into its preconditions, without properly acknowledging the fact. Action itself (in the sense that it occurs in a social context) disappears.

Thus, one of the problems in PNI is that of the "hyphenation" of very different domains, comprising types of phenomena that are not directly comparable. What is offered by PNI is a concatenation of terms that do not constitute a theoretical or experimental integration of domains – social, physical, functional. Thus, in the framework given, social forms of explanation cannot be brought to bear on biological mechanisms and vice versa.[2] This is an obvious point, yet it is frequently overlooked in discussion of the capacities of psychoneuroimmunology to bridge psycho-social and bodily domains.

How then can one move toward "locating" immune functioning, or indeed other biological functions, at the level of social relations? In medical anthropology, the question of the interrelationship of sociocultural and bodily mechanisms has typically been treated in terms of how symbolic phenomena, including metaphor, may be linked to, or given, embodied form. A number of authors have directly addressed the question of the integration of biological and cultural perspectives in this vein.[3] Among the earliest systematic accounts in medical anthropology are Hahn and Kleinman (1983a; 1983b), and Moerman (1983). Each treated what Hahn and Kleinman referred to as "the dialectic of nature and culture" (1983b: 321). For example, in an exploration and extension of the concept of placebo phenomena, Hahn and Kleinman construct a continuum of diverse "culturogenic" phenomena, placing voodoo death and faith healing at pathogenic and therapeutic poles, respectively. Their perspective, however, is somewhat narrowed by their emphasis on the question of "belief," and therefore heavily focused on the realm of ideas and meaning within the subject's awareness. (This is partly an artifact of the culturalist approach that treats the concept of culture as somehow primary, and encompassing all other domains.) Further, homeostatic assumptions underpin their continuum model. However, they do acknowledge the simultaneous role of sociocultural, psychological, and physiological factors. They then draw on a number of sources of the time to suggest a range of purely biological mechanisms which may underlie this interplay, e.g. autonomic activation, the role of hormones, immunoglobin production, etc. (1983: 18–19). Moerman (1983), in a somewhat different approach, discusses the "bimodal quality" of traditional healing, i.e. the simultaneity of matter and symbol, and seeks to establish its universality (1983: 157).[4] He draws on information about the hypothalamus' role in the production of hormones, thus making it "part" of the endocrine system (1983: 158). Moerman also appeals to Brody's notion of "person theory" as a means to bridge material and cultural being. In this, both "physical and mental predicates" are applied to the concept of person, but person is deemed to be "more basic" than those predicates (Brody 1977: 93 quoted in Moerman 1983: 163).

A related issue in PNI, and one that has been critiqued from the perspectives of anthropology, stems from the issue of the perceived locus of immune function within a "self." In the attempt to (re-)articulate and resituate the interrelationships between body, person, and society, it is necessary also to rethink the idea of the immune system as necessarily coterminous with "self." The conventional rhetoric of immunology has tended to place emphasis on understanding how immune function is ultimately concerned with the determination of "self" as opposed to "not self," i.e. how through complex processes of cellular interaction and recognition, it is engaged in defending the self against "foreign" invasion. In anthropology, these and certain other dominant metaphors commonly used in the construction of immune system discourse have been deconstructed, for example by Haraway (1989) and by Martin (1994). Such critiques are important, but they do not necessarily move us beyond the locus of immune function in the individual toward a more direct engagement with questions about the somatic side of the body-social interrelation.

Further, the approach to the body in anthropology has tended to emphasize its symbolic significance and the cultural construction of individual bodies in varying contexts.[5] But any real dialogue between fields as disparate as psychoneuroimmunology and anthropology – that is between processes that are within their respective disciplines construed as (or seen to be reducible to) either essentially bodily processes (including immune function), and/or as sociocultural processes – must come about through the development of alternative logical frameworks that can move debate outside conventional disciplinary boundaries. Purely constructionist approaches cannot do this, nor can other approaches that are grounded ultimately in conventional mind–body dualisms.

The above approaches have in common a linking of the cultural and biological that is primarily mediated through the construction of meaning, via the notions of symbol, belief, etc. I wish to suggest ways to move beyond this type of approach by foregrounding the import of the larger context of social structure and how, through emotion, both the phenomenological and social-relational come to be simultaneously embodied. We thus need to address "textured descriptions of embodied subjectivity" as well as "the part played by the whole living body interacting in particular social networks" (Freund

1990: 455). Most importantly, we must be aware of how subjectivity and these particular social networks are grounded in larger social structural forms that make up the "historically shaped, socially organized systems of human activity" in which we are all embedded (Freund 1990: 456). That is, these social networks must be seen as a function of particular social structural and institutional arrangements in a given society or social context. Such a shift toward a more sociological perspective will bring us closer to the question of the relationship between micro- and macro-, between individual and social milieu, and ultimately better able to address the question of their embodiment.

The question of emotion

What can the concept of emotion offer here? PNI, although acknowledging the importance of categories such as behavior and emotion in models of immune system functioning, leaves both categories underexamined, such that they remain implicitly reducible to imputed, underlying neurophysiological bases. Emotion in this context is primarily equated with psychological forces located wholly within the individual, a step which facilitates an implicit collapse of psychological (and thus emotional) into neurophysiological processes. Foss has pointed out that in biomedicine "the cognitive-affective states referenced are shorthand for certain complex neurophysiological (somatic) states that are their biological substrate" (Foss 1989: 177). Within the medical model, "[t]o conclude otherwise," he states, "is to commit a category mistake . . . [as] mental events *per se* cannot cause organic disease" (Foss 1989: 177). But, in the case of emotion, such a statement can be true only if emotion is regarded merely as a "mental" event, rather than conceptualized in more complex fashion. Thus, even within the framework of psychoneuroimmunology, emotion tends to be reduced to neuroendocrine and immune system response. This is because, as Foss and Rothenberg correctly point out in an earlier work, "while the psychoneuroimmunology position supersedes the conventional reductionist position, its interactionism is in the final analysis still limited to bodily systems" (1987: 125).

Many anthropological approaches to emotion tend to reinforce the view of emotion as inhering in individuals. Emotion is seen to be a product of cultural construction through an individual's socialization and through the dominant perceptual categories pertaining in a given sociocultural context, these constructions typically being explored through language categories as well as other cultural forms. The cognitive bias of cultural constructionist accounts tends to lead us to focus on meaning as mediated by these cultural or linguistic models that are necessarily seen as inhering in individuals. The term emotion, however, is an abstraction, encompassing many phenomenal realms. One of the chief functions of emotion is to situate individuals in particular social and material environments. Indeed, emotional capacities and emotional processes significantly *constitute* that situatedness. As such, an adequate concept or theory of emotion must include representation of its social ontology as well as its other dimensions including physiological, subjective feeling, expressive, and motivational components, etc. Such a broadened view of emotion has the capacity to provide a very different framework for the understanding of how social and biological being intertwine and emerge in the context of ongoing social processes.

In the sections below, I briefly discuss a series of concepts that in differing ways bridge bodily and social realms. I commence with the conceptions of conditioning and habit, then take up the concept of mimesis followed by a brief consideration of the notion of emotional contagion. I will show that emotion is fundamental in the operation of each. This in turn is used to explore the crucial role of emotion in understanding the processes through which social life comes to be embodied, including the place of human agency in these processes. The perspective presented here has implications for how we conceptualize various aspects of bodily being, including the understanding of phenomena such as immune function.

Bridging concepts

Conditioning

Conditioning is a form of learning and is important in perhaps all learning contexts including those involving highly complex behavior.[6] Evidence for the conditioning of immune system response was an important impetus in the early development of psychoneuroimmunology, and served to highlight the lack of understanding of the precise mechanisms for the operation of conditioning.

What is termed classical conditioning is typically characterized as the pairing of a neutral (or novel) stimulus with another stimulus that already elicits some response, such that the neutral stimulus comes to elicit a similar, or "conditional," response (Pavlov 1960 [1927]). It should be noted that Pavlov's original term is better rendered as "conditional" rather than "conditioned." The illustration of classical conditioning so frequently given is Pavlov's pairing of the sound of a bell (the conditional stimulus) with food (the unconditional stimulus) in experiments with laboratory dogs. The dogs came to salivate (the conditional reflex) at the sound of the bell as they did with the food (the unconditional reflex). The experience of a relationship or association between two previously unrelated stimuli constitutes the basis of the formation of the new conditional reflex.

The possibility that classical conditioning could affect immune system response raised important questions in immunology. In the early 1970s, University of Rochester researchers, Ader and Cohen, set out to disprove Soviet experimental work in immunology which purported to demonstrate that immune response was susceptible to classical conditioning methods. Critical of Soviet research design, they determined to replicate the work but under much stricter controls (Ader 1981; Spector and Korneva 1981). Contrary to expectation, their own carefully controlled experiments supported the earlier results, demonstrating that conditioning techniques could induce immunological changes. In their experiments, rats were given saccharin water (the conditional stimulus) in conjunction with cyclophosphamide, a chemical suppressor of antibody response (the unconditional stimulus). When the sweet-tasting saccharin water was given without the drug, the conditional response of suppression of immune function resulted.

The precise mechanisms through which immune suppression occurs, however, has remained a difficult question. Here, the conditional *expectation* of the effect of a cytotoxin is producing the same immunosuppression as the actual substance. The potential effects of the substance have been somehow interiorized through their *relationship* to another object or condition experienced by the subject (the sweetness of saccharin). Foss labels this conditioned expectation a "symbolic relationship" that somehow plays a demonstrable causal role in the production of disease (Foss 1989: 1). But the use of a cultural category may be premature, however, and perhaps unnecessary, as the category of emotion may offer a more satisfactory perspective.

The role of conditioning, not only in the production of disease but also in other aspects of behavior, has been largely ignored in medicine and psychology as well as in social science. This neglect "seems to be based largely upon the assumption that conditioning is a simple, automatic, and unconscious form of learning that underlies the acquisition of relatively trivial behavior" (Dickinson 1987: 159). In humans, it is thought, such mechanisms are irrelevant and indeed rarely occur because of the supposed awareness of association between the action or signal and the reinforcer (Dickinson 1987: 159). There is a further confusion: whereas behaviorist forms of explanation imply that persons or animals are conditioned, in fact it is always a *particular aspect of behavior in a particular context* which is subject to the conditional influence, not the person (Dickinson 1987). A further reason, perhaps, for the neglect of research on conditioning is that "the increasing focus on cognition and information processing [has meant that] the study of this form of learning has been consigned to a backwater of psychology" (Dickinson 1987: 159).

Although this neglect continues, conditioning processes are in fact implicated in the establishment of many of the bodily and behavioral patterns of social actors. These processes are complex, and most are not readily subject to conscious awareness or scrutiny. One overt example, though, is provided by the way in which certain autonomic processes of the body may be brought under volitional control through conditioning in the process typically called biofeedback. Gregory has suggested that the prevalence of conditioning phenomena in routine practices supports the argument for "strengthening the claims and widening the range of psychosomatic medical practice" (Gregory 1987: 66). It is now widely acknowledged, for example, that conditioning is implicated in the placebo effect; and placebo may in fact be a type of conditional response (Foss and Rothenberg 1987: 128). If this is so, and as placebo effect can be said to be involved at some level in all healing, then conditioning processes may be regarded as pervasively implicated in processes associated with sickness and healing.[7]

While the emotional component of conditioning is under-acknowledged, it is likely to have a high significance, for the impact of emotional states on learning and memory is well demonstrated today. Pavlov himself acknowledges emotional involvement. In his discussions of habit and rhythm, he referred to what he termed "purpose" as being of "great and vital importance" and the "fundamental form of the life energy of us all" (Pavlov 1928: 278, 279). Surprisingly, Darwin is clearer on this. In his *The Expression of the Emotions in Man and Animals* (1965 [1872]), Darwin refers to the form of learning that he called "association," a concept similar to classical conditioning as well as to the notion of state-dependent learning (Brown 1991: 23). His conception of "serviceable actions" also indicates the import of emotional orientation in given conditions such that "certain behavior becomes associated with a particular state of mind and will therefore occur whenever that state of mind is present" (Brown 1991: 23). In this light, then, emotional expression for Darwin, "is not random but part of a motor program that is an attempt to reach a goal motivated by the subjective experience of the individual" (Brown 1991: 23). Darwin thus recognized that "subjective experience is made up of particular combinations of cognitions, affects, and physiologic states" (Brown 1991: 23).[8]

I would describe the contribution of emotions to the conditioning process in the following terms. Conditioning necessarily occurs in a social environment or context, even when the context is constituted of transactions with objects that are incorporated into an experimental design. The primary emotional involvement in classical conditioning is through the subject's *expectation*, the latter being unavoidable if conditioning is to occur. The notion of expectation includes, indeed entails, action with a sense of what might be.[9] The emotional component of expectation is not unlike hope: both are future-oriented, both have objects, but the "object" of expectation may be negative, positive, or neutral. Further, although hope involves a projection or displacement into the future, expectation is about something immanent, and so always potentially in the present; that is, it is bound up with the self or the self's state in the present. In such an emotion as expectation, the body and mind are especially brought together. The individual has learned to, or come to, expect a particular event to happen. The fact of expectation means that the subject of conditioning is also an *agent* (with or without awareness) in the linking of different events, stimulus with response. This active process of interiorization of the consequences of a relationship which inheres in the notion of expectation helps explain why such processes operate below, or on the edge of, awareness.

In summary, conditioning involves the establishment, in social-relational contexts, of patterns of response. Emotion is central to this process and to the individual's agency within it. Indeed, conditioning experiments can be read to demonstrate the bodily impact of such social-emotional states (and vice versa). The real importance of the conditioning of responses cannot be overlooked. In multiple ways conditioning underlies the generation of patterns or order in social and bodily life.

Habit

The psychologist William James, writing at the end of the nineteenth century, was also concerned with the question of how the social world determines the order and shape of individual action. Such subjects come to the fore in his discussion of habit. Through its associative dimensions, habit can be seen to be linked logically to the concept of conditioning. In habit, the body is seen to be subject to educative processes; processes that are part of the creation and maintenance of social order. James felt that, once established, the ordering of patterns of action, for example those based on spatial memory, became rooted in lower centers, such that these centers "know the order of these movements, and show their knowledge by their surprise if the objects are altered so as to oblige the movement to be made in a different way" (1950 [1890]: 115). Yet our "higher thought-centers know hardly anything about the matter" (James 1950 [1890]: 115).

Inhering in the concept of habit is the wider sociocultural and historical setting within which habits are formed and within which the engagement of both psychological and bodily processes occurs. For James, patterns of response or action are at once grounded in the nervous system and in the social milieu in which we live. Writing later, the French sociologist, Mauss, too, argued that human action is made up of "physio-psycho-sociological assemblages" which are habitual as well as subject to historical, social, and cultural forces (Mauss 1973 [1935]).[10] Like Mauss after him, James saw the shaping of behavior through habit always as a function of a larger social structural and historical milieu. For James:

> Habit is thus the enormous fly-wheel of society, its most precious conservative agent. It alone is what keeps us all within the bounds of ordinance, and saves the children of fortune from the envious uprisings of the poor. It alone prevents the hardest and most repulsive walks of life from being deserted by those brought up to tread therein.
>
> (James 1950 [1890]: 121)

Habit is thus part of the foundations of more complex social phenomena. Emotion is implicated in the formation of habit through its place in associative and learning processes. Further, in that habit has a role in the routinization of behavior, it may also help in the redirection and maintenance of specific levels of emotional engagement, contributing perhaps to a sense of security, control, efficiency.[11] The topic of habit, if we follow James' point regarding the import of social milieu, takes us more clearly toward a macrosociological approach, that is, a concern with emotion's origins in macro-structures and relations, as well as simultaneously encompassing its functions in microsociological processes. It also raises the question of agency, both bodily and social.

At first glance, the notions of conditioning and habit would seem to indicate a relative absence of agency. Yet we can see how *agency is implicated in both these processes through emotion*. Expectation of what is to occur, the secure routine, or the sense of entrapment, deriving from patterns of habit, from the urge or requirement to conform, to imitate, within the constraints of patterns of structure and action of the group, all have to do with emotional orientation. Persons become agents through the engagement of feelings in particular contexts of group life. Habit and conditioning are processes that are part of the ordering of social life. By way of illustration, in every society there exist socially and culturally learned and perceived categories regarding relative status and power. These categories are also grounded in complex patterns of bodily behavior of which one may or may not be aware, for example in stance, head tilt, facial expression, etc. Perceived violations of status may elicit particular responses in particular contexts depending on the relative status and power of the actors, e.g. anger when one's status is violated by someone of similar or lesser status and power (Kemper 1984). Such affective responses, in that they entail also somatic dimensions, could be expected to bear a clear relationship to bodily states including those related to health. The engagement of feelings in particular contexts or in expectation of particular events is thus one crucial part of emotional agency implicated in these processes, and also part of processes of healing and sickness.

We need now to move toward concepts that give greater emphasis to complex social forms, and toward the further exploration of the question of the role of emotional (and bodily) processes in social agency. To this end, I take up the concept of mimesis, useful because of its emphasis on the person in continuous relation to context, and on movement – both imitative and transformative – as well as its potential for attention to visceral involvement in ongoing relational processes. We will see that the concept of mimesis gives emphasis to correspondences in bodily and social-processual components, in a way that social science concepts or theories grounded in more conventional dualist categories cannot.

Mimesis

Mimesis is a far broader and analytically less precise concept than conditioning or habit. This quality of imprecision is perhaps part of the attraction of the term to scholars who seek a way to encompass relationships across domains not conventionally bridged by categories within their disciplines. It is its attempt to capture the in-betweenness, the ongoing processual and transformative qualities of these relationships that is important here.

Mimesis most generally refers to imitation or modeling of an object or an other. It is a "movement of approximation between things and people," a capacity that is grounded simultaneously in bodily and cognitive processes, a *conditio humana*, say Gebauer and Wulf, that "plays a critical role in nearly all areas of human thought and action" (1995: 319: 1).[12] Taussig refers to the mimetic faculty as "the faculty to copy, imitate, make models, explore difference, yield into and become Other" (1993: xiii). Drawing on the work of Walter Benjamin, he points out the "two-layered character of mimesis: copying and the visceral quality of the percept uniting viewer with the viewed" (Taussig 1993: 24). My interest in the concept is precisely that it is at once bodily and social, i.e. oriented toward the relationship with other.

There is some conceptual overlap between mimesis, habit, and conditioning, in the sense that the latter two also include within them the idea of knowing and becoming through the body. Benjamin (1978), for example, like James, saw habit as a form of tactile knowing where "unconscious strata of culture are built into social routines as bodily dispositions" (Taussig 1993: 25). And, as Taussig notes, in "the very concept of 'knowing' something becomes displaced by a 'relating to'" (Taussig 1993: 26). Just as phenomena such as conditioning, habit, and – as we will see – emotional contagion, are grounded in the disposition toward relational processes, so also is mimesis grounded in the fundamental human capacity toward relationship, attachment, and thus the basis for the internalization, transformation, and expression of forms of relationship between human and object others.

Anthropology has been more frequently preoccupied with metaphor than with concepts such as conditioning, habit, or mimesis. Metaphor, too, is about relationship but though metaphor is a useful concept because it can be seen to be grounded in both bodily and social experience, its articulation in primarily linguistic form ultimately requires textual explication.[13] Although metaphor could perhaps be included here as a bridging concept, this would require an exploration of how emotion might be seen to function in understanding the agential nature of metaphoric process. In this chapter, I limit my focus to examples of concepts that foreground bodily and relational processes rather than linguistic or cognitive ones. Conditioning, habit, and mimesis are useful in that they can move us toward a more direct and explicit engagement with social context. They also, in their comparison, direct us toward a broader consideration of the processes through which complex relational structures come to be internalized, incorporated, or transformed.

Nevertheless, there are parallels between the concerns of the study of metaphor on the one hand, and mimesis, on the other. Metaphor might perhaps be conceived of as an (cognitive) abstraction, or a single dimension, of the more diffuse and complex phenomenon of mimesis. Metaphor, in a sense, works through mimetic processes. Metaphors are models of the world, according to Johnson, created from "conceptual frameworks that depend on the nature of human experience in a given culture" (Johnson 1987: xi). They are therefore about how this relationship between experience and conceptual framework can be seen to be transformed through metaphor into particular verbal or visual categories. Thus metaphor acts as a matrix for this transformation. Beck says that metaphor mediates between sensory and verbal categories via analogy. Verbal metaphors "inject the results of analogic reasoning processes into the semantic domain" (Beck 1978: 85). She states that "images and experiential associations" which "develop at a level where a network of sensory associations prevails are transferred to a level where thoughts are ordered according to a logic of verbal categories" (1978: 85). Johnson also sees metaphor as involving the projection or transformation of basic schemata, which are grounded in bodily experience, through analogy or metaphor, in a process that involves the mapping of "features of the source-domain onto the target domain via a metaphorical projection" (1987: 109). Beck is more specific about this transformation; she wants to see it as occurring through processes such as "synaesthesia or cross-sensory modality." But while this mechanism helps to explain the bodily bases of transformative processes, it would seem to be too narrow conceptually to explain the basis of the formation of metaphors or the force for their expression. In the end, the concept of metaphor itself is too narrow to fully encompass the complex interrelationship between social and bodily experience.

The mimetic capacity is implicated in the creation of both symbolic and somatic worlds. In the construction given mimesis in this chapter, the term can be said to articulate the process through which individual bodies produce, reproduce, or otherwise model the world and their position in it. Through mimetic processes relationships are displaced, reconstituted, and internally modeled through the harnessing of bodily functions and bodily capacities.

Gebauer and Wulf note that "[t]he human body has always been used to produce and express similarities, obvious examples being dance and spoken language, both of which are intimately bound up with the mimetic faculty" (1995: 269). But their emphasis is on the role of mimesis in aesthetic production. In what ways is it possible to represent the bodily dimensions of how "[e]xternal and internal worlds are continually approximating each other" (Gebauer and Wulf 1995: 275)? If "individuals make themselves similar to the outer world, changing themselves in the process . . . [t]he result is a mimetic developmental spiral" (1995: 275). This process of approximation is also occurring at a bodily and neurophysiological level. What is understood by Gebauer and Wulf as primarily a perceptual process must also be understood as a bodily one.

The bodily components of such mimetic processes, which would involve and include "subsidiary" processes such as habit, and conditioning, are largely outside normal awareness and would proceed of their own accord. Yet, the bodily system is not closed; its very being is always a product of its participation in its active relationship with a world. This is precisely the usefulness of the concept of mimesis, i.e. that it encompasses and embodies this reference to, this relationship with, a world outside (Gebauer and Wulf 1995: 315).

But although it captures the continual approximation between social and individual world, mimesis is analytically vague. It correctly foregrounds the import of the visceral dimension in the embodiment of relationships within and with the external world, but it doesn't adequately explore mechanisms or agency in these processes. The mimetic relationship is not unlike magic, and indeed, mimesis has been likened to sympathetic magic (Taussig 1993: xv; Gebauer and Wulf 1995). Magic seeks to enact such links, to create ritual or other conditions under which social forms may take other forms. "The precondition of the effectiveness of . . . rites and sacrifices is the laws of magic, as formulated by Marcel Mauss to designate contiguity, similarity, and opposition" (Gebauer and Wulf 1995: 283). Likewise, the principle of similarity is "the precondition for the effectiveness of mimesis" (ibid.). Gebauer and Wulf state that "[i]f the particular is the whole and the whole is in the particular, then there exists a mimetic relation among things, which makes it possible to influence the one by means of the other. Affinity among things and mimesis, which rests on the affinity, are responsible for the universal character of magic" (1995: 283).

Principles of sympathetic magic, however, do not explain the prevalence and power of mimetic processes. A social conception of emotion that foregrounds how emotion is a dimension of social relations, provides a means for understanding agency in mimetic process and therefore how social conditions come to be continually embodied. We referred above to the emotion of expectation that arises through an individual's relation with an object or other. Through the emotional orientation provided, the individual is an agent in mimetic processes just as in the case of conditioning and the formation of habit. In the case of expectation, the dimension of time is engaged through an orientation toward the future. In mimesis, the movement toward correspondences between inner and outer worlds is also rooted in emotions embodying a time dimension. Thus, fear, anxiety, expectation, hope, for example, are all future oriented. The time dimension of emotion, while often ignored, is crucial, and has been recognized by a number of authors, e.g. Lewin (1942) on time perspectives, and Tomkins (1962, 1963) on temporal interdependence of emotions: "Integral to most emotional experiences is an interlocking set of constituents relating to time and particularly to the future" (Aylwin 1985: 135, 137). Here we might again return to the emotion of expectation mentioned above in conjunction with the material on conditioning: "Many emotions reveal the extent to which we already exist in the future, projected through plans and intentions. . . . The temporality involved is not that of clock time, in which it would be sufficient just to wait; it is the time of Allport's (1955) *becoming*, of commitment and of action" (Aylwin 1985: 137).

But how is it that we "become"? We do so through being "moved," through emotion, as already stated. And, were we to extend Allport's notion of becoming to include a bodily dimension, in addition to social and psychological ones, we might better see the necessary relationship between emotion, action, and being.

I turn now to what is a primarily descriptive rather than analytical category, that of "emotional contagion." It is useful in foregrounding not only the unity of emotional and bodily phenomena but also the social contexts in which these phenomena arise and are experienced. Suitably interpreted, it is therefore useful in drawing out the import of emphasizing the social ontology of emotion, and how bodily processes are engaged in social being.

Emotional contagion

The notion of emotional contagion refers to the question of how emotional states might "spread" from one individual to another, and by implication through groups. The category of emotional contagion is really a collection of diverse phenomena that have been glossed under a single term. Explanation of emotional contagion generally grounds it in largely unconscious, imitative bodily processes. These processes, in turn, however, must be seen to be rooted in social and bodily dispositions such as attachment (MacDougall 1960 [1908]; Bowlby 1969) and synchrony (Byers 1976, 1982; Hall 1983), dispositions that are at the very foundation of social life, and which clearly demonstrate the interplay between bodily, emotional, and social phenomena.

The term contagion reflects the persistence of ideas rooted in the imitation or suggestion theories of crowd behavior of Gabriel Tarde (1890) and Gustave Le Bon (1947 [1911]). But its emphasis on how social influences determine the behavior of individuals, and the role of imitation in this process, can also be seen to be linked to the social psychology of George Herbert Mead (1962) and William James, for example. However, like the notion of imitation, the term emotional contagion can contribute little to analysis; indeed, it both reifies emotions and mystifies the nature of the underlying processes through which emotions might be supposedly spread or shared. A preferable perspective for the exploration of these processes, would be to approach emotional contagion rather in terms of how it is properly about the question of the *co-occurrence of emotions in specific settings*, that is, from the perspective of the social ontology of emotional experience. Only such an approach can take us beyond the obvious limitations of models based on notions of imitation or suggestion.

In a 1994 review of the evidence for what is termed emotional contagion, Hatfield, Cacioppo, and Rapson draw on sources from animal research, social and developmental psychology, cross-cultural psychology, and psychophysiology. Though primarily a review, the authors propose that the phenomenon is primarily grounded in what they term general imitative processes, a category in which they include phenomena such as mimicry, synchrony, and attunement. They see all of these as continually operating in the context of everyday relations, and thus characterize emotional contagion as a multi-level and multi-determined "family of psycho-physiological, behavioral, and social phenomena" (Hatfield *et al.* 1994: 4, 5).[14] My interest here is not in their model of these phenomena but in data from their review that can be used to draw attention to some of the bodily and emotional dimensions of such phenomena.

Beginning with data that demonstrate an unconscious tendency to "mimic and synchronize expressions, vocalizations, postures, and movements with those of another person," they show how such a function "coordinates and synchronizes social interactions while freeing the interactants to think about other issues" (Hatfield *et al.* 1994: 48). Most of these processes are "relatively automatic," they tell us, "unintentional, uncontrollable, and largely inaccessible to conversant awareness" (1994: 5). From their perspective, persons thus tend to synchronize automatically and this synchronization results in the tendency "to experience emotions consistent with the facial, vocal, and postural expressions they adopt" (Hatfield *et al.* 1994: 5). The mechanisms given for the convergence of emotions between interactants include conscious processes, conditioned and unconditioned emotional responses, mimicry and feedback of facial, postural, and other forms of information. Such phenomena are underpinned by autonomic nervous system coordination. These processes also underlie the organization of social systems (Chapple 1982 cited by Hatfield *et al.* 1994: 27–30). Further, the authors show that mere thoughts are sufficient to generate different forms of bodily mimicry (1994: 23).

Of greater interest for our purposes here, and as already indicated in the section on habit, such underlying capacities are implicated in higher order feelings such as sympathy and empathy. Empathy is the "feeling of belonging to, associating ourselves with, or being carried along with something" (Gregory 1987: 220), or, in Hatfield *et al.*, "to feel one's way into" another person's experience (1994: 81). Hatfield *et al.* cite Titchener (1909) who "argued that people could never know what another felt by reasoning; they could only know by feeling themselves into the other's feelings" (Hatfield *et al.* 1994: 81). Empathy can also include identifying with objects, the basis of the notion of empathy in theories of aesthetics (Gregory 1987: 221). Similarly, there is sympathy which involves "a heightened awareness of the feelings of the other person" and often the "urge to take whatever actions are necessary to alleviate the other person's plight" (Wispe 1991 quoted in Hatfield *et al.* 1994: 82).

Hatfield *et al.*, of course, do not explicitly extend their analysis to encompass how larger social structural forms might be factors in the genesis of particular emotions. The authors' stated focus is on what they term "rudimentary" or "primitive emotional contagion" among individuals (1994: 5). However, in their discussion of the role of focus in reference to the susceptibility to emotional contagion, they point to how people "construe themselves in terms of their interrelatedness" to others (1994: 123). Although their arguments are explicitly psychological rather than sociological, a number of their examples suggest how a sense of common identity and common interests are sufficient to facilitate, and thus be a crucial aspect of, emotional contagion, and that these operate also at the bodily level. As argued in this paper, this is an important point in considering the emotional consequences of social structural arrangements and an individual's position within them, that is, that one's position within given structural forms is inextricably bound up with the generation of emotion in ongoing social relational contexts. The perception of common interests may not be consciously articulable, or indeed perceived at all, but rather lurk in the sense of shared feeling, e.g. the feeling of resentment or anger when those interests are not being served, whether or not these feelings are consciously acknowledged. Further, shared emotion resulting from common social conditions may lead to group or individual actions which further foster emotional contagion.

Conclusion

We have reviewed a series of concepts that, each in its own way, addresses or bears on the bridging of bodily and social being. Each of these – conditioning, habit, mimesis, and finally, emotional contagion, in partial ways, demonstrates the simultaneous interpenetration of bodily life and social context – both macro and micro, real and imagined – that constitutes being.

These processes are deeply rooted in the fundamental fact of human sociality, and the drive toward association, attachment, attunement. What is of import here, and what I have tried to demonstrate in the above, is that emotional processes are implicit in, are an integral part of, these associative and bodily processes. Emotions arise in social contexts, in our relationship with others. Emotional processes are therefore constitutive of ongoing social relational processes and also the basis of agency within them. The emotion of expectation, for example, seen in reference to conditioning and habit, the complex processes involved in "becoming" the other in mimesis, the experiences of empathy and common interest associated with phenomena such as synchrony and co-rhythm in social context as explored through the notion of emotional contagion, provide examples of this phenomenon.

As we have seen, the body is also always engaged in ongoing social-emotional processes; these processes are always embodied.[15] The concepts taken up here indeed demonstrate the interrelationship, through emotion, of bodily and social processes. Emotion acts to situate people in social and material context. It is thus always emergent in ongoing social life and is so constitutive of that situatedness. This expanded perspective on emotions then becomes the basis of the reframing of how we see bodily processes as emergent within social ones, including deeper processes such as immune function in which complex and abstract relations may somehow come to be interiorized. Further, emotion makes possible the explanation of agency in these mimetic processes, that is, as the basis for social and bodily action. A social perspective on emotion, then, is a linking concept for the analysis of the interpenetration of physical and social domains. Emotional processes embody the movement between them.

Notes

1 I refer to the attempt to actually model the nature of these interrelationships, not the simple experimental demonstration of correlations between psychological states or actions and immune function.

2 A similar dilemma occurs in social science's attempts to deal with the interrelationship of biological and social domains.

3 I cite here only representative early sources in medical anthropology that directly address the question of interaction between cultural and biological domains.

4 See Moerman's chapter in this volume.

5 For a review and critique of constructionist approaches in the anthropology of emotion, see Lyon 1995.

6 For a review of the literature on learning and emotion, see, for example, Livesey 1986.

7 For reviews of the placebo phenomenon see Brody 1977 and Shapiro 1960. For a recent review of nocebo phenomena, see Hahn 1997.

8 I have used the example of Darwin here to illustrate the import of the larger social context of emotional associations.

9 Action doesn't necessarily imply motor action, nor does it imply conscious cognitive awareness of structures of action.

10 James' work was well known in France. Durkheim lectured on American pragmatism and on James' writings on religion in 1913–1914, and Mauss would have been aware of this. Mauss's thought has of course been extended in the work of Bourdieu (1977). Bateson's (1975) work on the patterning of response in reference to the socialization of trance is perhaps also relevant here.

11 On the other side of this equation, it is instructive to consider the social and bodily consequences of the disruption of patterns of habit in the context of major social structural change, e.g. social and economic upheavals wrought by economic globalization. Such a consideration again requires deeper analysis of the interrelationship between social and bodily states. It would lead us also toward a

critique of concepts such as stress that so frequently "blackbox" or mystify the relationship between social life and disease. The author addresses this topic further in a book manuscript currently in preparation.

12 It might be noted here that the ability to imaginatively take the role of another including that of an object seems to be confined to humans. While higher primates in general make and use tools, and imaginatively impugn motives to others, it is apparently only humans who can make an object stand for something else. This is easily observed in play, as when a child makes any object at hand stand for, and so be, something else either animate or inanimate, e.g. "let this piece of wood be a car."

13 See Kirmayer's (1992) development of the concept of metaphor in the representation and analysis of illness experience.

Ed. For a different view of metaphor and the relation of verbalization to somatic processes, see Wilce and Price, this volume.

14 Their concern is almost entirely with individual psychological processes in the context of micro-interaction. The term "family" as used by Hatfield *et al.* refers to the fact that emotional contagion can manifest as similar or complementary responses (1994: 5). Emotional contagion is said to be "multiply-determined" because it can "be produced by innate stimulus features (e.g. a mother's nurturing expressions and actions toward an infant), acquired stimulus features, and/or mental stimulations or emotional imagery" (1994: 4). It is multi-level, according to Hatfield *et al.* because it can act on one or more individuals, and because it may result in expressions ranging from neurophysiological or ANS (autonomic nervous system) activity to overt behavioral responses (1994: 5).

15 For an explication of one such embodied process, see Lyon 1994.

References

Ader, R. (1981). Introduction. In R. Ader (ed.), *Psychoneuroimmunology*. New York: Academic Press.

Allport, G. W. (1955). *Becoming: basic considerations for a psychology of personality*. New Haven: Yale University Press.

Aylwin, S. (1985). *Structure in thought and feeling*. London: Methuen.

Bateson, G. (1975). Components of socialization for trance. *Ethos* 3(2): 143–155.

Beck, B. (1978). The metaphor as mediator between semantic and analogic modes of thought. *Current Anthropology* 19(1): 83–97.

Benjamin, W. (1978 [1933]). On the mimetic faculty. In *Reflections: essays, aphorisms, autobiographical writings* (Edmund Jephcott, trans.). New York: Harcourt Brace Jovanovich.

Bourdieu, P. (1977 [1972]). *Outline of a theory of practice* (R. Nice, trans., vol. 16). Cambridge: Cambridge University Press.

Bowlby, J. (1969). *Attachment and loss* (vol. I, Attachment). New York: Basic Books.

Brody, H. (1977). *Placebos and the philosophy of medicine: clinical, conceptual, and ethical issues*. Chicago: University of Chicago Press.

Brown, P. (1991). *The hypnotic brain: hypnotherapy and social communication*. New Haven: Yale University Press.

Byers, P. (1976). Biological rhythms as information channels in interpersonal communication behavior. In P. P. G. Bateson and P. H. Klopfer (eds), *Perspectives in ethology* (vol. II). New York: Plenum.

—— (1982). Discussion. In M. Davis (ed.), *Interaction rhythms: periodicity in communicative behavior* (pp. 133–140). New York: Human Sciences Press.

Darwin, Charles. (1965 [1872]). *The expression of the emotions in man and animals.* Preface by Konrad Lorenz. Chicago: University of Chicago Press.

Dickinson, A. (1987). Conditioning. In R. L. Gregory (ed.), *The Oxford companion to the mind* (pp. 159–160). Oxford: Oxford University Press.

Engelhardt, H. T. Jr (1973). *Mind-body: a categorical relation.* The Hague: Martinus Nijhoff.

Foss, L. (1989). The challenge to biomedicine: a foundations perspective. *Journal of Medicine and Philosophy* 14: 165–191.

Foss, L. and Rothenberg, K. (1987). *The second medical revolution: from biomedicine to infomedicine.* Boston: New Science Library.

Freund, P. E. S. (1990). The expressive body: a common ground for the sociology of emotions and health and illness. *Sociology of Health and Illness* 12(4): 452–477.

Gebauer, G. and C. Wulf (1995). *Mimesis: culture, art, society* (Don Reneau, trans.). Berkeley: University of California Press.

Gregory, R. L. (ed.) (1987). *The Oxford companion to the mind.* Oxford: Oxford University Press.

Hahn, Robert A. (1997). The nocebo phenomenon: concept, evidence, and implications for public health. *Preventive Medicine* 26: 607–611.

—— and Kleinman, A. (1983a). Belief as pathogen, belief as medicine: "voodoo death" and the "placebo phenomenon" in anthropological perspective. *Medical Anthropology Quarterly* 14(4): 16–19.

—— and —— (1983b). Biomedical practice and anthropological theory: frameworks and directions. *Annual Review of Anthropology* 12: 305–333.

Hall, E. T. (1983). *The dance of life: the other dimensions of time.* New York: Anchor Books/Doubleday.

Haraway, D. (1989). The biopolitics of postmodern bodies: determination of self in immune system discourse. *Reflections* 1(1): 3–43.

Hatfield, E., Cacioppo, J. T., and Rapson, R. L. (1994). *Emotional contagion.* Cambridge: Cambridge University Press.

James, W. (1950 [1890]). *The principles of psychology* (2 vols). New York: Dover Publications.

Johnson, M. (1987). *The body in the mind: the bodily basis of meaning, imagination, and reason.* Chicago: University of Chicago Press.

Kemper, T. D. (1984). Power, status, and emotions: a sociological contribution to a psychophysiological domain. In K. R. Scherer and P. Ekman (eds), *Approaches to emotion* (pp. 369–383). Hillsdale, NJ: Lawrence Erlbaum.

Kirmayer, L. J. (1992). The body's insistence on meaning: metaphor as presentation and representation in illness experience. *Medical Anthropology Quarterly,* 6(4), 323–346.

Langman, R. E. (1989). *The immune system: evolutionary principles guide our understanding of this complex biological defense system.* San Diego: Academic Press.

Le Bon, G. (1947 [1911]). *The crowd: a study of the popular mind.* London: Benn.

Lewin, K. (1942). Time perspective and morale. In K. Lewin, G. W. Lewin, and G. W. Allport (eds), *Resolving social conflicts: selected papers on group dynamics* (pp. 103–124): London: Souvenir Press.

Livesey, Peter J. (1986). *Learning and emotion: a biological synthesis* vol. 1: Evolutionary processes. Hillsdale, NJ: Lawrence Erlbaum.

Locke, S., Ader, R., Besedovsky, H., Hall, N., Solomon, G., Strom, T. (eds), and Spector, N. H. (consulting editor) (1985). *Foundations of psychoneuroimmunology*. New York: Aldine.

Lyon, Margot L. (1993). Psychoneuroimmunology: the problem of the situatedness of illness and the conceptualization of healing. *Culture, Medicine and Psychiatry* 17(1): 77–97.

—— (1994). Emotion as mediator of somatic and social processes: the example of respiration. In W. Wentworth and J. Ryan (eds), *Social perspectives on emotion* (vol. 2, pp. 83–108). Greenwich, CT: JAI Press.

—— (1995). Missing emotion: the limitations of cultural constructionism in the study of emotion. *Cultural Anthropology*, 10(2): 244–263.

MacDougall, W. (1960 [1908]). *An introduction to social psychology*. London: Methuen.

Martin, E. (1994). *Flexible bodies: the role of immunity in American culture from the days of polio to the age of AIDS*. Boston: Beacon.

Mauss, M. (1973 [1935]). Techniques of the body. *Economy and Society* 2(1): 70–88.

Mead, G. H. (1962 [1934]). *Mind, self and society from the standpoint of a social behaviourist*. Chicago: University of Chicago Press.

Moerman, D. E. (1983). Physiology and symbols: the anthropological implications of the placebo effect. In L. Romanucci-Ross, D. E. Moerman, and L. R. Tancredi (eds), *The anthropology of medicine: from culture to method* (pp. 240–253). New York: Praeger.

Pavlov, I. P. (1960 [1927]). *Conditioned reflexes: an investigation of the physiological activity of the cerebral cortex* (G. V. Anrep, trans. and ed.). New York: Dover Publications.

—— (1928). *Lectures on conditioned reflexes: twenty-five years of objective study of the higher nervous activity (behaviour) of animals*, vol. 1 (W. Horsley Gantt, trans. and ed.). New York: International Publishers.

Pelletier, K. R., and Herzing, D. L. (1988). Psychoneuroimmunology: toward a mind-body model. A critical review. *Advances* (Institute for the Advancement of Health) 5(1): 27–56.

Shapiro, A. K. (1960). A contribution to the history of the placebo effect. *Behavioral Science* 5: 109.

Spector, H. N. and Korneva, E. A. (1981). Neurophysiology, immunophysiology, and neuroimmunomodulation. In R. Ader (ed.), *Psychoneuroimmunology* (pp. 449–474). New York: Academic Press.

Tarde, J. G. de (1890). *Les lois de l'imitation*. Paris: F. Alcan.

Taussig, M. (1993). *Mimesis and alterity: a particular history of the senses*. New York: Routledge.

Titchener, E. (1909). *Experimental psychology of the thought processes*. New York: Macmillan.

Tomkins, S. S. (1962). *Affect, imagery, consciousness* (vol. I, The Positive Affects). New York: Springer.

—— (1963). *Affect, imagery, consciousness* (vol. II, The Negative Affects). New York: Springer.

Wispe, L. (1991). *The psychology of sympathy*. New York: Plenum Press.

Part II

PNI in the wild

Anthropological fieldwork using endocrine and immune variables

Chapter 6: Editor's note

Flinn has conducted longitudinal ethnographic and biomedical research in the Dominican village of Bwa Mawego, a study in which Decker (this volume) has also participated. Whereas Decker's chapter focuses on levels of stress and cortisol in the village's adult population, Flinn and England focus on children. In providing ethnographic detail and some immunological measures, Flinn and England's chapter is an apt bridge between Decker's, which provides cortisol data associated with stressful events, and McDade's, which provides PNI data from Samoa.

Note that first author, Mark Flinn, played a key role in organizing the conference panels that led to this volume, introducing the editor to contributors Decker, McDade, and Worthman. Flinn has been a pioneer in asserting the relevance of anthropology to context-sensitive investigations of human immune function.

Childhood stress

Endocrine and immune responses to psychosocial events

Mark V. Flinn and Barry G. England

Introduction

This chapter presents an overview of a study of social environment, stress, and health among children living in a rural Caribbean village. The fieldwork is unusual in that it is long-term, naturalistic, and combines detailed ethnographic observation with physiological monitoring and health assessment. The research paradigm involves examination of relations among hormonal measures of stress response, naturally occurring "stressful" events, morbidity, growth, and immune function. The study population consisted of 283 residents, aged between two months and 20 years, of a village on the East Coast of Dominica. Fieldwork was conducted over a 15-year period (1988–2002). Research methods and techniques included: immunoassays from saliva samples of cortisol ($N = 27,871$), interleukins-1 and -8, neopterin, secretory immunoglobulin-A, and microglobulin β_2; systematic behavioral observations, psychological questionnaires, anthropometric measures, daily health evaluations, medical histories, and physical examinations.

Analyses of data indicate that psychosocial events were associated with stress hormones and health. Abnormal cortisol profiles, diminished immunity, and poor health were associated with household composition and unstable mating relationships of parents/caretakers. Traumatic family events temporarily elevated cortisol levels, but low or blunted levels often occurred subsequently. Chronically stressed children in difficult family environments usually had high average cortisol levels when they were at home, but some had reduced cortisol response to activities such as physical games and attending school. Individual differences and variable longitudinal patterning of cortisol response complicated analysis. Temporal patterns of cortisol suggest that children undergoing stressful events were at higher risk for illness (diarrhea, influenza, common cold, asthma, rashes, etc.) during a two–six day period following unusually high cortisol levels.

Concomitant with abnormal cortisol profiles was altered immune function; some chronically stressed children appear to have had reduced cell-mediated (neopterin, microglobulin β_2), humoral (secretory-immunoglobulin-A), and/or

Plate 6.1 Children from the study village playing in a tree.

non-specific (neutrophil recruitment via interleukin-8) immunity. Interpretation of these immune function results, however, is speculative.

Although elevated stress hormone levels may provide short-term benefits, the body needs to replenish energy reserves to provide for immunity, growth, and other functions. Chronic high levels of cortisol and/or sympathetic activation may deplete energy and immune reserves. Protection of active peripheral tissues – including the Central Nervous System (CNS) – from autoimmunity may present additional problems, particularly during growth and development.

Results suggest that naturally occurring psychosocial events associated with stress hormones have significant short- and long-term effects on child health. This finding is consistent with a large body of clinical and retrospective studies that indicate "stress" has negative effects on health. The remarkable sensitivity of the human CNS to psychosocial stressors and consequent release of cortisol with its apparent health costs presents an unresolved evolutionary paradox. We do not have satisfying explanations for how natural selection might have favored these complex associations among energy regulation, immune function, and cognition. And we have only begun to explore the ontogenetic responses of this system to different social environments faced by the developing child.

Family and stress

The family is of paramount importance in a child's world. Throughout human evolutionary history, parents and close relatives provided calories, protection, and information necessary for survival, growth, health, social success, and eventual reproduction. The human mind is therefore likely to have evolved special sensitivity to interactions with family caretakers, particularly during infancy and early childhood (Baumeister and Leary 1995; Daly and Wilson 1995; Belsky *et al.* 1996; Geary and Flinn 2001).

The family and other kin provide important cognitive "landmarks" for the development of a child's understanding of the social environment. The reproductive interests of a child overlap with those of its parents more than with any other individuals. Information (including advice, training, and incidental observation) provided by parents is important for situating oneself in the social milieu and developing a mental model of its operations. A child's family environment may be an especially important source and mediator of "stress,"[1] with consequent effects on health.

Psychosocial stressors are associated with increased risk of infectious disease (Mason *et al.* 1979; Cohen *et al.* 1991) and a variety of other illnesses (Ader *et al.* 2001; Glaser and Kiecolt-Glaser 1994). Physiological stress responses regulate the allocation of energetic and other somatic resources to different bodily functions via a complex assortment of neuroendocrine mechanisms. Changing, unpredictable environments require adjustment of priorities. Digestion, growth, immunity, and sex are irrelevant while being chased by a predator (Sapolsky 1994). Stress hormones help shunt blood, glucose, etc. to tissues necessary for the task at hand. Chronic and traumatic stress diminish health, evidently because resources are diverted away from important health functions. Such diversions may have special significance during childhood, because of the additional demands of physical and mental growth and development, and possible long-term consequences.

Investigation of physiological stress responses, social environment, and health has been hampered by the lack of non-invasive techniques for measurement of stress hormones and immune function. Frequent collection of plasma samples to assess temporal changes in endocrine and immune function is not feasible in non-clinical settings. The development of saliva immunoassay techniques (Walker *et al.* 1978; Hiramatsu 1981; Riad-Fahmy *et al.* 1983), however, presents new opportunities for stress research (Kirschbaum *et al.* 1992). Saliva is relatively easy to collect and store, especially under adverse field conditions faced by anthropologists (Ellison 1988). Concomitant monitoring of a child's daily activities, stress hormones, health, and psychological conditions provides a powerful research design for investigating the effects of naturally occurring psychosocial events ("stressors") on child health (Figure 6.1).

a.

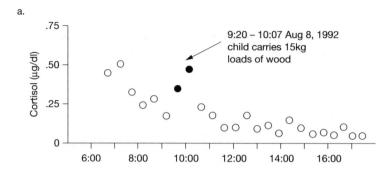

b.

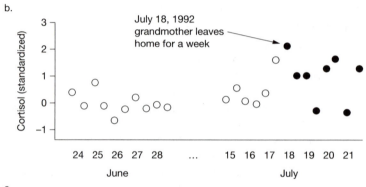

c.

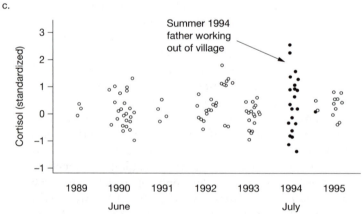

Figure 6.1 Longitudinal monitoring of cortisol levels as a tool for investigating stress response among children in a Caribbean village. (a) Hourly sampling of a 12-year-old male demonstrating elevation of cortisol levels associated with carrying heavy loads of wood. (b) Twice-daily sampling of a 13-year-old girl demonstrating change in pattern of cortisol levels associated with temporary absence of caretaking grandmother. (c) Twice-daily sampling over a 7-year period of a male born in 1985 demonstrating the change in pattern of cortisol levels associated with the absence of his father.

Stress response mechanisms and theory

Physiological response to environmental stimuli perceived as "stressful" is modulated by the limbic system (amygdala and hippocampus) and basal ganglia. These components of the CNS interact with the sympathetic and parasympathetic nervous systems and two neuroendocrine axes, the sympathetic–adrenal–medullary system (abbreviated as SAM), and the hypothalamic–anterior pituitary–adrenal cortex system (abbreviated as HPA). The SAM and HPA systems affect a wide range of physiological functions in concert with other neuroendocrine mechanisms and involve complex feedback regulation. The SAM system controls the catecholamines norepinephrine and epinephrine (adrenalin). The HPA system regulates glucocorticoids, primarily cortisol (for reviews see McEwen 1995; Sapolsky *et al.* 2000; Weiner 1992).

Cortisol is a key hormone produced in response to physical and psychosocial stressors (Mason 1968; Selye 1976). It is produced and stored in the adrenal cortex. Release into the plasma is primarily under the control of pituitary ACTH (adrenocorticotropic hormone). The free or unbound portion of the circulating cortisol may pass through the cell membrane and bind to a specific cytosolic glucocorticoid receptor. This complex may induce genes coding for at least twenty-six different enzymes involved with carbohydrate, fat, and amino acid metabolism in brain, liver, muscle, and adipose tissue (Yuwiler 1982).

Cortisol modulates a wide range of somatic functions, including: (a) energy release (e.g. stimulation of hepatic gluconeogenesis in concert with glucagon and inhibition of the effects of insulin), (b) immune activity (e.g. regulation of inflammatory response and the cytokine cascade), (c) mental activity (e.g. alertness, memory, and learning), (d) growth (e.g. inhibition of growth hormone and somatomedins), and (e) reproductive function (e.g. inhibition of gonadal steroids, including testosterone). These complex, multiple effects of cortisol muddle understanding of its adaptive functions. The demands of energy regulation must orchestrate with those of immune function, and so forth. Mechanisms for localized targeting (e.g. glucose uptake by active *versus* inactive muscle tissues, and neuropeptide-directed immune response) provide fine-tuning of the above general physiological effects. Cortisol regulation allows the body to respond to changing environmental conditions by preparing for *specific* short-term demands (Mason 1971; Munck *et al.* 1984; Weiner 1992).

These temporary beneficial effects of glucocorticoid stress response, however, are not without costs. Persistent activation of the HPA system is associated with immune deficiency, cognitive impairment, inhibited growth, delayed sexual maturity, damage to the hippocampus, and psychological maladjustment (Dunn 1989, 1995; Glaser and Kiecolt-Glaser 1994; Ader *et al.* 2001). Chronic stress may diminish metabolic energy (Ivanovici and Wiebe 1981; Sapolsky 1986, 1991) and produce complications from autoimmune protection (Munck *et al.* 1984; Munck and Guyre 1991). Stressful life events – such as divorce, death of a family member, change of residence, or loss of a job – are associated with infectious disease and other health problems (House *et al.* 1988; Kaplan 1991; Herbert and Cohen 1993; Maier *et al.* 1994).

Current psychosocial stress research suggests that cortisol response is stimulated by uncertainty that is perceived as significant[2] and for which behavioral responses will have unknown effects (Fredrikson *et al.* 1985; Levine 1993; Haggerty *et al.* 1994; Kirschbaum and Hellhammer 1994; Weiner 1992). That is, important events are going to happen, the child does not know how to react, but is highly motivated to figure out what should be done. Cortisol release is associated with unpredictable, uncontrollable events that require full alert readiness and mental anticipation. In appropriate circumstances, temporary moderate increases in stress hormones (and associated neuropeptides) may enhance mental activity for short periods in localized areas, hence improving cognitive processes for responding to social challenges (cf. Coe *et al.* 1985a; Martinez 1986; Breier *et al.* 1987; Martignoni *et al.* 1992; McEwen and Sapolsky 1995). Other mental processes may be inhibited, perhaps to reduce external and internal "noise" (Servan-Schreiber *et al.* 1990; cf. Wolkowitz *et al.* 1990; Newcomer *et al.* 1994; Kirschbaum *et al.* 1996).

Relations between cortisol production and emotional distress, however, are difficult to assess because of temporal and inter-individual variation in HPA response (Tennes and Mason 1982; Kagan 1983; Nachmias *et al.* 1996). Habituation may occur to repeated events for which a child acquires an effective mental model. Attenuation and below-normal levels of cortisol may follow a day or more after emotionally charged events. Chronically stressed children may develop abnormal cortisol response, possibly via changes in binding globulin levels, and/or reduced affinity or density of glucocorticoid or CRH/vasopressin receptors in the brain (Fuchs and Flugge 1995). Early experience – such as perinatal stimulation of rats (Meaney *et al.* 1991), prenatal stress of rhesus macaques (Schneider *et al.* 1992; Clarke 1993), prenatal exposure to cocaine among humans (Magnano *et al.* 1992) and sexual abuse among humans (De Bellis *et al.* 1994; Heim *et al.* 2000) – may permanently alter HPA response.[3] And personality may affect HPA response (and vice versa), because children with inhibited temperaments tend to have higher cortisol levels than extroverted children (Kagan *et al.* 1988; cf. Gunnar *et al.* 1995; Hertsgaard *et al.* 1995; Nachmias *et al.* 1996).

Further complications arise from interaction between HPA stress response and a wide variety of other neuroendocrine activities, including modulation of catecholamines, melatonin, testosterone, serotonin, β-endorphins, cytokines, and enkephalins (Axelrod and Reisine 1984; De Kloet 1991; Sapolsky 1992b; Scapagnini 1992; Saphier *et al.* 1994). Changes in cortisol for energy allocation and modulation of immune function may be confused with effects of psychosocial stress. Oxytocin and vasopressin intracerebral binding sites are associated with familial attachment in mammals (Insel and Shapiro 1992; Levy *et al.* 1992; Winslow *et al.* 1993), and may influence distress involving caretaker–child relationships. Other components of the HPA axis, such as corticotropin releasing hormone (CRH) and melanocyte stimulating hormone, have effects that are distinct from cortisol. Concurrent monitoring of all these neuroendocrine activities would provide important information about stress response, but is not possible in a non-clinical setting with current techniques.

Relations between stress-induced cortisol response and immunosuppression are perhaps even more complex and enigmatic (Cohen and Crnic 1982; Campbell and Cohen 1985; Besedovsky and del Rey 1991; Ader *et al.* 2001; Dunn 1995; Kiecolt-Glaser and Glaser 1995; McDade this volume). Stress is associated with a variety of illnesses, including infectious disease, reactivation of latent herpes virus, cancer, and cardiovascular problems. The wide range of health effects of stress suggests that a number of immune mechanisms are involved. Cortisol influences many functions of lymphocytes, macrophages, and leukocytes, and as with energy use, may direct their movement to specific locations. Cortisol also inhibits the production of some cytokines (e.g., interleukin-1) and mediates several components of the inflammatory response. In concert with the sympathetic–adrenal-medullary system (SAM), which generally down-regulates lymphocyte and monocyte functions, HPA stress response affects all of the major components of the immune system. However, the effects of neuroendocrine stress response are not all inhibitory, and may involve temporary up regulation and/or localized enhancement of some immune functions (Smith 1988; Jefferies 1991).

Munck *et al.* (1984) hypothesize that some effects of stress on health may be incidental consequences of the immune regulatory functions of cortisol. Because cortisol modulates both (1) immune response, including protection from autoimmune reactions, and (2) mental processes (energy allocation to the CNS?), immunity is inadvertently turned off during psychosocial stress. An alternative hypothesis suggests that stress response involves an optimal allocation problem (Tinbergen 1971; Sapolsky 1987). Energy resources are diverted to mental and other short-term (stress emergency) functions, at cost to long-term functions of growth, development, and immunity (Sapolsky 1992a, 1994). Under normal conditions of temporary stress, there would be little effect on health. Persistent stress, however, may result in pathological immunosuppression.

Assessment of relations among psychosocial stressors, hormonal stress response, and health is complex, requiring (a) longitudinal monitoring of hormone levels, immune measures, and health, (b) control of extraneous effects from physical activity, circadian rhythms, and food consumption, (c) knowledge of individual differences in temperament, experience, and perception, and (d) awareness of cultural context. Anthropological research that integrates human biology and ethnography is particularly well suited to

Plate 6.2 General oral examination and a check for throat infection conducted for this study.

these demands (e.g., Panter-Brick *et al.* 1996; Dressler and Bindon 1997). Physiological and medical assessment in concert with ethnography and co-residence with children and their families in a small village over a fifteen-year period can provide intimate, prospective, naturalistic information unavailable to clinical studies.

Research design

Longitudinal monitoring of cortisol, family environment, behavior, events, immune measures, growth, and illness in a natural (non-clinical) environment is used to identify associations between health and psychosocial stressors. Data analyses examine both long-term (cumulative) and short-term (day-to-day, hour-by-hour) associations among cortisol levels, family composition, socioeconomic conditions, behavioral activities, events, temperament, growth, medical history, immune measures, and illness.

Variables and measures are as follows: *Physiological stress response* is assessed by radioimmunoassay (RIA) of cortisol levels in saliva. Analyses examine mean values, variation, and day-to-day and hour-by-hour profiles of standardized (circadian time control) cortisol data. *Family composition* is assessed by age, sex, genealogical relationship, and number of individuals in the caretaking household. *Socioeconomic conditions* include household income, material possessions, land ownership, occupations, and educational attainment. *Caretaking attention* is assessed by (a) frequencies and types of behavioral interaction, (b) informant ratings of caretaking that children receive, and (c) informant interviews. *Personality and temperament* are assessed by (a) culturally appropriate versions of Emotionality-Activity-Sociability (Buss and Plomin 1984) and five-factor (Goldberg 1992, 1993) instruments, (b) interviews with peers, parents, teachers, and neighbors, and (c) behavioral observation. *Immune response* is assessed by RIA of neopterin and interleukins-1 and 8, turbidimetric immunoassay of secretory-immunoglobulin A, and microparticle enzyme immunoassay of micro-globulin β_2 from saliva samples. *Health* is assessed by (a) observed type, frequency, and severity of medical problems (diarrhea, influenza, common cold, asthma, abrasions, rashes, etc.), (b) informant (parents, teachers, neighbors) ratings, (c) medical records, (d) growth (weight for age, height for age, and fluctuating asymmetry) patterns, and (e) physical examination by a medical doctor. In this paper the primary measure of health used is *percentage of days ill*, the proportion of days that a child was observed (directly by researchers) with common benign temporary infectious disease (89 percent appeared to be common upper respiratory tract infections – e.g. rhinovirus, adenovirus, parainfluenza, and influenza; 6 percent were diarrheal; 5 percent were miscellaneous indeterminate – e.g. febrile without other symptoms). *Daily activities* and *emotional states* are assessed from (a) caretaker and child self-report questionnaires, and (b) systematic behavioral observation (focal follow and instantaneous scan sampling). Multiple sources of information are cross-checked to assess reliability (Bernard *et al.* 1984).

The primary focus of this chapter is on relations among: *percentage of days ill, cortisol levels, family composition*, and *immune function. Caretaking attention, socioeconomic conditions, temperament, daily activities*, and *emotional states* are analyzed as secondary or control variables; they are presented in more detail in other publications.

Study site

Bwa Mawego is a rural village located on the East Coast of Dominica. The approximately 600 residents live in roughly 200 structures/households that are loosely clumped into five "hamlets" or neighborhoods. The population is of mixed African, Carib, and European descent. The village is isolated because it sits at the dead-end of a rough road passable by small trucks except for occasional periods during the rainy season (the road was improved and partially paved in 1991, 1993 and 1999). Part-time residence is common, with many individuals emigrating for temporary work to other parts of Dominica or off-island (e.g. seasonal farm work in the United States and

Canada). Most residents cultivate bananas and/or bay leaves as cash crops, and plantains, dasheen (taro), and a variety of fruits and vegetables as subsistence crops. Fish are caught by free diving with spear guns and from small boats (hand-built wooden "canoes" of Carib design) using lines and nets. Land is communally "owned" by kin groups, but parceled for long-term individual use.

Most village houses are strung close together along roads and tracks. Older homes are constructed of wooden planks and shingles hewn by hand from local forest trees; concrete block and galvanized roofing are more popular today. Most houses have one or two sleeping rooms, with the kitchen and toilet as outbuildings. Children usually sleep together on foam or rag mats. Wealthier households typically have "parlors" with sitting furniture. Electricity became available in 1988; during the summer of 1995 about 70 percent of homes had "current," 41 percent had telephones, 11 percent had refrigerators, and 7 percent had televisions. Water is obtained from streams, spring catchments, and run-off from roofs.

The village of Bwa Mawego is appropriate for the study of relations among psychosocial stress and child health for the following reasons: (1) there is substantial temporal and permanent variability among individuals in the factors under study (socioeconomic conditions, family environments, cortisol response, and child health), (2) the village and housing are relatively open, hence behavior is easily observable, (3) kin tend to reside locally, (4) the number of economic variables is reduced relative to urban areas, (5) the languages (French-based "Kweyol" and English) and culture are familiar to the investigator, (6) there are useful medical records, and (7) local residents welcome the research and are most helpful.

The study involves 282 individuals, aged between two months and 20 years, residing in 82 households. This is a nearly complete sample (> 95 percent) of all children living in four of the five village hamlets during the period of fieldwork. Research was conducted during June–August 1988, June–August 1989, May–December 1990, May–August 1992, June–August 1993, December 1993–February 1994, May–August 1994, June–August 1995, and June–July 1996, August 1997, June–August 1998, December 1998–January 1999, June–July 1999, January 2000, July–August 2000, December 2000–January 2001, July–August 2001 and June–August 2002.[4] Cortisol data are from saliva samples collected during July–December 1990, June–August 1992, June–August 1993, December 1993–January 1994, June–August 1994, July 1995, June–July 1996, August 1997, June–August 1998, December 1998–January 1999, and January 2000.[5]

Methods and field techniques

Information on socioeconomic conditions, household environment, caretaking attention, temperament, and health was collected by standard ethno-

graphic techniques including interviews, behavioral scans, participant observation, and questionnaire instruments. These methods are described in more
detail in other publications (Flinn 1988; Quinlan 2000).

Data on physiological stress response are derived from RIA of saliva
samples (see below). Saliva is collected by two routines. The primary routine
was a twice-daily collection in which an anthropologist and research assistant walked set routes from house to house, once in the morning (5:30 a.m. –
9:00 a.m.) and once in the afternoon (3:00 p.m. – 6:30 p.m.). Most ($N =$
16,652 of 27,871) saliva samples were collected in this way. A secondary
routine used a "focal follow" technique in which (a) children were observed
from dawn until early afternoon or evening, or (b) infants were observed from
dawn until early afternoon, both with hourly saliva samples ($N = 7,655$).
Saliva samples from some parents and other caretakers were collected at the
same time as their children. Because the majority of saliva samples were
collected at the child's household during periods when family interactions
were common (early morning and late afternoon), the effects of family
environment on cortisol response may be accentuated.

Our saliva collection protocol was as follows: First, each child rinsed
her/his mouth with fresh water. At this point, children were checked for oral
bleeding. Both food and blood contamination may affect the integrity of
samples (Ellison 1988). Next, children were given a small amount of chewing
gum (spearmint) to stimulate saliva production. After chewing the gum for
about one minute and "swallowing the sugar," saliva was deposited in disposable plastic cups for about three minutes. For infants, saliva was collected by
swabbing with cotton rolls (Turner 1995). Approximately four milliliters of
saliva was pipetted into labeled (name, date, time, number) polystyrene test
tubes and preserved using sodium azide and refrigeration. Analysis of cortisol
levels requires precise information on *time of collection*, *time of waking up
from sleep*, and *individual sleep schedule* because there is a circadian pattern
to cortisol release (Fredrikson *et al.* 1985; Van Cauter 1990). Some hourly
samples were taken for finer-grained analysis of temporal fluctuation in
cortisol levels. Daily activity, emotional state, and health questionnaires were
administered concomitant with saliva collection (see below).

Children readily acclimated to the collection procedure. However, shy or
inhibited children in particular tended to have cortisol levels that were higher
than normal for the first few days of saliva collection. Multiple samples (more
than 50 days of morning and afternoon samples over several years) from each
child provide a more effective indication of stress response than a single
collection design, because it allows for habituation and provides data for
longitudinal analyses.

Cortisol levels in saliva samples were determined by standard immunoassay techniques. Salivary cortisol is a reliable measure of adrenal cortical
function (Walker *et al.* 1978: Hiramatsu 1981; Umeda *et al.* 1981; Vining
et al. 1983, 1984; Vining and McGinley 1984; Landon *et al.* 1984; Bolufer

1989; Kirschbaum *et al.* 1992). All samples were analyzed at the Ligand Assay Laboratory at the University of Michigan Hospitals.

Cortisol release follows a circadian pattern, with highest levels around waking up in the morning, diminishing to low levels during evening hours and a nadir just before or during sleep. For example, mean cortisol levels when children have been awake for ten minutes is 0.578 µg/dl; after two hours it is 0.222 µg/dl; and after eight hours it is 0.071 µg/dl. To control for time (circadian) effects, raw cortisol measures were standardized by five-minute time intervals from wake-up time.[6] For each time interval, mean values and standard deviations were computed. Standardized values were generated as time-controlled measures of cortisol response as with the following hypothetical example: the mean cortisol level of children that have been awake for 60 minutes = 0.3 µg/dl with standard deviation of 0.1 µg/dl. A cortisol measure of 0.4 µg/dl from this time period would have a standardized value of 1.0, i.e. 0.4 µg/dl is one standard deviation (0.1 µg/dl) from the average (mean) value of 0.3 µg/dl. This procedure allows comparison of cortisol values from saliva collected at different times. All cortisol data presented in this paper are time-standardized.

During saliva collection, children and their caretakers were interviewed concerning what activities the child did that day, and how the child felt during these activities (e.g. "Did you cry?" "Were you angry?" "How many runs did you score?" with follow-up questions regarding the specifics). This self-report and caretaker-report information on daily activities was compared with behavioral observation data. Health evaluations were also conducted daily during saliva collection. If illness was indicated, body temperature was checked using an oral thermometer. Blood pressure was measured once a week.[7]

Most individuals exhibit a slight rise (about 0.01 µg/dl at lunch, or 13 percent) in cortisol levels after eating a meal or drinking caffeinated beverages. This post-prandial rise is most significant for the midday meal. Data were not adjusted for eating and caffeine intake because very few samples were taken during lunch time, the effect is small, and eating and caffeine intake are presumed random with regard to hypotheses tested.[8] Individuals commonly have small elevations in cortisol levels during midday, usually in association with potential minor stressors (Holl *et al.* 1984).

Some individuals show a rise in cortisol levels during and shortly after intensive physical exertion (e.g. carrying heavy loads of wood, water, bananas, or bay leaf). Physical exertions involving social interaction, such as competitive sports, are associated with more substantial elevation of cortisol levels, particularly for males. Data are not adjusted for physical activity because only a small proportion of samples were collected when children exerted themselves, it was difficult to determine the extent of exertion, and such activities are presumed random with regard to hypotheses tested. Because general activity levels are associated with cortisol, this presents a confounding effect. Some children may exhibit increased cortisol response when they are healthy, active, and have abundant energetic resources, compared to when they are inactive and have depleted energy reserves.[9]

Results and discussion

Stress response and family environment

Human infants and juveniles cannot survive, let alone develop effective social skills, without assistance from parents or other caretakers. Relationships within the caretaking household are essential for the developing child (Bowlby 1969, 1973). Composition of the family or caretaking household may have important effects on child development (Kagan 1984; Whiting and Edwards 1988). For example, in Western cultures, children with divorced parents may experience more emotional tension or "stress" than children living in a stable two-parent family (Wallerstein 1983; Pearlin and Turner 1987; Gottman and Katz 1989).

Associations between average cortisol levels of children and household composition are presented in Figure 6.2. Children living with non-relatives, stepfathers + half-siblings (stepfather has children by the stepchild's mother), or single parents without kin support had higher average levels of cortisol than children living with both parents, single mothers with kin support, or grandparents.[10] A further test of this hypothesis is provided by comparison of step and genetic children residing in the same households (Figure 6.3).

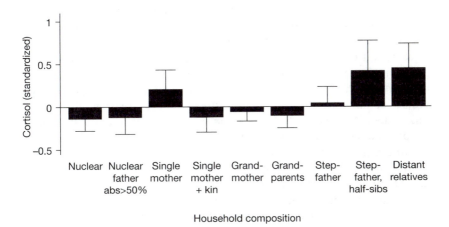

Figure 6.2 Household composition and cortisol. Vertical bars represent 95 percent confidence intervals (1.96 SE). Sample sizes (N of children, N of cortisol saliva assays) are: 89, 6,905; 28, 2,234; 30, 2,296; 31, 2,581; 32, 2,645; 16, 1,341; 5, 279; 24, 1,870; 9, 482. Figure adapted from Flinn and England (1997).

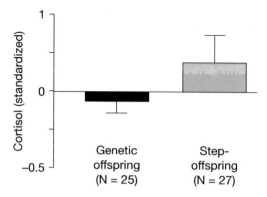

Figure 6.3 Average (mean) cortisol levels of step and genetic children residing in the same household. In 38 of 43 dyads, stepchildren had higher mean cortisol levels than their co-resident half-siblings who are genetic offspring of both resident parents. Average age of stepchildren is 11.3 years, genetic children 8.4 years. 95 percent confidence intervals are shown by vertical lines. Figure adapted from Flinn and England (1997).

Stepchildren had higher average cortisol levels than their half-siblings residing in the same household who were genetic offspring of both parents.

Several caveats need emphasis. First, not all children in difficult family environments have elevated cortisol levels. Second, household composition is not a uniform indicator of family environment. Some single-mother households, for example, appear more stable, affectionate, and supportive than some two-parent households. And third, children appear differentially sensitive to different aspects of their caretaking environments, reflecting temperamental and other individual differences.

These caveats, however, do not invalidate the general association between household composition and childhood stress. There are several possible reasons underlying this result. Children in difficult caretaking environments may experience chronic stress resulting in moderate–high levels of cortisol (i.e. a child has cortisol levels that are above average day after day). They may experience more acute stressors that substantially raise cortisol for short periods of time. They may experience more frequent stressful events (e.g. parental chastisement or marital quarreling – see Wilson *et al.* 1980; Flinn 1988; Finkelhor and Dzuiba-Leatherman 1994) that temporarily raise cortisol. There may be a lack of reconciliation between parent and child. And they may have inadequate coping abilities, perhaps resulting from difficult experiences in early development. The following case examples present temporal analyses of family relations and cortisol levels that illustrate some of the above possibilities.

"Jenny" was a twelve-year-old girl who lived with her grandparents, aunt, and uncle. Her mother had lived in Guadeloupe for the past ten years. At 9:17 a.m. on July 17, 1994, I (MVF) observed the following events: "Wayonne," a six-year-old male cousin who was visiting for the week, threw a stone at Jenny, who was sweeping in front of the house. She responded by scolding Wayonne, who pouted and retreated behind a mango tree. Wayonne found a mango pit, and lobbed it towards Jenny, but missed and hit a dress hanging on a clothesline, marking it with a streak of red dirt. Jenny ran to Wayonne, and struck him on the legs with her broom. He began to cry, arousing the interest of "granny Ninee," who emerged from the cooking room asking what happened, and upon hearing the story, scolded Jenny for "beating" Wayonne. Jenny argued that she was in the right, but granny Ninee would not hear of it, and sent her into the house. Jenny appeared frustrated, but looked down and kept quiet despite a quivering lip.

Jenny's cortisol levels were substantially elevated that afternoon, followed by subnormal levels the next day (a possible recovery period?). Three days after the incident she reported feeling ill and had a runny nose and oral temperature of 99.9°F (Figure 6.4).[11]

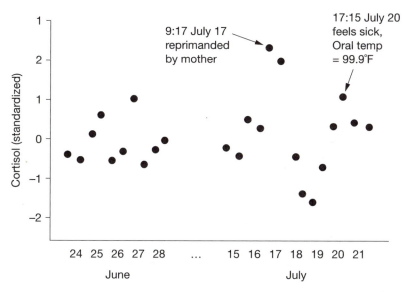

Figure 6.4 Morning and afternoon cortisol levels of "Jenny" during summer 1994. Late June cortisol levels are normal, but after being reprimanded by her grandmother on the morning of July 17, she has elevated cortisol levels for one day, followed by depressed cortisol levels for two days. Jenny exhibits symptoms of an upper respiratory infection with slight fever (common cold, probably rhinovirus) on the afternoon of July 20. Figure adapted from Flinn and England (1997).

On June 28, 1992, a serious marital conflict erupted in the "Franklin" household. "Amanda" was a 34-year-old mother of six children, five of whom (ages 2, 3, 5, 8, and 14) were living with her and their father/stepfather, "Pierre Franklin." Amanda was angry with Pierre for spending money on rum. Pierre was vexed with Amanda for "shaming" him in front of his friends. He left the village for several weeks, staying with a relative in town. His three genetic children (ages 2, 3, and 5) showed abnormal cortisol levels (in this case elevated) for a prolonged period following their father's departure (Figure 6.5). Children usually became habituated to stressful events but absence of a parent often resulted in abnormal patterns of elevated and/or subnormal cortisol levels. Following the return of their father, the Franklin children's cortisol levels resumed a more normal profile. Children living in families with high levels of marital conflict (observed and reported serious quarreling, fighting, residence absence) were more likely to have abnormal cortisol profiles than children living in more amiable families were.

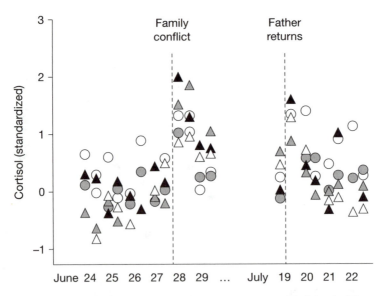

Figure 6.5 Marital conflict and cortisol levels in the "Franklin" family. Three genetic children (2-, 3-, and 5-year-old males) are represented by △ ▲ ▲ and two stepchildren (8- and 14-year-old females) are represented by ○ ● respectively. Cortisol levels of three genetic children are normal before the conflict, rise during the conflict and during father's absence, briefly rise upon his return, and return to normal (lower) levels. The younger of the two stepchildren has a pattern of abnormally high cortisol, although her levels are moderate during stepfather's absence. The older stepdaughter has a similar, but more normal pattern of cortisol levels. Figure adapted from Flinn and England (1997).

The events in children's lives that were associated with elevated cortisol were not always traumatic or even "negative." Eating meals, hard physical work, routine competitive play such as cricket, basketball, and "king of the mountain" on ocean rocks, and return of a family member that was temporarily absent (e.g. father returning from a job in town for the weekend) were associated with temporary moderate increases (about 10 percent – 100 percent) in cortisol among healthy children. These moderate stressors usually had rapid attenuation (< one hour) of cortisol levels (some stressors had characteristic temporal "signatures" of cortisol level and duration).

High stress events (cortisol increases from 100 percent – 2000 percent), however, most commonly involved trauma from family conflict or change (Flinn and England 1995, 1997; Flinn et al. 1996). Punishment, quarreling, and residence change substantially increased cortisol levels, whereas calm affectionate contact was associated with diminished (–10 percent to –50 percent) cortisol levels. 19.2 percent of all cortisol values that were more than two standard deviations above mean levels (i.e. indicative of substantial stress) were temporally associated with traumatic family events (residence change of child or parent/caretaker, punishment, "shame," serious quarreling, and/or fighting) within a 24-hour period. 42.1 percent of traumatic family events were temporally associated with substantially elevated cortisol (i.e. at least one of the saliva samples collected within 24 hours was > 2 S.D. above mean levels). Chronic elevations of cortisol levels, as in the above example of the Franklin family, may also occur, but are more difficult to assess quantitatively.

It is important to note that there was considerable variability among children in cortisol response to family disturbances. Not all individuals had detectable changes in cortisol levels associated with family trauma. Some children had significantly elevated cortisol levels during some episodes of family trauma but not during others. Cortisol response is not a simple or uniform phenomenon. Numerous factors, including preceding events, habituation, specific individual histories, context, and temperament, might affect how children respond to particular situations.

Nonetheless, traumatic family events were associated with elevated cortisol levels for all ages of children more than any other factor that we examined. These results suggest that family interactions were a critical psychosocial stressor in most children's lives, although the sample collection during periods of intense family interaction (early morning and late afternoon) may have exaggerated this association.

Although elevated cortisol levels are associated with traumatic events such as family conflict, long-term stress may result in diminished cortisol response. In some cases chronically stressed children[12] had blunted response to physical activities that normally evoked cortisol elevation. Comparison of cortisol levels during "non-stressful" periods (no reported or observed: crying, punishment, anxiety, residence change, family conflict, or health problem during 24-hour period before saliva collection) indicates a striking reduction and, in many cases, reversal of the family environment–stress association (Figure 6.6). Chronically stressed children sometimes had subnormal cortisol levels when they were not in stressful situations. For example, cortisol levels immediately after school (walking home from school) and during non-competitive play were lower among some chronically stressed children (cf. Long *et al.* 1993). Some chronically stressed children appeared socially "tough" or withdrawn, and exhibited little or no arousal to the novelty of the first few days of the saliva collection procedure.

Some children exhibited longitudinal change in cortisol profiles concomitant with an improved family environment, but others did not. Unlike their responses to many other potential stressors, most children did not seem to habituate readily to family trauma. Some parental actions may lack predictability and controllability necessary for development of actions or perceptions that reliably alleviate stress response (Garmezy 1983; Rutter 1983; Hinde and Stevenson-Hinde 1987; Pennebaker, this volume).

Longitudinal analysis of caretaking histories indicates that children may have "sensitive periods" for development of stress response. Children with severe caretaking problems during infancy (neglect, parental alcoholism, and/or maternal absence) and/or growth disruptions (weight loss of >10 percent of body weight) during the first two years of life (see black dots in Figure 6.10) usually exhibit one of two distinct cortisol profiles: (1) unusually

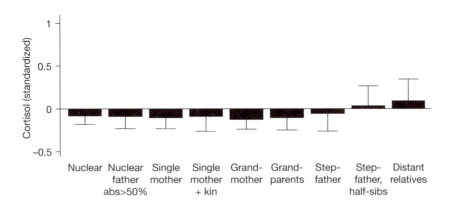

Figure 6.6 Household composition and cortisol during "non-stressful" periods. Vertical bars represent 95 percent confidence intervals (1.96 SE). Sample sizes (number of children, number of cortisol saliva assays) are: 89, 4,387; 28, 1,309; 30, 1,322; 31, 1,651; 32, 1,878; 16, 934; 5, 181; 24, 864; 9, 256. There are no significant differences among household types. Figure adapted from Flinn (1999).

low basal cortisol levels with occasional high spikes, or (2) chronically high cortisol levels. The first type (low basal, high spikes) is associated with hostility and antisocial behavior (e.g. theft, running away from home) and is more common among males. The second type (chronically high) is associated with anxiety and withdrawal behavior and is more common among females. These profiles are suggestive of diminished glucocorticoid regulatory function of the hippocampus (cf. Gray 1987; Sapolsky 1991; Yehuda *et al.* 1991).

Stress response and illness

A large and convincing research literature confirms commonsense intuition that psychosocial stress affects health (Black 1994; Glaser and Kiecolt-Glaser 1994; Ader *et al.* 2001). Retrospective studies indicate that traumatic life events – such as divorce or death of a close relative – are associated with subsequent health problems – such as cancer or cardiovascular disease (Rabkin and Struening 1976).[13] Clinical studies indicate that individuals with stressful lives are more susceptible to the common cold (Mason *et al.* 1979; Cohen *et al.* 1991; Evans and Pitts 1994; Stone *et al.* 1992; Boyce *et al.* 1995a).

Stress response may deplete cellular energy and immune reserves (perhaps involving protection from autoimmunity). Although cortisol may provide short-term benefits, the body needs to replenish energy reserves to provide for immunity, growth, and other functions. Hence chronic stress and high average cortisol levels may be predicted to be associated with frequency of illness. Data suggest that chronically stressed children with high cortisol levels tend to be ill more frequently than children in normal stress environments (Figure 6.7).[14]

Short-term temporal patterns of cortisol and observed stressful events also are associated with increased risk of illness, as anecdotally illustrated in the above example of Jenny (Figure 6.4), in which illness follows a high-stress event. Children in Bwa Mawego have a nearly two-fold increased risk of illness for several days following naturally occurring high-stress events (Figure 6.8).

These prospective data suggest that stress increases vulnerability to infectious disease; however, they do not demonstrate a direct effect of cortisol. Sleep disruption and poor nutrition often accompany social trauma. Stressful events may be associated with increased exposure to pathogens, resulting, for example, from trips to town by family members, or residence changes. Stressful events may be more likely when family members are ill. Common infectious diseases are more prevalent during stressful seasonal periods such as Christmas, start of school, and carnival. A more direct causality would be indicated by immunosuppressive effects of stress (Palmblad 1991; Glaser and Kiecolt-Glaser 1994).

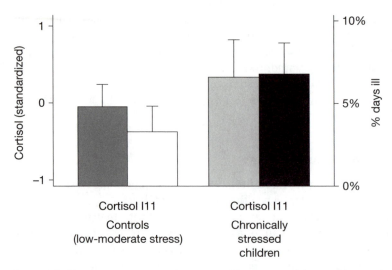

Figure 6.7 Chronic stress, cortisol levels, and frequency of illness. Chronically stressed children (N = 36) had higher average cortisol levels and were ill more often than controls (N = 141). Chronically stressed children were defined as having two or more major risk factors, including: parental conflict, mild abuse or neglect, high frequency (upper 10 percent) of reported daily stressors, inhibited or anxious temperament, parental alcoholism, low (bottom 10 percent) peer friendship ranking, and reported antisocial (theft, fighting, or runaway) behaviors. Figure adapted from Flinn (1999).

Immune function

Numerous (hundreds) of specific interactions between stress endocrinology and immune function have been identified (e.g. Herbert and Cohen 1993; Biondi *et al.* 1994; Dunn 1995; Booth and Davison this volume; McDade this volume; Decker this volume). Indeed, so many different and complex mechanisms appear to be involved in psychoneuroimmunological (PNI) interactions that a general explanation remains elusive. It seems paradoxical that an organism would suppress immune response during periods of stress when exposure and vulnerability to pathogens may be high.

Several non-exclusive, complementary hypotheses appear feasible. Allocation of energy to "emergency" demands may favor diversion from immunity (Sapolsky 1994). Overactive defensive responses to stress can result in autoimmunity; anti-inflammatory effects of glucocorticoid stress hormones may be protective of some types of tissues (Munck *et al.* 1984). The possibility of damage to peripheral tissues generating novel antigens (e.g. collagen in joints) during exposure to stressors – such as disease and strenuous physical or mental activity – may require particular suppression of

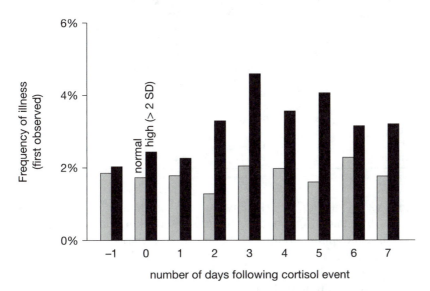

Figure 6.8 Temporal association between naturally occurring stress events and frequency of illness. Children had higher frequencies of illness for 3-5 days following a stress event (observed or reported stressor that was accompanied within an eight-hour period by an elevated cortisol level of more than two standard deviations above mean levels – illustrated by solid black bars), than when no stress event had occurred (diagonally striped bars). Figure adapted from Flinn (1999).

immune function. Finally, the movements of immune cells may be enhanced or focused by localized overrides of the general suppressive effects of cortisol.

The complexity and dynamics of the immune system make assessment of immune function extraordinarily difficult. Measures of immune function include: lymphocyte proliferation to novel antigens (e.g. phytohemagglutinin, concanavalin A, and keyhold limpet hemocyanin); circulating CD-4 (helper T-cells), CD-8 (suppressor/cytotoxic T-cells) and CD-15/56 (natural killer) cells; and levels of immunoglobulins (e.g. see McDade this volume) and cytokines (e.g. interleukins). A battery or panel of different measures provides a broad assessment of immune function, and allows for examination of possible mechanism-specific effects of glucocorticoid stress response on immunity. Blood samples are required for many of these measures, however, making non-invasive study of immune function problematic.

We have begun an exploratory investigation of several components of immune function among children in Bwa Mawego using saliva samples. Levels of neopterin and microglobulin β_2 are examined as indicators of

Table 6.1 Associations between measures of immune function, stress, and illness conditions among children in a Caribbean village

	Average cortisol	Chronically stressed vs. controls when both healthy	Chronically stressed vs. controls when both ill	Post-stress	During illness
s-Immunoglobulin A	n.s.	–	n.s.	n.s.	+
Interleukin-1	n.s.	n.s.	n.s.	n.s.	+
Interleukin-8	n.s.	n.s.	+	n.s.	n.s.
Neopterin	n.s.	n.s.	n.s.	–	n.s.
Microglobulin β_2	n.s.	n.s.	n.s.	–	n.s.

cell-mediated (cytotoxic T-cell) activity, secretory-immunoglobulin-A as an indicator of humoral (antibody) response, interleukin-8 as a measure of non-specific (neutrophil recruitment) immunity, and interleukin-1 as an indicator of general immune activation (cytokine cascade). Preliminary analyses of these data suggest that psychosocial stress may have different effects on these components of immune function (Table 6.1 and Figure 6.9).

In Table 6.1, significant elevations of immune measures from saliva samples are indicated by +, significant decreases by –, and non-significant associations by n.s. Data indicate: (1) no significant association between a child's average (mean) cortisol levels and any of the five immune measures (R^2 = –0.18, 0.04, –0.07, –0.01, –0.02); (2) chronically stressed children have lower s-immunoglobulin A levels than controls when they are healthy (two-tailed *t*-tests, $p < 0.05$); (3) chronically stressed childen have lower interleukin-8 levels than do controls when they are sick (two-tailed *t*-tests, $p < 0.05$); (4) children have lower neopterin and microglobulin β_2 levels for at least two days after a stress event (two-tailed *t*-tests, $p < 0.05$); and (5) children have higher s-immunoglobulin A and interleukin-1 levels when they are sick (two-tailed *t*-tests, $p < 0.05$).

Apparent differences between immune functioning of chronically stressed and normal children include lower levels of s-IgA (Figure 6.10, neopterin (Figure 6.11), and Il-8 (Figure 6.12). These measures change in response to stress events and illness. Temporal patterns of immune function differ slightly between normal (Figure 6.13) and chronically stressed children (Figure 6.14). We do not know if these differences affect morbidity for any specific pathogen, but they are suggestive of possible links among psychosocial stress, immune function, and illness.

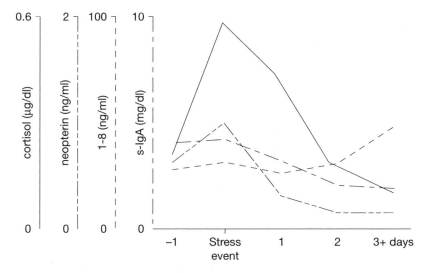

Figure 6.9 Temporal changes in salivary cortisol, neopterin, interleukin-8 and s-immunoglobulin A levels of a 12-year-old male over a five-day period (25–29 July, 1994). Elevated cortisol levels were associated with a fight with a peer ("stress event"); subsequent moderate changes occurred in neopterin, interleukin-8, and s-immunoglobulin A levels. Figure adapted from Flinn (1999).

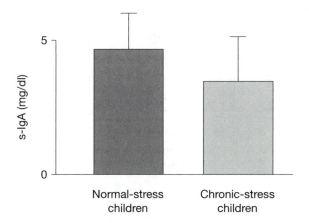

Figure 6.10 Cortisol and s-IgA levels. Chronically stressed individuals have lower s-IgA. Saliva samples collected when subjects had no apparent illness.

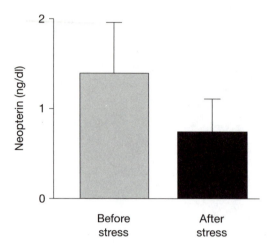

Figure 6.11 Neopterin and stress. Neopterin levels are lower for a two-day period following stress (observed or reported events and elevated cortisol levels). Sample includes seven individuals.

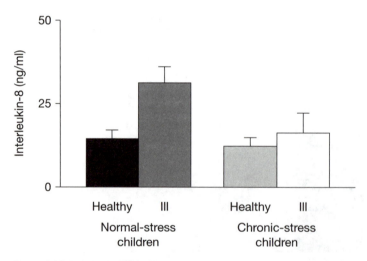

Figure 6.12 Interleukin-8 (Il-8) response to illness and chronic stress. Il-8 levels of normal stress children (N = 6) are more elevated during illness than are those of chronically stressed children (N = 9). The definition of chronic stress is the same as in Figure 6.7.

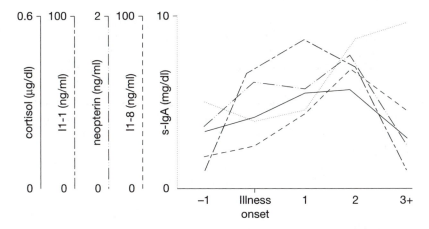

Figure 6.13 Temporal changes in immune measures during illness. Sample includes five individuals.

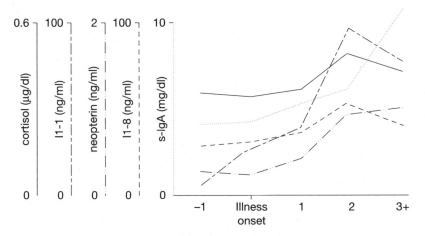

Figure 6.14 Temporal changes in immune measures during illness for chronically stressed children. Sample includes six individuals.

Summary and concluding remarks

Glucocorticoid stress response may be viewed as an adaptive mechanism that allocates energy resources to different bodily functions, including immunity, growth, muscle action, and cognition (Maier *et al.* 1994; Sapolsky 1994; McEwen 1995). Understanding the algorithms for stress response allocation decisions is important, because of consequences for health and psychological development (Tinbergen 1974). Release of cortisol and other stress hormones in response to traumatic family events may modulate energy and mental activity to resolve perceived psychosocial problems, but may diminish immunity and other health functions.

The objective of our long-term ethnographic study in Bwa Mawego is to monitor children's social and physical environment, behavioral activities, health, mental perceptions, and physiological states in a naturalistic setting so as to better understand relations among family environment, stress responses, and health. Analyses of data indicate that children living in households with intensive, stable caretaking usually had moderate cortisol levels (Figure 6.2) and low frequency of illness (Figures 6.7 and 6.8). Children living in households with non-intensive, unstable caretaking were more likely to have abnormal (usually high and variable, but sometimes low) cortisol levels. Traumatic family events were associated temporally with elevated cortisol levels (Figure 6.5). Some children with caretaking and growth problems during infancy had unusual cortisol profiles. These associations indicate that family environment was a significant source of stress and illness risk for children living in Bwa Mawego. The variability of stress response, however, suggests a complex mix of each child's perceptions, neuroendocrinology, temperament, and specific context.

Relations between family environment and cortisol stress response appear to result from a combination of factors. These include: frequency of traumatic events, frequency of positive "affectionate" interactions, frequency of negative interactions such as irrational punishment, frequency of residence change, security of "attachment," development of coping abilities, and availability or intensity of caretaking attention. Probably the most important correlate of household composition that affects childhood stress is maternal care. Mothers in socially "secure" households (i.e. permanent amiable co-residence with mate and/or other kin) appeared more able and more motivated to provide physical, social, and psychological care for their children. Mothers without mate or kin support were likely to exert effort attracting potential mates, and may have viewed dependent children as impediments to this. Hence, co-residence of the father may provide not only direct benefits from paternal care, but also may affect maternal care (Lamb *et al.* 1987; Scheper-Hughes 1988; Belsky *et al.* 1991; Flinn 1992; Hurtado and Hill 1992). Young mothers without mate support usually relied extensively upon their parents or other kin for help with childcare.

Children born and raised in household environments in which mothers have little or no mate or kin support were at greatest risk for abnormal cortisol profiles and associated health problems. Because socioeconomic conditions influence family environment, they have consequences for child health that extend beyond direct material effects. And because health in turn may affect an individual's social and economic opportunities, a cycle of poor health and poverty may be perpetuated generation after generation.

Notes

1 "Stress" or "stressful" are terms that have elusive meanings; a recent review called the attempt to define stress "an exercise in futility" (Levine *et al.* 1989: 341). Some of the confusion may be semantic, but much of the problem originates with the misconception that there is a uniform, general physiological response to a variety of "stressors" that perturb the organism (see critiques by Mason 1971; Levine *et al.* 1989). In this chapter I attempt to avoid this quagmire by referring to "cortisol response" as a specific, measurable phenomenon. An evolutionary perspective of physiological stress responses and their effects may help clarify the definitional issue. I hypothesize that human psychosocial stress response has evolved to be sensitive to conditions for which the physiological/neurological effects were advantageous; see also note 4.

2 In evolutionary terms, "significant" is used in the sense of a fitness-altering event, an event that alters the likelihood that one will successfully reproduce. As a product of natural selection, cognitive processing of information in regard to "stress" involves assessment by the CNS of fitness consequences of potential "stressors." "Positive" or "negative" affect is irrelevant. The criterion is whether stimulation of stress response is perceived (consciously or unconsciously – see Mann this volume for further discussion) as advantageous. "Arousal" may be a more appropriate term than "stress," because physiological response can be associated with positive emotional states of excitement as well as negative emotional states of anxiety.

3 And, for comparable long-term cardiovascular effects, see Mann, this volume.

4 MVF was assisted in the field by: Eric Durbrow in 1988, 1989, and 1990; Tomasz Beer, M.D., Ingrid Bozoky, and Carol Ward in 1990; Seamus Decker in 1992, 1993, and 1994; David Tedeschi in 1992 and 1993, Robert Quinlan and Marsha Quinlan in 1993, 1994, and 1996; Mark Turner in 1993, 1994, 1995, and 1996, David Leone in 1998, 1999, 2000, and 2001; Connie Carpenter in 2001, and Chris Worthen in 2001.

5 During August–December 1990, saliva was collected twice daily from each child for four six-day periods. Because saliva must be collected during a limited time period, the study population was divided into two roughly equal halves, with collection periods alternating between them (i.e. six days with one half, then six days with the other; hence saliva was collected for a total of four + four = eight six-day periods). All-day "focal follows" with hourly saliva collection were conducted with two children to provide more precise information on cortisol variation. During the 1992 field season, I was assisted by two graduate students, and saliva was collected concurrently (each of us took one of three separate routes) from all children during two six-day periods. During the 1993 and 1994 field seasons, three graduate students assisted me, and saliva was collected concurrently from all children during six six-day periods. All-day focal follows

were conducted with four children. During 1995, 1996, June–August 1998, and June–August 1999 saliva was collected three times at approximately two-hourly intervals from all children over a six-day period. Additional all-morning focal follows were conducted with 30 infants and mothers by Mark Turner in 1994, and by Mark Turner and Mark Flinn in 1995. During August 1997, January 1998, January 1999, July 2000, January 2001, and August 2001 saliva was also collected from children during anthropometric measurement sessions.

The effect of family interactions on cortisol levels is probably accentuated in our sample because most of the samples were collected during time periods (early morning at home, late afternoon at home) that are likely to involve family inter-actions. Hence, many of the observed "traumatic family interactions" occurred within one to two hours of saliva collection. We are currently investigating such time effects in more detail.

6 Wake-up time is used because individuals have different sleep schedules; some children arise habitually at 5:30 a.m., whereas others sleep until 7:00 or later. Hence circadian time controls must include individual differences, and are most appropriately based on wake-up time, rather than absolute time. Five-minute time intervals are necessary because of the quick drop in cortisol levels during the morning: approximately a one-hour half-life; from about 0.6 µg/dl 30 minutes after wake-up to 0.22 µg/dl at 120 minutes after wake-up. The half-life of cortisol is about 1 hr. However, we have discovered that this is dependent on several factors, including level of physical exertion (activity shortens the half-life), and the "type" of "stressor" (some psychosocial stressors seem to involve longer-term release patterns). Hence there is not an easy answer to this important issue. This time-standardization technique requires a large number of samples (> 100 samples per time interval). We further suspect that individual children differ in the circa-dian pattern of cortisol release stimulated by the paraventricular nucleus on the one hand, and the pattern of cortisol release stimulated by the limbic system in response to perceived stressors on the other.

7 Blood pressure was systematically measured during the 1990 and 1992 field seasons only.

8 An exception to this apparently was caused by the practice by some families of making a sweetened coffee and milk drink for their children on school day morn-ings, resulting in higher cortisol levels. Because these families were mostly of high socioeconomic position, there was a slight association between wealth and cortisol levels on school day mornings.

9 Our RIA protocol was as follows: (1) Saliva tubes were decapped and centrifuged at 2,400 rpm for 10 minutes at 6°C. (2) Tubes were placed in a rack for an auto-matic pipetting robot, which pipetted 200 µl of saliva from each sample tube into receiver tubes from DPC 125I cortisol solid phase radioimmunoassay kits. Each sample was duplicated. (3) Radioactive label was added, and tubes were vortexed. (4) Receiver tubes were placed in 37°C water baths for 45 minutes after which they were aspirated (twice). (5) Receiver tubes were run through a gamma counter. And (6) data from the counter were analyzed with a statistical program (StatLIA). Six standards (0.2 µg/dl – 50 µg/dl) diluted 8:1 were used to deter-mine the assay curve. B/B0 ratios, covariance of duplicates, and interassay variation using these techniques are of high quality (e.g. covariance of duplicates for 1993–5 samples averaged 1.9 percent; covariance of interassay duplicates averaged 4.1 percent).

10 The relation between cortisol levels and household composition for infants (one to fourteen months) is less certain. Preliminary analyses indicate infants in house-holds without fathers had lower cortisol levels than infants in households with

co-resident fathers (Turner *et al.* 1995). However, this may reflect higher activity levels, different sleeping patterns, age effects, and/or more frequent breastfeeding among father-resident infants rather than higher levels of psychosocial stress.

11 *Ed. Immunosuppressive effects of the cortisol surge probably mediated her getting sick.*

12 Chronically stressed children were defined as having two or more major risk factors, including: parental conflict, mild abuse or neglect, high frequency (upper 10 percent) of reported daily stressors, inhibited or anxious temperament, parental alcoholism, low (bottom 10 percent) peer friendship ranking, and reported anti-social (theft, fighting, or runaway) behaviors.

13 *Ed. Pennebaker and Susman found these negative health effects associated with traumatic experiences that had not been disclosed, and found great prospective benefit in disclosure. See Pennebaker, this volume.*

14 *Ed. The emphasis here on chronicity of stress, and the need for longitudinal data, accords with Mann's chapter in this volume.*

References

Ader, R. (1991). Psychoneuroimmunology. In R. Ader, D. L. Felten, and N. Cohen (eds), *Psychoneuroimmunology* (pp. 653–670). New York: Academic Press.

—— , Cohen, N. and Felten, D. L. (1995). Psychoneuroimmunology: interactions between the nervous system and the immune system. *The Lancet* 345(8942): 99–103.

——, Felten, D. L., and Cohen, N. (2001). *Psychoneuroimmunology* (3rd edn). San Diego: Academic Press.

Axelrod, J. and Reisine, T. D. (1984). Stress hormones: their interaction and regulation. *Science* 224(4648): 452–459.

Baumeister, R. F. and Leary, M. R. (1995). The need to belong: desire for interpersonal attachments as a fundamental human motivation. *Psychological Bulletin* 117(3): 497–529.

Belsky, J., Steinberg, L., and Draper, P. (1991). Childhood experience, interpersonal development, and reproductive strategy: an evolutionary theory of socialization. *Child Development* 62(4): 647–670

Bernard, H. R., Killworth, P. D., Kronenfeld, D., and Sailer, L. (1984). The problem of informant accuracy: the validity of retrospective data. *Annual Review of Anthropology* 13: 495–517.

Besedovsky, H. O. and del Rey, A. (1991). Feedback interactions between immunological cells and the hypothalamus-pituitary-adrenal axis. *Netherlands Journal of Medicine* 39: 274–280.

Biondi, M., Peronti, M., Pacitti, F., Pancheri, P., Pacifici, R., Altieri, I., Paris, L., and Zuccaro, P. (1994). Personality endocrine and immune changes after eight months in healthy individuals under normal daily stress. *Psychotherapy and Psychosomatics* 62(3–4): 176–184.

Black, P. H. (1994). Central nervous system-immune system interactions: psychoneuroendocrinology of stress and its immune consequences. *Antimicrobial Agents and Chemotherapy* 38(1): 1–6.

Bowlby, J. (1969). *Attachment.* New York: Basic Books.

—— (1973*). Separation – anxiety and anger.* New York: Basic Books.

Boyce, W. T., Chesney, M., Alkon, A., Tschann, J. M., Adams, S., Chesterman, B., Cohen, F., Kaiser, P., Folkman, S., and Wara, D. (1995a). Psychobiologic reactivity to stress and childhood respiratory illnesses: results of two prospective studies. *Psychosomatic Medicine 57*(5): 411–422.

Breier, A., Albus, M., Pickar, D., Zahn, T. P., Wolkowitz, O. M., and Paul, S. M. (1987). Controllable and uncontrollable stress in humans: alterations in mood and neuroendocrine and psychophysiological function. *American Journal of Psychiatry 144*(11): 1419–1425.

Buss, A. H. and Plomin, R. (1984). *Temperament: early developing personality traits.* Hillsdale, NJ: Erlbaum.

Campbell, P. A. and Cohen, J. J. (1985). Effects of stress on the immune response. In T. M. Field, P. M. McCabe, and N. Schneiderman (eds), *Stress and coping* (pp. 135–145). Hillsdale, NJ: Erlbaum.

Clarke, A. S. (1993). Social rearing effects on HPA axis activity over early development and in response to stress in rhesus monkeys. *Developmental Psychobiology 26*(8): 433–446.

Coe, C. L., Wiener, S. G., Rosenberg, L. T., and Levine, S. (1985a). Physiological consequences of maternal separation and loss in the squirrel monkey. In L. A. Rosenblum and C. L. Coe (eds), *Handbook of squirrel monkey research.* New York: Plenum.

Cohen, J. J. and Crnic, L. S. (1982). Glucocorticoids, stress and the immune response. In D. R. Webb (ed.), *Immunopharmacology and the regulation of leukocyte function* (pp. 69–91). New York: Marcel Dekker.

Cohen, S., Tyrrell, D. A., and Smith, A. P. (1991). Psychological stress and susceptibility to the common cold. *New England Journal of Medicine 325*(9): 606–612.

Daly, M. and Wilson, M. (1995). Discriminative parental solicitude and the relevance of evolutionary models to the analysis of motivational systems. In M. S. Gazzaniga (ed.), *The cognitive neurosciences* (pp. 1269–1286). Cambridge, MA: MIT Press.

De Bellis, M., Chrousos, G. P., Dorn, L. D., Burke, L., Helmers, K., Kling, M. A., Trickett, P. K., and Putnam, F. W. (1994). Hypothalamic-pituitary-adrenal axis dysregulation in sexually abused girls. *Journal of Clinical Endocrinology and Metabolism 78*(2): 249–255.

De Kloet, E. R. (1991). Brain corticosteroid receptor balance and homeostatic control. *Frontiers in Neuroendocrinology 12*(2): 95–164.

Dressler, W. A., Grell, G. A. C., Gallagher Jr, P. N., and Viteri, F. E. (1988). Blood pressure and social class in a Jamaican community. *American Journal of Public Health 78*: 714–716.

Dunn, A. J. (1989). Psychoneuroimmunology for the psychoneuroendocrinologist: a review of animal studies of nervous system-immune system interactions. *Psychoneuroendocrinology 14*: 251–274.

—— (1995). Interactions between the nervous system and the immune system: implications for psychopharmacology. In F. R. Bloom and D. J. Kupfer (eds), *Psychopharmacology: the fourth generation of progress.* New York: Raven Press.

Ellison, P. (1988). Human salivary steroids: methodological considerations and applications in physical anthropology. *Yearbook of Physical Anthropology 31*: 115–142.

—— (1994). Advances in human reproductive ecology. *Annual Review of Anthropology 23*: 2255–2275.

Evans, P. and Pitts, M. (1994) Vulnerability to respiratory infection and the four-day desirability dip: comments on Stone, Porter and Neale (1993). *British Journal of Medical Psychology* 67: 387–389.

Finkelhor, D. and Dzuiba-Leatherman, J. (1994) Victimization of children. *American Psychologist* 49(3): 173–183.

Flinn, M. V. (1988). Step and genetic parent/offspring relationships in a Caribbean village. *Ethology and Sociobiology* 9(3): 1–34.

—— (1992). Paternal care in a Caribbean village. In B. Hewlett (ed.), *Father–child relations: cultural and biosocial contexts (*pp. 57–84). Hawthorne, NY: Aldine.

—— (1999). Family environment, stress, and health during childhood. In C. Panter-Brick, and C. Worthman (eds), *Hormones, health, and behavior* (pp. 105–138). Cambridge: Cambridge University Press.

—— and England, B. G. (1995). Family environment and childhood stress. *Current Anthropology* 36(5): 854–866.

—— and —— (1997). Social economics of childhood glucocorticoid stress response and health. *American Journal of Physical Anthropology* 102: 33–53.

——, Turner, M. T., Quinlan, R., Decker, S. D., and England, B. G. (1996). Male-female differences in effects of parental absence on glucocorticoid stress response. *Human Nature* 7(2): 125–162.

Fredrikson, M., Sundin, Ö., and Frankenhauser, M. (1985) Cortisol excretion during the defense reaction in humans. *Psychosomatic Medicine* 47(4): 313–319.

Fuchs, E. and Flugge, G. (1995). Modulation of binding sites for corticotropin-releasing hormone by chronic psychosocial stress. *Psychoneuroendocrinology* 30(1): 33–51.

Garmezy, N. (1983). Stressors of childhood. In N. Garmezy, and M. Rutter (eds), *Stress, coping, and development in children* (pp. 43–83). New York: McGraw-Hill.

Geary, D.C. and Flinn, M.V. (2001). Evolution of human parental behavior and the human family. *Parenting: Science and Practice* 1(1 and 2): 5–61.

Glaser, R. and Kiecolt-Glaser, J. K. (eds) (1994). *Handbook of human stress and immunity.* New York: Academic Press.

Goldberg, L. R. (1992). The development of markers for the big-five factor structure. *Psychological Assessment* 4: 26–42.

—— (1993). The structure of phenotypic personality traits. *American Psychologist* 48(1): 26–34.

Gottman, J. M. and Katz, L. F. (1989). Effects of marital discord on young children's peer interaction and health. *Developmental Psychology* 25(3): 373–381.

Gray, J. A. (1982). *The neuropsychology of anxiety: an enquiry into the functions of the septo-hippocampal system.* New York: Oxford University Press.

Gunnar, M., Porter, F. L., Wolf, C. M., Rigatuso, J., and Larson, M. C. (1995). Neonatal stress reactivity: predictions to later emotional temperament. *Child Development* 66(2): 1–13.

Haggerty, R. J., Sherrod, L. R., Garmezy, N., and Rutter, M. (eds) (1994). *Stress, risk, and resilience in children and adolescents.* Cambridge: Cambridge University Press.

Heim, C., Newport, D. J., Heit, S., Graham, Y. P., Wilcox, M., Bonsall, R., Miller, A. H., and Nemeroff, C. B. (2000). Pituitary-adrenal and autonomic responses to stress in women after sexual and physical abuse in childhood. *Journal of the American Medical Association 284*(5): 592–597.

Herbert, T. B. and Cohen, S. (1993) Stress and immunity in humans: a meta-analytic review. *Psychosomatic Medicine 55*(4): 364–379.

Hertsgaard, L., Gunnar, M., Erickson, M. F., and Nachmias, M. (1995). Adrenocortical responses to the strange situation in infants with disorganized/disoriented attachment relationships. *Child Development 66*(4): 1100–1106.

Hinde, R. A. and Stevenson-Hinde, J. (1987) Interpersonal relationships and child development. *Developmental Review 7*: 1–21.

Hiramatsu, R. (1981) Direct assay of cortisol in human saliva by solid phase radioimmunoassay and its clinical applications. *Clinical Chimica Acta 117*(2): 239–249.

Holl, R., Fehm, H., Voigt, K., and Teller, W. (1984). The "mid-day surge" in plasma cortisol induced by mental stress. *Hormones and Metabolism Research 16*(3): 158–159.

House, J. S., Landis, K. R., and Umberson, D. (1988). Social relationships and health. *Science 241*(4865): 540–544.

Hurtado, A. M. and Hill, K. R. (1992). Paternal effect on offspring survivorship among Ache and Hiwi hunter-gatherers: implications for modeling pair-bond stability. In B. Hewlett (ed.), *Father–child relations: cultural and biosocial contexts* (pp. 31–55). New York: Aldine De Gruyter.

Insel, T. R. and Shapiro, L. (1992). Oxytocin receptor distribution reflects social organization inmonogamous and polygamous voles. *Proceedings of the National Academy of Sciences USA 89*: 5981–5985.

Ivanovici, A. M. and Wiebe, W. J. (1981). Towards a working "definition" of "stress": a review and critique. In G. W. Barrett and R. Rosenberg (eds), *Stress effects on natural ecosystems* (pp. 13–17). New York: Wiley.

Jefferies, W. M. (1991). Cortisol and immunity. *Medical Hypotheses 34*: 198–208.

Kagan, J. (1983). Stress and coping in early development. In N. Garmezy and M. Rutter (eds), *Stress, coping, and development in children* (pp. 191–215). New York: McGraw-Hill.

—— (1984). *The nature of the child*. New York: Basic Books.

——, Resnick, J. S., and Snidman, N. (1988). Biological bases of childhood shyness. *Science 240*(4849): 167–171.

Kaplan, H. B. (1991). Social psychology of the immune system: a conceptual framework and review of the literature. *Social Science and Medicine 33*(8): 909–923.

Kiecolt-Glaser, J. K. and Glaser, R. (1995). Measurement of immune response. In S. Cohen, R. C. Kessler and G. L. Underwood (eds), *Measuring stress* (pp. 213–229). Oxford: Oxford University Press.

Kirschbaum, C. and Hellhammer, D. H. (1994). Salivary cortisol in psychoneuroendocrine research: recent developments and applications. *Psychoneuroendocrinology 19*(4): 313–333.

——, Read, G. F., and Hellhammer, D. H. (eds) (1992). *Assessment of hormones and drugs in saliva in biobehavioral research*. Seattle: Hogrefe and Huber.

——, Wolf, O. T., May, M., Wippich, W., and Hellhammer, D. H. (1996). Stress- and treatment-induced elevations of cortisol levels associated with impaired declarative memory in healthy adults. *Life Sciences 58*(17): 1475–1483.

Lamb, M., Pleck, J., Charnov, E., and Levine, J. (1987). A biosocial perspective on paternal behavior and involvement. In J. B. Lancaster, J. Altmann, A. Rossi, and

L. Sherrod (eds), *Parenting across the lifespan: biosocial dimensions* (pp. 111–142). Hawthorne, NY: Aldine de Gruyter.

Levine, S. (1993). The influence of social factors on the response to stress. *Psychotherapy and Psychosomatics 60*(1): 33–38.

——, Coe, C. and Wiener, S. G. (1989). Psychoneuroendocrinology of stress: a psychobiological perspective. In R. Ader (ed.), *Psychoneuroendocrinology* (pp. 341–377). New York: Academic Press.

Long, B., Ungpakorn, G., and Harrison, G. A. (1993). Home-school differences in stress hormone levels in a group of Oxford primary school children. *Journal of Biosocial Sciences 25*(1): 73–78.

Magnano, C. L., Gardner, J. M., and Karmel, B. Z. (1992). Differences in salivary cortisol levels in cocaine-exposed and non-cocaine-exposed NICU infants. *Developmental Psychobiology 25*(2): 93–103.

Maier, S. F., Watkins, L. R., and Fleshner, M. (1994). Psychoneuroimmunology: the interface between behavior, brain, and immunity. *American Psychologist 49*(12): 1004–1017.

Martignoni, E., Costa, A., Sinforiani, E., Luzzi, A., Chiodini, P., Mauri, M., Bono, G., and Nappi, G. (1992). The brain as a target for adrenocortical steroids: cognitive implications. *Psychoneuroendocrinology 17*(4): 343–354.

Martinez, J. L. (1986). Memory: drugs and hormones. In J. L. Martinez and R. P. Kesner (eds), *Learning and memory: a biological view* (pp. 127–163). New York: Academic Press.

Mason, J. W. (1968). A review of psychoendocrine research on the pituitary-adrenal cortical system. *Psychosomatic Medicine 30*(5): 576–607.

—— (1971). A re-evaluation of the concept of "non-specificity" in stress theory. *Journal of Psychosomatic Research 8*(3): 323–334.

——, Buescher, E. L., Belfer, M. L., Artenstein, M. S., and Mougey, E. H. (1979). A prospective study of corticosteroids and catecholamine levels in relation to viral respiratory illness. *Journal of Human Stress 5*(3): 18–28.

McEwen, B. S. (1995). Stressful experience, brain, and emotions: developmental, genetic, and hormonal influences. In M. S. Gazzaniga (ed.), *The cognitive neurosciences* (pp. 1117–1135). Cambridge, MA: MIT Press.

Meaney, M., Mitchell, J., Aitken D., Bhat Agar, S., Bodnoff, S., Ivy, L., and Sarriev, A. (1991). The effects of neonatal handling on the development of the adrenocortical response to stress: implications for neuropathology and cognitive deficits later in life. *Psychoneuroendocrinology 16*(1–3): 85–103.

Munck, A. and Guyre, P. M. (1991). Glucocorticoids and immune function. In R. Ader, D. L. Felten, and N. Cohen (eds), *Psychoneuroimmunology*. San Diego: Academic Press.

——, ——, and Holbrook, N. J. (1984). Physiological functions of glucocorticoids in stress and their relation to pharmacological actions. *Endocrine reviews 5*(1): 25–44.

Nachmias, M., Gunnar, M., Mangelsdorf, S., Parritz, R. H., and Buss, K. (1996). Behavioral inhibition and stress reactivity: the moderating role of attachment security. *Child Development 67*(2): 508–522.

Newcomer, J. W., Craft, S., Hershey, T., Askins, K., and Bardgett, M. E. (1994). Glucocorticoid-induced impairment in declarative memory performance in adult humans. *Journal of Neuroscience 14*(4): 2047–2053.

Palmblad, J. (1981). Stress and immunologic competence: studies in man. In R. Ader (ed.), *Psychoneuroimmunology*. New York: Academic Press.

Panter-Brick, C., Todd, A., Baker, R., and Worthman, C. (1996). Heart rate monitoring of physical activity among village, school, and homeless Nepali boys. *American Journal of Human Biology 8*(2): 661–672.

Pearlin, L. I. and Turner, H. A. (1987). The family as a context of the stress process. In S. V. Kasl and C. L. Cooper (eds), *Stress and health: issues in research methodology*. New York: John Wiley.

Quinlan, R. (1995). Father absence, maternal care, and children's behavior in a rural Caribbean village. Unpublished M.A. thesis. Columbia: University of Missouri.

Rabkin, J. G. and Streuning, E. L. (1976). Life events, stress, and illness. *Science 194*: 1013–1020.

Riad-Fahmy, D., Read, G. F., and Hughes, I. A. (1983). Corticosteroids. In C. H. Gray and V. H. T. James (eds), *Hormones in the blood* (pp. 285–315). New York: Academic Press.

Rutter, M. (1983). Stress, coping, and development: some issues and some questions. In N. Garmezy and M. Rutter (eds), *Stress, coping, and development in children* (pp. 1–41). New York: McGraw-Hill.

Saphier, D., Welch, J. E., Farrar, G. E., Ngunen, N. Q., Aguado, F., Thaller, T. R., and Knight, D. S. (1994). Interactions between serotonin, thyrotropin-releasing hormone and substance P in the CNS regulation of adrenocortical secretion. *Psychoneuroendocrinology 19*(8): 779–797.

Sapolsky, R. M. (1987). Stress, social status, and reproductive physiology in free-living baboons. In D. Crews (ed.), *Psychobiology of reproductive behavior: an evolutionary perspective*. New York: Prentice Hall.

—— (1991). Effects of stress and glucocorticoids on hippocampal neuronal survival. In M. R. Brown, G. F. Koob, and C. Rivier (eds), *Stress: neurobiology and neuroendocrinology* (pp. 293–322). New York: Dekker.

—— (1992a) Neuroendocrinology of the stress-response. In J. B. Becker, S. M. Breedlove, and D. Crews (eds), *Behavioral endocrinology* (pp. 287–324). Cambridge, MA: MIT Press.

—— (1992b). *Stress, the aging brain, and the mechanisms of neuron death*. Cambridge, MA: MIT Press.

—— (1994). *Why zebras don't get ulcers*. New York: W. H. Freeman and Co.

Scapagnini, V. (1992) Psychoneuroendocrinoimmunology: The basis for a novel therapeutic approach in aging. *Psychoneuroendocrinology. 17*(4): 411–420.

Scheper-Hughes, N. (ed.) (1988). *Child survival: anthropological perspectives on the treatment and maltreatment of children*. Boston: Reidel.

Schneider, M. L., Coe, C. L., and Lubach, G. R. (1992). Endocrine activation mimics the adverse effects of prenatal stress on the neuromotor development of the infant primate. *Developmental Psychobiology 25*(6): 427–439.

Selye, H. (1976). *The stress of life* (rev. edn). New York: McGraw-Hill.

Servan-Schreiber, D., Printz, H., and Cohen, S. D. (1990). A network model of catecholamine effects: gain, signal-to-noise ratio, and behavior. *Science 249*(4971): 892–895.

Smith, K. A. (1988). Interleukin-2: inception, impact, and implications. *Science 240*(4586): 1169–1176.

Stone, A. A. L., Bovbjerg, D. H., Neale, J. M., Napoli, A., Valdimarsdottir, H., Cox, D., Hayden, F. G., and Gwaltney, J. M. Jr (1992). Development of the common cold symptoms following experimental rhinovirus infection is related to prior stressful life events. *Behavioral Medicine 13*: 70–74.

Tennes, K. and Mason, J. (1982). Developmental psychoendocrinology: an approach to the study of emotions. In C. Izard (ed.), *Measuring emotions in infants and children* (pp. 21–37). Cambridge, New York: Cambridge University Press.

Tinbergen, N. (1974). Ethology and stress diseases. *Science 185*: 20–27.

Turner, M. T. (1995). Mother and infant cortisol response in a Dominican village. Unpublished M.A. thesis. Columbia: University of Missouri.

——, Flinn, M. V., and England, B. G. (1995). Mother-infant glucocorticoid stress response in a rural Caribbean village. *American Journal of Physical Anthropology* Supplement 19: 191.

Van Cauter, E. (1990). Diurnal and ultradian rhythms in human endocrine function: a mini-review. *Hormone Research 34*(2): 45–53.

Walker, R. Riad–fahmy, D. and Road, G. F. (1978) Adrenal status accessed by direct radioimmunoassay of cortisol in whole saliva or parotid saliva. *Clinical Chemistry 24*(9): 1460–3.

Wallerstein, J. S. (1983). Children of divorce: Stress and developmental tasks. In N. Garmezy and M. Rutter (eds), *Stress, coping, and development in children* (pp. 265–302). New York: McGraw-Hill.

Weiner, H. (1992) *Perturbing the organism.* Chicago: University of Chicago Press.

Whiting, B. B. and Edwards, C. P. (1988). *Children of different worlds: the formation of social behavior.* Cambridge, MA: Harvard University Press.

Wilson, M. I., Daly, M., and Weghorst, S. J. (1980). Household composition and the risk of child abuse and neglect. *Journal of Biosocial Sciences 12*(3): 333–340.

Winslow, J. T., Hastings, N., Carter, C. S., Harbaugh, C. R., and Insel, T. R. (1993). A role for central vasopressin in pair bonding in monogamous prairie voles. *Nature 365*: 545–548.

Wolkowitz, O. M., Reus, V. I., Weingartner, H., Thompson, K., Breier, A., Doran, A., Rubinow, D., and Pickar, D. (1990). Cognitive effects of corticosteroids. *American Journal of Psychiatry 147*(10): 1297–1303.

Yehuda, R., Giller, E. L., Southwick, S. M., Lowy, M. T., and Mason, J. W. (1991). Hypothalamic-pituitary-adrenal dysfunction in posttraumatic stress disorder. *Biological Psychiatry 30*(10): 1031–1048.

Yuwiler, A. (1982). Biobehavioral consequences of experimental early life stress: effects of neonatal homones on monoaminergic systems. In L. J. West and M. Stein (eds), *Critical issues in behavioral medicine* (pp. 59–78). Philadelphia: J. P. Lippincott.

Further reading

Adler, N. E., Boyce, T., Chesney, M. A., Cohen, S., Folkman, S., Kahn, R. L., and Syme, S. L. (1994). Socioeconomic status and health. *American Psychologist 49(1)*: 15–24.

Alexander, R. D. (1974). The evolution of social behavior. *Annual Review of Ecology and Systematics 5*: 325–383.

Angelucci, L., Patachioli, F. R., Chieriechetti, C., and Laureti, S. (1983). Perinatal mother-offspring pituitary-adrenal interrelationship in rats: corticosterone in milk may affect later life. *Endocrinologia Experimentalis 17*(3–4): 191–205.

Armelagos, G. J., Leatherman, T., Ryan, M., and Sibley, L. (1992). Biocultural synthesis in medical anthropology. *Medical Anthropology 14*(1): 35–52.

Asterita, M. E. (1985). *The physiology of stress.* New York: Human Services Press.

Atkinson, D. E. (1977). *Cellular energy metabolism and its regulation.* New York: Academic Press.

Baxter, J. D. and Rousseau, G. G. (1979). *Glucocorticoid hormone action.* New York: Springer-Verlag.

Bertrand, P. V., Rudd, B. T., Weller, P. H., and Day, A. J. (1987). Free cortisol and creatinine in urine of healthy children. *Clinical Chemistry, 33*(11): 2047–2051.

Bober, J. F., Weller, E. B., Weller, R. A., Tait, A., Fristad, M. A., and Preskorn, S. H. (1988). Correlation of serum and salivary cortisol levels in prepubertal schoolaged children. *Journal of the American Academy of Child and Adolescent Psychiatry, 27*(6): 748–750.

Born, J., Hitzler, V., Pietrowsky, R., Pauschinger, P., and Fehm, H. L. (1989). Influences of cortisol on auditory evoked potentials (AEPs) and mood in humans. *Neuropsychobiology 20*(3): 145–151.

Boyce, W. T., Adams, S., Tschann, J. M., Cohen, F., Wara, D., and Gunnar, M.R. (1995b). Adrenocortical and behavioral predictors of immune responses to starting school. *Pediatric Research 38*(6): 1009–1017.

Brown, D. (1981). General stress in anthropological fieldwork. *American Anthropologist 83*(1): 74–91.

—— (1982). Physiological stress and culture change in a group of Filipino-Americans: a preliminary investigation. *Annals of Human Biology 9*(6): 553–563.

Brown, G. L., Ebert, M. H., Goyer, D. C., Jimerson, D. C., Klein, W. J., Bunney, W. E., and Goodwin, F. K. (1982). Aggression, suicide, and serotonin: relationships to CSF amine metabolites. *American Journal of Psychiatry 139*(6): 741–746.

Ciaranello, R. D. (1983). Neurochemical aspects of stress. In N. Garmezy and M. Rutter (eds), *Stress, coping, and development in children* (pp. 85–105). New York: McGraw-Hill.

Coe, C. L., Lubach, G., and Ershler, W. B. (1989). Immunological consequences of maternal separation in infant primates. *New Directions for Child Development 45*: 65–78.

——, ——, Schneider, M. L., Dierschke, D. J., and Ershler, W. B. (1992). Early rearing conditions alter immune responses in the developing infant primate. *Pediatrics 90*(3, pt. 2): 505–509.

——, Rosenberg, L. T., Fischer, M., and Levine, S. (1987). Psychological factors capable of preventing the inhibition of antibody responses in separated infant monkeys. *Child Development 58*: 1420–1430.

——, Wiener, S. G. Rosenberg, L. T. and Levine, S. (1985b). Endocrine and immune responses to separation and maternal loss in nonhuman primates. In M. Reite and T. Field (eds), *The psychobiology of attachment and separation* (pp. 163–199). New York: Academic Press.

Cohen, P., Velez, C. N., Brook, J., and Smith, J. (1989). Mechanisms of the relation between perinatal problems, early childhood illness, and psychopathology in late childhood and adolescence. *Child Development 60*: 701–709.

Cohen, S. (1988). Psychosocial models of the role of social support in the etiology of physical disease. *Health Psychology* 7(3): 269–297.

——, Kessler, R. C., and Underwood, G. L. (eds) (1995). *Measuring stress*. Oxford: Oxford University Press.

——, ——, and —— (1993). Negative life events, perceived stress, negative effect, and susceptibility to the common cold. *Journal of Personality and Social Psychology* 64(1): 131–140.

Daly, M. and Wilson, M. (1988). Evolutionary social psychology and family homicide. *Science* 242(4878): 519–524.

Danon, A. and Assouline, G. (1978). Inhibition of prostaglandin synthesis by corticosteroids requires RNA and protein synthesis. *Nature* 273: 552.

Daynes, R. A. and Araneo, B. A. (1989). Contrasting effects of glucocorticoids on the capacity of T cells to produce the growth factors interleukin-2 and interleukin-4. *European Journal of Immunology* 19(12): 2319–2325.

de Vries, M. W. (1984). Temperament and infant mortality among the Masai of East Africa. *American Journal of Psychiatry* 141(10): 1189–1194.

Draper, P. and Harpending, H. (1988). A sociobiological perspective on the development of human reproductive strategies. In K. MacDonald (ed.), *Sociobiological perspectives on human development* (pp. 340–372). New York: Springer-Verlag.

Ellis, L. (1994). Social status and health in humans: the nature of the relationship and its possible causes. In L. Ellis (ed.), *Social stratification and socioeconomic inequality* (vol. 2, pp. 123–144). Westport, CT: Praeger.

Emlen, S. T. (1995). An evolutionary theory of the family. *Proceedings of the National Academy of Sciences USA 92*: 8092–8099.

Everly, G. S. and Sobelman, S. A. (1987). *Assessment of the human stress response: neurological, biochemical, and psychological foundations*. New York: AMS.

Flinn, M. V. (1986). Correlates of reproductive success in a Caribbean village. *Human Ecology* 14(2): 225–243.

——, Baerwald, C., Decker, S. D., and England, B. G. (1998). Evolutionary functions of neuroendocrine response to social environment. *Behavioral and Brain Sciences* 20(3): 372–374.

——, England, B. G., and Beer, T. (1992). Health condition and corticosteroid stress response among children in a rural Dominican village (abstract). *American Journal of Physical Anthropology Supplement 14*: 73.

——, Quinlan, M., Quinlan, R., Turner, M., and England, B. G. (1995). Glucocorticoid stress response, immune function, and illness among children in a rural Caribbean village (abstract). *American Journal of Human Biology 7*: 122.

Fukunaga, T., Mizoi, Y., Yamashita, A., Yamada, M., Yamamoto, Y., Tatsuno, Y., and Nishi, K. (1992). Thymus of abused/neglected children. *Forensic Sciences International* 53(1): 69–79.

Geiser, D. (1989) Psychosocial influences on human immunity. *Clinical Psychology Review* 9(6): 689–715.

Glaser, R., Mehl, V. S., Penn, G., Speicher, C. E., and Kiecolt-Glaser, J. K. (1986a). Stress-associated changes in serum immunoglobulin levels. *International Journal of Psychosomatics 33*: 41–42.

——, Rice, J., Speicher, C. E., Stout, J. C., and Kiecolt-Glaser, J. K. (1986b). Stress depresses interferon production concomitant with a decrease in natural killer cell activity. *Behavioral Neuroscience 100*(5): 675–678.

Goodman, A. H., Thomas, R. B., Swedlund, A. C., and Armelagos, G. J. (1988). Biocultural perspectives on stress in prehistoric, historical, and contemporary population research. *Yearbook of Physical Anthropology 31*: 169–202.

Gould, E. and Tanapat, P. (1999). Stress and hippocampal neurogenesis. *Biological Psychiatry 46*(46): 1472–1479.

Gray, J. A. (1987). *The psychology of fear and stress* (2nd edn). Cambridge: Cambridge University Press.

Gunnar, M. (1986). Human developmental psychoneuroendocrinology: a review of research on neuroendocrine responses to challenge and threat in infancy and childhood. In M. Lamb, A. Brown, and B. Rogoff (eds), *Advances in developmental psychology* (pp. 51–103). Hillsdale, NJ: Erlbaum.

—— (1992). Reactivity of the hypothalamic-pituitary-adrenocortical system to stressors in normal infants and children. *Pediatrics 90*: 491–497.

——, Marvinney, D., Isensee, J., and Fisch, R. O. (1989). Coping with uncertainty: new models of the relations between hormonal, behavioral and cognitive processes. In D. Palermo (ed.), *Coping with uncertainty: biological, behavioral, and developmental perspectives*. Hillsdale, NJ: Erlbaum.

Hamburg, D. A., Elliot, G. R., and Parron, D. L. (1982). *Health and behavior: frontiers of research in the biobehavioral sciences*. Washington, DC: National Academy Press.

Hanna, J. M., James, G. D., and Martz, J. M. (1986). Hormonal measures of stress. In P. T. Baker, J. M. Hanna, and T. S. Baker (eds): *The changing Samoans* (pp. 203–221). New York: Oxford University Press.

House, J. S., Kessler, R., Herzog, A. R., Mero, R., Kinney, A., and Breslow, M. (1991). Social stratification, age, and health. In K. W. Scheie, D. Blazer, and J. S. House (eds), *Aging, health behaviors, and health outcomes* (pp. 1–32). Hillsdale, NJ: Erlbaum.

Hubert, W. and de Jong-Meyer, R. (1989). Emotional stress and saliva cortisol response. *Journal of Clinical Chemistry and Clinical Biochemistry 27*(4): 235–237.

Illsley, R. and Baker, D. (1991). Contextual variations in the meaning of health inequality. *Social Science and Medicine 32*(4): 359–365.

Insel, T. R. (1990). Long-term neural consequences of stress during development: is early experience a form of chemical imprinting? In B. J. Carroll (ed.), *The brain and psychopathology*. New York: Raven Press.

Irons, W. (1983). Human female reproductive strategies. In S. Wasser and M. Waterhouse (eds), *Social behavior of female vertebrates* (pp. 169–213). New York: Academic Press.

James, G. D., Crews, D. E., and Pearson, J. (1989). Catecholamines and stress. In M. A. Little and J. D. Haas (eds), *Human population biology: a transdisciplinary science* (pp. 280–295). Oxford: Oxford University Press.

Kagan, J. (1992) Behavior, biology, and the meanings of temperamental constructs. *Pediatrics 90*(3 pt 2): 510–513.

Kiecolt-Glaser, J. K., Kennedy, S., Malkoff, S., Fisher, L., Speicher, C. E., and Glaser, R. (1988). Marital discord and immunity in males. *Psychosomatic Medicine 50*(3): 213–229.

——, Malarkey, W. B., Cacioppo, J. T. and Glaser, R. (1994). Stressful personal relationships: immune and endocrine function. In R. Glaser and J. K. Kiecolt-Glaser (eds), *Handbook of human stress and immunity* (pp. 301–319). New York: Academic Press.

Kirschbaum, C. and Hellhammer, D. H. (1989). Salivary cortisol in psychobiological research: an overview. *Neuropsychobiology 22*(3): 150–169.

——, ——, and Strasburger, C. J. (1989). Pyschoendocrinological and psychophysiological response patterns to experimental stress in children. In H. Weiner, I. Florin, and R. Murison (eds), *Frontiers in stress research* (pp. 383–387). Toronto: Huber.

Kobasa, S. C. and Puccetti, M. C. (1983). Personality and social resources in stress-resistance. *Journal of Personality and Social Psychology 45*(4): 839–855.

Konner, M. J. (1981). Evolution and human behavior development. In R. H. Munroe, R. L. Munroe, and B. B. Whiting (eds), *Handbook of cross-cultural human development*. New York: Garland Press.

Lancaster, J. (1989). Evolutionary and cross-cultural perspectives on single-parenthood. In R. W. Bell and N. J. Bell (eds), *Sociobiology and the social sciences* (pp. 63–71). Lubbock, TX: Texas Tech University Press.

—— and Lancaster, C. S. (1987). The watershed: change in parental-investment and family-formation strategies in the course of human evolution. In J. B. Lancaster, J. Altmann, A. S. Rossi, and L. R. Sherrod (eds), *Parenting across the lifespan: biosocial dimensions* (pp. 187–206). New York: Aldine de Gruyter.

Lazarus, R. S. (1971). The concepts of stress and disease. In L. Levi (ed.), *Society, stress, and disease* (pp. 53–58). London: Oxford University Press.

Leventhal, H. and Tomarken, A. (1987). Stress and illness: perspectives from health psychology. In S. V. Kasl and C. L. Cooper (eds), *Stress and health: issues in research methodology* (pp. 27–55). New York: John Wiley.

Levine, S. (1983). A psychobiological approach to the ontogeny of coping. In N. Garmezy and M. Rutter (eds), *Stress, coping, and development in children* (pp. 107–131). New York: McGraw-Hill.

—— (1985). A definition of stress? In G. P. Moberg (ed.), *Animal stress* (pp. 51–69). Bethesda, MD: American Physiological Society.

—— and Coe, C. L. (1985). The use and abuse of cortisol as a measure of stress. In T. M. Field, P. M. McCabe, and N. Schneiderman (eds), *Stress and coping* (pp. 149–159). Hillsdale, NJ: Erlbaum.

Maclean, D. and Reichlin, S. (1981). Neuroendocrinology and the immune process. In R. Ader (ed.), *Psychoneuroimmunology*. New York: Academic Press.

Margolis, P. A., Greenberg, R. A., Keyes, L. L., Lavange, L. M., Chapman, R. S., Denny, F. W., Bauman, K. E., and Boat, B. W. (1992). Lower respiratory illness in infants and low socioeconomic status. *American Journal of Public Health 82*(8): 1119–1126.

Marmot, M. G., Kogenivas, M., and Elston, M. A. (1987). Social/economic status and disease. *Annual Review of Public Health 8*: 111–135.

——, Smith, G. D., Stansfield, S., Patel, C., North, F., Head, J., White, I., Brunner, E., and Feeney, A. (1991). Health inequalities among British civil servants: the Whitehall II study. *Lancet 337*(8754): 1387–1393.

McBurnett, K., Lahey, B. B., Frick, P. J., Risch, C., Loeber, R., Hart, E. L., Christ, M. A., and Hanson, K. S. (1991). Anxiety, inhibition, and conduct disorder in children: II. Relation to salivary cortisol. *Journal of the American Academy of Child and Adolescent Psychiatry 30*(2): 192–196.

McGaugh, J. L. (1989). Involvement of hormonal and neuromodulatory systems in the regulation of memory storage. *Annual Review of Neuroscience 12*: 255–287.

Monjan, A. A. and Collector, M. I. (1977). Stress-induced modulation of the immune response. *Science 196*(4287): 307–308.

Montager, H., Restoin, A., and Henry, J. C. (1982). Biological defense rhythms, stress, and communication in children. In W. Hartup, and H. Pick (eds), *Reviews of child development research* (pp. 291–319). Chicago: University of Chicago Press.

Mormede, P. (1990). Psychobiology of stress and immune functions. In S. Puglisi-Allegra and A. Oliverio (eds), *Psychobiology of stress*. Dordrecht, The Netherlands: Kluwer Academic Publishers.

O'Leary, A. (1990). Stress, emotion, and human immune function. *Psychological Bulletin 108*(3): 363–382.

Paul, W. E. and Seder, R. A. (1994). Lymphocyte responses and cytokines. *Cell 76*: 241–251.

Pearson, J. D., James, G. D., and Brown, D. E. (1993). Stress and changing lifestyles in the Pacific: physiological stress responses of Samoans in rural and urban settings. *American Journal of Human Biology 5*(1): 49–60.

Petrovich, S. B. and Gewirtz, J. L. (1985). The attachment learning process and its relation to cultural and biological evolution: proximate and ultimate considerations. In M. Reite and T. Fields (eds), *The psychobiology of attachment and separation* (pp. 259–291). New York: Academic Press.

Plaut, S. M. and Friedman, S. B. (1981). Psychosocial factors in infectious disease. In R. Ader (ed.), *Psychoneuroimmunology*. New York: Academic Press.

Pollard, T. M. (1995). Use of cortisol as a stress marker: practical and theoretical problems. *American Journal of Human Biology 7*(2): 265–274.

Robins, L. N. (1983). Some methodological problems and research directions in the study of the effects of stress on children. In N. Garmezy, and M. Rutter (eds), *Stress, coping, and development in children* (pp. 335–346). New York: McGraw-Hill.

Rose, R. M. (1980). Endocrine responses to stressful psychological events. *Psychiatric Clinics of North America 3*: 251–276.

Rutter, M. (1991). Childhood experiences and adult psychosocial functioning. In G. R. Bock and J. Whelan (eds), *The childhood environment and adult disease* (pp. 189–200). Chichester: John Wiley.

Sapolsky, R. M. (1986). Glucocorticoid toxicity in the hippocampus: reversal by supplementation with brain fuels. *Journal of Neuroscience 6*: 2240–2245.

—— (1990a). Stress in the wild. *Scientific American* (262): 116–123.

—— (1990b). Adrenocortical function, social rank, and personality among wild baboons. *Biological Psychiatry 28*(10): 862–878.

——, Romero, L. M., Munck, A. U. (2000). How do glucocorticoids influence stress responses? *Endocrine Reviews 21*(1): 55–89.

Scott, P. (1993) Selective differentiation of CD4+ T helper cell subsets. *Current Opinions in Immunology 5*(3): 391–397.

Shell-Duncan, B. (1993). Cell-mediated immunocompetence among nomadic Turkana children. *American Journal of Human Biology 5*(2): 225–235.

—— (1995). Impact of seasonal variation in food availability and disease stress on health status of nomadic Turkana children: a longitudinal analysis of morbidity, immunity, and nutritional status. *American Journal of Human Biology 7*(3): 339–355.

Sklar, L. S. and Anisman, H. (1979). Stress and coping factors influence tumor growth. *Science 205*(4405): 513–515.

Suomi, S. J. (1997). Long-term effects of differential early experiences on social, emotional, and physiological development in nonhuman primates. In: M. S. Keshevan and R. M. Murra (eds), *Neurodevelopmental models of adult psychopathology* (pp. 104–116). Cambridge: Cambridge University Press.

Takahashi, L. K. (1992). Prenatal stress and the expression of stress-induced responses throughout the life span. *Clinical Neuropharmacology 15*(suppl. 1 pt. A): 153–154.

Tennes, K. (1982). The role of hormones in mother-infant interaction. In R. N. Emde and R. J. Harmon (eds), *The development of attachment and affiliative systems* (pp. 75–88). New York: Plenum Press.

van Wimersma Greidanus, T. J. B. and DeWied, D. (1977). The physiology of the neurohypophyseal system and its relation to memory processes. In A. M. Davison (ed.), *Biochemical correlates of brain structure and function* (pp. 215–248). New York: Academic Press.

Vickers, R. R. J. (1988). Effectiveness of defense: a significant predictor of cortisol excretion under stress. *Journal of Psychosomatic Research 32*(1): 21–29.

Werner, E. E. (1985). Stress and protective factors in children's lives. In A. R. Nicol (ed.), *Longitudinal studies in child psychology and psychiatry*. New York: John Wiley.

Wiebe, D. J. (1991). Hardiness and stress moderation: a test of proposed mechanisms. *Journal of Personality and Social Psychology 60*(1): 89–99.

Williams, G. C. and Nesse, R. M. (1991). The dawn of Darwinian medicine. *The Quarterly Review of Biology 66*(1): 1–22.

Wright, P., Gill, M., and Murray, R. M. (1993). Schizophrenia: genetics and the maternal immune response to viral infection. *American Journal of Medical Genetics 48*(1): 40–46.

Young, E. A., Haskett, R. F., Murphy-Weinberg, V., Watson, S. J., and Akil, H. (1991). Loss of glucocorticoid fast feedback in depression. *Archives of General Psychiatry 48*(8): 693–699.

Chapter 7: Editor's note

Decker has long been associated with a longitudinal, ethnographic, and medically sophisticated study (see Flinn, this volume) of human immune function in a particular cultural context quite far removed from the American university or hospital contexts in which many psychoneuroimmunological studies have been carried out. Working in the Dominican village of Bwa Mawego, Decker combined ethnographic and laboratory-analytic methods to isolate a physiological marker of stress – HPA activation – and associate it with four primary sociocultural variables. Among these, the first – participation in culturally approved activities (which have no direct health impact) – might seem an unlikely candidate for affecting stress, HPA activation, and thus (indirectly) immune function. But Decker succeeds in presenting a coherent model to explain the correlations he uncovered between cortisol levels, social status, and cultural consonance (Dressler and Bindon 2000).

Chapter 7

Cultural congruity and the cortisol stress response among Dominican men

Seamus A. Decker, Mark V. Flinn,
Barry G. England, and Carol M. Worthman

Introduction to the research problem: social status and stress

A growing body of research contributes to new conceptions of stress and immune responses – physiological axes which have traditionally been regarded as separate – as elements in an integrated life-history resource allocation process. According to this new understanding of mind and body, biology and culture, physiology and symbol, "systems" which have previously been regarded as being relatively autonomous aspects of human experience (e.g. stress-response, worldview, emotion, decision-making, immune function, social identity, and power) are being redefined as integrated but dynamically interacting elements in the complex human biocultural phenotype. The give and take in this process occurring between evolved predispositions and sociocultural opportunities are poorly understood.

For example, among nonhuman primates, social dominance (measured as frequency of victories in competitive bouts) associates negatively with baseline HPA activation and immunosuppression (Coe *et al.* 1979; Cohen *et al.* 1992; Cunnick *et al.* 1991; Golub 1979; Keverne 1990; Manogue 1975; Sapolsky 1982, 1983a; Sapolsky and Mott 1987). In other words, animals who are subordinate – those with less competent behavioral styles, who win less, are harassed more, and have less predictable and lower-quality access to food, mates, nesting sites, and other "resources" – show evidence of higher chronic stress response, and immunosuppression. In contrast, two studies of humans indicate that military and/or socioeconomic rank associate *positively* with HPA activation (Bourne *et al.* 1968; Brandstadter *et al.* 1991; Seeman and McEwen 1996). These differences demonstrate that, at present, we have a poor understanding of the degree to which homologous aspects of psychosocial intelligence, emotional sensitivity, and responsiveness among humans and nonhuman primates account for human social experience, psychosocial stress, and psychoneuroimmunological function compared to more evolutionarily novel cultural factors particular only to humans. Moreover, cultural factors may influence psychosocial stress not only by shaping differences in social status structure and thus mediating exposure to stressors, but also because of how cultural models are integral to individual psychological appraisal of stressors (Brown *et al.* 1998). As such, one of the most important gaps in understanding the social lives of psychoneuroimmunological (PNI) systems is a lack of information on the psychosomatic effects of relative differences in culturally defined power, social rank, or dominance.

Cultural consensus and stress

Hypothetically, the most basic cultural effects on psychosomatic processes involve inter-group or inter-individual differences emerging through different interpretations of similar experience because of differences in cultural models or worldview (Baratta *et al.* 1990; Jacobson 1987). One of the most exciting recent themes in biocultural anthropological investigations is the role that cultural consensus or sociocultural congruity plays in psychosomatic processes such as stress-response, immune function and other aspects of well being (e.g. depression or other forms of psychopathology). Congruity or consensus is typically conceived of as a continuously varying quantitative phenomenon, i.e. not as a threshold on/off or yes/no effect. Congruity can be conceived in at least three rather different ways.

First, because of acculturation, migration, or simply cultural evolution, individuals may experience degrees of incongruity or poor-fit among specific cultural models or schema which they have mentally-internalized or enact. For example, Brown (1982) found that Filipino immigrants to Honolulu with an intermediate degree of acculturation to modern urban Hawaiian culture had higher 24-hour urinary catecholamine output than did immigrants who were either more-acculturated or less-acculturated. In other words, internalizing roughly equal mixtures of traditional Filipino and opposing modern Hawaiian cultural models was associated with greater stress. The idea is that, believing in, or otherwise following, opposing schema produces internal psychosomatic tension manifested as higher stress.

In a somewhat different view of cultural consensus as an intervening variable in social experience and, in particular, in the experience of social support and affiliation, congruity has been operationalized as "the degree of cultural sharing (or consensus) among informants" or members of an interacting social group (Dressler 1995: 3; Dressler and Bindon 2000; Romney *et al.* 1986). In this conceptualization, the tension leading to higher stress and immunosuppression emerges from how well an individual's worldview fits with that of others in the group. A third alternative to cultural incongruity is an operationalization of the degree of disparity in actual resource control, or means of resource control, and expectations of resource control (Bindon *et al.* 1997: 7), i.e. having higher status expectations than one can actually achieve, which has typically been referred to as status incongruity. Several studies have successfully established empirical associations between physiological measures of stress (e.g. blood pressure, catecholamine secretions, or cortisol secretions) and these various conceptualizations and operationalizations of cultural congruity, consensus, or inconsistency.

Summary of the study

We investigated these questions with data on salivary cortisol, and various social status measures from 30 adult male Dominican villagers. Products of the hypothalamic–pituitary–adrenal axis (HPA), including cortisol, comprise one strand in a web of neuroendocrinological forces which mediate immunoregulation in humans (Falaschi et al. 1994; O'Leary 1990; Ursin 1994). Actions of the central nervous system, the autonomic nervous system, and the sympathetic–adrenal–medullary axis are also known to mediate immune function. However, HPA secretions – cortisol in particular – have received considerable attention as immunoregulators (Ahmed et al. 1974; Arnetz et al. 1991; Coe 1994; Cohen 1994; Cohen et al. 1993; Cunnick et al. 1991; Cupps and Fauci 1982; Fauci and Dale 1975; Dale et al. 1974; Flinn and England 1996, 1997; Gatti et al. 1987; Gillis et al. 1979; Glaser et al. 1994; Gordon and Nouri 1981; Herbert and Cohen 1993; Kiecolt-Glaser et al. 1984; Kimzey 1975; Kimzey et al. 1976; Meuleman and Katz 1985; Onsrud and Thorsby 1981; Panter-Brick et al. 1996; Schleifer et al. 1984; Weidenfeld et al. 1990). As such, baseline salivary cortisol is a highly salient and efficient proxy measure of PNI function.

Circadian variation in salivary cortisol values was standardized using residuals from a curvilinear regression by time of day. Mean cortisol residuals for each individual were used in a multivariate linear regression analysis to examine associations between individuals' chronic level of HPA activation and various social status measures including indicators of cultural congruity.

Results indicate that individuals' mean level of HPA activation associates negatively with the following four social characteristics: (i) engaging in culturally sanctioned religious and political institutions as opposed to illicit activities; (ii) infrequent reports of distressed mood; (iii) being rated highly by peers on affiliative or cooperative characteristics; and (iv) having grown up with a father who was present as a caretaker more often than he was absent. These findings support two hypotheses, (i) that affiliational or cooperative social status associates negatively with HPA activation, and (ii) that social or behavioral incongruity with the predominant representational models in a culture associates positively with HPA activation. No clear association was found between other measures of social status (education, income, property, age, number of dependents, or children) and HPA activation. These findings are congruent with a large body of theory and evidence in developmental psychobiology in which a harsher childhood environment canalizes individual life-history toward more short-term allocational tendencies with elevated long-term costs (e.g. relatively greater immunosuppression; see Mann, this volume).

Study site and sample

The data used in this research were collected during two brief ethnographic surveys in the remote rural village of Bwa Mawego[1] on the Caribbean island of Dominica. Dominica is an underdeveloped Caribbean nation economically dependent on small-scale agriculture and informal work arrangements (Gomes 1985; Hunte 1972; Trouillot 1988). The village comprises 600 inhabitants, grouped into about 100 households where Flinn and colleagues have conducted more than 31 months of longitudinal research on childhood, family organization, and stress since 1988 (Flinn 1999; Flinn *et al.* 1995; Flinn and England 1996, 1997, and in this volume; Flinn *et al.* 1996). Bwa Mawego lies at the end of a poor-quality road at the most remote corner of the southeastern coast of Dominica. Small-scale agriculture, fishing, and migrant labor are the primary means of subsistence in the village. Modern infrastructure and associated social reorganizations are incipient, "about 60 per cent of homes have electricity, 23 per cent have telephones, 11 per cent have refrigerators, and 7 per cent have televisions" (Flinn and England 1996).

The study involves 30 adult males, aged 17 to 49 years, residing in 28 different households. This is a nearly complete sample of adult men living permanently in two adjoining hamlets of the village during the period of fieldwork. Field research was conducted during June and July, 1992 and December and January of 1993–1994. Laboratory analyses were conducted at the University of Michigan, Department of Pathology, Ligand Research Laboratory during November 1992, and at Emory University, Department of Anthropology, Laboratory for Comparative Human Biology in 1994. Details of the radioimmunoassay protocol for measurement of salivary concentrations of cortisol have been published in Decker (2000).

Cultural context

Many of the predominant cultural themes in Bwa Mawego derive from Dominica's colonial past and intensive missionization by various Christian denominations. Christian values of temperance, monogamy, nuclear family coherence, hard work, and piety are the most powerful models in the society, though alternative models such as Rastafarianism exist. Many families are matrifocal, but there appears to be an unspoken distinction associated with intact nuclear families, and members of such families seem to possess a distinct form of cultural capital. Illicit drug use is not uncommon, but again, the sanctioned representational models in the village are set in opposition to drug use, and other non-Christian behaviors such as gambling, drinking, or "partying" at local pubs.

The village was particularly well suited for this research because subjects comprise a long-term social group in which direct reciprocal relations are paramount for economic and social success (Decker 1993). Wage labor comprises a largely supplementary economic role to small-scale cash crop production and subsistence gardening executed through reciprocal work arrangements.

Methods

Results reported here derive from three sets of interviews with all 30 subjects, and two sets of multiple-day longitudinal ambulatory observations of salivary cortisol levels and mood. Salivary cortisol is considered a superior measure of adrenal function compared to serum cortisol, and is far easier to collect, store and analyze (Bolufer *et al.* 1989; Reid *et al.* 1992; Shinkai *et al.* 1993). These methods were supplemented with information gained through regular participant observation during five months of field research, and with insights of two key informants who were members of the research cohort.

The first interview was a semi-structured interview of about one hour in length, conducted in each subject's home. During this interview we collected information about a variety of institutional and material status dimensions, as well as information on differences in social roles, for example, whether a man was married or not; the presence of co-residing children and other kin; each man's occupation; estimated yearly income; a checklist of material property and livestock, and estimates of the quantity and quality of agricultural land controlled; number of years of education or vocational training, and special skills; roles of religious and political institutional power; and a brief life history focused on residential and work history and other salient life events. These data formed the basis for several scales of social status.

Following completion of the first round of interviews, a second round of unstructured interviews was conducted with all 30 subjects to investigate the cultural models of status in Bwa Mawego. Subjects were asked to discuss what sort of characteristics in other men were preferential for friendships or cooperative affiliations. After this interview, facial photographic prints were taken of all 30 subjects. Responses to these interviews were used in concert with key-informant responses to devise a four-item peer-rating scale of social status: trustworthiness; agreeableness; influence; and helpfulness, shown in Table 7.1. Ratings on these four scales were obtained for all subjects from all 29 of their peers during the final interviews.

During the final round of interviews all 30 subjects rated all 29 other subjects on the 4-item scale of social status using a five-point Likert scale with the facial photographs as prompts. These interviews were conducted in complete privacy in the researchers' living quarters. First, subjects were told that they would be asked how well they liked other men in the village and that they could respond using a Likert-scale with five potential responses,

Table 7.1 Four-item peer-rating of social status scale

| • How much do you trust this man? |
| • How much do you agree with this man? |
| • How much influence does this man have on you? |
| • How much help does this man give you? |

Five-point Likert scale for response to four peer-rating items:

1	2	3	4	5
None	Not much	Average	A lot	The most

shown in Table 7.1. Next subjects were told the four questions on which they would rank other men, also shown in Table 7.1.

Using the facial photographs taken of each man, each of the four peer-rating questions was addressed to all 30 research subjects once for each of his 29 peers who were also participants in the study. Using these peer ratings, mean social ranks were calculated for each of the 30 subjects. Calculation of Cronbach's Alpha equal to 0.948 indicated a high internal consistency for this four-item scale of social status. This instrument appears to be a reliable measure, and based on qualitative information gathered through participant observation and key informant discussions, this scale is a valid indicator of individuals' overall social power in Bwa Mawego. Men rated highly by peers tended to have more stable economic and social relationships, and had reputations for integrity and industriousness. In contrast, low-rated men often had little or no income, infrequent opportunity for work, and in some cases limited access to garden products which complicated their daily subsistence. Low-rated men had reputations for failed social relationships (for example divorces, breakups, and disagreements), frequent fighting or arguing, criminal activity, excessive drug-use, and/or indolence.

Each individual's baseline HPA activation was assessed by collecting saliva samples twice daily for eight contiguous days in 1992 and for four contiguous days in 1993. Radioimmunoassay analyses were conducted on the 471 saliva samples collected from the 30 subjects in this study. Each salivary cortisol value was standardized by time of day using a linear model of diurnal decline shown in Figure 7.1. Details of the RIA procedure, as well as the linear regression analysis are described in Decker (2000) (see also Appendix to Flinn chapter in this volume). The intercept for this model was 0.766 micrograms per deciliter; the time slope coefficient was –0.072; and the time squared slope coefficient was 0.002. This linear model accounts for 53.1 percent of the observed variation in cortisol. Using the intercept and slope estimates, we calculated a residual score for all 471 cortisol samples. These residuals are indicative of individuals' cortisol levels above or below the mean level at a specified time of day given the mean circadian decline in

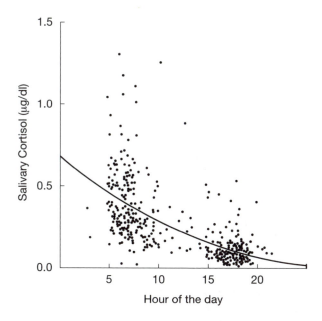

Figure 7.1 Salivary cortisol [μg.dL] by time of day (*n* = 471). The linear model shown (Cortisol = 0.766 + (−0.072×Time) + (0.002×Time²)) is derived from a regression using only the 219 samples prior to which no alcohol or tobacco had been consumed, health and mood status were reported to be positive, and − for PM samples − no naps had occurred. Adjusted R^2 = 0.531; P (F > 124.299) = 0.0009 with $F \approx F_{2, 216}$

cortisol level for the entire sample. In the next step of analysis, individuals' mean HPA levels were estimated using each subject's mean cortisol residuals from this regression analysis.

The research hypotheses were tested by examining associations between subjects' mean cortisol residuals, and various measures of peer-rated affiliative, cultural congruity, and socioeconomic status (income, land ownership, education) in a backward stepwise multivariate linear regression. We also examined associations of cortisol with cultural consensus using two categorical variables derived from life-history interview responses. Table 7.2 describes the criterion for categorization in each of these two dichotomous variables.

Based on interview data, individuals were coded into the "More Absent" (Fathpres₁) category if, at minimum, their father had been absent as a caretaker during a roughly equal portion of their childhood as he was present. Subjects were coded into the "More Present" (Fathpres₀) category if their father had been present as a caretaker during the majority of their childhood. Individuals who had reputations for engaging in illicit behavior, for example,

Table 7.2 Two dichotomous measures of childhood developmental environment and social role

Variable	Category	Description
Father presence	> Absent	Subject's biological father was absent as a caretaker as often as or more often than he was present
	> Present	Subject's biological father was present as a caretaker during the majority of childhood
Social conduct	Illicit	Reputations for criminality, drug-abuse, polygyny, and no participation in culturally-sanctioned religious or political institutions
	Sanctioned	no reputation for criminality, drug-abuse, polygyny, and active participation in culturally-sanctioned religious and/or political institutions

theft, gun-running, drug-abuse, polygyny, and no participation in sanctioned religious or political institutions, were coded in the "Illicit" ($Conduct_1$) social conduct category. Individuals were coded in the "Sanctioned" ($Conduct_0$) social conduct category if they did not have reputations for such illicit behaviors, and were involved in sanctioned religious or political institutions. Variables were removed in a stepwise fashion, with alpha levels of 0.05 as criterion for entry and removal and tolerance minimums of 0.5. This stepwise procedure resulted in the following final model: Cortisol = 0.239 + $(0.103 \times Mood) - (0.067 \times Peermean) + (0.035 \times Fathpres_1) + (0.042 \times Conduct_1)$ as detailed in Table 7.3.

Results

Table 7.3 is the ANOVA table with regression statistics and model estimates for the final multivariate model resulting from this backward stepwise process. The final model includes frequency of distressed mood, mean peer rating, father absence, and illicit social conduct as linear predictors of mean cortisol residual. Overall, this model is highly statistically significant; we can be 99.99 percent confident in predicting at least 56.1 percent of an individual's variation in mean cortisol level using this model. Each of the independent variables in the model is separately a statistically significant predictor of cortisol, with frequency of distressed-mood accounting for 18.1 percent of the variance in cortisol, mean peer rating accounting for 10.3 percent, father absence accounting for 9.2 percent and social conduct accounting for 18.5 percent of the observed variation in cortisol. Variance inflation indices, tolerance values, and condition indices indicated

Table 7.3 Final ANOVA table for a backwards stepwise multivariate linear regression model of mean cortisol with nine psychosocial variables

Adjusted $R^2 = 0.561$; $N = 26$; Overall F-ratio: $P (F > 8.30) < 0.001$ with $F \approx F_{4, 26}$

Source	Sum of squares	DF	Mean square	Partial F-ratio	Partial P-value	Partial R^2
Mood	0.049	1	0.049	10.745	0.003	0.181
Peermean	0.028	1	0.028	6.171	0.020	0.103
Fathpres	0.025	1	0.025	5.492	0.027	0.092
Conduct	0.050	1	0.050	10.850	0.003	0.185
Error	0.119	26	0.005	–	–	0.439
Total	0.271	30	–	–	–	–

Final model: Cortisol = 0.239 + (0.103×Mood) – (0.067×Peermean) + (0.035×Fathpres$_1$) + (0.042×Conduct$_1$)

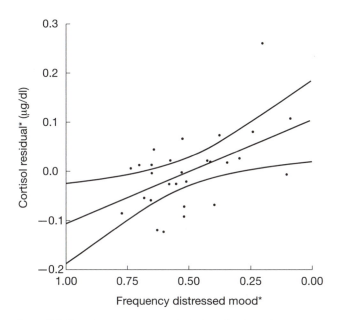

Figure 7.2 Partial regression residual plot of subjects' mean cortisol residuals and frequency of distressed mood with 95 percent confidence intervals. Men who reported distressed mood more frequently had significantly higher cortisol: $P (F > 10.745) = 0.003$ with $F_{1, 26}$.

no problems from multicollinearity in this model. Examination of linear regression standard diagnostics for each independent variable revealed no breaches of assumptions of homoscedasticity, independence, linearity, or normality.

Figure 7.2 shows the partial regression residual plot of subjects' mean cortisol residuals and frequency of distressed mood with 95 percent confidence intervals. This plot shows that there is a positive association between frequency of distressed mood and cortisol, when variation in cortisol and mood that is explained by other variables is controlled. Figure 7.3 shows the partial regression residual plot of cortisol and mean peer rating with 95 percent confidence intervals. Men considered more trustworthy, agreeable, influential, and helpful by their peers have significantly lower cortisol than men rated low in these qualities. Figure 7.4 shows the least squares means and standard errors of subjects' mean cortisol residuals for the "more absent" (Fathpres$_1$) and "more present" (Fathpres$_0$) categories of father presence. Men whose fathers were present as caretakers for the majority of their childhood have 0.07 micrograms per deciliter lower cortisol than do men whose fathers were absent. Figure 7.5 shows the least squares means and standard errors of

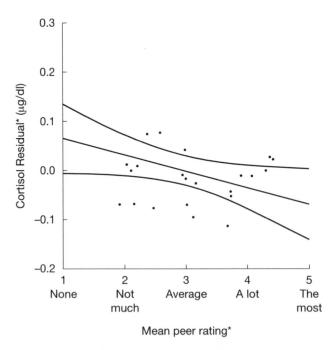

Figure 7.3 Partial regression of residual plot of cortisol and mean peer rating with 95 percent confidence intervals. Men considered the most trustworthy, agreeable, influential, and helpful by their peers have significantly lower cortisol than men rated low in these qualities.

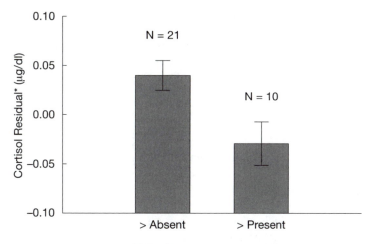

Figure 7.4 Least squares means and standard errors of subjects' mean cortisol residuals [μg/dL]. Men whose fathers were present as caretakers for the majority of their childhood have significantly lower cortisol than do men whose fathers were absent: $P (F > 6.171) = 0.020$ with $F \approx F_{1, 30}$, Tukey's HSD Multiple Means Comparison.

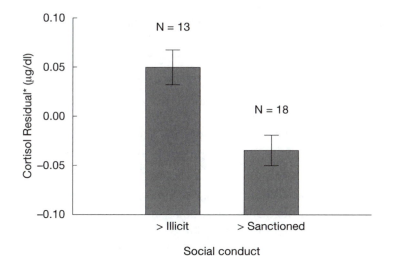

Figure 7.5 Least squares means and standard errors of subjects' mean cortisol residuals [μg/dL]. Men with reputations for illicit behavior (criminality, drug-abuse, polygyny, and/or no role in sanctioned religious and political institutions) have higher cortisol than men with reputations for more sanctioned social behavior: $P (F > 10.85) = 0.003$ with $F \approx F_{1, 30}$, Tukey's HSD Multiple Means Comparison.

subjects' mean cortisol residuals for the "Illicit" ($Conduct_1$) and "Sanctioned" ($Conduct_0$) groups of social conduct. Men with reputations for illicit behavior, that is, criminality, drug-abuse, or polygyny, and no role in culturally-sanctioned religious and political institutions, have 0.085 micrograms per deciliter higher cortisol than men with reputations for culturally-sanctioned social behaviors.

Conclusions

The results of this study support the hypothesis that high status in affiliative or cooperative social domains (as measured by the peer-rating instrument described here) associates negatively with chronic HPA activation whereas status in income, education, and land ownership exhibited no associations with salivary cortisol. This lack of association with traditional measures of SES and cortisol differs from findings in some studies which found higher cortisol among men with higher income or higher military rank (Bourne et al. 1968; Brandstadter et al., 1991; Seeman and McEwen 1996). Dominican men who were considered by their peers to be more helpful, influential and, in particular, more trustworthy and agreeable by other men have significantly lower chronic HPA levels as evidenced by mean salivary cortisol residual. Results are also supportive of the hypothesis that social and behavioral congruity with the predominant cultural models in a society associates negatively with stress. Men with reputations for engaging in socially accepted behaviors, and refraining from illicit behaviors also have lower cortisol. Results provided no support for the hypothesis that status in income, education, material wealth, or institutional rank associates with stress. Measures of education, income, and material wealth did not associate with chronic HPA level in a linear or any evident non-linear fashion in this study. Only two other studies have found a positive association between SES measures and chronic levels of salivary cortisol (Bourne et al. 1968; Brandstadter et al. 1991). Because of the distinct importance of cultural factors in shaping the meaning of these forms of status, our findings must be regarded as highly tentative and potentially varying across cultures (see McDade, this volume).[2]

Although pursuit of greater education, income, or material wealth may be associated with increased competitiveness and individualism in Western industrial societies (Bourdieu 1984; Durkheim 1951; Willis 1977) this may not be so true in cultures such as Dominica where extended families sometimes work together to concentrate resources into one high-potential family member (Burton 1990; Gonzalez 1969; Smith 1988; Trouillot 1988). It is quite likely that the relationship between these status domains and stress varies dramatically from one cultural context to the next. There may, indeed, be a strong contrast between the Dominican Bwa Mawego and Samoan contexts in regards to the relationship of status and stress.

Among monkeys changing, unstable, or conflictual social organization associates with elevated HPA activation among *both* dominant and subordinate animals (Coe 1994; Cunnick *et al.* 1991; Keverne 1990; Sapolsky 1983b, 1986). This may reflect the fact that lower cortisol among more powerful individuals – both in this study and in past nonhuman primate research – ultimately originates from feelings of control, and predictability higher status individuals (Breier *et al.* 1987; Ursin 1994). Corroboration of the low status–elevated cortisol link resulting from these feelings comes from Sapolsky, who marshaled evidence that negative associations between status and stress among wild baboons resulted from differences in central nervous system functioning, namely more sensitive hypothalamic negative feed-back sensitivity and faster pituitary response to CRF (cortisotropin releasing factor) among dominants compared to subordinants (Sapolsky 1983a, 1989, 1996; Sapolsky and Plotsky 1990).

Dominant animals exhibited more sensitive, flexible and labile physiological flexibility in their responses to stress. Although they have lower basal levels of HPA secretions, dominant animals exhibit faster, larger, and more ephemeral increases in HPA secretions in response to acute stressors, such as anesthesia-induced disorientation, live snakes, and physical restraint (Manogue 1975; Sapolsky 1982, 1983a).[3]

Chronically elevated levels of glucocorticoids damage hippocampal receptors integral to the negative feedback down-regulation of the HPA system (Sapolsky and Plotsky 1990: 946). Such neuronal damage results in dysregulation of HPA function manifested as chronically elevated cortisol levels, but also in relatively dampened response to acute stressors. Thus, past work among nonhuman primates indicates that permanent hippocampal receptor down-regulation resulting from particularly intense, or chronic stressors, in part accounts for differences in stress-response between dominant and subordinate animals. A similar effect could result from chronic stress-response among humans, and could in part explain the association between low affiliative status and elevated cortisol observed in this study. In other words, chronic stress, low affiliative social status, damaging effects of stress on hippocampal glucocortoid receptors, and resultant diminished ability to respond adaptively to social challenges may well be engaged in an interactive and self-perpetuating feedback loop.

Sapolsky's work among baboons (1990, 1996) also indicates that personality differences, or social affiliational capabilities influence the social-stress association both by predisposing individuals to different status attainment and by directly affecting HPA responsiveness (Coe *et al.* 1994; Cohen *et al.* 1992; Sapolsky 1990). Among most cercopithecines, individuals' status within group dominance hierarchies fluctuate to some degree during their adult lives, and not surprisingly, the status-stress association is not perfect. Sapolsky (1990) found that animals who were more frequently dominant tended to have certain personality characteristics, including: skill at forming alliances, and differentiating between neutral and threatening behaviors by others; infrequent unprovoked aggression; and high rates of affiliative behaviors. Similar conclusions have been reached by other investigators (Coe 1994; Cohen *et al.* 1992).

It appears that it is not simply the experience of being high-status, and the differential daily life that goes with such status. Individuals who are gregarious and socially skilled tend to occupy high-status positions more than those with more aggressive, anxious, antisocial, and hostile personalities (Jones *et al.* 1986; Lundberg *et al.* 1991; Spangler 1995). Even when they have been temporarily displaced from their high-status role, gregarious and socially skilled animals seem to be buffered against high stress by a placid behavioral style, and presumably more placid internal emotional state. Thus, how primates perceive or appraise stressors is as important to stress-response as the objective quality of stressors, a point which bears great significance for understanding stress among a profoundly cultural animal such as humans (Baratta *et al.* 1990; Brown 1981, 1982; D'Andrade 1992; Dressler 1984: 268; Dressler 1991, 1992; Jacobson 1987; Spradley and Phillips 1972).

Despite cultural prescriptions and symbolic value linked to forms of social status such as high income or rank, the social experience of high military or socioeconomic rank may exceed the threshold of human social predispositions derived from evolved psychological mechanisms (Tooby and Cosmides 1992). That is, despite the material and symbolic benefits of such status, it may be that such high-intensity roles are intrinsically stressful to human beings because they involve habitual social experiences that differ too much from our environment of evolutionary adaptedness. Bowlby suggested that such a conceptualization may help in understanding problematic mother–infant relations in post-industrial social settings by noting that "no system can be expected to operate effectively except in its environment of adaptedness" (Bowlby 1969: 58).

Among humans, individuals who pursue institutionalized power may have more competitive behavioral styles associated with higher physiological arousal (Jones *et al.* 1986: 699), and higher risk for coronary heart disease. Some have characterized such individuals as having a "Type A personality" comprising: "a success-oriented, challenge-induced, action-emotion complex with hostility, achievement striving and time urgency" and also "extremes of competitive achievement-striving, a strong sense of time urgency, impatience, easily aroused anger, and aggression" (Spangler 1995: 303).

In contrast to these psychosocial characteristics, dominant monkeys tend to have less competitive behavioral styles, styles that, among humans, have been characterized as "Type B personality."[4] During most of human natural history, social success, and evolutionary fitness may not have been increased by the behavioral styles that contribute to high SES or military rank in modern industrial society (Axelrod 1984; Konner 1972, 1982; Lee 1979; Shostak 1983; Tooby, and Cosmides 1989, 1990, 1992). Thus, the individualistic and competitive social organizations typical of post-Neolithic and post-industrial societies may represent a departure from the social environment to which our evolved allostatic load distributing systems are adapted.

A more traditional notion of culture suggests that stress will derive from individuals' unwillingness or inability to adhere to the predominant cultural values in their society. The growing field of practice theory has benefited from increasing conceptual complexity such as the distinction between representational and operational models. Representational models cover "what actors say about the nature of social reality, whereas operational models refer to the way they respond or act" (Karp and Kent 1983: 483). This distinction allows consideration of the vast interindividual disparity in interpretations of how things should be, and how to behave. Thus, practice theory leads us to recognize that cultures are not unitary sets of information embraced harmoniously, nor smoothly interacting hives of individuals. Rather, social structure is a set of rules and resources that actors can use to affect others (Karp 1986:135). Thus, an individual's congruity, or degree of fit within the predominant or hegemonic cultural models of his or her society appears to be an important source of stress among humans (Dressler 1988, 1991). Yet another interpretation is that the higher physiological arousal found by Brandstadter and Bourne among high SES and high ranking men is not actually stress in the sense of a maladaptive, chronically destructive response, but is actually adaptive arousal among individuals occupying a dynamic microniche (Pollard 1994; Napier, this volume).

Our findings are in line with a large body of theory and evidence in which quality of childhood developmental environment canalizes individual life-history trajectory (Mann, this volume; Belsky *et al.* 1991; Chisholm 1993, 1999; Gottlieb 1991; Greenough *et al.* 1987; LeVine 1990; MacDonald 1988; Robins 1994; Rutter 1994; Valsiner 1989; Wallace 1970), resulting in more short-term focused responses throughout the lifespan by those who experience harsh early environments. Absence of father during childhood may be a reliable proxy measure of harsh or inconsistent developmental environments (Flinn, this volume; Flinn *et al.* 1996; Flinn and England 1997). Such environments may cause lingering effects on individuals' psychosocial capacities through a number of "Carry Forward effects which may represent a combination of persistence of psychopathological consequences and a resulting increased vulnerability to later stress and adversity" (Rutter 1994: 374). Potential mechanisms of these carry forward effects include: (1) neural effects such as those known from studies of visual deprivation in infancy; (2) neuroendocrine effects; (3) predisposition of one type of social adversity to others; and (4) cognitive features such as self-esteem, self-efficacy, and cognitive models of relationships (ibid.).

At the proximal level, at least two distinct processes may be at work linking social status to elevated HPA activation. First, low social status individuals may experience objectively distinct socioecologies. That is to say, their social world is objectively more harsh and stressful. Second, higher HPA activation among low social status men may not reflect objective differences in their socioecologies relative to high social status men as much as it results from different sensitivities and responsiveness to social life. Psychosocial deficiencies stemming in part from harsh developmental environments may cause not only lower capacities to affiliate, cooperate, and reciprocate but also hypersensitivity to social interactions and false appraisal of neutral interactions as threatening. Support for this mechanism is found in findings of strong linear associations between frequency of distressed mood and chronic HPA activation.

A very different interpretation is also possible. The elevated HPA activation observed among some men may not be "stress" in the sense that it represents a failure of the organism to adapt. Despite the costs to long-term well-being which are probably imposed by chronically elevated HPA activation on immune system and other long-term physiological processes, compromise of these long-term goals in order to redirect resources toward short-term demands may actually be the best possible response to a bad situation.[5] For those whose social lives are harsh, inconsistent, and lack in support, higher stress and decreased immunocompetence may be the only viable option for adapting to frequent acute psychosocial crises. In order to answer this question, future studies must account for the cognitive, emotional, and social options available to individuals in different psychosocial contexts, and how stress processes relate to these options.

Notes

*   The asterisks next to the variable names for Figures 7.2 and 7.3 indicate –
      following common use by statisticians – that the variables being plotted are not
      original, unmodified data but are instead "partial residuals" from a common
      multiple-linear regression model that included other independent variables not
      shown in the figures.
1   Bwa Mawego is a pseudonym used to help protect the anonymity of research
      subjects.
2   McDade (this volume) finds SES moderating the impact of stress.
3   The possibility that homologous forces in late capitalism favor flexibility both at
      work and in immune responsiveness has long been a theme in the work of Emily
      Martin (Cone and Martin, this volume, and Martin 1994).
4   A meta-analytic review of research on hostility and physical health by Miller
      et al. (1996) problematizes the more global personality distinction postulated in
      the Type A/Type B model. T. W. Smith and collaborators find that, among the
      features thought to constitute "Type A" personality, both coronary heart disease
      (CHD) and all-cause mortality are significantly associated with only one in the
      main – hostility, especially "cynical hostility" according to co-author Smith's
      findings (Smith and Allred 1989, Christensen and Smith 1993).
5   *Ed. Such a re-examination of "stress" occupies much of Napier's chapter in this
      volume, though in his description of intense he envisions something other than
      the trade-off between short-term victories and long-term sacrifice of immuno-
      competence.*

References

Ahmed, A., C. Herman, and R. Knudsen (1974). Effect of exogenous and endogenous glucocorticoids on the in vitro stimulation of lymphocytes from sedated and awake-restrained healthy baboons. *Journal of Surgical Research*, 16, 172–182.

Arnetz, B. B., S.-O. Brenner, L. Levi, R. Hjelm, I.-L. Petterson, J. Wasserman, B. Petrini, P. Eneroth, A. Kallner, R. Kvetnansky, and M. Vigas (1991). Neuroendocrine and immunologic effects of unemployment and job insecurity. *Psychotherapy and Psychosomatics*, 55, 76–80.

Axelrod, R. (1984). *The evolution of cooperation*. New York: Basic Books.

Baratta, S., G. Interlandi, M. Giardinella, R. Micciolo, and C. Zimmermann-Tansella (1990). The perception of life events in two different cultural settings. *Journal of Affective Disorders*, 18, 97–104.

Belsky, J., L. Steinberg, and P. Draper (1991). Childhood experience, interpersonal development, and reproductive strategy: an evolutionary theory of socialization. *Child Development*, 62, 647–670.

Bindon, J. R., A. Knight, W. W. Dressler, and D. E. Crews (1997). Social context and psychosocial influences on blood pressure among American Samoans. *American Journal of Human Biology*, 103, 7–18.

Bolufer, P., A. Gandia, A. Rodriquez, and P. Antonio (1989). Salivary corticosteroids in the study of adrenal function. *Clinica Chimica Acta*, 183, 217–226.

Bourdieu, P. (1984). *Distinction: a social critique of the judgment of taste*. Cambridge, MA: Harvard University Press.

Bourne, P., R. Rose, and J. Mason (1968). 17-OHCS levels in combat Special Forces "A" Team under threat of attack. *Archives of General Psychiatry*, 19, 135–140.

Bowlby, J. (1969). *Attachment and loss*. Volume I, *Attachment*. New York: Basic Books.

Brandstadter, J., B. Baltes-Gotz, C. Kirschbaum, and D. Hellhammer (1991). Developmental and personality correlates of adrenocortical activity as indexed by salivary cortisol: observations in the age range of 35 to 65 years. *Journal of Psychosomatic Research*, 35(2–3), 173–185.

Breier, A., M. Albus, D. Pickar, T. Zahn, O. Wolkowitz, and S. Paul (1987). Controllable and uncontrollable stress in humans: alterations in mood and neuroendocrine and psychophysiological function. *American Journal of Psychiatry*, 144, 1419–1425.

Brown, D. E. (1981). General stress in anthropological research. *American Anthropologist*, 83, 74–91.

—— (1982) Physiological stress and culture change in a group of Filipino-Americans: a preliminary investigation. *Annals of Human Biology*, 9(6), 553–563.

——, G. D. James, and L. Nordloh (1998). Comparison of factors affecting daily variation of blood pressure in Filipino-American and Caucasian nurses in Hawaii. *American Journal of Human Biology*, 106, 373–383.

Burton, L. (1990). Teenage childbearing as an alternative life-course strategy in multigeneration black families. *Human Nature*, 1(2), 123–143.

Chisholm, J. (1993). Death, hope, and sex: life-history theory and the development of reproductive strategies. *Current Anthropology*, 34(1), 1–24.

—— (1999). *Death, hope, and sex: steps to an evolutionary ecology of mind and morality*. Cambridge: Cambridge University Press.

Christensen, A. J. and Smith, T. W. (1993). Cynical hostility and cardiovascular reactivity during self-disclosure. *Psychosomatic Medicine*, *55*, 193–202.

Coe, C. L. (1994) Psychosocial factors and immunity in nonhuman primates: a review. *Psychosomatic Medicine*, 55, 298–308.

——, S. Mendoza, and S. Levine (1979). Social status constrains the stress response in the squirrel monkey. *Physiology and Behavior*, 23, 633–641.

Cohen, S. (1994). Psychosocial influences on immunity and infectious disease in humans. In R. Glaser and J. K. Kiecolt-Glaser (eds), *Handbook of human stress and immunity* (pp. 301–319). San Diego: Academic Press.

——, J. R. Kaplan, J. E. Cunnick, S. B. Manuck, and B. S. Rabin (1992). Chronic social stress, affiliation, and cellular immune response in nonhuman primates. *Psychological Science*, 3(4), 301–304.

——, D. Tyrrell, and A. Smith (1993). Negative life events, perceived stress, negative affect, and susceptibility to the common cold. *Journal of Personality and Social Psychology*, 64(1), 131–140.

Cunnick, J. E., Sheldon Cohen, Bruce S. Rabin, A. Betts Carpenter, S. B. Manuck, and J. R. Kaplan (1991). Alterations in specific antibody production due to rank and social instability. *Brain, Behavior and Immunity*, 5, 357–369.

Cupps, T. and A. Fauci (1982). Corticosteroid-mediated immunoregulation in man. *Immunological Review*, 65, 133–155.

Dale, D., A. Fauci, and S. Wolff (1974). Alternate-day prednisone leucocyte kinetics and susceptibility to infections. *The New England Journal of Medicine*, 291, 1154–1158.

D'Andrade, R. G. (1992). Schemas and motivation. In R. D'Andrade and C. Strauss (eds), *Human motives and cultural models* (pp. 23–44). Cambridge: Cambridge University Press.

Decker, S. (1993) *Social networks, and daily patterns of cortisol and testosterone among adult males in a rural caribbean village*. Master's thesis, University of Missouri, Columbia.

—— (2000). Cortisol and social status among Dominican men. *Hormones and Behavior*, 38(1), 29–38.

Dressler, W. (1984). Hypertension and perceived stress. *Ethos*, 12(3), 265–283.

—— (1988) Social consistency and psychological distress. *Journal of Health and Social Behavior*, 29, 79–91.

—— (1991). *Stress and adaptation in the context of culture*. Albany, NY: State University of New York Press.

—— (1992). Culture, stress, and depressive symptoms: building and testing a model in a specific setting. In J. J. Poggie Jr, B. R. Dewalt, and W. W. Dressler (eds), *Anthropological research: process and application* (pp. 19–34). Albany, NY: State University of New York Press.

—— (1995). Modeling biocultural interactions: examples from studies of stress and cardiovascular disease. *Yearbook of Physical Anthropology*, 38, 27–56.

—— and Bindon, J. R. (2000). The health consequences of cultural consonance: cultural dimensions of lifestyle, social support, and arterial blood pressure in an African American community. *American Anthropologist*, 102(2), 244–260.

Durkheim, E. (1951). *Suicide: a study in sociology* (John A. Spaulding, trans.). Glencoe: The Free Press of Glencoe.

Falaschi, P., A. Martocchia, A. Proietti, R. Pastore, and R. D'Urso (1994). Immune system and the hypothalamus-pituitary-adrenal axis: common words for a single language. *Annals of the New York Academy of Sciences*, 741, 223–233.

Fauci, A. and D. Dale (1975). Alternate-day prednisone therapy and human lymphocyte subpopulations. *Journal of Clinical Investigations*, 55, 22–32.

Flinn, M. V. (1999). Family environment, stress, and health during childhood. In Catherin Panter-Brick and Carol M. Worthman (eds), *Hormones, health, and behavior*. Cambridge: Cambridge University Press.

——, S. A. Decker, and D. Tedeschi (1995). Male life histories, hormonal profiles, and reproductive strategies. In B. Campbell (ed.), paper presented at the *Annual Meeting of the American Association of Physical Anthropologists*, Oakland, CA: Wiley-Liss.

—— and B. G. England (1996). Childhood stress and family environment. *Current Anthropology*, 36, 854–866.

—— and —— (1997). The social economics of childhood glucocorticoid stress response and health. *American Journal of Physical Anthropology*, 102, 33–53.

——, R. J. Quinlan, S. A. Decker, M. T. Turner, and B. G. England (1996). Male-female differences in effects of parental absence on glucocorticoid stress response. *Human Nature*, 7, 125–162.

Gatti, G., R. Cavallo, M. Sartori, D. del Ponte, R. Masera, A. Salvadori, R. Carignola, and A. Angeli (1987). Inhibition by cortisol of human natural killer cell (NK) cell activity. *Journal of Steroid Biochemistry*, 26, 49–58.

Gillis, S., G. Crabtree, and K. Smith (1979). Glucocorticoid-induced inhibition of T cell growth factor production: I. The effect on mitogen-induced lymphocyte proliferation. *Journal of Immunology*, 123, 1624–1631.

Glaser, R., D. Pearl, J. Kiecolt-Glaser, and W. Malarkey (1994). Plasma cortisol levels and reactivation of latent Epstein-Barr virus in response to examination stress. *Psychoneuroendocrinology*, 19(8), 765–721.

Golub, M. (1979). Plasma cortisol levels and dominance in peer groups of rhesus monkey weanlings. *Hormones and Behavior*, 12, 50–59.

Gomes, P. (1985). Plantation dominance and rural dependency in Dominica. In P. Gomes (ed.), *Rural development in the Caribbean* (pp. 60–75). London: C. Hurst.

Gonzalez, N. L. S. (1969). *Black Carib household structure: a study of migration and modernization*. Seattle and London: University of Washington Press.

Gordon, D. and A. Nouri (1981). Comparison of the inhibition by glucocorticoids and cyclosporin A of mitogen-stimulated human lymphocyte proliferation. *Clinical and Experimental Immunology*, 44, 287.

Gottlieb, G. (1991). Experiential canalization of behavioral development: theory. *Developmental Psychology*, 27(1), 1–13.

Greenough, W. T., J. E. Black, and C. S. Wallace (1987). Experience and brain development. *Child Development*, 58, 539–559.

Herbert, T. B. and S. Cohen (1993). Stress and immunity in humans: a meta-analytic review. *Psychosomatic Medicine*, 55, 364–379.

Hunte, G. (1972). *The West Indian islands*. New York: Viking Press.

Jacobson, D. (1987). The cultural context of social support and support networks. *Medical Anthropology Quarterly*, 1, 42–67.

Jones, K., D. Copolov, and K. Outch (1986). Type A, test performance and salivary cortisol. *Journal of Psychosomatic Research*, 30, 699–707.

Karp, I. (1986) Agency and social theory: a review of Anthony Giddens. *American Ethnologist*, 13(1), 131–137.

—— and M. Kent (1983) Reading the Nuer. *Current Anthropology*, 24(4), 481–503.

Keverne, E. B. (1990). Primate social relationships: their determinants and consequences. *Advances in the Study of Behavior*, 21, 1–37.

Kiecolt-Glaser, J., J. Ricker, D. George, J. Messick, C. Speicher, C. Garner, and R. Glaser (1984). Urinary cortisol levels, cellular immunocompetency, and loneliness in psychiatric inpatients. *Psychosomatic Medicine*, 46, 15–23.

Kimzey, S. L. (1975). The effects of extended spaceflight on hematologic and immunologic systems. *Journal of the American Medical Women's Association*, 30, 218–232.

——, P. C. Johnson, S. E. Ritzman, and C. E. Mengel (1976). Hematology and immunology studies: the second manned Skylab mission. *Aviation, Space, and Environmental Medicine*, 47, 383–390.

Konner, M. (1972). Aspects of the developmental ethology of a foraging people. In N. Blurton-Jones (ed.), *Ethological Studies of Child Behavior* (pp. 285–304). Cambridge: Cambridge University Press.

—— (1982). *The tangled wing: biological constraints on the human spirit*. New York: Henry Holt.

Lee, R. B. (1979). *The !Kung San: men, women, and work in a foraging society*. Cambridge: Cambridge University Press.

LeVine, R. (1990). Enculturation: a biosocial perspective on the development of self. In D. Cicchetti and M. Beeghly (eds), *The self in transition: infancy to childhood* (pp. 99–117). Chicago: University of Chicago Press.

Lundberg, U., B. Rasch, and O. Westermark (1991). Physiological reactivity and Type A behavior in preschool children: a longitudinal study. *Behavioral Medicine*, 17(4), 149–157.

MacDonald, K. B. (1988). *Social and personality development: an evolutionary synthesis* (1st edn). New York: Plenum Press.

Manogue, K. (1975). Dominance status and adrenocortical reactivity to stress in squirrel monkeys (*Saimiri scuireus*). *Primates*, 16, 457–463.

Martin, E. (1994). *Flexible bodies: the role of immunity in American culture from the days of polio to the age of AIDS*. Boston: Beacon.

Meuleman, J. and P. Katz (1985). The immunologic effects, kinetics, and use of glucocorticosteroids. *Medical Clinics of North America*, 69, 805–816.

Miller, T. Q., T. W. Smith, C. W. Turner, M. L. Guijarro, and A. Hallet (1996). A meta-analytic review of research on hostility and physical health. *Psychological Bulletin*, 119(2), 322–348.

O'Leary, A. (1990). Stress, emotion, and human immune function. *Psychological Bulletin*, 108(3), 363–382.

Onsrud, M. and E. Thorsby (1981). Influence of *in vivo* hydrocortisone on some human blood lymphocyte populations: I. Effect on NK cell activity. *Scandinavian Journal of Immunology*, 13, 573–579.

Panter-Brick, C., C. M. Worthman, P. Lunn, R. Baker, and A. Todd (1996). Urban-rural and class differences in biological markers of stress among Nepali children. In *Annual Meeting of the Human Biology Council*, Durham, NC.

Pollard, T. M. (1995). Use of cortisol as a stress marker: practical and theoretical problems. *American Journal of Human Biology*, 7(2): 265–274.

Reid, J., R. Intrieri, E. Susman, and J. Beard (1992). The relationship of serum and salivary cortisol in a sample of healthy elderly. *Journal of Gerontology*, 47(3), 176–179.

Robins, L. N. (1994). Sociocultural trends affecting the prevalence of adolescent problems. In M. Rutter (ed.), *Psychosocial disturbances in young people*. Cambridge: University of Cambridge Press Syndicate.

Romney, A. K., S. C. Weller, and W. H. Batchelder (1986). Culture as consensus: a theory of culture and informant accuracy. *American Anthropologist*, 88: 313–338.

Rutter, M. (1994). Stress research: accomplishments and tasks ahead. In R. J. Haggerty, L. R. Sherrod, N. Gramezy, and M. Rutter (eds), *Stress, risk, and resilience in children and adolescents*. Cambridge: Cambridge University Press.

Sapolsky, R. M. (1982). The endocrine stress-response and social status in the wild baboon. *Hormones and Behavior*, 15, 279–285.

—— (1983a). Individual differences in cortisol secretory patterns in the wild baboon: role of negative-feedback sensitivity. *Endocrinology*, 113, 2263–2268.

—— (1983b). Endocrine aspects of social instability in the olive baboon. *American Journal of Primatology*, 5, 365–372.

—— (1986). Endocrine and behavioral correlates of drought in the wild baboon. *American Journal of Primatology*, 11, 217–224.

—— (1989). Hypercortisolism among socially subordinate wild baboons originates at the CNS level. *Archives of General Psychiatry*, 46, 1047–1052.

—— (1990). Adrenocortical function, social rank, and personality among wild baboons. *Biological Psychiatry*, 28, 862–878.

—— (1996). Stress, glucocorticoids, and damage to the nervous system: the current state of confusion. *Stress*, 1, 1–19.

—— and G. E. Mott (1987). Social subordinance in a wild primate is associated with suppressed HDL-cholesterol concentrations. *Endocrinology*, 121, 1605–1610.

—— and P. M. Plotsky (1990). Hypercortisolism and its possible neural bases. *Biological Psychiatry*, 27, 937–952.

Schleifer, S., S. E. Keller, A. T. Meyerson, M. Raskin, K. Davis, and M. Stein (1984). Lymphocyte function in major depressive disorder. *Archives of General Psychiatry*, 41, 484–486.

Seeman, T. E. and B. S. McEwen (1996). Impact of social environment characteristics on neuroendocrine regulation. *Psychosomatic Medicine*, 58, 459–471.

Shinkai, S., S. Watanabe, Y. Kurokawa, and J. Torii (1993). Salivary cortisol for monitoring circadian rhythm variation in adrenal activity during shiftwork. *Archives of Occupational and Environmental Health*, 64, 499–502.

Shostak, M. (1983). *Nisa: the life and words of a !Kung woman*. New York: Vintage Books.

Smith, R. T. (1988). *Kinship and class in the West Indies: a genealogical study of Jamaica and Guyana*. Cambridge: Cambridge University Press.

Smith, T. W. (1992). Hostility and health: current status of a psychosomatic hypothesis. *Health Psychology*, 11, 139–150.

—— and K. D. Allred (1989). Blood pressure responses during social interaction in high- and low-cynically hostile males. *Journal of Behavioral Medicine*, 12, 135–143.

Spangler, G. (1995). School performance, Type A behavior and adrenocortical activity in primary school children. *Anxiety, Stress, and Coping*, 8, 299–310.

Spradley. J. P. and Phillips, M. (1972). Culture and stress: a quantitative analysis. *American Anthropologist, 74*, 518–529.

Tooby, J. and L. Cosmides (1989). Evolutionary psychology and the generation of culture, Part I. *Ethology and Sociobiology*, 10, 29–49.

—— and —— (1990). On the universality of human nature and the uniqueness of the individual: the role of genetics and adaptation. *Journal of Personality*, 58(1), 17–26.

—— and —— (1992). The psychological foundations of culture. In J. Barkow, L. Cosmides, and J. Tooby (eds), *The adapted mind*. Oxford: Oxford University Press.

Trouillot, M.-R. (1988). *Peasants and capital: Dominica in the world economy*. Baltimore and London: The Johns Hopkins University Press.

Ursin, H. (1994). Stress, distress, and immunity. *Annals of the New York Academy of Sciences*, 741, 204–211.

Valsiner, J. (1989). *Child development in cultural context*. Toronto: Hogrefe and Huber Publishers.

Wallace, A. (1970). *Culture and personality* (2nd edn). New York: Random House.

Weidenfeld, S., A. O'Leary, A. Bandura, S. Brown, S. Levine, and K. Raska (1990). Impact of perceived self-efficacy in coping with stressors on components of the immune system. *Journal of Personality and Social Psychology*, 59, 1082–1094.

Willis, P. (1977). *Learning to labor: how working class kids get working class jobs*. New York: Columbia University Press.

Chapter 8: Editor's note

McDade's chapter breaks new ground in supplying hard PNI data from a non-Western society. Indeed his study indicates that "PNI research based in western populations cannot simply be replicated in new populations around the world. Rather, it must consider the unique ethnographic and ecological contexts that may shape stress-immune function relationships in unexpected ways." It raises the possibility that "social support" or high levels of involvement in, and dependence on, social networks do not (by buffering stress) bear a linear relationship to health measures such as EBV antibody titer. It thus contributes to rethinking the relationship between health and fundamental social and cultural realities in which persons live, and through which, the experience of stress is mediated.

Life event stress and immune function in Samoan adolescents

Toward a cross-cultural psychoneuroimmunology

Thomas W. McDade[1]

Introduction

Life events research represents a major behavioral science paradigm for investigating the relationship between psychosocial stress and health, and has consistently reported significant – though relatively small – correlations with multiple physical and psychological health outcomes (Johnson 1986). Complementing the life events paradigm is a parallel emphasis on the role of social support in mitigating stress, where low social support has been associated with a two- to three-fold increased risk of death, an effect that is comparable to other health risk factors, including smoking, obesity, and physical activity (House *et al.* 1988).

Psychoneuroimmunology (PNI) has employed a number of enumerative and functional measures of immunity in an attempt to quantify the physiological effects of psychosocial stress and social relationships in humans (Schleifer *et al.* 1986, Glaser and Kiecolt-Glaser 1994, Uchino *et al.* 1996). Psychosocial stress has been significantly associated with decreased numbers of T, B, and NK cells, suppressed lymphocyte proliferation and cytotoxic activity, lower levels of secretory IgA and IgM, as well as elevated levels of herpesvirus antibodies (indicating suppressed cell-mediated immune function) (Herbert and Cohen 1993).

Some of the earliest PNI work investigated changes in immune function surrounding bereavement, and found consistent impairments in immune function following the loss of a loved one (Irwin *et al.* 1987). Immune suppression has also been associated with other negative life events, including divorce (Kiecolt-Glaser *et al.* 1994), caring for a loved one with Alzheimer's disease (Kiecolt-Glaser *et al.* 1996), natural disasters (Ironson *et al.* 1997, Solomon *et al.* 1997), and medical school exams (Glaser *et al.* 1985, Glaser *et al.* 1994). A number of these studies also show stress-buffering effects of social support.

Psychoneuroimmunology has been critical in demonstrating the relevance of psychosocial experience to human immunity, but a shortcoming of current research is the fact that the vast majority of studies include only opportunistic, homogeneous, Western middle-class samples.[2] In part this reflects a limitation of currently available methods for assessing immune function that require blood collection via venipuncture and prompt access to laboratory facilities for the processing and analysis of samples.

It also reflects the fact that the nature of the stressor and the quality of the individual's psychosocial experience are not of fundamental interest to most psychoneuroimmunologists. Rather, a stressor is a means to investigate the mechanisms and health consequences of stress in general. Although PNI may in many ways be considered an integrative discipline (Ader 1999), from an anthropological perspective it is constrained by its emphasis on mechanisms and laboratory models, and resists interpretive discussions of human psychosocial experience that are situated in diverse ethnographic contexts (Lyon 1993). Previous work in PNI linking human physiology and psychosocial stress has built a solid foundation upon which such an anthropological perspective can be built.

This study attempts to expand the range of current PNI research through an analysis of life events, social relationships, and immune function in Samoan adolescents. Samoa was selected due to its high rates of adolescent suicide – suggesting an exceptionally high level of adolescent distress – and due to its low rates of malnutrition and endemic disease, two factors that may obscure stress-immune function relationships. By bringing an anthropological perspective to PNI and to the notion of "social support," this study recognizes that the experience of life event stress is locally constructed and given meaning within a unique Samoan cultural context (Young 1980, O'Neil 1986). Nevertheless, this experience has measurable physiological consequences. The tools of PNI are used to assess the immunological effects of life event stress, and to provide insight into the experience of stress for adolescents in Samoa. Just as importantly, the tools of anthropology are used to explore the complex meanings of local stressors and social relationships. It is hoped that this study will lay the groundwork for future cross-cultural, anthropologically informed PNI research.

Ethnographic context: Samoa[3]

The Independent State of Samoa is a sovereign Polynesian nation, composed of a chain of islands in the South Pacific. The islands are mountainous and lush, and currently support over 160,000 people in three primary geographic areas: the urban capital of Apia, where economic development has created extensive commercial activity and opportunities for wage labor; rural Upolu, composed of coastal villages outside of Apia, but with relatively easy access to its commercial and educational opportunities; and the island of Savai'i, where people live in small villages and engage primarily in cultivation of family-owned lands. Despite strong colonial and post-colonial encroachments, Samoans have managed to maintain a strong cultural identity, and

Plate 8.1 Drinking kava on the island of Savai'i.

Samoa is recognized as one of the most conservative remaining Polynesian societies (Holmes 1980, O'Meara 1990). People take pride in the *fa'aSamoa* (Samoan way of life), and the *'aiga* (extended family) continues to play a fundamental role in everyday life.

Samoans are currently experiencing an unprecedented period of cultural diversification: non-traditional legal, political, and economic institutions continue to encroach, and Western consumer goods and services are increasingly available and desired. These changes appear to be having a disproportionate impact on the youth of Samoa: the number of suicides increased steadily from 1970 through the early 1980s, and the most recent figures report that Samoan males between the ages of 15 and 24 are committing suicide at a rate of over two per 1,000, nearly four times the rate in American males of the same age (Bowles 1985).

Although the effects of life events on immune function have yet to be evaluated in Samoa, Howard (1986) has explored the local meanings of various life events in a survey of American Samoan adults. The following events were reported to elicit an "extremely strong" reaction – death of a child, spouse, close relative, or close friend; birth of a child or miscarriage; serious illness of a relative, marriage, argument with a relative, or having a child leave home. When compared to similar rankings provided by a group of Mexican-Americans, the Samoan rankings appear to reflect a fundamental concern with social relationships (Howard 1986). For example, "serious illness of relative" is ranked 8, while personal illness is ranked much lower at 16. Similarly, Samoans rank "marriage" higher than "divorce," suggesting concern over the new set of social obligations that follow marriage, while divorce frees one from these obligations.

In addition to events such as these, the practice of *faalavelave* was hypothesized in this study to be a significant life event that may be a source of stress. *Faalavelave* is a system of public, formalized gift exchange associated with community events such as weddings, funerals, and building dedications (O'Meara 1990). Through gifts of food, money, and weaved mats, the host family and their guests attempt to demonstrate their wealth and generosity, and to bolster their social and political position within the community. Careful attention is paid to the size and type of gifts exchanged, and host families draw upon the resources of their extended kin networks to fulfill their obligations. Increasingly, *faalavelave* is forcing families to incur large financial and social debts. One mother from Apia discussed the current state of *faalavelave*:

> Traditional gift giving during times of mourning such as funerals used to be something beautiful. People donated food, money, and fine mats in the true spirit of giving – without weighing up if they will lose or gain in this. Nowadays, it is like a business deal. Many donate so much because of their sense of pride in their social status. But they then expect to get just as much or even more from the grieving family. Before *faalavelave* used to provide real financial support for the family. Nowadays, many families run into big debts after the *faalavelave*.

In addition to life events, previous work has highlighted the complex and conflicted nature of social relationships in Samoa. In western industrialized societies, social involvement or integration of any degree is often assumed to represent social "support." However, in cultures with extended kin-based networks of interaction and exchange, social relationships can entail considerable expectation and obligation (Janes 1990). This is the case for Samoans at home and overseas, where kin networks are a critical source of material, social, and emotional support, but they also demand contributions to the household economy, attendance at family ceremonies, respect for the authority of elders, and maintenance of the family's status within the community (Janes and Pawson 1986, O'Meara 1990, Hanna and Fitzgerald 1993). For these reasons, social relationships have been cited as a significant source of stress for Samoans (Graves and Graves 1985).

It is hypothesized that locally meaningful life events will be associated with suppressed immune function in Samoan adolescents. In addition, socio-economic status is considered as a moderator of life event stress, since the life events considered here often entail considerable financial costs. Social relationships are also considered as a potential moderator of life event stress, but it is not assumed that they will buffer individuals from its negative physiological impact.

Methods

Data collection

Participants for this study were recruited from 14 villages across the three main geographic regions of Samoa. Overall, 295 individuals between the ages of 10 and 20 years provided data for these analyses, with comparable age and sex distributions in each of the three regions (Table 8.1). The study was conducted under conditions of informed consent, as approved by the Emory University Human Investigations Committee and the Western Samoa Health Research Council.

Demographic and psychosocial information was collected in interviews, and standard anthropometric measurements were taken. Dried spots of whole blood were collected for later analysis of immune function. A sterile disposable lancet was applied to the participant's finger and 2–5 drops were placed directly on standardized filter paper (#903 Schleicher and Schull, Keene, NH). This relatively non-invasive blood collection protocol minimizes pain and inconvenience to the participants, and facilitates the collection of large numbers of blood samples despite the constraints of field conditions. Samples were allowed to dry, and then stored refrigerated prior to shipment to the laboratory in the US, where they were frozen at $-23°C$ until analysis.

Analysis of immune function

Building on previous PNI research, antibodies against the Epstein-Barr virus (EBV) were used as a marker of cell-mediated immune function. Details of the logic and physiology behind this method are presented elsewhere (Glaser et al. 1991, Glaser et al. 1993, McDade et al. 2000a). Briefly, EBV is a ubiquitous herpesvirus to which 98.8 percent of Samoans under the age of 20 have been exposed (McDade et al 2000b), and adequate cell-mediated immune function is critical for maintaining the virus in a latent state. Stress-induced immunosuppression allows EBV to reactivate and release viral antigens into circulation, to which a humoral antibody response may emerge (Glaser *et al.* 1991). As a result, levels of antibodies against EBV antigens provide an indirect measure of cell-mediated immune function, such that increased EBV antibody levels indicate lower immunity.

This model may seem counterintuitive at first, as an *increase* in EBV anti-body level – itself an aspect of immune function – is interpreted as indicating a *decrease* in cell-mediated immune performance. However, it is important to keep in mind that the immune system is comprised of multiple integrated subsystems that play complementary roles in protecting the body against pathogens. With respect to viruses such as EBV, cell-mediated immunity represents the first, and most important, line of defense. Humoral-mediated immunity involving the production of antibodies represents a second line of defense that kicks in when cell-mediated processes fail to control the virus. Therefore, increases in specific antibody levels can indicate a relative failure on the part of cell-mediated immunity.

Following this logic, previous work has linked increases in EBV antibody levels to stress associated with negative life events (McDade *et al.* 2000a), medical school exams (Glaser *et al.* 1987, Glaser *et al.* 1993), involvement in a poor quality marriage (Kiecolt-Glaser *et al.* 1987a, Kiecolt-Glaser *et al.* 1988), and caring for a family member with Alzheimer's disease (Kiecolt-Glaser *et al.* 1987b). In addition, loneliness, defensiveness, and anxiety have all been positively associated with EBV antibodies (Glaser *et al.* 1985, Esterling *et al.* 1993). Conversely, stress management interventions and disclosure of previously repressed trauma are associated with decreases in EBV antibody levels (Esterling *et al.* 1992, Lutgendorf *et al.* 1994; compare chapters by Booth and Davison, Mann, and Pennebaker, this volume). These studies validate the EBV model as an indirect measure of stress-induced cell-mediated immune suppression such that higher stress burdens are reflected in higher levels of EBV antibodies. Samples were analyzed using a previously developed ELISA method for assaying anti-viral capsid antigen EBV antibodies in dried blood spots (McDade *et al.* 2000a).

Since the model linking stress to suppressed cell-mediated immune function and increased EBV antibody level does not apply to individuals who have not been exposed to EBV, analyses must be limited to seropositive individuals. Previous comparison of matched plasma and blood spot samples for seronegative and seropositive individuals established a blood spot seropositivity cut-off value of 20 ELISA units (McDade *et al.* 2000a). Individuals with EBV antibody levels below this value were assumed to be seronegative for EBV, and were excluded from analysis.

Poor nutrition and current infection can potentially confound the effects of psychosocial stress on immune function (Kiecolt-Glaser and Glaser 1988). This poses a challenge to PNI research in developing countries where food shortages and endemic disease may be unfortunate realities. However, previous analysis of this dataset has shown that Samoans under the age of 20 years are well-nourished, and no significant relationships were found between EBV antibody level and multiple markers of nutritional status (McDade *et al.* 2000b). To verify this finding in the sample of adolescents used in this study, body mass index (BMI = weight in kg/height in meters^2) and sum of skin-folds (SSF = triceps skinfold (mm) + subscapular skinfold (mm)) measures were considered. These measures are used as global markers of nutritional status, although it is recognized that intake of specific micro- and macro-nutrients can have important implications for immune function (Gershwin *et al.* 2000).

Blood spot samples were also used to measure levels of C-reactive protein (CRP). This acute phase protein provides the body's first line of defense against infection: trace amounts of CRP are normally undetectable in circulation, but concentrations increase by a factor of 100 to 1,000 during the 24 to 72 hours following an injury or infectious challenge (Fleck 1989, Baumann and Gauldie 1994). CRP has been shown to increase in response to a wide range of viral, bacterial, and parasitic agents, making it a potentially useful marker of pathogen exposure and infection status. Samples were analyzed for CRP using a previously developed ELISA blood spot method (McDade *et al.* 2000b).

Based on previous work in this population (McDade *et al.* 2000b), a CRP level greater than or equal to 5 mg/L was used as a cut-off value to identify individuals with a current or recent infection. Participants with elevated CRP were removed from the sample prior to analysis to minimize the possibility of confounding. This is a conservative step that biases results toward the null, as individuals with current infection may be the same individuals who are suffering from the infectious consequences of stress-induced immunosuppression.

Scale construction and statistical analysis

A summary life events variable was constructed from responses to questions regarding the occurrence of the following events over the year preceding the interview: death of a family member or close friend; serious illness in the family; hospitalization of a family member; and the number of *faalavelave* hosted by the family (0 = none, 1 = one, 2 = two or more). These events were chosen based on previous analysis of the importance of such events in Samoa (Howard 1986). Number of *faalavelave* was included as a potentially stressful life event based on the observation in 29 in-depth, semi-structured interviews that *faalavelave* can be a significant drain on a family's economic as well as social resources.

Each household's position with respect to socioeconomic status was summarized by the occupational rank of the father and mother as follows:

1 = planter/housewife (no cash income); 2 = unskilled wage labor (domestic help, factory work, security, etc.) 3 = skilled labor/professional (teacher, government employee, engineer, etc.). In addition, adolescents were asked if their family received remittances from relatives working overseas, as this has become an important source of income. Scores on this item were assigned as follows: 0 = no remittances; 1 = money regularly received from one family member; 2 = 2 family members; 3 = 3 or more family members. A summary score of household socioeconomic status was obtained by adding remittances, mother's occupational rank, and father's occupational rank.

Two aspects of social relationships were considered: social orientation, and satisfaction with social relationships. Participants were asked upon whom they rely when given a task, or when in need of help. Answers were coded as 1 for self, 2 for others (family and/or friends), and summed to provide a measure of social orientation. Higher scores indicate a more pro-social orientation, while lower scores indicate a preference of self-reliance.[4] To assess satisfaction with social relationships, individuals were asked to rate on a 3-point scale their happiness with their family and their friends (0 = not happy; 1 = happy; 2 = very happy). Responses were summed, with higher scores representing higher reported relationship satisfaction.

Analyses were conducted using Statistical Analysis Software (SAS Institute, Release 6.12, Cary, NC). Prior to analysis, EBV antibody levels were log-transformed to normalize the distribution. Age was broken down into three groups (10–12, 13–15, 16–20 years) and entered as a categorical variable due to its non-linear association with EBV antibody level. Number of life events was entered into general linear models as a main effect (the independent variable of primary interest), and in interaction with age, sex, and region, with EBV antibody as the dependent variable. In addition, the potentially moderating roles of socioeconomic status and social relationships were evaluated in interaction with life events.

Table 8.1 Distribution of participants across region, as well as mean (standard deviation) values of selected variables

	Total sample	Apia	Rural Upolu	Savai'i
N	278	91	128	59
Sex (% female)	55.8	57.1	57.0	50.8
Age (years)	14.0 (3.0)	13.7 (2.9)	14.3 (2.9)	13.6 (3.4)
BMI (kg/m²)	20.9 (3.9)	20.7 (3.8)	21.3 (3.9)	20.3 (3.9)
SSF¹ (mm)	23.3 (11.0)	23.0 (10.8)	24.0 (11.9)	22.5 (9.0)
Number of life events	1.9 (1.3)	2.1 (1.7)	1.7 (1.0)	1.9 (1.1)
EBV antibody level (ELISA units)²	102.3 (71.2)	117.3 (78.0)	102.1 (66.5)	79.5 (64.5)

¹ SSF = sum of skinfolds (triceps skinfold + subscapular skinfold)
² ELISA = enzyme-linked immunoabsorbent assay

Results

Life events, socioeconomic status, and social orientation

Table 8.1 displays the distribution of participants across the three regions of Samoa, as well as mean scores for BMI, total skin folds, life events, and EBV antibody level. Samoan adolescents in this study reported on average 1.9 life events in the year preceding interview. Slightly more life events were reported for Apia than Upolu or Savai'i, largely due to the higher frequency of *faalavelave*. Of the 295 10- to 20-year-olds, two were not seropositive for EBV, and 15 showed evidence of current or recent infection (CRP ⩾ 5 mg/L). These 17 individuals were removed from subsequent analyses. Neither BMI (Pearson $r = -0.019$, $p = 0.75$) nor SSF ($r = -0.012$, $p = 0.84$) was significantly related to EBV antibody level, consistent with previous analyses from this population indicating no effect of nutritional status on immune function due to low rates of undernutrition (McDade *et al.* 2000b).

When number of life events was added to a linear regression model including age, sex, and region, no significant effect of events on EBV antibody level was found ($F_{1,275} = 0.49$; $p = 0.49$). Interaction terms for life events with age, sex, and region did not approach significance. However, when socioeconomic status was added to the model, a significant life events × SES interaction emerged ($F_{1,275} = 5.66$; $p = 0.018$), and the main effect of life events reached significance ($F_{1,275} = 4.12$; $p = 0.043$). As expected, the association between life events and EBV antibody level was positive ($\beta = 0.082$, SE = 0.040), such that individuals with more life events had elevated antibody levels, indicating reduced cell-mediated immunity. The interaction between life events and SES is presented in Figure 8.1. For low SES individuals, there was a positive association between life events and EBV antibodies, while a negative association was found for high SES individuals.

The effect of specific types of life events was explored by breaking the life events variable down into its constituents. With the exception of family illness, each life events variable (death, hospitalization, *faalavelave*) reached or approached statistical significance in predicting EBV antibody levels. In each case, the pattern was the same as the summary life events measure: there was a positive main effect of events on EBV antibodies, and a significant interaction with SES such that a positive effect was found with low SES, and a negative effect with high SES. These results indicate that death of a friend or family member, hospitalization of a family member, or the pressures associated with *faalavelave* are significant stressors for adolescents in low SES families.[5]

In order to investigate the potential role of social relationships in moderating the effects of stress, life events were included in general linear models with variables representing social orientation and satisfaction with social relationships. A significant interaction between life events and social

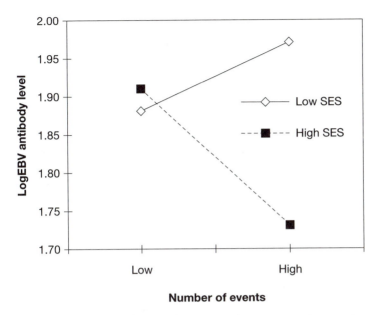

Figure 8.1 Interaction between life events and socioeconomic status in predicting EBV antibody level. Higher antibody levels indicate lower cell-mediated immune function.

relationships was taken as evidence for a moderating role. No such role was found for satisfaction with social relationships: neither the main effect ($F_{1,257}$ = 0.08, p = 0.78) nor the interaction with life events ($F_{1,257}$ = 0.46, p = 0.50) approached significance.

However, the effect of life events was found to differ significantly according to social orientation ($F_{1,259}$ = 4.54, p = 0.034). For individuals with a more pro-social orientation, there was a strong positive relationship between life events and EBV antibody levels. A negative relationship was found for more self-reliant adolescents. The interaction between social orientation and life events is presented in Figure 8.2. When the specific types of life events (death, family member sick, hospitalization, *faalavelave*) were considered separately in interaction with social orientation, the same general pattern of findings emerged such that these events were particularly stressful for socially-reliant adolescents, but not self-reliant adolescents.

Lastly, life events, SES, and social orientation were included in a single model to confirm the pattern of relationships discovered above (Table 8.2). The interaction between life events and SES, and between life events and social orientation, remained significant after controlling for age, sex, and region, while the main effect of life events lost significance. Regional differences in

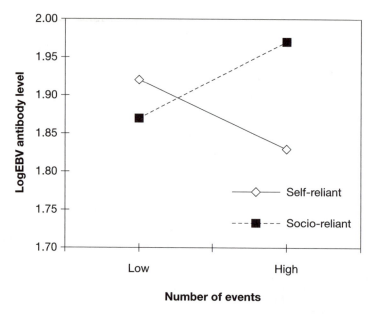

Figure 8.2 Interaction between life events and social orientation in predicting EBV antibody level.

Table 8.2 Linear model results indicating the effects of life events, SES, and social orientation on log-transformed EBV antibody levels

	DF	MS	F	P value
Model	10	0.363	3.94	0.0001
Age group	2	0.399	4.33	0.014
Sex	1	0.266	2.89	0.090
Region	2	0.534	5.81	0.003
Life events	1	0.014	0.15	0.70
Social orientation	1	0.199	2.16	0.14
SES	1	0.038	0.41	0.52
Life events × social orientation	1	0.415	4.51	0.035
Life events × SES	1	0.539	5.85	0.016

Model R^2 = 0.13

EBV antibody level have been discussed previously in terms of differential levels of exposure to non-traditional ways of life (McDade *et al.* 2000b), and the significant effect of age is due to elevated antibody levels in 13–15 year olds. Overall, these results demonstrate a significant effect of life events on EBV antibodies. In particular, low SES, socio-reliant individuals with a high number of life events have the highest EBV antibody levels, indicating the lowest level of cell-mediated immune function.[6]

Discussion

In this sample of 10- to 20-year olds from Samoa, life events are significantly related to immune function, as measured by antibodies against EBV. But life event stress is not universally experienced: SES and social orientation are important moderators of the stress–immune function relationship in this population. In particular, there is a positive association between life events and EBV antibodies in individuals from low SES households, and a negative association in high SES households. Further, social orientation also interacts with life events: with a high number of life events, socio-reliant individuals have significantly higher EBV antibody levels than self-reliant individuals.

These findings are consistent with previous research linking life events to increased EBV antibody levels in Western adolescents (McDade *et al.* 2000a) and adults (Kiecolt-Glaser and Glaser 1991, Herbert and Cohen 1993, Kiecolt-Glaser *et al.* 1993). In children, adverse life events have previously been associated with reduced NK cell activity (Birmaher *et al.* 1994), while parental separation or divorce has been correlated with reduced bacterial lysis (Bartlett *et al.* 1997).[7]

The interaction between life events and SES may reflect stress associated with financial obligations that accompany these events in Samoa. In particular, SES may provide a measure of a household's financial ability to meet the social expectations associated with life events such as *faalavelave*, where visiting members of the community and distant family may expect to be housed, fed, and honored with a gift. With low economic resources, a family may have difficulty affording the high costs associated with these events, and may be forced to draw on the resources of extended kin networks in order to maintain its status within the community. The economic and social debts that follow are likely to make these experiences more stressful for all members of the household.

Conversely, families with high SES have sufficient resources to cover these costs, and may even enjoy an opportunity to elevate their status within the community through culturally appropriate demonstrations of wealth and generosity. The importance of SES for moderating the experience of *faalavelave* is underscored by the large difference in EBV antibody level between individuals from high versus low SES families experiencing one or more *faalavelave*: the mean untransformed EBV antibody level for low SES individuals is 83.2 ELISA units, compared to 56.2 ELISA units for high SES individuals, a 48 percent difference.

Previous life events research in Western cultural contexts has emphasized the protective role of social relationships in buffering individuals from psychosocial stress. Obviously, the positive association between life events and EBV antibody levels in socio-reliant individuals runs counter to that model. For adolescents in Samoa, it appears as though *self*-reliant individuals are the ones who are buffered from life event stress, not those with a more pro-social orientation as might be expected.

Samoan ethnography consistently emphasizes the obligations of extended kin networks, and the financial, psychological, and social burdens they can impose (Shore 1982, Janes 1990, O'Meara 1990). In this study, social orientation may provide a measure of an individual's integration into such networks of obligation. A more pro-social orientation suggests greater integration and interdependence, while a more self-reliant orientation might lighten some of the burdens associated with such integration. It should be remembered that this study deals with adolescents – not heads of households – who are in relatively subordinate positions within the family. As such, the stress associated with a life event is likely to be shared by the family, and transduced to the individual through the actions and attitudes of parents, or the position of the family within the community. If this is the case, then perhaps socio-reliant adolescents are more "tuned in" to household and community dynamics, and are therefore more likely to share the stress associated with a life event. Self-reliant individuals, in contrast, may be relatively buffered from life event stress by "tuning out."[8] A similar pattern of results was found in this population in response to stress associated with lifestyle incongruity (McDade 2001).

The findings linking social orientation and SES to the experience of life event stress triangulate on the following point: social relationships in Samoa can be a burden, as well as a buffer. Most psychological and epidemiological approaches to stress and social relationships are embedded in Western industrial cultural contexts where individualism and independence are valued, and high degrees of relative isolation are assumed. Therefore, any degree of social involvement has historically been positively valenced as social "support."[9]

However, Samoans live in a qualitatively different social milieu, where socialization erodes a sense of subjective self, and emphasizes one's identification with, and dependence upon, the community (Shore 1982, Mageo 1988, 1989). Indeed, obligations to kin and community have been linked to reports of health problems in Samoan migrants to New Zealand (Graves and Graves 1985), and to increased blood pressure in Samoan migrants to California after controlling for changes in diet and activity (Janes 1990). It is likely that Samoans would perceive the lives of even the most socially integrated Westerners as relatively alienated.[10]

This study has found evidence for a significant effect of life events on immune function in Samoan adolescents, but this effect emerges in a social and cultural environment that is qualitatively different from that considered in previous PNI research. This underscores the point that PNI research based in Western populations cannot simply be replicated in new populations around the world. Rather, it must consider the unique ethnographic and ecological contexts that may shape stress–immune function relationships in unexpected ways.[11]

Future directions: toward a cross-cultural psychoneuroimmunology

Stress is an important area of research for behavioral and physiological scientists, and an issue of central concern to all subfields of anthropology. In particular, biological anthropologists have systematically investigated the health effects of bioecological stressors such as malnutrition, poverty, seasonality, disease, and high altitude, while others have focused exclusively on psychosocial stress, looking specifically at the endocrine or cardiovascular correlates of stress in an attempt to identify locally relevant stressors, and to illuminate the quality of individual psychosocial environments in a range of cultural and ecological conditions.

As such, it seems as though PNI and anthropology have much to gain from one another. Psychoneuroimmunology has demonstrated that stress resulting from the loss of a loved one, from loneliness or abrasive social relationships, or from the uncertainty following a disaster, suppresses multiple parameters of immune function in Western, middle class populations. Are these not universal human experiences? Is there reason to believe that similar events would not suppress immune function cross-culturally? Indeed, this study shows that life events are associated with suppressed cell-mediated immune function in Samoan adolescents, but in a manner and for reasons that are unique to the Samoan cultural context.

As this study has demonstrated, anthropology can benefit from the incorporation of PNI tools for measuring stress. These methods complement those currently employed by biological anthropologists (e.g. self-reports of morbidity, blood pressure, cortisol, catecholamines) which are subject to a number of limitations. They may provide an additional biomarker of stress that can actually serve as an ethnographic tool that assays the quality of individual psychosocial environments, and identifies vulnerable individuals. In addition, immunological measures of stress provide direct links to risk for infectious disease, a health issue of considerable importance in many anthropological populations, especially among children.

In turn, anthropology can expand current PNI models to explore the contextual and constitutional variables that define the relationships between stress and immune function around the world. With an emphasis on human variation and cultural diversity, anthropology can build on PNI's solid mechanistic foundation and introduce naturalistic models of stress located within meaningful sociocultural and human ecological contexts.

In addition, while methodological constraints have limited most psychoneuroimmunologists to clinic or lab-based studies of opportunistic Western samples, the field expertise of biological anthropology can move PNI research into new cultural and ecological settings. In particular, the development of "field-friendly" blood spot methods for assessing immune function opens up the possibility of future studies in a range of populations around the world (McDade *et al.* 2000a). Blood spot assays for EBV antibodies and C-reactive protein provide a starting point, and future work should consider a range of additional immune markers.

Research in Samoa represents a solid first step in promoting cross-cultural studies of stress and immune function. The potentially confounding effects of undernutrition and infection were minimized in this relatively healthy population, and significant associations between life events and immune function were revealed in a cultural context that is radically different from our own.

Future work should move beyond life events to consider additional stressors that may be associated with suppressed immune function. For example, the concept of lifestyle incongruity (inconsistency between socioeconomic status and material style of life) has been linked to elevated blood pressure in diverse cultures around the world (Dressler 1990, 1995, Decker, this volume), but its impact on immune function has only recently been considered (McDade 2001). As PNI research is taken to new locations, it must be grounded in an ethnographic understanding of the tensions, issues, and processes that may be sources of stress in a given cultural context.

In addition to considering new stress models, future cross-cultural PNI research will be forced to address the following question: how do psychosocial stressors interface with ecological stressors in modulating immune function? That is, to what extent do the stress–immune function relationships documented in Western populations (and in Samoa) manifest under conditions of malnutrition or high pathogen load? Up to this point, these nuisance factors have been controlled for by limiting research to healthy individuals. Do malnutrition and infection obscure the effects of psychosocial stress, or are their effects additive? Integrative, field-based studies of stress and immune function will be necessary to address this and other questions. It is hoped that this study will facilitate that work.

Notes

1 Correspondence: Northwestern University, Department of Anthropology, 1810 Hinman Ave., Evanston, IL 60208-1310.
2 *Ed. Nor have psychoneuroimmunologists or health psychologists addressed the cultural variability of what constitutes social support.*

3 This study was conducted in the islands formerly known as "The Independent State of Western Samoa." In 1997 Parliament voted to drop "Western" and officially change the country's name to "The Independent State of Samoa."

4 *Ed. Future ethnographic research in Samoa should investigate the empirical correlates of this attitudinal phenomenon. Are such self-reliant people excused from upholding their part of reciprocal obligations? Do they get (but not give) support at, e.g. funerals? Do they receive psychosocial but not economic support, and is there a local discourse recognizing the difference (which would entail a sign of modernity, separating material from psychological dimensions of relationship)? Do they psychologize the nature of "support," a form of modernization (Giddens 1991)?*

5 It may seem counterintuitive to posit that *faalavelave* and deaths are related to stress in a similar manner, and that a death in the family could be associated with lower EBV antibody level in high SES individuals. However, the reader should keep in mind that there were relatively few individuals with deaths in the family, and that such events are typically followed by *faalavelave*; hence this result should not be overinterpreted.

6 *Ed. Self-reliant individuals are culturally deviant or dissonant vis-à-vis Samoan norms. Dressler's model (Dressler and Bindon 2000) shows that such individuals with low cultural consonance have higher levels of stress. This would lead to a prediction that they would have higher EBV antibody levels; this prediction was not confirmed in this study. However, Dressler's model is not at all interchangeable with the life events model here, and the explanation the author offers.*

7 *Ed. The possibility that such traumatic events have long-term effects such as essential hypertension are explored by Mann, this volume.*

8 Interview responses from adolescents regarding their attitudes toward *faalavelave* indicate a general consensus that it is an expensive and burdensome practice.

9 There are a number of recent exceptions to this trend, where the potentially negative health implications of social relationships have been explicitly considered in Western contexts (e.g. Rook 1997, Cohen *et al.* 1998 Berkman *et al.* 2000).

10 The results reported herein emphasize the contingent nature of the relationship between life events and social orientation. Social orientation alone is not related to EBV, but when the interaction with life events is considered, a significant effect emerges. Initially, based on my reading of the Samoan literature and studies by others, I had predicted that self-reliant individuals would have higher EBV levels than socio-reliant individuals, and that this difference would be exacerbated by life event stress. However, this was not the case. The finding challenges such preconceptions, and forces us to reconsider the cultural context within which these relationships emerge.

Ed. The most recent publication of Dressler (Dressler and Bindon 2000) indicates a remarkably similar – nonlinear – correlation between stressors (in McDade's case, life events) and a measure of health (hypertension for Dressler, EBV for McDade), one conditioned in both cases by relation to support networks. "The nonlinear association between cultural consonance in lifestyle and blood pressure is evident only under conditions of low reported kin support" (Dressler and Bindon 2000: 255). Dressler's argument – that researchers must take into account status (defined in the African-American community he studied in terms of ownership of basic comfort items and participation in church), consonance with cultural values in relation to maintaining social support networks, stress and health measures in a single model – is congruent with McDade's argument. Both address the nonlinearity of relations sometimes taken to be linear in the PNI literature.

11 *Ed. I believe that one of the significant ramifications of the finding is its challenge to universal notions of social support. McDade's findings relativize the*

notion of "social support" in two ways – in relation to culture (Samoan versus Euro-American) and socioeconomic status.

References

Ader, R. (1999). *Psychoneuroimmunology* (3rd ed.). New York: Academic Press.

Bartlett, J. A., Demetrikopoulos, M. K., Schleifer, S. J., and Keller, S. E. (1997). Phagocytosis and killing of *Staphylococcus aureus*: effects of stress and depression in children. *Clinical and Diagnostic Laboratory Immunology, 4*(3), 362–366.

Baumann, H. J. and Gauldie, J. (1994). The acute phase response. *Immunology Today, 15*(2), 74–80.

Berkman, L., Glass, T., Brisette, I. and Seeman, T. (2000). From social integration to health: Durkheim in the new millenium. *Social Science and Medicine 51*(6): 843–857.

Birmaher, B., Rabin, B. S., Garcia, M. R., Jain, U., Whiteside, T. L., Williamson, D. E., Al-Shabbout, M., Nelson, B. C., Dahl, R. E., and Ryan, N. D. (1994). Cellular immunity in depressed, conduct disorder, and normal adolescents: role of adverse life events. *Journal of the American Academy of Child and Adolescent Psychiatry, 33*(5), 671–678.

Bowles, J. R. (1985). Suicide and attempted suicide in contemporary Western Samoa. In F. X. Hezel, D. H. Rubinstein, and G. M. White (eds), *Culture, youth and suicide in the Pacific: papers from an East-West Center conference* (pp. 15–34). Honolulu: University of Hawaii.

Cohen, S., Frank, E., Doyle, W., Skoner, D., Robin, B., and Gwaltney, J. (1998). Types of stressors that increase susceptability to the common cold in healthy adults. *Health Psychology 17*(3) 214–223.

Dressler, W. W. (1990). Culture, stress, and disease. In T. M. Johnson and C. F. Sargent (eds), *Medical anthropology: a handbook of theory and method* (pp. 248–268). New York: Greenwood Press.

—— (1995). Modeling biocultural interactions: examples from studies of stress and cardiovascular disease. *Yearbook of Physical Anthropology, 38*, 27–56.

—— and Bindon, J. (2000). The health consequences of cultural consonance: cultural dimensions of lifestyle, social support, and arterial blood pressure in an African American Community. *American Anthropologist 102*(2): 244–260.

Esterling, B. A., Antoni, M. H., Kumar, M., and Schneiderman, N. (1993). Defensiveness, trait anxiety, and Epstein-Barr viral capsid antigen antibody titers in healthy college students. *Health Psychology, 12*(2), 132–139.

——, ——, Schneiderman, N., Carver, C. S., LaPerriere, A., Ironson, G., Klimas, N. G., and Fletcher, M. A. (1992). Psychosocial modulation of antibody to Epstein-Barr viral capsid antigen and human Herpesvirus Type-6 in HIV-1-infected and at-risk gay men. *Psychosomatic Medicine, 54*(3), 354–371.

Fleck, A. (1989). Clinical and nutritional aspects of changes in acute-phase proteins during inflammation. *Proceedings of the Nutrition Society, 48*(3), 347–354.

Gershwin, M., German, J., and Keen, C. (2002). *Nutrition and immunology: principles and practice.* Totowa: Humana.

Glaser, R. and Kiecolt-Glaser, J. K. (eds). (1994). *Handbook of human stress and immunity.* San Diego: Academic Press.

——, ——, Speicher, C. E., and Holliday, J. E. (1985). Stress, loneliness, and changes in herpesvirus latency. *Journal of Behavioral Medicine, 8*(3), 249–260.

——, Pearl, D. K., Kiecolt-Glaser, J. K., and Malarkey, W. B. (1994). Plasma cortisol levels and reactivation of latent Epstein-Barr virus in response to examination stress. *Psychoneuroendocrinology, 19*(8), 765–772.

——, Pearson, G. R., Bonneau, R. H., Esterling, B. A., Atkinson, C., and Kiecolt-Glaser, J. K. (1993). Stress and the memory T-cell response to the Epstein-Barr virus in healthy medical students. *Health Psychology, 12*(6), 435–442.

——, ——, Jones, J. F., Hillhouse, J., Kennedy, S., Mao, H., and Kiecolt-Glaser, J. K. (1991). Stress-related activation of Epstein-Barr virus. *Brain, Behavior, and Immunity, 5*(2), 219–232.

——, Rice, J., Sheridan, J., Fertel, R., Stout, J., Speicher, C. E., Pinsky, D., Kotur, M., Post, A., Beck, M., and Kiecolt-Glaser, J. K. (1987). Stress-related immune suppression: health implications. *Brain Behavior and Immunology, 1*(1), 7–20.

Graves, T. D. and Graves, N. B. (1985). Stress and health among Polynesian migrants to New Zealand. *Journal of Behavioral Medicine, 8*(1), 1–19.

Hanna, J. M. and Fitzgerald, M. H. (1993). Acculturation and symptoms: a comparative study of reported health symptoms in three Samoan communities. *Social Science and Medicine, 36*(9), 1169–1180.

Herbert, T. B. and Cohen, S. (1993). Stress and immunity in humans: a meta-analytic review. *Psychosomatic Medicine, 55*(4), 364–379.

Holmes, L. D. (1980). Factors contributing to the cultural stability of Samoa. *Anthropological Quarterly, 53*(3), 188–197.

House, J. S., Landis, K. R., and Umberson, D. (1988). Social relationships and health. *Science, 241*(4865), 540–545.

Howard, A. (1986). Questions and answers: Samoans talk about happiness, distress, and other life experiences. In P. T. Baker, J. M. Hanna, and T. S. Baker (eds), *The changing Samoans: behavior and health in transition* (pp. 174–202). New York: Oxford University Press.

Ironson, G., Wynings, C., Schneiderman, N., Baum, A., Rodriguez, M., Greenwood, D., Benight, C., Antoni, M., LaPerriere, A., Huang, H., Klimas, N., and Fletcher, M. A. (1997). Posttraumatic stress symptoms, intrusive thoughts, loss, and immune function after Hurricane Andrew. *Psychosomatic Medicine, 59*(2), 128–141.

Irwin, M., Daniels, M., Smith, T. L., Bloom, E., and Weiner, H. (1987). Impaired natural killer cell activity during bereavement. *Brain, Behavior, and Immunity, 1*, 98–104.

Janes, C. R. (1990). *Migration, social change, and health: a Samoan community in urban California.* Stanford: Stanford University Press.

—— and Pawson, I. G. (1986). Migration and biocultural adaptation: Samoans in California. *Social Science and Medicine, 22*(8), 821–834.

Johnson, J. H. (1986). *Life events as stressors in childhood and adolescence.* Newbury Park: Sage.

Kiecolt-Glaser, J. K. and Glaser, R. (1988). Methodological issues in behavioral immunology research with humans. *Brain, Behavior, and Immunity, 2*(1), 67–78.

—— and —— (1991). Stress and immune function in humans. In R. Ader, D. L. Felten, and N. Cohen (eds), *Psychoneuroimmunology* (pp. 849–67). New York: Academic Press.

——, Fisher, L. D., Ogrocki, P., Stout, J. C., Speicher, C. E., and Glaser, R. (1987a). Marital quality, marital disruption, and immune function. *Psychosomatic Medicine, 49*(1), 13–34.

——, Glaser, R., Gravenstein, S., Malarkey, W. B., and Sheridan, J. (1996). Chronic stress alters the immune response to influenza virus vaccine in older adults. *Proceedings of the National Academy of Sciences, 93*(7), 3043–3047.

——, ——, Shuttleworth, E. C., Dyer, C. S., Ogrocki, P., and Speicher, C. E. (1987b). Chronic stress and immunity in family caregivers of Alzheimer's disease victims. *Psychosomatic Medicine, 49*, 523–535.

——, Kennedy, S., Malkoff, S., Fisher, L., Speicher, C. E., and Glaser, R. (1988). Marital discord and immunity in males. *Psychosomatic Medicine, 50*(3), 213–229.

——, Malarkey, W. B., Cacioppo, J. T., and Glaser, R. (1994). Stressful personal relationships: immune and endocrine function. In R. Glaser and J. K. Kiecolt-Glaser (eds), *Handbook of human stress and immunity* (pp. 321–339). San Diego: Academic Press.

——, ——, Chee, M. A., Newton, T., Cacioppo, J. T., Mao, H. Y., and Glaser, R. (1993). Negative behavior during marital conflict is associated with immunological down-regulation. *Psychosomatic Medicine, 55*(5), 395–409.

Lutgendorf, S. K., Antoni, M. H., Kumar, M., and Schneiderman, N. (1994). Changes in cognitive coping strategies predict EBV-antibody titre change following a stressor disclosure induction. *Journal of Psychosomatic Medicine, 38*(1), 63–78.

Lyon, M. L. (1993). Psychoneuroimmunology: the problem of the situatedness of illness and the conceptualization of healing. *Culture, Medicine and Psychiatry, 17*(1), 77–97.

Mageo, J. M. (1988). Malosi: a psychological exploration of Mead's and Freeman's work and of Samoan aggression. *Pacific Studies, 11*(2), 25–65.

—— (1989). "Ferocious is the centipede": a study of the significance of eating and speaking in Samoa. *Ethos, 17*(4), 387–427.

O'Meara, J. T. (1990). *Samoan planters: tradition and economic development in Polynesia*. Fort Worth: Holt, Rinehart and Winston.

O'Neil, J. D. (1986). Colonial stress in the Canadian Arctic: an ethnography of young adults changing. In C. R. Janes, R. Stall, and S. M. Gifford (eds), *Anthropology and epidemiology: interdisciplinary approaches to the study of health and diseases* (pp. 249–274). Boston: D. Reidel.

Rook, K. (1997). Positive and negative social exchange: weighing their effects in later life. *Journals of Gerontology, Series B, Psychological Sciences and Social Sciences 52*(4): S 167–9.

Schleifer, S. J., Scott, B., Stein, M., and Keller, S. E. (1986). Behavioral and developmental aspects of immunity. *Journal of the American Academy of Child and Adolescent Psychiatry, 26*(6), 751–763.

Shore, B. (1982). *Sala'ilua: a Samoan mystery*. New York: Columbia University Press.

Solomon, G. F., Segerstrom, S. C., Grohr, P., Kemeny, M., and Fahey, J. (1997). Shaking up immunity: psychological and immunologic changes after a natural disaster. *Psychosomatic Medicine, 59*(2), 114–127.

Uchino, B. N., Cacioppo, J. T., and Kiecolt-Glaser, J. K. (1996). The relationship between social support and physiological processes: a review with emphasis on underlying mechanisms and implications for health. *Psychological Bulletin, 119*(3), 488–531.

Young, A. (1980). The discourse on stress and the reproduction of conventional knowledge. *Social Science and Medicine, 14B*(3), 133–146.

Part III

Civilization and its stressed discontents

From individual stress to cross-national comparisons

Chapter 9: Editor's note

Blood pressure, like salivary cortisol (Flinn and England, and Decker et al., this volume), provides a measure of the physiologic impact of stress that is highly relevant to health and often correlates with immune function (Pennebaker et al. 1988, Mills et al. 1995). Thus this chapter, with its focus on emotion, social support (McDade, this volume), and the sense of isolation in the experience of emotions related to life trauma (Flinn, this volume), raises questions central to theorizing variation and universals in the culture and psychobiology of health. Mann's methods are tested in relation to hypertension (high blood pressure); but, as he makes clear, they offer lessons for the study of psychoneuro-immunology as well.

There is substantial, though of course not complete, concord between the arguments in Mann's and Pennebaker's chapters. Pennebaker and colleagues have collected blood pressure data showing how it drops when a subject in their interventions writes about trauma that moves the emotional experience toward new levels of understanding. Mann's model is not only relevant for understanding the benefits of writing traumatic experiences (Pennebaker, Booth, and Davison, this volume), but also raises questions about the structural model of PNI and stress implicit in those very writing interventions. Mann emphasizes the role of painful emotions that have been kept from awareness, whereas any traumatic experience about which a subject chooses to write is by definition conscious (though some of the emotional impact of the experience is often – as Pennebaker acknowledges – unconscious). Perhaps most importantly, the research on interethnic and intra-ethnic (class) variation in hypertension which Mann discusses illustrates questions and methods highly relevant to building a cultural PNI.

Finally, there is fascinating room for dialogue between the work of Mann as a psycho-analytically oriented cardiologist and that of the medical anthropologist specializing in hypertension in African communities in the New World, William Dressler – and rich implications for cultural theories of immune function. Dressler (2000) argues that the markedly higher average blood pressure of African Americans in large part reflects the social constraints on their ability to achieve "cultural consonance" – self-perceived consonance with what African Americans value, especially achieving a basic level of domestic comfort and a strong network of support from kin and others. Individuals who fail to gain these valued forms of comfort and social support experience dissonance with key cultural values – and have higher blood pressure than their community peers. Mann, in this chapter, argues that objective stressors working over the long term have higher effects than short-term stressors that may be more subjectively salient. Dressler, similarly, finds that the effects of a lack of consonance with a widely shared model of the successful life depend on objective and long-term shortcomings in relation to durable local ideals.

Psychoneuroimmunologists should investigate the hypothesis that immune measures, like blood pressure, reflect long-term, objective stressors that include a failure to achieve cultural norms in terms of both lifestyle and social support.[1] Mann and Pennebaker would argue that, among these norms, we should include the ideal of safety from trauma and – when trauma does occur – the ideal presence of an outlet (be it writing, psychotherapy, or an intimate relationship) in which to bring the trauma to light and to some resolution (Brison 1999).

The enigma of hypertension and psychosomatic illness

Lessons for psychoneuroimmunology from beyond the conscious mind

Samuel J. Mann

Introduction

For several decades, a focus on perceived emotional distress has dominated psychosomatic research in the study of medical conditions such as hypertension. However, such studies have not clarified the link between emotions and hypertension. Clinical observations and reported studies suggest instead that this link can be found in emotions hidden from conscious awareness. These can be traced either to trauma-related emotions that have been repressed or dissociated, particularly events that occurred during childhood (Flinn, this volume), or to a lifelong coping style characterized by minimization of perceived emotional distress. The absence of emotional support, either at the time of trauma or during childhood years, contributes greatly to the need to defend against conscious awareness of such emotions, and ultimately to the physical manifestations that can result.

These findings suggest that greater emphasis on childhood history and coping style are needed in understanding the mind/body link in hypertension and in other unexplained medical conditions, for which a link to emotions is suspected but unproven.

While advances in genetics and molecular biology have enabled us to better understand the origin of many medical illnesses, the origin of many others, including many prevalent conditions such as those listed in Table 9.1, remains unknown. Science has discovered drugs that can treat the manifestations of many of these disorders, but cannot provide a cure.

Many of these disorders are believed to be related to emotions, but "mind-body" research has not clarified their origin. Most of this research has focused on the relationship between perceived emotional distress and physical illness. The role of emotions that are not consciously perceived, i.e. that are hidden from awareness, has received scant attention.

This report focuses on the role of such emotions in causing hypertension (sustained high blood pressure). Hypertension is the most important risk factor for stroke, and a leading risk factor for heart attacks. Its link to emotions, particularly perceived emotional distress, has been extensively

Table 9.1 Common largely unexplained medical
conditions believed to be at least partly
emotion-related

back pain	chronic fatigue syndrome
chronic pain	colitis
fibromyalgia	hypertension
insomnia	irritable bowel syndrome
migraine	obesity
psoriasis	rheumatoid arthritis
tension headache	tinnitus

studied, but not clarified. Based primarily on clinical experience, and supported by growing evidence from psychosomatic research, this report will argue for greater consideration of repressed rather than manifest emotions. It will suggest that it is time for a paradigm shift in how we look at the relationship between emotions and physical health, in hypertension and in other physical disorders with a suspected link to emotions.

The traditional view of emotions and hypertension, and accumulating evidence against it

The traditional view that has driven psychosomatic research in hypertension postulates that perceived emotional distress repeatedly raises blood pressure, leading over time to structural changes in blood vessels and thus to sustained hypertension. This view also postulates that treatment aimed at reducing such emotional distress will alleviate hypertension.

This view is based on powerful and consistent evidence that emotional distress, such as anger or anxiety, acutely elevates blood pressure. However, beyond this widely established and accepted observation, the trail of evidence linking such emotions to sustained blood pressure elevation, i.e. hypertension, is weak.

It should be noted that:

1   As recently reviewed, the evidence of a link between anger and hypertension is weak and inconsistent (Jorgensen *et al.* 1996, Suls *et al.* 1995). Evidence for a link between anxiety and hypertension is similarly inconsistent (Jorgensen *et al.* 1996, Monk 1980). Even among individuals with severe hypertension, in whom a link between perceived emotional distress and hypertension should be most evident, anger and anxiety scores are not higher than those of individuals with a normal blood pressure (Mann and James 1998).

2   The hypothesis that repeated bouts of blood pressure elevation caused by recurrent emotional distress leads eventually to structural vascular

damage and sustained hypertension has not been confirmed by research to date, as recently reviewed (Weder and Julius 1985, Weiner and Sapira 1987). Further, if repeated bouts of elevation of blood pressure and sympathetic tone did lead to sustained hypertension, physical laborers, who experience such changes repeatedly would also be prone to developing hypertension. But that is not the case.

3   The hypothesis that we can understand the link between stress and hypertension by assessing acute changes in blood pressure in response to laboratory stressors has not been validated. Studies have failed to document a link between the magnitude of blood pressure reactivity to acute stressors in the laboratory, and the development of essential hypertension (Hunyor and Henderson 1996). Blood pressure reactivity to laboratory stressors is highly variable, differs from stressor to stressor, and is not predictive of the response to real life stress (Floras *et al.* 1987, Parati *et al.* 1988, Pickering and Gerin 1990).

4   Although uncontrolled studies suggested that interventions such as biofeedback and relaxation techniques, designed to reduce perceived emotional distress, can favorably affect hypertension, well-controlled studies have not confirmed this, as recently reviewed (Eisenberg *et al.* 1993).

Thus the widely-held belief that perceived emotional distress causes hypertension, and that reducing this distress alleviates it, has not been validated despite decades of research. Perceived anger and anxiety clearly have short-term effects on blood pressure in anyone, but studies have failed to document long-term effects.

This distinction between short-term and long-term effects is also highly relevant to study of the mind/body relationship in many other disorders. Too often, measurement of the effect of acute stressors on physiologic parameters such as blood pressure, stress hormone levels, or immune function, are assumed to be representative of long-term effects. Hypertension research indicates the fallacy of this assumption.[2]

Ironically, there is considerable evidence to suggest, almost counterintuitively, that hypertension is not related to perceived emotional distress, and may even be inversely related to it. For example, a study by Winkleby, of 1,429 bus drivers in San Francisco, found, contrary to what the investigators expected, that hypertensive bus drivers reported less job-related emotional distress than did bus drivers with a normal blood pressure (Winkelby *et al.* 1988). The Alameda County Blood Pressure Study reported that people who subjectively rated a given stressor as milder than objective measures of that stress, had higher blood pressure levels than those who did not (Borhani and Borkman 1968). A review by Nyklicek reports similarly that blood pressure varies directly with objective measures of stress, and inversely with subjective measures (Nyklicek *et al.* 1996). James, in a study employing ambulatory monitoring, found the highest blood pressure levels in subjects who reported stressful lives but claimed little distress (James *et al.* 1999). Finally, in a recent study, African Americans who had hypertension were less likely to report being victims of discrimination than those with a normal blood pressure (Krieger and Sidney 1996).[3]

Repressed emotions and hypertension

The effect on blood pressure of emotions that have been kept out of awareness has received much less attention (Mann 1999a). Many terms have been used in describing the process of keeping emotions out of conscious awareness. These include denial, dissociation, repression, alexithymia,[4] defensiveness, isolation of affect and others. Delineation of the differences between these terms is not central to this discussion. What is central is the association between such processes and hypertension.

Studies indicate a consistent relationship between hypertension and emotional "defensiveness," (Jorgensen *et al.* 1996, Sommers-Flanagan and Greenberg 1989), a term defined as the tendency to withhold, deny, or repress aversive emotion and personal information. Studies using the Marlowe-Crowne Scale of Social Desirability as a measure of emotional defensiveness consistently find defensiveness to be greater among hypertensive than among normotensive individuals (Mann and James 1998).[5] There is disagreement as to whether defensiveness represents unconscious self-deception, i.e. unknowingly hiding emotions from oneself, or conscious deception of others, i.e. feeling emotions but hiding them from others. Studies by Weinberger support the former interpretation (Weinberger and Davidson 1994). Studies show that in defensive individuals, in response to laboratory stressors, there is an inverse relationship between the magnitude of the emotional response and the magnitude of the blood pressure response (Warrenberg *et al.* 1989).

Regrettably, the importance of clinical observations as a driving force for mind/body research in hypertension has greatly declined in recent decades, having been largely supplanted by computer-derived statistical associations. Although clinical observations provide uncontrolled data, they can nevertheless provide dramatic evidence that is not readily observable in the laboratory. The role of repressed emotions is hard to assess in the laboratory. Clinical observations can help fill that void. Thus, with regard to the mind/body link in hypertension, clinical observations provide needed new directions.

Clinical observations

Two recent reports provide observational evidence of a link between repressed emotions and severe hypertension. In one reported case, a patient with longstanding severe and uncontrollable hypertension experienced a dramatic and sustained improvement in blood pressure control following the disclosure of a rape that had been unmentioned and virtually forgotten for decades (Mann and Delon 1995). Another report finds such a link in a series of patients with unexplained severe and symptomatic paroxysmal hypertension. Most patients in this series reported having survived severe trauma or abuse that they uniformly insisted had had no lingering impact on them (Mann 1999b). The manifestations of the trauma are physical rather than emotional.[6] The remaining patients did not describe a history of severe trauma, but uniformly manifested a prominent pattern of minimizing distressful emotions. This observation on patients with paroxysmal hypertension provides further evidence that the process of repression can affect blood pressure even in the absence of a history of overt trauma. It indicates that the notion that hypertension is related to repression need not be limited to individuals with a history of overt emotional trauma. Measurement of plasma catecholamine levels (epinephrine and norepinephrine) during a hypertensive episode revealed an increase in blood levels (see Table 9.2 for clinical examples) (Mann 1996), consistent with increased activation of the sympathoadrenal system (compare Decker, this volume). These findings suggest that paroxysmal hypertension is linked to repressed emotions and is mediated by the sympathoadrenal system.

This proposed link between repressed emotions and paroxysmal hypertension is not merely of theoretical interest. Whereas the cause and treatment of this disorder have been a longstanding mystery, appreciation of the role of repressed emotions enables a successful treatment approach with interventions including psychotherapy, blockade of alpha and beta adrenergic receptors, and/or treatment with an antidepressant agent (Mann 1999a).

To study the relationship between traumatic events and more routine cases of essential hypertension is difficult. Most human beings are exposed to potentially traumatic life events at some point in their lives. In addition, the circumstances particular to those events, and the manner in which emotions related to them were processed bear greater importance than the history of having endured those events per se. A check list of events is less relevant than the details concerning those events, details which are harder to quantify for research analyses.

Another major issue is the age of the individual at the time he or she is exposed to a traumatic event or period. Most psychosomatic research focuses on the effects of recent events, experienced in adulthood, whereas the impact of childhood trauma on adult physical health has been the subject of less research. A recent study reported an association between childhood sexual abuse and adult irritable bowel syndrome (Drossman et al. 1990). Another study suggests that a history of childhood trauma is more often reported by hypertensive than by normotensive individuals (Ekeberg et al. 1990). Thus more study of the unexplored role of childhood trauma is suggested both by clinical observations and by studies.

Table 9.2 Blood pressure recordings and plasma catecholamine values during a hypertensive crisis in three patients with paroxysmal hypertension

	Blood pressure	Heart rate	Epinephrine (pg/ml)	Norepine-phrine (pg/ml)	Dopamine (pg/ml)
	Normal supine values < 50			110–410	<85
Case 6					
Baseline (*)	154/90	84	<14	160	<15
15 min	228/130	54	<14	362	<15
90 min	226/130	54	36	883	53
150 min	130/80	54	<14	991	<15
Case 7					
Baseline(*)	140/60	68	75	248	31
15 min	196/84	76	24	432	<25
90 min	146/80	68	66	229	<25
Case 8					
Baseline(#)	120/83	89	39	53	<25
15 min	145/90	96	340	40	<25

(*) One hour before episode
(#) Random baseline value, on a different day

Psychosocial history and ethnic variability

Essential hypertension is known to be more prevalent in Westernized and urban societies, attributable to many lifestyle factors, including, perhaps most importantly, diet.[7] Differences between ethnic groups in the prevalence of hypertension are less clear, with the most notable exception being the extensively studied difference in hypertension prevalence between whites and African Americans. Studies indicate that in the United States, the prevalence of essential hypertension is 33 percent among African Americans versus 24 percent among whites (Burt *et al.* 1995). Several factors appear to contribute to this difference.

A widely held assumption is the existence of genetic differences in predisposition to develop hypertension. This is most evident in studies that demonstrate that the blood pressure of African Americans is more likely to rise with increased salt intake than is that of whites (Luft *et al.* 1979). Many believe that psychosocial factors also play a considerable role. The prevalence of hypertension is inversely proportional to socioeconomic status (Tyroler 1989), a factor which would favor an increased incidence of the condition in African Americans. Other areas of study include the concept of John Henryism, characterized by a work ethic associated with a belief that hard work can overcome the disadvantages of low status (James 1983).

Other proposed factors include "status incongruence" characterized by frustrated hopes for socioeconomic gain, and repressed anger (Dressler 1996).

The concepts proposed in this paper offer another perspective on the social differences encoded in our culture as racial differences in both the prevalence and severity of essential hypertension. It focuses on the childhood experiences that shape the adult psyche. It proposes that trauma occurring in childhood constitutes more of the driving force of hypertension than does day-to-day psychosocial stress. Consistent with this are reports that indicate a greater incidence of childhood abuse in African American children (Pelton 1994). Child abuse is associated inversely with socioeconomic status, and this factor may explain much of the disparity between white and African American communities in this regard (ibid.). In assessing the causative factors of hypertension, the role of childhood trauma, and the lifelong repression of emotions related to that trauma, remain to be investigated.

The protective value of hiding emotions

The human psyche is programmed to keep from awareness emotions that could be overwhelming if consciously perceived (Lazarus 1983). Emotions related to severe emotional trauma, for example, could be overwhelming because of either the severity of the trauma, or because of factors such as its suddenness, the helplessness or young age of the victim, the absence of emotional support, or other factors. Keeping these emotions from awareness, at the time, is protective.

A defensive coping style is similarly protective at the time it is formed. Usually acquired in early childhood, it is characterized by an incongruity between stress and perceived distress, in which individuals feel less distress than would be expected. It is likely linked to an inability to confide emotions, acquired in a childhood environment in which emotions were not confided, resulting in a need for, and a pattern of, keeping distressful emotions from awareness.

Keeping overwhelming emotions from awareness protects against their psychological impact. The child who was abused or whose parent died suddenly, particularly if unable to confide his emotional distress, can be spared the consequences of a serious psychological break by unknowingly defending himself from awareness of those emotions. However, studies and clinical observations suggest that the maintenance of these defenses, over decades, when often they are no longer needed, puts an individual at risk of physical consequences, such as hypertension.

Emotional and physical healing may be possible if and when those emotions are experienced and confided. However, this potential for healing is not widely recognized. Whereas mind/body research that follows the reigning stress model focuses on the reduction of perceived emotional distress, the value of increasing awareness of repressed emotions receives little attention.

In addition, this avenue of healing is available to some, but not to others, who either lack access to these emotions, or who are survivors of particularly severe trauma, or who lack social support or the ability to utilize the social support that is available to them. Emotional awareness is widely advocated in popular culture (Wilce and Price, Booth and Davison, this volume). Yet there are some who are survivors of such overwhelming trauma that continued repression, even if it is the cause of hypertension or other physical disorders, may be preferable to being emotionally overwhelmed.

Psychosocial history and the treatment of essential hypertension

For decades, psychosomatic research in hypertension and other disorders has sought to identify the means to improve treatment of these disorders. There have been great hopes that relaxation and stress management interventions could play a role in treating hypertension.[8] However, this hope has not been borne out, as recent reviews cast doubt on the efficacy of such interventions (Eisenberg *et al.* 1993). A major problem in this research has been that placebo or expectation effects (Lyon, Moerman, this volume) confound assessment of the effect of interventions on clinic blood pressure. More recent study designs have incorporated the more informative use of ambulatory or home blood pressure measurement. These studies have provided further evidence that stress reduction techniques are of limited efficacy in treating hypertension (Van Montfrans *et al.* 1990, Johnston *et al.* 1993).

A major flaw in psychosomatic studies is that study designs focus almost exclusively on obtaining group data, and do not look at individual data. Since it is extremely likely that psychological factors are contributory to hypertension in some individuals and not in others, the relevance to clinical management of looking at individual patterns cannot be overstated. Studies have not adequately addressed the heterogeneity of the mind/body link in hypertension, and have not provided guidelines for how to determine in whom psychological factors are contributory to hypertension and in whom they are not.

Another area that has been the subject of conspicuously little research is the question of whether the psychological heterogeneity of the hypertensive population contributes to a heterogeneity in responses to pharmacologic therapy of hypertension. Do psychological factors affect the responsiveness to all agents? Do they affect the response to certain agents but not others?

In a recent study, we provide data suggesting that psychological factors are an important determinant of responses to antihypertensive agents (Mann and Gerber 2002). The hypothesis of this study was that emotion-driven hypertension, which is mediated by the sympathetic nervous system, will have a reduced response to agents such as ACE inhibitors or diuretics, which do not target the sympathetic nervous system. In contrast, individuals whose hypertension is driven more by genetics than by emotional factors, will have a greater response to such agents. In the study, subjects completed psychological questionnaires assessing self-perceived anger anxiety, emotional defensiveness, and trauma history, and were then treated, in crossover fashion, with an ACE inhibitor (quinapril), a diuretic (hydrochlorothiazide) and a combination of an alpha blocker + a beta blocker (doxazosin + betaxolol).

Data analysis revealed that of subjects reporting childhood trauma (Childhood Trauma Questionnaire (Bernstein *et al.* 1994, The Psychological Corporation 1998)), only 25 percent achieved the target systolic blood pressure of 130 mmHg (Mann and Gerber 2002). In contrast, 79 percent of subjects without childhood trauma achieved the target blood pressure (p = 0.03). Responses to alpha + beta blockade did not differ between groups. Thus the study suggests that childhood trauma history may be an important determinant of responses to antihypertensive treatment. The role of childhood history in the treatment of other disorders may similarly be an important, yet unstudied, variable.

Emotional support and physical illness in Western societies

Evolution provided us with the ability to keep emotions from awareness when we need to. It also provided us with the ability to face those emotions by deriving strength through emotional and spiritual support. There is growing evidence that emotional support has important effects on physical health.[9] Recent studies have documented that emotional support is more relevant to survival in the months and years following myocardial infarction than are any of the traditional risk factors such as cholesterol, blood pressure, or smoking (Berkman *et al.* 1992). Western societies, and families within each society vary in the degree to which emotional support is available for its members. When it is not available, and severe emotional distress is borne in isolation, of necessity it is often barred from awareness, albeit with a different set of consequences to our health.

In modern Western society, many factors promote emotional isolation. Work, intellectual pursuits, and recreational pleasures dominate the attention of most people. Although medical research is beginning to document the medical benefits of emotional support, the breakdown of both the nuclear and extended family, geographic mobility, and the breakneck pace of life, act in concert to reduce its availability. A "be happy" philosophy also promotes diversion of attention from unwanted emotions, instead of promoting their processing in an atmosphere of emotional support.

Defenses that keep distressful emotions from awareness do not constitute psychopathology in a society or family in which emotional isolation is rampant. They are, by default, a necessity for psychological homeostasis. However, although they help minimize emotional consequences, they might be importantly related to medical consequences.[10]

The challenge for the future

Decades of psychosomatic research have amply documented the absence of a strong relationship between perceived emotions and hypertension. Despite the small but growing body of evidence that repressed emotions can better explain the mind/body link of hypertension, the resistance, at both a societal and individual level, to consideration of their role has perpetuated the focus of psychosomatic research on perceived emotions. A new paradigm, paying more attention to repressed and unreported emotions and their physiologic effects, and to the emotional isolation that lies beneath them in a society – unlike India or Japan (where middle class and expert discourses valorize emotional disclosure) is needed.

Research in other mind/body areas of investigation, such as psychoneuro-immunology, is similarly focusing on the relationship between perceived emotions and physiologic changes. Responses to transient emotional stress, and the relationship between perceived emotions and immunological para-meters are easier to study, than are relationships to repressed emotions. However, the lessons of hypertension research suggest that here as well, better understanding of the mind/body link will require consideration of the emotions we harbor without awareness.

In the absence of consideration of the role of repressed emotions, the cause of many medical conditions has remained, and will remain, a mystery. A shift in our view of the mind/body link is needed, if we are to unlock the mystery of their origin.

Notes

1 *Ed. Indeed, the contributors to Part II have already begun such investigations.*
2 *Ed. One study whose focus is, unfortunately, of this short-term nature, is nonethe-less worth noting because it links psychoneuroimmune function with hypertension and with ethnicity (Mills et al. 1995). The responsiveness of all ethnic groups to laboratory stressors (measured in terms of immune and cardiovascular functions) would seem to indicate what Mann has been arguing – the panhuman effect of objective stressors. They also note, in keeping with Mann's emphasis on the need to study individuals as well as groups, that individuals with the highest cardiovascular response to acute stress also "have the highest immune changes" (1995: 61).*
3 *Ed. Krieger and Sidney interpret their findings in terms consistent with health psychology's emphasis on assertiveness, but in terms that are also unavoidably political:*

> Systolic blood pressure among working-class Black adults reporting that they typically *accepted* unfair treatment and had experienced racial discrimina-tion in none of seven situations was about 7 mm Hg higher than among those reporting that they *challenged* unfair treatment and experienced racial discrimination in one or two of the situations. Among professional Black adults, systolic blood pressure was 9 to 10 mm Hg lower among those reporting that they typically *challenged* unfair treatment and had not

experienced racial discrimination. Black-White differences in blood pressure were substantially reduced by taking into account reported experiences of racial discrimination and responses to unfair treatment.

Krieger and Sidney conclude, "Research on racial/ethnic distributions of blood pressure should take into account how discrimination may harm health" (1996: 1370, emphasis added).

4 *Ed. Volume contributor Kirmayer has made essential, and critical, contributions to our understanding of alexithymia as "personality factor" or as a cultural construction (1987).*

5 *Ed. There is a long history of research on the immunological correlates of trait repression or defensiveness, research of particular relevance to chapters here by Pennebaker and Booth and Davison. Esterling et al. (1994) found that students who wrote unemotionally about a stressful event that they had not previously disclosed to many people (which correlated with their pre-intervention scores on a repression scale) experienced an elevation in their Epstein-Barr Virus titers (the PNI measure on which McDade relied, this volume). Writers who revealed emotions experienced a decrease.*

6 *Ed. See discussion of embodiment in this volume (especially chapters by Lyon, Wilce and Price, and Kirmayer).*

7 *Ed. On diet, social class, urbanization, and immune disorders see Cone and Martin, this volume.*

8 *Ed. For a review of hopeful research, see Hall and O'Grady 1991.*

9 *Ed. Questions remain about the extent of cross-cultural variation in the shape and meaning of "emotional support" and "isolation," and McDade (this volume) demonstrates interesting sociocultural variability in the meanings of social support. A certain behavior might receive sociocultural or widespread ideological support. Values and ideologies vary widely across cultures such that Indonesians tend to hear messages encouraging them to forget stressful events while Americans tend to hear messages encouraging disclosure (Wilce and Price, this volume). Bangladeshis asked by the editor to define "sympathy" offered the example of telling someone to "harden themselves" – quite different from the definition a middle-class American (Kusserow 1999) might offer (perhaps "telling them it's OK to cry or talk about how awful it was"). The hypothesis that familiar values form a cushion of comfort and that violating those values – for some Asian persons this might entail talking about distress or encouraging a loved one to do so – would provoke a stress of its own, needs testing but finds some support in Dressler's work on cultural consonance (Dressler et al. 1998; Dressler 2000).*

None of this is to say that cultural ideologies (such as middle-class American encouragement to work or talk through grief or trauma) are consistently reflected in the actual behavior of those called upon to offer this admittedly variable "support." On this point, see Pennebaker 1993.

10 *Ed. When a gap exists between ideological and empirical support for certain coping behaviors like venting, individuals who fail to follow ideologically validated strategies – for lack of empirical support for them – can be expected to experience a particularly destructive form of stress from lack of cultural consonance (Dressler 2000). Where a particular society's ideal notion of emotional support (see earlier note and Wilce and Price, this volume) is exemplified by utterances like "Forget about it, get over it" – with no dominant conflicting messages from experts such as "Let it all out" – at least the stress resulting from the conflict entailed in the competing messages (Bateson 1972) would be absent.*

References

Bateson, G. (1972). *Steps to an ecology of mind*. Scranton, PA: Chandler.

Berkman, L. F., Leo-Summers, L., and Horwitz, R. I. (1992). Emotional support and survival after myocardial infarction: a prospective, population-based study of the elderly. *Annals of Internal Medicine, 117*(12), 1003–1009.

Bernstein, D. P., Fink, L., Handelsman, L., Foote, J., Lovejoy, M., Wenzel, K., Saparet, E., and Ruggiero, J. (1994). Initial reliability and validity of a new retrospective measure of child abuse and neglect. *American Journal of Psychiatry, 151*(8), 1132–1136.

Borhani, N. O., and Borkman, T. S. (1968). *The Alameda county blood pressure study*. Berkeley, CA: State of California Department of Public Health.

Brison, S. J. (1999). Trauma narratives and the remaking of the self. In M. Bal, J. Crew, and L. Spitzer (eds), *Acts of memory: cultural recall in the present* (pp. 39–54). Hanover, NH: University Press of New England/Dartmouth College.

Burt, V. L., Whelton, P., *et al.* (1995). Prevalence of hypertension in the US adult population. Results from the third National Health and Nutrition Examination Survey. *Hypertension, 25*(3), 305–313.

Dressler, W. W. (1996). Hypertension in the African American community: social, cultural, and psychological factors. *Seminars in Nephrology, 16*(2), 71–82.

——, Balieiro, M. C., and Dos Santos, J. E. (1998). Culture, socioeconomic status, and physical and mental health in Brazil. *Medical Anthropology Quarterly, 12*(4), 424–446.

—— and Bindon, J. (2000). The health consequences of cultural consonance: cultural dimensions of lifestyle, social support, and arterial blood pressure in an African American community. *American Anthropologist, 102*(2), 244–260.

Drossman, D. A., Lesserman, J., Nachman, G., Li, Z. M., Gluck, H., Toomes, T. C., and Mitchell, C. M. (1990). Sexual and physical abuse in women with functional or organic gastrointestinal disorders. *Annals of Internal Medicine, 113*(11), 828–833.

Eisenberg, D. M., Delbanco, T. L., Berkey, C. S., Kaptchuk, T. J., Kupelnick, B., Kuhl, J., and Chalmers, T. C. (1993). Cognitive behavioral techniques for hypertension: are they effective? *Annals of Internal Medicine, 118*(12), 964–972.

Ekeberg, O., Kjeldsen, S. E., Eide, I., and Leren, P. (1990). Childhood traumas and psychosocial characteristics of fifty-year-old men with essential hypertension. *Journal of Psychosomatic Research, 34*(6), 643–649.

Esterling, B., Antoni, M., Fletcher, M., Margulies, S., and Schneiderman, N. (1994). Emotional disclosure through writing or speaking modulates latent Epstein-Barr virus antibody titers, *Journal of Consulting and Clinical Psychology, 62*(1), 130–140.

Floras, J. S., Hassan, M. O., Jones, J. V., and Sleight, P. (1987). Pressure responses to laboratory stresses and daytime blood pressure variability. *Journal of Hypertension, 5*(6), 715–719.

Hall, N. R. S. and O'Grady, M. P. (1991). Psychosocial interventions and immune function. In R. Ader, D. L. Felten, and N. Cohen (eds), *Psychoneuroimmunology* (2nd edn). San Diego: Academic Press.

Hunyor, S. N. and Henderson, R. J. (1996). The role of stress management in blood pressure control: why the promissory note has failed to deliver. *Journal of Hypertension, 14*(4), 413–418.

James, G. D., Bovbjerg, D. H., and Pickering, T. G. (1999). Stress and denial independently increase ambulatory blood pressure at work and home in women. *American Journal of Hypertension*, *12*, 167A.

James, S. A. (1983). John Henryism and blood pressure differences among black men. *Journal of Behavioral Medicine*, *6*(3), 259–278.

Johnston, D. W., Gold, A., Kentish, J., Smith, D., Vallance, P., Shah, D., Leach, G., and Robinson, B. (1993). Effect of stress management of blood pressure in mild primary hypertension. *British Medical Journal*, *306*(6883), 963–966.

Jorgensen, R. S., Johnson, B. T., Kolodziej, M. E., and Schreer, G. E. (1996). Elevated blood pressure and personality: a meta-analytic review. *Psychological Bulletin*, *120*, 293–320.

Kirmayer, L. J. (1987). Languages of suffering and healing: alexithymia as a social and cultural process. *Transcultural Psychiatric Research Review*, *24*(2), 119–136.

Krieger, N. and Sidney, S. (1996). Racial discrimination and blood pressure: the CARDIA study of young black and white adults. *American Journal of Public Health*, *86*(10), 1370–1378.

Kusserow, Adrie Suzanne (1999) De-homogenizing American individualism: socializing hard and soft individualism in Manhattan and Queens. *Ethos*, *27*(2), 210–234.

Lazarus, R. S. (1983). The costs and benefits of denial. In S. Bresnitz (ed.), *The denial of stress* (pp. 1–33). New York: International Universities Press.

Luft, F. C., Rankin, L. I., Bloch, R., Weyman, A. E., Willis, L. R., Murray, R. H., Grim, C. E., and Weinberger, M. H. (1979). Cardiovascular and humoral responses to extremes of sodium intake in normal black and white men. *Circulation*, *60*(3), 697–706.

Mann, S. J. (1996). Severe paroxysmal hypertension: an autonomic syndrome and its relationship to repressed emotions. *Psychosomatics*, *37*(5), 444–450.

—— (1999a). *Healing hypertension: a revolutionary new approach*. New York: Wiley.

—— (1999b). Severe paroxysmal hypertension (pseudopheochromocytoma): understanding its cause and treatment. *Archives of Internal Medicine*, *159*(7), 670–674.

—— and Delon, M. A. (1995). Improved blood pressure control following disclosure of decades-old trauma. *Psychosomatic Medicine*, *57*(5), 501–505.

—— and Gerber, L. M. (2002). Psychological characteristics and responses to antihypertensive drug therapy. *Journal of Clinical Hypertension*, *4*(1), 25–34.

—— and James, G. D. (1998). Defensiveness and essential hypertension. *Journal of Psychosomatic Research*, *45*(2), 139–148.

Mills, P. J., Berry, C. C., Dimsdale, J. E., Ziegler, M. G., Nelesen, R. A., and Kennedy, B. P. (1995). Lymphocyte subset redistribution in response to acute experimental stress: effects of gender, ethnicity, hypertension, and the sympathetic nervous system. *Brain, Behavior, and Immunity*, *9*(1), 61–69.

Monk, M. (1980). Psychologic status and hypertension. *American Journal of Epidemiology*, *112*(2), 200–208.

Nyklicek, I., Vingerhoets, A. J. J. M., and Van Heck, G. L. (1996). Hypertension and objective and self-reported stresses exposure:a review. *Journal of Psychosomatic Research*, *40*(6), 585–601.

Parati, G., Pomidossi, G., Casadei, R., Ravogli, A., Groppelli, A., Cesana, B., and Mancia, G. (1988). Comparison of the cardiovascular effects of different laboratory stressors and their relationship to blood pressure variability. *Journal of Hypertension*, *6*(6), 481–488.

Pelton, L. H. (1994). The role of material factors in child abuse and neglect. In G. B. Melton and F. D. Barry (eds), *Protecting children from abuse and neglect: foundations for a new national strategy* (pp. 131–181). New York: Guilford Press.

Pennebaker, J. W. (1993). Social mechanisms of constraint. In D. M. Wegner and J. W. Pennebaker (eds), *Handbook of mental control* (pp. 200–219). Englewood Cliffs, NJ: Prentice Hall.

——, Barger, S. D., and Tiebout, J. (1989). Disclosure of traumas and health among Holocaust survivors. *Psychosomatic Medicine*, *51*(5), 577–589.

——, Kiecolt-Glaser, J., and Glaser, R. (1988). Disclosure of traumas and immune function: health implications for psychotherapy. *Journal of Consulting and Clinical Psychology*, *56*(2), 239–245.

Pickering, T. G. and Gerin, W. (1990). Cardiovascular reactivity in the laboratory and the role of behavioral factors in hypertension: a critical review. *Annals of Behavioral Medicine*, *12*(1), 3–16.

The Psychological Corporation (1998). *Childhood trauma questionnaire*. San Antonio.

Socha, T. J., Sanchez-Hughes, J., Bromley, J., and Kelly, B. (1995). Invisible parents and children: exploring African American parent-child communication. In T. J. Socha and G. H. Stamp (eds), *Parents, children, and communication: frontiers of theory and research* (pp. 127–145). Malwah, NJ: Erlbaum.

Sommers-Flanagan, J., and Greenberg, R. P. (1989). Psychosocial variables and hypertension: a new look at an old controversy. *Journal of Nervous and Mental Disease*, *177*(1), 15–24.

Suls, J., Wan, C. K., and Costa, P. T. (1995). Relationship of trait anger to resting blood pressure: a metaanalysis. *Health Psychology*, *14*(5), 444–456.

Tyroler, H. A. (1989). Socioeconomic status in the epidemiology and treatment of hypertension. *Hypertension*, *13*(5) (supplement), I-94–I-97.

Van Montfrans, G. A., Karemaker, J. M., Wieling, W., and Dunning, A. J. (1990). Relaxation therapy and continuous ambulatory blood pressure in mild hypertension: a controlled study. *British Medical Journal*, *300*(673), 1368–1372.

Warrenberg, S., Levine, J., Schwartz, G. E., Fontana, A., Kerns, R. D., Delaney, R., and Mattson, R. (1989). Defensive coping and blood pressure reactivity in medical patients. *Journal of Behavioral Medicine*, *12*, 407–424.

Weder, A. B. and Julius, S. (1985). Behavior, blood pressure variability and hypertension. *Psychosomatic Medicine*, *47*(5), 406–414.

Weinberger, D. A. and Davidson, M. N. (1994). Styles of inhibiting emotional expression: distinguishing repressive coping from impression management. *Journal of Personality*, *62*(4), 587–613.

Weiner, H. and Sapira, J. D. (1987). Hypertension: a challenge to behavioral research. In S. Julius and D. R. Bassett (eds), *Handbook of hypertension: behavioral factors in hypertension* (vol. 9, pp. 259–284). New York: Elsevier Science Publishers.

Winkleby, M. A., Ragland, D. R., and Syme, S. L. (1988). Self-reported stressors and hypertension: evidence of an inverse association. *American Journal of Epidemiology*, *127*(1), 124–134.

Chapter 10: Editor's note

In this chapter, Moerman explores fascinating cross-national differences in placebo-controlled trials of remedies for, among other things, ulcers. These introductory remarks will serve to highlight the relevance of the phenomena described herein to psychoimmunology. The PNI links with hypertension are mentioned in notes to Mann's chapter (this volume), and I will not speculate here on the immunologic correlations of Generalized Anxiety Disorder. Rather, my comments will focus on ulcer disease.

Moerman notes that "peptic ulcer disease has come to be seen as caused by infection from a bacterium, Helicobacter pylori *(Hp)." In other forms of ulcer disease, auto-immunity or at least an inflammatory response is involved (Schiffer and Hoffman 1991). All three of these factors have been shown, in relation to other disease conditions, to be responsive to changes in immunocompetence, which is in turn influenced by psychosocial factors. So, the effects of placebos on patients' immune systems may be significant in relation to tests of various interventions for ulcer disease.*

Peptic ulcers can be related to an immune deficiency. In their study of ulcer disease induced in mice that were genetically deficient in T and B cells, von Freeden-Jeffry et al. (1998) found that "IL-7 plays a critical role in exacerbating a non-T cell/non-B cell-mediated chronic inflammatory response." Ibraghimov and Pappo (2000) found that H. pylori *infects about half the people in the world, and elicits a very particular immune response. "Some infected individuals remain asymptomatic, while others develop significant gastroduodenal disease." There is, in the latter group an "underlying host immune response to* H. pylori *which programs for persistence and evolution of gastroduodenal disease" (Ibraghimov and Pappo 2000: 1073). Likewise, Smagina (2000: 57) finds that, "In peptic ulcer the immunological characteristics of gastric juice were found to essentially differ from those of saliva by a lower content of mucin, IgA and a higher content of SIgA and IgM in gastric secretions, which may form prerequisites for the colonization of the gastric mucosa by* H. pylori." *Shirai and colleagues (2000: 749), studying the effectiveness of oral vaccination against* H. pylori *infection, note that "saliva is necessary for both the induction and maintenance of optimal immunity in the stomach. Effective immunity was associated with an increased number of neutrophils and lymphocytes in gastric tissue." Relaxation is a well reviewed intervention in psychoneuroimmunology studies (Hall and O'Grady 1991). Aksenova et al. (1999) found one relaxation method to work as well as conventional drug therapy in the treatment of ulcers in Russia. Given the strong evidence for the mediating role of the immune response in bacterial infections related to ulcer disease, evidence points to a significant role for psychosocial factors at work in the immune response to* H. pylori.

To address the specific mechanisms – including PNI – that underlie the placebo effects noted in this meta-analysis of those effects in randomized clinical trials is outside the scope of this chapter, especially since those underlying mechanisms are not revealed by the previous studies Moerman re-analyzes. Still, although all the desired evidence is not in to confirm the pyogenic-bacterial causation of some ulcers and the specific PNI links in ulcer disease are also understudied, Moerman provides some evidence of the sort needed to substantiate claims that cultural differences mediate PNI effects.

Cultural variations in the placebo effect

Ulcers, anxiety, and blood pressure[1]

Daniel E. Moerman

> [N]ocebo and placebo effects are integral to all sickness and healing, for
> they are concepts that refer in an incomplete and oblique way to the inter-
> actions between mind and body and among the three bodies: individual,
> social and politic.
>
> (Scheper-Hughes and Lock 1987)

Some years ago I reported on an analysis of 31 double-blind controlled trials
of the anti-ulcer drug cimetidine (Moerman 1982). I recently reviewed those
data, added to them, and repeated the process for several other conditions and
drugs. The analysis of these new data materially expands and complicates the
original conclusions.

The placebo effect

The placebo effect is an important part of the human healing process that has
been considered several times in the anthropological literature (Moerman
1979, 1997, 2002; van der Geest and Whyte 1989); I will, therefore, only
briefly indicate some of the dimensions of the placebo effect here.

I define placebo effects as the desirable[2] psychological and physiological
effects of meaning in the treatment of illness.[3] Participating in a healing
process, regardless of its content, can lead to healing. While this is clearly
true, it is much easier to assert than to demonstrate to a skeptic.[4] One of the
clearest demonstrations comes from what is known as a "three-arm trial" of
medical treatment. In such a trial, after a diagnosis, patients are randomly
allocated to one of three groups. The first group typically receives some sort
of (presumably) active medication. The second receives placebo treatment,
(presumably) indistinguishable from the active one but lacking the item being
tested. The third, untreated, "natural history" group serves to represent what
happens to patients who receive no treatment. If the group receiving placebos
(inert pills, perhaps) does substantially better than the untreated group, one
can attribute the difference to the placebo effect. Trials of this sort show just

how difficult it is to create, or even conceptualize, an "untreated group." Every part of an intervention – taking a history, stating a diagnosis, making repeated blood pressure readings or multiple endoscopic observations of the gut, having patients keep symptom diaries – may well have therapeutic value.[5]

Few three-arm trials have been carried out, but the ones that have are very interesting. One well-designed study compared ultrasound therapy to sham ultrasound therapy (the machine is applied but not turned on) for swelling following third molar extraction; the study included a third group that received ordinary dental care (as did the patients in the two study groups), but neither real nor sham ultrasound treatment. "The placebo [ultrasound] treatment . . . reduced [swelling] in all conditions in which the dentist applied the equipment to the patient's face" compared with the results in the untreated group (Ho *et al.* 1988: 203; see also Hashish *et al.* 1986). In another study, placebo treatment was shown to improve both exercise duration and functional class in patients with congestive heart failure compared with patients receiving no treatment (Archer and Leier 1992). In trials of this sort, it is not uncommon that the untreated group improves, too. Things often do heal by themselves; these are often called "natural history effects."[6]

It is also often the case that people seek treatment (and are enrolled in trials) when their (fluctuating) symptoms are at their worst; improvement in such patients is (awkwardly) called "regression to the mean" (McDonald and McCabe 1989).

In any event, the placebo effect is most unambiguously evident when a group receiving sham treatment heals significantly faster than an untreated group. A number of additional three-arm studies have recently been reviewed (Ernst and Resch 1995). It is also possible to infer the existence of a placebo effect in many controlled trials where placebo groups but no "natural history" groups are utilized. A number of controlled trials are considered in this article.

Controlled trials are of many types. The simplest trial treats two groups of patients using two different drugs and compares the outcome. If there is a difference in improvement between the two groups, it may indicate that the drug taken by one group is somehow better than the other drug. Other factors, however, may intrude. The conclusion of superior effectiveness can only be true if the patients in both groups are "the same." Typically achieving equivalence is attempted by randomization – people are randomly assigned to one group or another, and, subsequently, an analysis is done to see if indeed they are the same on relevant measures like sex, age, degree of illness, and so on.[7] This comparability ensures that the "only difference" between the two groups is the drug they receive. The second major factor in such a study is "blinding." Studies are occasionally "single blind" – the patients are not told what medication they are receiving. Since physician bias is a strong element in many such situations, a "double-blind" trial – where neither the patients nor the physicians treating the patients know who is receiving what drug – is usually required to demonstrate drug efficacy. Minimally, double-blinding prevents physicians from evaluating the improvement of those taking the new drug more favorably than others. The third important element of controlled trials is the use of a control. While one can compare two active drugs (cimetidine versus ranitidine, for example), such tests are often inconclusive, especially if both drugs work reasonably well. Many trials, especially in the absence of widely recognized effective treatments, compare treatment groups with placebo control groups; one of the groups is given drugs that appear and taste the same as the drug being tested, but lack the active ingredient under study. Putting all these elements together, one then would have a "randomized, double-blind, placebo-controlled trial," which is often referred to as the "gold standard" of modern medicine. Such trials are understood to demonstrate how the drug under study differs from "no treatment." I have already noted that the control group in such a trial has had far more than "no treatment," and, not surprisingly, perhaps, many control group patients get better, too.

There is another interesting situation where one can detect placebo effects. The randomized controlled trial (RCT) has only become common in conventional medical practice since the early 1970s. Before then, there was much serious scientific investigation of drugs that did not control for the bias and enthusiasm of the clinicians. This led to the widespread use of treatments that were only later put to the test of the RCT. In a number of such cases, drugs with high levels of effectiveness in actual practice could not be shown to be more effective than inert treatment in subsequent trials. There are two major reviews of cases of this sort. The first examined a number of "subsequently discredited" treatments for angina pectoris. "The pattern is consistent: the initial 70 to 90 per cent effectiveness in the [early] enthusiasts' reports decreases to 30 to 40 per cent 'base-line' placebo in the [later] skeptics' reports" (Benson and McCallie 1979: 1424). The second such study considered five medical procedures once considered efficacious (mostly for treating viral infections) but subsequently abandoned when they could not outperform a placebo in trials. For these five treatments combined, "40 percent excellent, 30 percent good, and 30 percent poor results were reported by proponents" (Roberts *et al.* 1993: 375). There is remarkable agreement in these two studies. Both report good to excellent effects of apparently inert substances that are much higher – 70 percent or more – than those usually attributed to such treatment – about 30 to 35 percent. A primary ingredient in the effectiveness of the earlier experience is probably physician enthusiasm. Several studies have manipulated clinician enthusiasm and shown significant effect on patient response (Gryll and Katahn 1978; Uhlenhuth *et al.* 1966). There is good reason to believe that placebo effects are generally lower in RCTs than in the ordinary practice of medicine. In an RCT, everyone knows that half the patients are not going to receive the "exciting new drug." This may dim the overall enthusiasm of the investigators in that clinical context. In addition, the process of eliciting informed consent may diminish patient expectations. The "naive enthusiasm" of both doctor and patient in these cases from the 1950s and 1960s was a compelling factor in the improvement of serious sickness.

In July, 1999, the BBC reported in the business section of its World Wide Web Site, that the share price of a biotech company had dropped 33 percent on news that its new food allergy drug, which had been successful in 75 percent of patients trying it, had been shown to be no more effective than a placebo treatment for the same allergies. Three-quarters of placebo-treated patients were able to eat foods that had previously made them ill. The company announced that it would drop development of the drug. There is no indication that anyone is going to follow up this quite remarkable result (BBC 1999).

In addition to such effects, which seem to follow from the relationship between clinician and patient,[8] there are other sorts of mechanisms that also may play a role. A group of American medical students was asked to partic-ipate in a study of two new drugs, one a tranquilizer and the other a stimulant (Blackwell *et al.* 1972). Each student was given a packet containing either one or two blue or red tablets; the tablets were inert. Hours later, the students' responses to a questionnaire indicated that the red tablets tended to act as stimulants, while the blue ones acted as depressants, and two tablets had more effect than one. The response of these students was not to the inertness of the tablets and cannot be easily accounted for by natural history or by clin-ician enthusiasm. While the *fact* of their experience may have had something to do with the authority of their professors, the *directions* of their experience and its intensity can be accounted for by the "meanings" in the experiment: red means "up," "hot," "danger," while blue means "down," "cool," "quiet," and two means "more than one."[9] A recent Dutch study has shown that stimulant medications tend to be marketed in "hot" colors – red, yellow, or orange tablets – while depressants tend to be marketed in "cool" colors – blue, green, or purple tablets (de Craen *et al.* 1996). One can consider "one-a-day" vitamins to be among the most neutral of medications; they are not imagined to have immediate or dramatic effects at all. Observations suggest that vitamins are marketed in tablets with pale pastel tones.[10]

An elaborate British study demonstrated that aspirin tablets labeled with a widely advertised brand name are more effective against headache than generically labeled aspirin tablets; similarly, inert tablets with the same brand name are more effective against headache than generically labeled inert tablets (Branthwaite and Cooper 1981). Aspirin is more effective than a placebo, and advertised pills are more effective than generic ones. Aspirin relieves headaches, but so does the knowledge and/or belief that surrounds medication; people know from watching the television that brand X is better, and, as a result, it may well be.

More direct kinds of discourse can also affect the healing process. Several studies have shown that short conversations can have substantial effects on the healing course of surgical procedures.[11] In one study, short pre-operative conversations with an anesthetist, which described frankly the typical post-operative course, led to substantially reduced analgesic use and shortened hospital stays for abdominal surgery patients (Egbert *et al.* 1964). In another study, equally short, frank conversation between mothers and nurses substantially reduced objective and subjective discomfort for children having tonsillectomy (Skipper and Leonard 1968).[12] More recently, 200 British patients who presented in a general practice with symptoms but with no abnormal signs, and for whom, therefore, no firm diagnosis could be made, were randomly given a positive or negative consultation. "In the positive consultation, the patient was given a firm diagnosis and told confidently that he would be better in a few days." In the negative consultation, the doctor said, "I cannot be certain what is the matter with you." "A total of 64 (64 percent) of those receiving a positive consultation [reported two weeks later that they] got better compared with only 39 (39 percent) of those who received a negative consultation" (Thomas 1987: 1201).

Similar, but more significant, variations have been shown on a cultural level. A large study examined the deaths of 28,169 adult Chinese Americans and nearly half a million randomly selected matched "white" controls. It was found that "Chinese Americans, but not whites, die significantly earlier than normal (1.3–4.9 years) if they have a combination of disease and birthyear which Chinese astrology and medicine consider ill fated" (Phillips *et al.* 1993: 1142). For example, among the Chinese Americans whose deaths were attributed to lymphatic cancer ($n = 3,041$), those who were born in "Earth years" – and consequently were deemed especially susceptible to diseases involving lumps, nodules, or tumors – had an average age at death (AAD) of 59.7 years; among those born in other years, AAD was 63.6 years, nearly four years longer. Similar differences were found for other sorts of cancers, for heart attack, and for a series of other diseases. No such differences were evident in a large series of "whites" who died of similar causes in the same period. The intensity of the effect was shown to be correlated with "the strength of commitment to traditional Chinese culture." This study is phrased negatively, but the terms might be reversed, with certain astrological characteristics being associated with AAD greater [or later] than "normal."

Finally, there is evidence that shows, at least in some circumstances, that the adherence (or "compliance") of patients to their drug or placebo regime can substantially influence the outcome of treatment. For example, in a very large study of beta blockers to prevent heart attack after myocardial infarction, it was found that "good adherers" – patients who took more than 80 percent of their prescribed medication – had a five-year mortality rate of 15 percent compared to "poor adherers" – patients who took less than 80 percent of their medication – who had a five-year mortality rate of 25 percent. The more startling result was that "virtually identical findings were noted for patients who received a placebo (15 percent mortality for good adherers and 28 percent for poor adherers)" (Horwitz *et al.* 1990: 542).[13] "Taking your medicine" may be construed as a sort of autodiscourse, a confession of faith that can affect the body.

These effects are not, as some would have it, only "psychological." In the previous two cases, the outcome variable is not some sort of patient preference or other psychological measure; it is mortality. In addition, placebo analgesia, induced by injection of sterile saline, can be reversed by a subsequent injection of the opiate antagonist naloxone (Levine *et al.* 1978), thus indicating that the symbolic act has led the patient to produce endorphins, endogenous opiates. There are many other similar examples.[14]

In sum, many things shape the placebo response (more than have been considered here). Placebo effects follow from, and are shaped by, factors that influence the meanings patients attribute to their illnesses and to the treatments they receive. These include clinical factors such as physician enthusiasm and provider–patient interaction, and cultural factors such as patients' understandings of colors, forms, and names of medications, as well as their understandings of fate and faith. Reflexively, these can, in turn, influence additional clinical factors such as the patients' adherence, mood, and attitude. The placebo effect is of particular interest to anthropologists because it is a clear case of symbolic and meaningful events – involving relationship, discourse, form, belief, knowledge, commitment, history – having an apparently direct effect on human biology. From an anthropological perspective, these processes may best be labeled the "meaning response." There is no better single demonstration of the force (Rosaldo 1993) of the mindful body (Scheper-Hughes and Lock 1987) than the placebo effect. In what follows, I will examine in more detail how cultural factors may be at play in these engagements.

Measuring placebo effects

Regardless of how omnipotent the placebo effect is (or perhaps because of that omnipotence), it is not a simple or straightforward process to recognize and isolate it for analysis. In part, the difficulty of measuring placebo effects is a consequence of the complexity of the human healing process and the complexity of *measuring* the various elements of this process. Generally speaking, there are three sorts of healing processes: *autonomous ones* based on the immunological and homoeostatic processes of the body, *specific ones* based on the pharmacological or physical dimensions of the healing process, and *meaningful ones*, based on knowledge and interaction (Kleijnen *et al.* 1994; Moerman 1979; Moerman and Jonas 2002). It is often difficult to differentiate these processes.

Consider an elaborate Australian study of the treatment of moderate hypertension: tens of thousands of Australians were screened for high blood pressure. Only those with systolic pressure (SBP) greater than 200 or diastolic pressure (DBP) greater than 90 millimeters of mercury (mm Hg) were entered in the study. Various drugs or placebos were provided in a double-blind manner, and blood pressure in the participants generally dropped, as shown in measurements made every four months. The study wisely included a relatively small group of 237 untreated people with moderate hypertension whose blood pressure was also measured every four months. Their blood pressure dropped, too. The mean DBP in this group dropped from 101.5 mm Hg (mildly elevated) to about 80 mm Hg (normal) in 32 months, and then stabilized at that level (plus or minus 1 mm Hg) for the next two years (MCATT 1982). This may be evidence of "regression to the mean" in this group of people, who were selected for study because one of their vital signs was extreme; the vital sign may simply have returned to "normal" as the result of human homoeostatic processes. There are other explanations. It may be that these individuals were, when first enrolled into the study, responding nervously to having their blood pressure taken, which gave them higher blood pressure; "doctor's office hypertension" is a common phenomenon. Subsequent (tri-annual) blood pressure readings may have gradually desensitized them to this event, and their blood pressure then no longer increased with the approach of the cuff. This would be a case of a distinct "measurement effect," where the measurement created the object of study (at least for a while). There is another possibility: this may be an example of the placebo effect. There is ample evidence to indicate that the use of various medical instruments and machines can have significant healing effects. It has been suggested that this is particularly true of any instrument with the word "laser" in its name (Johnson 1994).[15] Repeated blood pressure readings may have a similar effect, lowering pressure to normal levels.

These matters are necessarily complex, and every case requires careful analysis. Measurement – which can act as treatment – is an important element in the entire situation.

The case of ulcer disease

Ulcer disease has, since the development of gastroenterology, been recognized as a classic disease of unknown origin; despite recent enthusiasm for new and simpler explanations, they have their own problems, which are addressed below. Ulcers are generally characterized as one of two main types: gastric (or stomach) ulcers or duodenal ulcers, which together constitute the class "peptic ulcers." Duodenal ulcers are generally understood to be relatively easier to treat than gastric ulcers, which are often associated with carcinoma of some sort and can be more dangerous. Pain often varies independently of ulcer disease (pain relief from treatment has a varying association with actual ulcer healing); another painful condition known as duodenitis may account for some of this variation, but that remains unclear.

Popular explanations for ulcer disease are usually of two sorts and are based on commonsense notions of "stress" and "acid." There is little evidence to support either factor; both vary independently of the incidence of ulcer disease. It is widely recognized that cigarette smoking inhibits ulcer healing under almost any treatment scheme, but the great majority of smokers do not develop ulcers. Although ulcers seem to heal more quickly in an acid-reduced or acid-neutralized environment, acid seems not to cause the ulcers in the first place. In the past decade or so, peptic ulcer disease has come to be seen as caused by infection from a bacterium, *Helicobacter pylori* (Hp). Most, but not all, ulcer patients are infected with this bacteria: infection rates for duodenal ulcer patients range from 80 to 100 percent; gastric ulcer infection rates are somewhat lower. However, only 15 or 20 percent of people with Hp infections will ever have an ulcer in their lifetime (Walsh and Peterson 1995). Ulcer disease remains a serious matter: in 1994, 6,088 deaths from ulcer of stomach and duodenum occurred in the United States (Singh *et al.* 1996).

For many years, the primary treatment option for ulcers was antacids. The effectiveness of antacids is unclear; some studies have shown some effectiveness (Lublin *et al.* 1985), and others have not (Butler and Gersh 1975), but this treatment was all that was available, and, at least for some patients, antacids reduced pain. Refractory cases (then as now) were treated surgically. In the mid 1970s, a new approach to ulcer treatment appeared with a class of drugs called "histamine H2 receptor antagonists." These drugs, commonly called hydrogen blockers, reduce the ability of the gut to produce hydrogen ions, hence limiting the amount of acid that can be produced. The first widely used drug of this type was cimetidine, sold under the trade name Tagamet® in the United States by the manufacturer Smith Kline & French. After a number of trials demonstrated its effectiveness, Tagamet® became, for some years, the leading drug in world sales. Subsequently, several additional drugs of this class and related ones were developed. The most significant was ranitidine, another hydrogen blocker sold in the United States as Zantac® by the manufacturer Glaxo Pharmaceuticals. There were many trials of this new drug as well. It is these two sets of drug trials that I describe here.[16]

Variability in randomized, double-blind, placebo-controlled trials in ulcer disease

In the earlier article on this topic, I gathered 31 trials of cimetidine treatment of ulcer. Using more powerful search techniques that are now available, I have found a total of 72 such trials from 28 different countries. In all these trials, ulcers were diagnosed and ulcer healing was confirmed by endoscopic examination;[17] patients were randomly assigned, under double-blind conditions, to either cimetidine or placebo treatment. In most cases, the drug (or placebo) was taken four times a day. Usually, tablets contained 200 mg of cimetidine, and patients were to take one at each meal[18] and two at bedtime, for a total daily dose of 1,000 mg. Some trials called for four 300-mg tablets; a few others used somewhat different dosing regimens. The outcome was clearly defined as "endoscopically observed healed ulcer craters." In all cases where it was possible, sample size was the number of patients enrolled in the trial ("intention to treat" analysis) rather than the number who completed it ("per protocol" analysis). Although this more conservative measure of drug (and placebo) effectiveness is more or less standard today, it was not in the 1970s and 1980s when most of these studies were done.[19] In many cases, it was possible to determine sample size reasonably easily; in some it was not, for example when investigators reported a total number of patients that dropped out, but did not report how many dropped out from each group. I have also gathered results from an additional 45 trials of ranitidine from 16 countries. In most of these trials, the same considerations as those of the cimetidine trials applied, except that medication was usually taken twice a day, usually 300 mg per day. A total of 32 countries are represented in the 117 trials. I eliminated from consideration other trials because they did not meet the criteria of randomization, blinding, endoscopic diagnosis, or the like.

Figure 10.1 displays the enormous variation in the placebo healing rate in these trials. The mean placebo healing rate in the 117 trials is 35.3 percent; but the rates vary enormously, from zero to 100 percent.

Figure 10.2 shows the relationship between the placebo healing rates and the drug healing rates in duodenal and gastric ulcer using cimetidine and

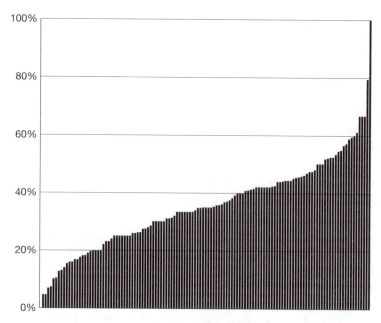

Figure 10.1 Variations in placebo healing rates in 117 different drug trials.

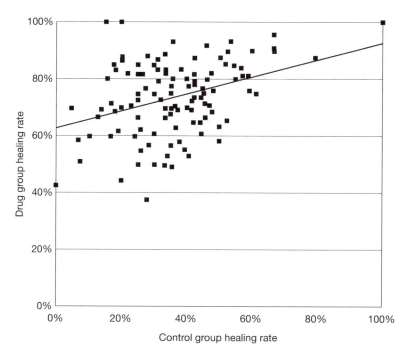

Figure 10.2 Relationship between placebo healing rates and the drug healing rates in duodenal and gastric ulcer using cimetidine and ranitidine.

ranitidine. Overall, it is clear that the effectiveness of the drug treatment and placebo treatment are related – as placebo effects increase, overall drug effects increase, too; the correlation between the rates is 0.40 ($p = 0.00001$).

This finding is highly counterintuitive for medical researchers who usually consider placebo effects to be constant – sort of like "noise" in the system – and orthogonal, unrelated, to medical effects. Both of these notions are clearly incorrect. Even those whose only interest in therapy is the use of drugs ought to be interested in the placebo effect.

These two figures stimulate several interesting questions. First, what might account for the enormous variation in placebo effect (note that the effect of placebo treatment is far more variable than is drug treatment)? Second, how can so many ulcers be healed with "nothing?"

Accounting for variability in placebo healing rates

To what can we attribute the healing of placebo-treated patients in these studies? Many factors are probably involved, but just exactly what those factors might be is a difficult question.

Autonomous healing

Ulcers just might "go away all by themselves." Perhaps there is a medical version of the "Heisenberg principle" at work here, where the observation of a phenomenon changes the phenomenon itself. The presenting symptom of ulcers is usually very sharp pain, the source of which, at least for first-time sufferers, is probably quite terrifying, raising images of potentially catastrophic disease. The diagnosis of "ulcers," rather than, say, heart disease or cancer, is likely a calming, perhaps even therapeutic or analgesic, event, reminding us of Howard Brody's classic argument that "Diagnosis is Therapy" (Brody and Waters 1980). By labeling the condition, we necessarily change it.

Another explanation is that ulcer disease is often said to be cyclical, and ulcers often may "heal by themselves." But not always or even often; recall that over 6,000 Americans died of ulcer disease in 1994. It is often the case that gastroenterologists speak of treating ulcer patients to "hasten ulcer healing." And it is clear that medication might facilitate this process.

One study that addresses the issue is a fascinating one. A Danish group diagnosed duodenal ulcers endoscopically in 91 patients who were then subjected to "passive observation for 2 weeks," whereupon they were endoscoped again. Twenty-nine patients (32 percent) had healed ulcers in two weeks. Unhealed patients were checked again, at two-week intervals, two more times. By six weeks, 52 (75 percent) had healed. (Four-week healing rates, like those in most of the studies shown in Figure 10.1, were not reported.) Can we say that these patients were "untreated?" Patients gave informed consent, although of what they were informed the report does not indicate. They received a substantial physical examination and two or more endoscopies and were asked not to consume aspirin or other nonsteroidal anti-inflammatory drugs; they were given antacids (which may have appeared to them little different than the placebos in normal double-blind trials) and were required to keep diaries noting presence of pain and antacid consumption. The authors conclude that "less than half of the ulcer patients need active treatment," although they note that they are unable to predict which half it is (Fredriksen *et al.* 1984). It is clear enough that these patients did not experience "nothing," and the attention they received is not well described by the phrase "passive observation."

Antacid treatment

One assertion made occasionally is that uncontrolled medical treatment in trials like this – particularly with antacids – could account for placebo healing in ulcer disease (Keinle and Kiene 1996). Indeed, in many of the studies shown in Figure 10.1, patients were allowed unlimited access to antacid tablets for pain relief. The situation is somewhat different regarding ulcer pain and ulcer healing.

Antacid treatment for ulcer pain

Ulcer pain is relatively easy to treat. Several gastroenterologists have argued that "it is likely that any white medicine sold as an 'antacid' will give relief of ulcer pain" (Butler and Gersh 1975: 805; see also Baume and Hunt 1969).[20] Moreover, in what might have been a more daring past, researchers demonstrated that they could relieve ulcer pain with injections of sterile saline solution (Flood and Mullins 1936). Pain relief could also facilitate ulcer healing, although I am aware of no data that demonstrate this proposition. Unfortunately, there is only a modest relationship between the presence of ulcers and pain in ulcer patients; one study, for example, notes that "the severity of 'ulcer' symptoms after four weeks' antacid/placebo treatment was a poor indicator of whether the ulcer was healed or not" (Berstad *et al.* 1982: 958; see also Peterson *et al.* 1977).

Antacid treatment for ulcer healing

The effect of antacids on ulcer healing is much less clear than their effect on pain relief. The standard treatment for acute ulcers from about 1920 until the 1970s was the "Sippy regimen," which consisted of hourly feeding of milk and antacids (Sippy 1915). The effectiveness of this treatment was always controversial. For example, as recently as the 1970s, a popular handbook for physicians on gastroenterology listed 16 reasons why "acid-pepsin cannot be responsible" for ulcer disease, which the author calls a "whole-body disease. The patient has trouble with people (ulcer is caused by people)" (Palmer 1975). In addition, a number of double-blind trials of antacid for ulcer disease have had highly variable outcomes, and outcomes in the control groups were nearly as high as those reported for the treatment groups (Gudjonsson and Spiro 1978).

In some studies, no supplementary antacids were allowed to patients in the placebo group. In one, endoscopically diagnosed ulcer patients were randomly assigned to antacid or placebo treatment; no supplementary antacids were allowed. In addition, patients were told to avoid caffeine, alcohol, and milk, but were otherwise advised to continue life normally. Twenty-four of 27 patients (89 percent) taking antacids were healed after four weeks, but so were 17 of 23 patients (74 percent) taking placebos; this is not a statistically significant difference with $X^2 = 1.89$, p $= 0.17$ (Hollander and Harlan 1973).[21] At least six of the 117 acid blocker studies reviewed here did not allow any supplementary antacids (Collen *et al.* 1980; Frank *et al.* 1989; Mach and Bogdal 1992; Moshal *et al.* 1977; Salgado *et al.* 1981). Placebo healing rates in these studies ranged from 10 percent to 74 percent and averaged 39 percent; it seems unlikely that antacid medication can account for much of the placebo effectiveness seen in these trials.

Finally, antacids are easily available over the counter in most of the world; by one estimate for Great Britain, £30,000,000 were spent annually on antacids in the early 1980s (Faizallah *et al.* 1984). Recognizing that these drugs may effectively relieve pain, one imagines that if they were all that effective for healing ulcer disease, few people would show up at the gastroenterologist's office to enter those controlled trials.

Generally, it seems that, while antacid medication may reduce some of the pain of ulcer patients, it is unlikely that systematic differences in antacid consumption can account for the substantial variations in ulcer healing seen in these trials.

Age, gender, and length of study

A few additional factors also do *not* account for differences in any substantial way. Placebo healing rates (PHR) are not related to length of study time; studies lasting four weeks have the same outcome (mean PHR = 36 percent, 86 studies) as those lasting six weeks (PHR = 33 percent, 25 studies). Age of the participants in the studies also does not affect the outcome: the correlation between average age of participants and drug healing rate is 0.02, and between age and placebo healing rate is 0.03 (neither figure is statistically significant with data available for 90 studies). Gender, likewise, has no relationship to the outcome; correlation between male/female gender ratio and drug healing rate is 0.05, and between gender ratio and placebo healing rate is –0.21 (neither is statistically significant with data available from 82 studies).

Dosing regimen

It is possible to show a small difference in outcome depending on the number of times per day that individuals take their placebos: 201 of 618 patients (32.5 percent) who took placebos twice a day were healed after four weeks, while 405 of 1,058 patients (38.2 percent) who took placebos four times a day were healed after four weeks; this difference is statistically significant (c_2 = 5.6, p = 0.018).

This finding is an important one in that it is the only one that I know of outside a psychological experiment,[22] and within a real medical setting, where one can see this meaning affecting outcome: "More pills, more healing." The difference, however, is obviously a modest one.[23]

National differences

By contrast, it is possible to show a number of substantial and significant variations in outcome when studies from different countries are compared. Three studies from Brazil demonstrate that placebo healing rates there are much lower than in other countries. The placebo healing rate is 7 percent in Brazil versus 36 percent in the rest of the world (t = 3.13, p = 0.0016).

Similarly, the placebo healing rate in six studies in Germany averages 59 percent, twice as high as in the rest of the world ($t = 3.88$, $p = 0.00018$) and three times that of two of its neighboring countries, Denmark and the Netherlands, where, in five studies, it averages 22 percent ($t = 3.21$, $p = 0.011$).

In summary, the placebo rate is very low in Brazil and in northern Europe (Denmark, Netherlands). The German placebo rate is extremely high.

Some other conditions and treatments

Are cultural variations in placebo effectiveness constants? Are the rates of placebo healing in Germany always high, and in Brazil always low? To address this, I will briefly describe data for two other medical conditions, the treatment of hypertension and generalized anxiety disorder.[24]

Hypertension

I examined more than 400 studies of drugs for the treatment of moderate hypertension; 32 studies provided comparable data.[25] Overall, active drug treatment reduced diastolic blood pressure (DBP) by an average of 10.9 mm Hg (range 7 to 21) while placebo treatment reduced DBP by 3.5 mm Hg (range –5 to 9; in two studies, placebo-treated patients had an increase in mean DBP). Active drug treatment reduced systolic blood pressure (SBP) by 15.9 mm Hg (range 7 to 28), while placebo treatment reduced SBP by 3.9 mm Hg (range –6 to 15). The correlations between drug- and placebo-induced changes in blood pressure are modest: 0.20 for SBP and 0.10 for DBP; neither is statistically significant. The clearest international variation in these data is opposite to the findings in the ulcer data. The mean placebo group change in DBP in four German trials is 0.25 mm Hg, while in the remaining 29 trials it is 3.9 ($t = 2.6$, $p = 0.013$); one study that showed an *increase* of 5 mm Hg in DBP with placebo treatment was done in Germany. The drug group change in the German studies is the same as in the remaining trials. Hence, Germany, with the highest placebo healing rates in ulcer disease, shows the least improvement in placebo treatment of hypertension. High rates of placebo effect seem to vary by medical condition within cultures. (I was unable to find any usable trials for hypertension from Brazil.)

Generalized anxiety disorder

I examined over 400 studies of a broad range of treatments for Generalized Anxiety Disorder (GAD) and extracted 37 more or less comparable trials. In all of them, individuals had some approximation of GAD as defined in DSM-III or DSM-IV[26] (see section 300.02) plus an elevated score on the Hamilton Anxiety Scale (HAS),[27] usually above 17 to 20 (of a maximum of 56). The outcome measure was the decrease in the Hamilton score. The correlation of change in HAS by placebo treatment with change by drug treatment is 0.39 ($p = 0.017$), the same as the ulcer trials; this can be interpreted to mean that the placebo effect contributes to the improvement of those patients treated with active drugs.

The mean drop in HAS in the placebo-treated groups in four Italian studies is 4.3, while the mean drop for the remaining 33 studies is 7.1 ($t = 2.06$, $p = 0.046$). Italians seem more resistant to placebo treatment for anxiety than others. The German studies are in the middle of the list, and the American ones are found all along the scale (two of the bottom five, five of the top seven). While there are some national variations in these data, they seem unrelated to the ones noted for ulcer treatment and for hypertension.

The Germans, with their extraordinarily high placebo rates for ulcer, have middling rates for treatment of anxiety and are among the lowest for treatment of hypertension. Just because placebo effects are high for one condition in some setting they need not be high for other conditions in that setting. Placebo effects vary between national cultures, they vary within them, and sometimes they seem to be unaffected by national culture. Placebo effects seem to be highly variable regardless of the axis on which you examine them.

The placebo effect in Germany and Brazil

Among the strangest findings in this study are the very low placebo effects in Brazil and high placebo effects in Germany for ulcer disease. Why do these occur? I do not know. Colleagues and students, when apprized of the German data, often break into their best "Hogan's Heroes" accent and assert that German doctors must tell their patients that "You vill get better!" The notion that medicine is somehow more authoritarian in Germany than elsewhere is not, however, borne out by others who know more about the situation. German medicine is probably the most holistic of any western European country and shows a strong concern with emotional balance; regular spa treatment is still routinely covered by the national health care system (Maretzki 1987; Payer 1996). Germany is well known for widespread use of herbal medicines and a broad range of constitutional cures.

And the data reported here for hypertension suggest that, at least for Germany, the high or low placebo effect is not a generalized phenomenon, but specific to different diseases. For example, German medicine and culture have an unusually strong concern with the "heart" and its workings; I put the word in quotation marks to indicate that I am describing an emic category (Ots 1993).

Payer (1996) notes that Germans, but not the French, British, or Americans, regularly diagnose and treat low blood pressure; in the United States, such treatment in otherwise normal individuals would probably be considered malpractice. This uncommon German view of blood pressure may be related to the low placebo effect in the treatment of high blood pressure there;

concern about their blood pressure getting too low may inhibit their response to antihypertensive treatment.

Regarding ulcer disease, Payer (personal communication) has suggested that a variable that may account for some of these cultural variations is adherence. As noted earlier, there is evidence to show that patients who take all their placebos do better than those who do not. It is possible that there may be systematic differences in adherence among patients in different Western nations (perhaps different for different medical conditions) that might account for some of the variation in healing seen here. Or, there might be persistent differences in the doctor–patient relationship or in patients' understanding of various illnesses, which could influence these different healing rates. These different factors could all be at play, and they might vary independently. For the moment, without sustained field research, there is simply no way to tell.

When I have described these findings to Brazilian colleagues, they have, essentially, denied them. "It can't be true," they have said. Further research is clearly needed to answer these fascinating questions and to address both the empirical differences reviewed here and their relationship to national self-understandings like those of my Brazilian colleagues.

Conclusions

I have shown that:

1 in three different conditions – ulcer disease, anxiety disorder, and hypertension – placebo effects are highly variable;
2 in two of these cases, there is a functional relationship between placebo effects and drug effects; as placebo effects are higher, drug effects are higher;
3 at least some portion of this variation is due to factors involving what medical treatments "mean" (for example, "4 is more than 2");
4 variations in national culture can account for some of this variation;
5 more research will be required to account for these variations.

Medicine's symbolic reality is the first principle of medical anthropology (Kleinman 1973). Meaning is the inescapable complementary medical treatment, accompanying all specific treatments – pharmacological, herbal, surgical, or manipulative. Symbolic, meaningful acts in a medical context can have a substantial effect on the sick person's experience of illness; they can have a substantial effect on actual physical lesions and, indeed, on mortality. The intervening processes (in any such case) are not at all clear and likely vary in different circumstances, probably from individual to individual, from illness to illness, and probably also from society to society. To specify these processes in more detail will require a very thick description indeed, one as sensitive to immune processes and gastric secretions as it is to metaphor and symbol.

Notes

1 Acknowledgments. The research for this paper was supported by NSF grant number SBR-9421128. Barry Bogin and Robert Hahn read the manuscript and improved it significantly. Ton de Craen provided very helpful discussion, especially regarding methodology, and Lynn Payer gave useful counsel on German medicine. The editor and several anonymous reviewers from MAQ provided useful advice. I also wish to acknowledge the unceasing support, financial and moral, of the University of Michigan-Dearborn in my work for a quarter century.
  For my grandson, Spencer.

2 The negative effects of meaning are called "nocebo effects"; I do not deal with these effects, except in passing, in this article. Anthropologist Robert Hahn has written extensively about the nocebo effect (Hahn 1997).

3 The definition of placebos and the placebo effect is an extremely vexing and difficult matter. Since the essential problem (and promise) of the placebo effect appears to be getting something (healing) from nothing (inert pills), the matter seems inherently paradoxical. For a demonstration (unwitting?) of these paradoxes, see Gøtzsche 1994. The definition adopted here differs from many others in that it differentiates placebo effects from other non-drug elements of the medical process that may account for healing (some things go away by themselves, for example). It posits a cause (meaning). It is not said to be nonspecific, or, as I have said in the past, "general." Note that, if placebo effects are said to be nonspecific, and if, subsequently, the mechanisms are identified so that the effects became "specific," they would no longer be placebo effects. To specify that something (meaning, mass) has an effect (healing, gravitational attraction) is not to specify exactly what that effect is or how it happens to be.
  Ed. Placebo effects might in part be explained by the ability of meaning per se (Moerman and Jonas 2002) to affect immune response. While "Medicine's symbolic reality is the first principle of medical anthropology" (Moerman), solid evidence about the semiosis (see Introduction to this volume) of placebo effects is still very much needed.

4 It may be worth noting that many are, indeed, intensely skeptical; while the placebo effect is commonplace, it also poses a serious challenge to much of the ideology of biomedicine, in particular, the reductionist notion that disease is a mechanical phenomenon. Much of the literature about the placebo effect is, in effect, an effort to debunk, confuse, or minimize it (Gøtzsche 1994). Even much of the more positive work usually simply suggests that the placebo effect exists, and that physicians should try to enhance its workings in their patients (Chaput de Saintonge and Herxheimer 1994, for example). Efforts to try to actually move forward our understanding of this fundamental human phenomenon are very rare.

5 This is illustrated in a rather complex study of the effect of biofeedback training on migraine headache (Kewman and Roberts 1980). Several different training groups were established along with a group that received no training; all groups kept diaries of their headaches for six weeks. All groups, regardless of the presence or absence or effectiveness of training, had fewer headaches at the end of the study than at baseline. Diary-keeping was quite elaborate and included symptom checklists, impairment ratings, and so on; subjects were reminded with phone calls every ten days or so to continue their diaries. The one thing always associated with improvement in migraines was diary-keeping. A similar three-arm trial of treatment of nausea and vomiting during pregnancy showed that patients wearing acupressure bands, those wearing acupressure bands improperly placed, and an "untreated group" all improved over the study period;

all participants kept diaries and were telephoned daily by a research assistant who recorded symptoms (O'Brien *et al.* 1996). Keeping a record of symptoms in a diary may be the minimal form of psychotherapy.

Ed. For the possibility that writing itself mobilizes immune responses that facilitate health and healing, see Pennebaker (this volume).

6 In an article that accompanied my earlier paper on this subject, Howard Brody persuasively argued that human diseases do not have "natural histories," but only meaningful and symbolic ones (Brody 1983).

7 Note that in an extended treatment of this argument, the phrase "were the same on relevant measures" would have to be unpacked; it would be shown to be a shorthand for "were the same on measures agreed upon to be construed as relevant." For a review, see Romanucci-Ross and Moerman 1997.

8 There is some evidence to indicate that the gender of clinician and patient, which can condition their relationship, might also affect the outcome of treatment (von Kerekjarto 1967).

9 *Ed. Such attributions of meaning to colors are, of course, culturally variable. For example, white can signify innocence in the West or bereavement in China.*

10 Thanks to my student Edward Gould for this observation. Color and form are not invariably this clear: Viagra, for example, is marketed in a blue tablet.

11 Surgery itself can have significant placebo effects that will not be reviewed here. This was first clearly pointed out by Beecher (1961). For a more recent review, see Moerman 1997. Placebo-controlled trials of surgical procedures are rare; for a recent one, see Moseley *et al.* 1996.

12 The children, ages 3–9, were present during these conversations, though they were not focal participants. The authors hypothesized that children's stress was "reduced indirectly by reducing the stress of the mothers."

13 Similar observations of higher success in patients taking all their placebos have been made in studies of treatments for excessive cholesterol, schizophrenia, and alcoholism, and for antibiotic treatment in cancer patients. For a review, see Horwitz and Horwitz 1993.

14 *Ed. There is very little doubt – unfortunately also very little evidence – that other mechanisms are at work here. Ader and Cohen (1991) found evidence for the classical conditioning of the immune response; the conditioned response allowed lower and lower doses of medication (e.g. antibiotic) to produce the same effect. If that is indeed the case, Moerman's evidence for cross-cultural variability of placebo response becomes evidence for cultural mediation of psychoneuroimmune links. On conditioning and PNI, see Lyon, this volume.*

15 A newly developed treatment for serious and otherwise untreatable angina pectoris is called "transmyocardial laser revascularization." With this technique, the surgeon uses a carbon dioxide or holmium laser to create 20 to 50 small channels on the epicardial surface of the left ventricle, small holes in the heart. Two studies in *The New England Journal of Medicine* have reported significant and sustained improvement in up to 75 percent of patients. However, in an editorial accompanying the articles, Hillis argues that there is no acceptable mechanism for how this treatment might work except a "marked placebo effect." "For laypersons and physicians alike, the word 'laser' is synonymous with state-of-the-art, successful therapy" (Hillis 1999).

16 *Ed. Again, bacterial infection plays a role in some, though not all, ulcer disease. Hydrogen blockers are unlikely to attack or control bacteria, but seem to have a secondary placebo function, whatever their specific effects are. The placebo process triggered by the H-blockers may involve the body's own immunocompetence helping it to overcome the bacterial infection. How to model this medicating*

process is a difficult question. Whereas Lyon (this volume) views the process as involving expectation effects, Moerman (2002) prefers to view it as a function of the meaning of the medical interaction, a meaning response. It should not, in the case of ulcer disease, be difficult in principle to learn just how this meaning response occurs, but no one has ever done the relevant experimentation. Typically biomedical researchers are more interested in attempting to "eliminate" or "control for" the responses of patients to meaningful treatment. Of course eliminating meaning from human medical encounters is about as likely as eliminating respiration or digestion.

17 An endoscope is an instrument constructed essentially of a fiber-optic tube that allows visual examination of the gut. Endoscopy is a complex procedure usually requiring anesthesia, which may have placebo effects of its own.

18 Western medical researchers seem to assume that people around the world eat three meals a day.

19 Suppose 40 patients are entered in a trial of a new drug for ulcers. Half get the drug, half get a placebo. In each group, ten patients have healed ulcers after four weeks. But suppose five patients in the drug treatment group drop out of the study because the drug causes serious headaches. On a "per protocol basis," ten of 20 (half) of placebo-treated patients are cured, while ten of 15 (two-thirds) of drug-treated patients are cured. On an "intent to treat basis," the healing rates are the same in both groups (ten of 20).

20 This may not be simply a placebo effect. It is often the case that antacid medications are flavored with mint. Mint has long been used as medication for the treatment of dyspepsia, and may have some influence on gastric pain. Various species of the genus *Mentha* and their constituents (menthol, thymol) have been listed as useful carminatives, antinausea, antivomiting, and antispasmodic agents in the *United States Pharmacopoeia* since the first edition of that work in 1820.

21 This study had another interesting twist. "Seven patients were switched to a [randomly selected] second batch of medications because of continuing peptic discomfort of high intensity after three days of therapy. Due to lack of pain relief after the first switch, one patient was switched twice. The sequence of switching was from placebo to placebo to placebo again. On the third batch of placebos, the patient obtained pain relief and his ulceration healed after four weeks of therapy" (Hollander and Harlan 1973: 1183).

22 The (experimental) case of two red or blue pills being more effective than one has already been described (Blackwell *et al.* 1972).

23 Ton de Craen of the University of Amsterdam has done a similar analysis using more sophisticated statistical methods. He included studies with drugs (proton pump inhibitors, synthetic prostaglandins) in addition to ranitidine and cimetidine, but he considered only duodenal ulcers. In 80 eligible trials, 805 of 1,821 ulcer patients taking placebos four times a day (44.2 percent) were healed after four weeks, while 564 of 1,554 (36.5 percent) of patients taking placebos twice a day were healed (c2 = 20.41, p = 0.0000) (de Craen *et al.*, in press).

24 Data used in this section are available from the author.

25 The patients are more variable in these than in the ulcer studies: mean initial systolic blood pressure (SBP) on entry to the trial, for example, varied from 140 millimeters of mercury (mm Hg) to 200 mm Hg. Mean diastolic blood pressure (DBP) ranged from 76 to 107. Most of these studies began with some sort of "placebo washout" or "run-in" stage; in these cases, patients were given inert medication for a week or two before the study actually began. During this period, individuals whose blood pressure fell below the low-level cutoff point for entry into the study were then usually dropped. Such studies have a bias against indi-

viduals responsive to meaningful treatment. These "washout/run-in" rates can be substantial. In one study from Hong Kong, 16 of 52 patients (31 percent) originally recruited were excluded because the blood pressure dropped below entry requirements for the study after four weeks of placebo treatment (Chan *et al.* 1992). In a study in the United States, 125 of 507 recruited patients (25 percent) were dropped during the four-to-six week placebo lead-in phase, "most often because their diastolic blood pressure fell below 92 mmHg" (Schoenberger and Wilson 1986: 381). Note that these run-ins are "single blind," that is, the physicians, but not the patients, are aware that the patients are receiving inert treatment. The run-in phase is usually understood as a period during which other drugs the patients might have been taking are being cleared from their systems. Since physician bias inevitably leans toward some sort of treatment, even if not the treatments the patient might have been taking, these substantial effects seem all the more remarkable and indicate how physiologically effective it can be for people to be entered into a trial. A rigorous study of the effects of placebo washout phases would be very interesting to do; it would be difficult, however, as the reports of washout effects in the literature are almost always incomplete and hard to interpret. Nonetheless, in all of these studies, patients were treated for hypertension with drugs generally deemed to be effective, or with inert placebos, and both groups usually responded with blood pressure declines.

26   DSM-III and DSM-IV are the third and fourth editions of the *Diagnostic and Statistical Manual of Mental Disorders*, published by the American Psychiatric Association. They are standardized listings of characteristics of a broad range of mental disorders (American Psychiatric Association 1987, 1994).

27   The Hamilton Anxiety Scale has a number of minor variants, and sometimes investigators modify it for their particular interests, usually by deleting a question or two. Generally, as used, the scale has 14 items (Anxious mood; Fears; Insomnia; etc.), which are each rated from 0 to 4 points in terms of a series of fairly explicit definitions (Bech *et al.* 1986). Most of these studies of GAD have a short placebo run-in phase after which patients who have dropped below the entry boundary are eliminated from the trial; usually this is 5 or 10 percent of patients, although sometimes it is more than that. As in the case of hypertension, this biases the studies against placebo effects. After the test period, the HAS is determined again, often along with a battery of other measures of mood. A number of the trials examined included two active drugs and placebo; the active drug considered here in those cases was the more effective of the two in that trial.

References

Ader, R. and Cohen, N. (1991). The influence of conditioning on immune responses. In R. Ader, D. L. Felten, and N. Cohen (eds), *Psychoneuroimmunology* (2nd edn, pp. 653–670). San Diego: Academic Press.

Aksenova, A. M., Teslenko, O. I., and Boganskaia, O. A. (1999). Changes in the immune status of peptic ulcer patients after combined treatment including deep massage [Russian]. *Voprosy Kurortologii, Fizioterapii i Lechebnoi Fizicheskoi Kultury*, 2, 19–20.

American Psychiatric Association (1987). *Diagnostic and statistical manual of mental disorders (III)*. Washington, DC: American Psychiatric Press.

—— (1994). *Diagnostic and statistical manual of mental disorders: DSM-IV*. Washington, DC: American Psychiatric Association.

Archer, T. P. and Leier, C. V. (1992). Placebo treatment in congestive heart failure. *Cardiology*, *81*(2–3), 125–133.

Baume, P. E. and Hunt, J. H. (1969). Failure of potent antacid therapy to hasten healing in chronic gastric ulcers. *Australasian Annals of Medicine*, *18*(2), 113–116.

BBC (1999) Placebo effect shocks drug makers. Electronic document. http://news2. thls.bbc.co.uk/hi/english/business/the%5Fcompany%5Ffile/newsid%5F386000/ 386773.stm

Beecher, H. K. (1961). Surgery as placebo: a quantitative study of bias. *Journal of the American Medical Association*, *176*, 1102–1107.

Benson, H. K. and McCallie Jr., D. P. (1979). Angina pectoris and the placebo effect. *New England Journal of Medicine*, *300*(25), 1424–1429.

Berstad, A., Rydning, A., Aadland, E., Kolstad, B., Frislid, K. and Aaseth, J. (1982). Controlled clinical trial of duodenal ulcer healing with antacid tablets. *Scandinavian Journal of Gastroenterology*, *17*(2), 953–959.

Blackwell, B., Bloomfield, S. S., and Buncher, C. R. (1972). Demonstration to medical students of placebo responses and non-drug factors. *Lancet*, *1*, 1279–1282.

Branthwaite, A. and Cooper, P. (1981). Analgesic effects of branding in treatment of headaches. *British Medical Journal (Clin Res Ed)*, *282*(6276), 1576–1578.

Brody, H. (1983). Does disease have a natural history? *Medical Anthropology Quarterly*, (o.s.) *14*((4):3), 19–22.

—— and Waters, D. B. (1980). Diagnosis is treatment. *Journal of Family Practice*, *10*(3), 445–449.

Butler, Melvin L. and Gersh, Harvey (1975). Antacid vs. placebo in hospitalized gastric ulcer patients: a controlled therapeutic study. *American Journal of Digestive Diseases*, *20*(9), 803–807.

Chan, T. Y., K. S. Woo, and Nicholls, M. G. (1992). The application of nebivolol in essential hypertension: a double-blind, randomized, placebo-controlled study. *International Journal of Cardiology*, *35*(3), 387–395.

Chaput de Saintonge, D. M. and Herxheimer, A. (1994). Harnessing placebo effects in health care. *Lancet*, *344*(8928), 995–998.

Collen, M. J., Stubrin, S. E., Hanan, M. R., Maher, J. A., and Rent, M. (1980). Cimetidine vs placebo: complete gastric ulcer pain relief. Six week controlled double blind study without any antacid therapy. *Acta Gastroenterologica Latino-americana*, *10*(4), 291–295.

de Craen, A. J., Kleijnen, J., Moerman, D. E., Tytgat, G. N. J., and Tijssen, P. G. (1999). Placebo effect in duodenal ulcer healing: the more the better? *British Journal of Clinical Pharmacology*, *48*(6), 853–860.

——, Roos, P. J., Leonard de Vries, A., and Kleijnen, J. (1996). Effect of colour of drugs: systematic review of perceived effect of drugs and of their effectiveness. *British Medical Journal*, *313*(7072), 1624–1626.

Egbert, L. D., Battit, G. E., Welch, C. E., and Bartlett, M. K. (1964). Reduction of postoperative pain by encouragement and instruction of patients: a study of doctor-patient rapport. *New England Journal of Medicine*, *270*, 825–827.

Ernst, E. and Resch, K. L. (1995). Concept of true and perceived placebo effects. *British Medical Journal*, *311*(7004), 551–553.

Faizallah, F., de Haan, H. A., Krasner, N., Walker, R. J., Morris, A. I., Calam, M. J., and Budgett, D. A. (1984). Is there a place in the United Kingdom for intensive antacid treatment for chronic peptic ulceration? *British Medical Journal*, *289*(6449), 869–871.

Flood, C. and Mullins, D. (1936). Treatment of peptic ulcer by means of injections. *American Journal of Digestive Diseases*, *3*, 303–305.

Frank, W. O., Young, M. D., Palmer, R., Rockhold, F., Karlstadt, R., Mounce, W., and O'Connell, S. (1989). Acute treatment of benign gastric ulcer with once-daily bedtime dosing of Cimetidine compared with placebo. *Alimentary Pharmacology and Therapeutics*, *3*(6), 573–584.

Fredriksen, H.-J. B., Matzen, P., Kragelund, E., Krag, E., Christiansen, P. M., and Bonnevie, O. (1984). Spontaneous healing of duodenal ulcers. *Scandinavian Journal of Gastroenterology*, *19*(3), 417–421.

Gøtzsche, P. C. (1994) Is there logic in the placebo? *Lancet*, *344*, 925–926.

Gryll, S. L. and Katahn, M. (1978). Situational factors contributing to the placebo effect. *Psychopharmacology*, *57*, 253–261.

Gudjonsson, B. and Spiro, H. M. (1978). Response to placebos in ulcer disease. *American Journal of Medicine*, *65*(3), 399–402.

Hahn, R. A. (1997). The nocebo phenomenon: concept, evidence, and implications for public health. *Preventive Medicine*, *26*(5), 607–611.

Hall, N. R. S. and O'Grady, M. P. (1991). Psychosocial interventions and immune function. In R. Ader, D. L. Felten, and N. Cohen (eds), *Psychoneuroimmunology* (2nd edn). San Diego: Academic Press.

Hashish, I., Harvey, W., and Harris, M. (1986). Anti-inflammatory effects of ultrasound therapy: evidence for a major placebo effect. *British Journal of Rheumatology*, *25*(1) 77–81.

Hillis, L. D. (1999) Transmyocardial laser revascularization. *The New England Journal of Medicine*, *341*(14), 1075–1077.

Ho, K. H., Hashish, I., Salmon, P., Freeman, R., and Harvey, W. (1988). Reduction of post-operative swelling by a placebo effect. *Journal of Psychosomatic Research*, *32*(2), 197–205.

Hollander, D. and Harlan, J. (1973) Antacids vs. placebos in peptic ulcer therapy: a controlled double-blind investigation. *JAMA*, *226*(10), 1181–1185.

Horwitz, R. I. and Horwitz, S. M. (1993). Adherence to treatment and health outcomes. *Archives of Internal Medicine*, *153*(16), 1863–1868.

——, Viscoli, C. M., Berkman, L., Donaldson, R. M., Horwitz, S. M., Murray, C. J., Ransohoff, D. F., and Sindelar, J. (1990). Treatment adherence and risk of death after myocardial infarction. *Lancet*, *336*, 542–545.

Ibraghimov, A. and Pappo, J. (2000). The immune response against *Helicobacter pylori* – a direct linkage to the development of gastroduodenal disease. *Microbes and Infection*, *2*(9), 1073–1077.

Johnson, Alan G. (1994). Surgery as a placebo. *Lancet*, *344*(8930), 1140–1142.

Keinle, G. S. and Kiene, H. (1996). Placebo effect and placebo concept: a critical methodological and conceptual analysis of reports on the magnitude of the placebo effect. *Alternative Therapies*, *2*(6), 39–54.

Kewman, D. G. and Roberts, A. H. (1980). Skin temperature biofeedback and migraine headaches: a double-blind study. *Biofeedback and Self-regulation*, *5*(3), 327–345.

Kleijnen, J., de Craen, A. J., Everdingen, J. V., and Krol, L. (1994). Placebo effect in double-blind clinical trials: a review of interactions with medications. *Lancet*, *344*(8933), 1347–1349.

Kleinman, A. (1973) Medicine's symbolic reality. *Inquiry*, *16*(2), 203–216.

Levine, J. D., Gordon, N. C., and Fields, H. L. (1978). The mechanism of placebo analgesia. *Lancet*, *2*(8103), 654–657.

Lublin, H., Amiri, S., and Jensen, H. E. (1985). Antacids in the treatment of duodenal ulcer. *Acta Medica Scandinavica*, *217*(1) 111–116.

Mach, T. and Bogdal, J. (1992). Low-dose antacids versus ranitidine in the short-term treatment of patients with duodenal ulcer. Endoscopic and histologic placebo-controlled study. *Materia Medica Polona*, *24*(3), 201–204.

Maretzki, T. W. (1987). The Kur in West Germany as an interface between naturopathic and allopathic ideologies. *Social Science and Medicine*, *24*(12), 1061–1068.

MCATT (Management Committee of the Australian Therapeutic Trial in Mild Hypertension) (1982). Untreated mild hypertension. *Lancet*, *1*(8265), 185–191.

McDonald, C. J. and McCabe, G. P. (1989). How much of the placebo "effect" is really statistical regression? [Letter]. *Statistics in Medicine*, *8*(10), 1301–1302.

Moerman, D. E. (1979). Anthropology of symbolic healing. *Current Anthropology*, *20*(1), 59–80.

—— (1982). General medical effectiveness and human biology: placebo effects in the treatment of ulcer disease. *Medical Anthropology Quarterly* (o.s.), *14*(4), 13–15.

—— (1997). Physiology and symbols: the anthropological implications of the placebo effect. In L. Romanucci-Ross, D. E. Moerman, and L. R. Tancredi (eds), *The anthropology of medicine: from culture to method* (pp. 240–253). Westport, CT: Bergin and Garvey.

—— (2002) *Meaning Medicine and the "Placebo Effect"*. Cambridge: Cambridge University Press.

—— and Jonas, W. B. (2002). Deconstructing the placebo effect and finding the meaning response. *Annals of Internal Medicine*, *136*(6), 471–476.

Moseley, J. B., Jr, Wray, N. P., Kuykendall, D., Willis, K., and Landon, G. (1996). Arthroscopic treatment of osteoarthritis of the knee: a prospective, randomized, placebo-controlled trial. Results of a pilot study. *American Journal of Sports Medicine*, *24*(1), 28–34.

Moshal, M. G., Spitaels, J. M., and Bhoola, R. (1977). Treatment of duodenal ulcers with Cimetidine. *South African Medical Journal*, *52*(19), 760–763.

O'Brien, Beverley, Relyea, M. Joyce, and Taerum, Terry (1996). Efficacy of P6 acupressure in the treatment of nausea and vomiting during pregnancy. *American Journal of Obstetrics and Gynecology*, *174*(2), 708–715.

Ots, T. (1993). A heart is not a heart is not a heart is not a heart: semantics of medical practice in four western countries [review of Payer 1988]. *Semiotica*, *95*, 397–401.

Palmer, E. D. (1975). *Practical points in gastroenterology* (2nd edn). Flushing, NY: Medical Examination Publishing.

Payer, L. (1996). *Medicine and culture: varieties of treatment in the United States, England, West Germany, and France* (2nd edn). New York: Henry Holt.

Peterson, W. L., Sturdevant, R. A., Frankl, H. D., Richardson, C. T., Isenberg, J. I., Elashoff, J. D., Sones, J. Q., Gross, R. A., McCallum, R. W., and Fordtran, J. S. (1977). Healing of duodenal ulcer with an antacid regimen. *New England Journal of Medicine*, *297*(7), 341–345.

Phillips, D. P., Ruth, T. E., and Wagner, L. M. (1993). Psychology and survival. *Lancet*, *342*(8880), 1142–1145.

Roberts, A. H., Kewman, D. B., Mercier, L., and Hovell, M. (1993). The power of nonspecific effects in healing: implications for psychosocial and biological treatments. *Clinical Psychology Review*, *13*(5), 375–391.

Romanucci-Ross, L. and Moerman, D. E. (1997). The extraneous factor in Western medicine. In L. Romanucci-Ross, D. E. Moerman, and L. R. Tancredi (eds), *The anthropology of medicine: from culture to method* (pp. 351–368). Westport, CT: Bergin and Garvey.

Rosaldo, Renato (1993). *Culture and truth: the remaking of social analysis*. Boston, MA: Beacon Press.

Salgado, J. A., de Oliveira, C. A., Lima Jr., G. F., and Castro de P., L. (1981). Endoscopic findings after antacid, Cimetidine and placebo for peptic ulcer – importance of staging the lesions. *Arquivos de Gastroenterologia*, *18*(2), 51–53.

Scheper-Hughes, N. and Lock, M. (1987). The mindful body: a prolegomenon to future work in medical anthropology. *Medical Anthropology Quarterly*, *1*(1), 6–41.

Schiffer, R. B. and Hoffman, S. A. (1991). Behavioral sequelae of autoimmune disease. In R. Ader, D. L. Felten, and N. Cohen (eds), *Psychoneuroimmunology* (2nd edn). New York: Academic Press.

Schoenberger, J. A. and Wilson, D. J. (1986). Once-daily treatment of essential hypertension with Captopril. *Journal of Clinical Hypertension*, *2*(4), 379–387.

Shirai, Y., Wakatsuki, Y., Kusumoto, T., Nakata, M., Yoshida, M., Usui, T., Iizuka, T., and Kita, T. (2000). Induction and maintenance of immune effector cells in the gastric tissue of mice orally immunized to *Helicobacter pylori* requires salivary glands. *Gastroenterology*, *118*(4), 749–759.

Singh, G. K., Kochanek, K. D., and MacDorman, M. F. (1996). Advance report of final mortality statistics, 1994. *Monthly Vital Statistics Report*, *45*(3) (Supplement), 1–78.

Sippy, B (1915) Gastric and duodenal ulcer: medical cure by an efficient removal of gastric juice corrosion. *JAMA*, *64*, 1625–1630.

Skipper, J. K., Jr and Leonard, R. C. (1968). Children, stress, and hospitalization: a field experiment. *Journal of Health and Social Behavior*, *9*(4), 275–287.

Smagina, N. V. (2000). The immunity characteristics of men with gastric and duodenal peptic ulcer associated with *Helicobacter pylori*. *Zhurnal Mikrobiologii, Epidemiologii i Immunobiologii*, *2*, 57–60.

Thomas, K. B. (1987) General practice consultations: is there any point in being positive? *British Medical Journal*, *294*(6581), 1200–1202.

Uhlenhuth, E. H., Rickels, K., Fisher, S., Park, L. C., Lipman, R. S., and Mock, J. (1966). Drug, doctor's verbal attitude and clinic setting in symptomatic response to pharmacotherapy. *Psychopharmacology*, *9*, 392–418.

van der Geest, S. and Whyte, S. R. (1989). The charm of medicines: metaphors and metonyms. *Medical Anthropology Quarterly*, *3*, 345–367.

von Kerekjarto, M. (1967). Studies on the influence of examiner's sex on the effects of drugs. In H. Brill (ed.), *Neuro-Psycho-Pharmacology: proceedings of the Fifth International Congress of the Collegium Internationale Neuro-Psychopharmacologicum* (pp. 552–556). Amsterdam: Elsevier.

Walsh, J. H. and Peterson, W. L. (1995). The treatment of *Helicobacter pylori* infection in the management of peptic ulcer disease [see comments]. *New England Journal of Medicine*, *333*(15), 984–991.

Further reading

Agnihotri, N., Bhasin, D. K., Vohra, H., Ray, P., Singh, K., and Ganguly, N. K. (1998). Characterization of lymphocytic subsets and cytokine production in gastric biopsy samples from *Helicobacter pylori* patients. *Scandinavian Journal of Gastroenterology*, *33*(7), 704–709.

Blanchard, T. G., Czinn, S. J., and Nedrud, J. G. (1999). Host response and vaccine development to *Helicobacter pylori* infection. *Current Topics in Microbiology and Immunology*, *241*, 181–213.

de Boer, O. J., van der Wal, A. C., and Becker, A. E. (2000). Atherosclerosis, inflammation, and infection. *Journal of Pathology*, *190*(3), 237–243.

Duchmann, R., Scherer, H., Neurath, M., Knolle, P., and Meyer zum Buschenfelde, K. H. (1997). Normal interleukin-12 production in individuals with antibodies to *Helicobacter pylori*. *APMIS*, *105*(11), 824–830.

Ernst, P. B., Jin, Y., Reyes, V. E., and Crowe, S. E. (1994). The role of the local immune response in the pathogenesis of peptic ulcer formation. [Review]. *Scandinavian Journal of Gastroenterology – Supplement*, *205*(22–28).

Fiocca, R., Luinetti, O., Villani, L., Chiaravalli, A. M., Capella, C., and Solcia, E. (1994). Epithelial cytotoxicity, immune responses, and inflammatory components of *Helicobacter pylori* gastritis. *Scandinavian Journal of Gastroenterology – Supplement*, *205*, 11–21.

Fixa, B., Komarkova, O., Krejsek, J., Nozicka, Z., and Bures, J. (1990). Specific cellular immune response in patients with *Helicobacter pylori* infection. *Hepato-Gastroenterology*, *37*(6), 606–607.

Knipp, U., Birkholz, S., Kaup, W., and Opferkuch, W. (1993). Immune suppressive effects of *Helicobacter pylori* on human peripheral blood mononuclear cells. *Medical Microbiology and Immunology*, *182*(2), 63–76.

van Doorn, N. E., van Rees, E. P., Namavar, F., and de Graaf, J. (1998). Local cellular immune response in the acute phase of gastritis in mice induced chemically and by *Helicobacter pylori*. *Journal of Medical Microbiology*, *47*(10), 863–870.

von Freeden-Jeffry, U., Davidson, N., Wiler, R., Fort, M., Burdach, S., and Murray, R. (1998). IL-7 deficiency prevents development of a non-T cell non-B cell-mediated colitis. *Journal of Immunology*, *161*(10), 5673–5680.

Chapter 11: Editor's note

In earlier work Martin (1990, 1993) and others (Sontag 1977–78) have noted the prevalence of invidious metaphoric uses of disease and the immune system, rhetorical phenomena that buttressed classism, sexism, and nationalism. Here Cone and Martin describe the social distribution of dietary and environmental factors that have non-metaphorical impacts on people around the world, but particularly the inner city poor.

 Cone and Martin propose that human immune systems benefit maximally from consuming locally grown foods and are weakened by consuming what most of us increasingly consume – products of a global food distribution system. They argue that autoimmune disorders are more likely to arise among those whose diets are non-local. Abstracting from this model produces interesting parallels with the theoretical models invoked in other chapters. Dressler (cited by Wilce and Price, Decker, and McDade) finds evidence that behavior that is consonant with sociocultural ideals carries some benefits best explained by recourse to the meaning of the behavior rather than its "specific effects." An example of a culturally valued behavior without specific health effects would be the accumulation of status symbols (Dressler 1998). Culturally dissonant behavior leads to greater stress and has health costs. While recognizing the risk of the leap I make – namely, the political and theoretical shadiness of reifying culture and its ties to a locality – there does seem to be a natural parallel between the Cone–Martin model arguing the benefits of the local (in diet) and the Dressler model arguing the benefits of consonance with local values. Where the one emphasizes soil, air, and foodstuffs as substances, the other emphasizes food, material, and actions as symbols. The functionalist nature of these models becomes even clearer when we compare them with Booth and Davison's (this volume) "harmony of purpose" or "teleological coherence" model, which finds immune and psychosocial systems sharing the common aim of maintaining self-identity.

 Several chapters, including this one, Decker's (touching missionization), and McDade's (touching individualism), raise interesting questions about globalizing modernity. Modernist assumptions of universalism underlie globalization – that is, globalization both presumes and "demonstrates" the modernist presupposition that "people are people, wherever they live." The uniformity of global food-industry products might have its parallel in universalist assumptions that certain behaviors, such as writing stress, might work for all people. The evidence on writing is, in the editor's opinion, still wanting; the evidence about the dangers of global distribution of foods is coming in more rapidly.

Chapter 11

Corporeal flows

The immune system, global economies of food, and new implications for health

Richard Cone and Emily Martin

Allergies and autoimmune disorders are increasing in incidence, especially among the urban poor. This chapter,[1] which results from conversations and research that bring together knowledge and methods from anthropology and immunology,[2] considers the interrelated biological and social implications of the increasing incidence of immune dysfunctions, and the ways in which changes in food production, transport, and consumption, circulating through global markets, may be contributing to immune dysfunctions, especially through changes in "oral tolerance."

Is collaboration between a biologist and a cultural anthropologist possible today? Would bringing insights from biological science and cultural studies together produce a synergy that scholars on both sides would find enlightening? This chapter could be seen as a test case for these questions. Richard Cone is a biophysicist who, for the first half of his career studied the fluid properties of membranes in the cell in order to further basic science. For the second half of his career he has been studying the physiological properties of sperm, the vagina, and the rectum, in order to develop a topical substance for the penis or vagina that would kill sperm and any pathogen found in human sexual orifices. Emily Martin is an anthropologist who, for the first half of her career studied cultural and social organization in the Taiwanese countryside. For the second half of her career, she has been studying the complex interplay among sciences like reproductive biology and immunology and concepts and practices that permeate the wider culture in the United States in order to understand, and influence, contemporary conceptions and practices related to health.

Reactions to drafts of this paper from our respective colleagues surprised us. We were both anxious that immunologists might be affronted by non-immunologists' suggesting new questions about the immune system. But we both felt confident that anthropologists and other students of culture would react with interest, the more so because the text is experimental in form and content. In spite of our worries, immunologists who read the paper were immensely encouraging, excitedly offering us related thoughts and references. One immunologist immediately made copies of the paper and assigned it to his students in an advanced immunology class, which he invited us to attend. Again confounding our expectations, colleagues in cultural studies were disapproving. Many felt that the paper conceded too much ground to science, and that it needed a stronger interpretive voice. No doubt future readers from the sciences will find many things to add or correct in this account, and we welcome that; but it would be dismaying if the chapter were dismissed by students of culture because it speaks too much with the voice of science. In an effort to prevent this reaction, we would suggest that this account *is* an interpretation, of the body, of the globe, and of what it means to be healthy. It is an interpretation that dramatically rearranges in importance the parts of the body that biologists think have something to do with health, and it is an interpretation that postulates dramatic connections among things that ordinarily belong to separate disciplines: *the culture and economy of food production and consumption, the recent rise of autoimmune diseases,* and *the surfaces of our bodies that produce mucus.*

Prologue

This morning I awake with another stupefyingly painful headache, which I have been told is probably caused by an allergy to something in the air. Faced with the impossible choice of taking medicine that will make me unable to stay awake or trying to work in spite of the pain, I read the New York Times' Science Times instead. I get absorbed in an article about a new form of treatment for autoimmune disorders, in which patients are fed orally the part of the body their immune systems are reacting to wrongly (i.e., since arthritis is caused by the immune system attacking and destroying collagen in the joints, arthritis sufferers are fed collagen from animal joints), and I am brought up short by the results: patients experience remission or significant relief from their symptoms.

I am electrified by the implications of this. Isn't my immune system reacting to particles in the air that are harmless (pollen or mold), wrongly treating them as harmful substances that should be attacked, producing swelling and pain in my sinuses? Maybe I can simply eat whatever is causing this reaction. . . .

I call my husband, Richard, a biophysicist, in Baltimore and ask him how I can eat what is in the air imagining pollinating flowers in soup, flowering grass on sandwiches, and spore forming molds on bread.

(EM)

Eat what is in the air? [short pause] Well, you could eat local, unfiltered honey straight from the hive. The bees have done all the work of gathering up pollen of every kind along with all sorts of airborne particles. Whatever you are allergic so, it might be in there, and you would certainly be eating it.

(RAC)

I immediately buy honey gathered from hives kept in a hamlet near Princeton (wondering why I never thought about how health food stores always seem to carry local, unfiltered honey) and after a few days of eating it, I experience profound relief from sinus pain. Ever since then, as long as I eat honey from the place I am in, my sinus problems have been dramatically reduced. Wanting to spread the news, Richard and I devise recipes so our friends who have allergies and autoimmune disorders can try oral tolerance, since the experiment might provide significant benefits at little risk or effort. One friend, whose immune system is attacking the melanin in her skin, tries eating melanin. Since melanin is found in high concentration in the eyes of any animal we suggest she can eat fish stock made out of fish heads. Same goes for another friend who has an autoimmune reaction to the vitreous fluid in her eyes. Still another friend, suffering from sinus congestion caused by allergy to molds, tries leaving her dishes out on the counter (where mold spores in the house will land on them) and then eating food from the dishes without rinsing them first.

(EM)

Introduction

Immune disorders give rise to a diverse array of health problems, some of which, especially allergies and asthma, not only cause major suffering, but also are increasing in incidence. There are few effective therapies for immune disorders, and over the past few years immunologists have begun to investigate whether food ("oral exposure") might be used to help treat autoimmune diseases such as arthritis, multiple sclerosis, and diabetes. The results are promising. The recently demonstrated effects of oral exposures on immune functions also raise the possibility that major alterations in food production, transport, and diet may be playing a role in altering the incidence and severity of immune disorders. In this chapter we describe some aspects of how food helps "instruct" the immune system to distinguish between what to attack, what to ignore, and what to protect. Occasionally the immune system can make false associations in this learning process and may start to attack something normal or innocuous as if it were a pathogen or toxin. In light of these recent immunological findings, we describe major changes in food transport, preparation, and consumption that might influence the incidence of immune disorders. Investigations of the connections between diet and immune function, "immuno-nutrition," may suggest ways to reduce the incidence or severity of immune disorders by changes in diet as well as changes in the global system of food production, processing, and transport.

Incidence of allergy and autoimmune disease

What is the evidence the incidence is rising?

The most thoroughly documented rise in incidence of these maladies is in asthma. The prevalence rate of asthma in the United States rose by 30 percent from 1980 to 1987 (Moslehi 1995). The National Institute of Allergy and Infectious Diseases reports that from 1990 to 1992 the number of people with self-reported asthma in the United States increased from 10.4 million to 12.4 million (Yunginger et al. 1992). Asthma has also been found to be more common by far (26 percent more prevalent) in African American children than in white children (Evans 1992).

In addition there is evidence that rates of death from asthma are increasing alarmingly despite recent advances in methods for treating asthma: while earlier treatments were based on the use of bronchodilators to relax the sphincter muscles that control the airways in the lungs, current therapies are based on the realization that asthma is an immune-dysfunction and hence include the use of anti-inflammatory drugs (such as cortico-steroids). Despite the resulting symptomatic improvements from this therapy, rates of death from asthma in the United States increased from 0.8 per 100,000 in 1977 to 2.0 in 1991 (Sly 1994). Another study showed that from 1980 to 1987 the rate of deaths from asthma increased by 30 percent (Moslehi 1995). Increases in death from asthma are also documented for Australia, Canada, Great Britain, and New Zealand, though Australia and New Zealand's rates have been falling recently (Sly 1994). As with the rates for asthma itself, the rates of death from asthma are highest in minorities in the United States. African Americans were three times as likely to die from asthma as whites in the period 1982–92 (CDC 1995). (See also Malveaux et al. 1993.)

Data on the incidence of allergies and autoimmune diseases are more difficult to come by. In the case of autoimmune disease, there is a pervasive impression among medical practitioners as well as the general public that they are dramatically increasing. But this impression is complicated because the number of maladies defined as autoimmune has itself been increasing, making it hard to prove an actual statistical increase in the number of cases.

Allergies are certainly pervasive. The National Institute of Allergy and Infectious Diseases says that, "while there are no solid statistics, estimates from a skin test survey suggest that allergies affect as many as 40 to 50 million people in the US" or one in five people (Gergen et al. 1987). Data are again scarce, but there are multiple indications that both allergies and autoimmune diseases affect women more than men (Schwartz and Datta 1989; CDC 1994). Not many statistics are available, but those we have indicate a rise in allergies in recent years. The number of children diagnosed with allergic dermatitis in the United States has increased from three percent in the 1960s to ten percent in the 1990s (Horan *et al.* 1992). In other countries, efforts have begun to document the widespread impression that the incidence of allergies is on the increase. Data from Sweden, Switzerland, Germany, Denmark, Japan, show a definite increase in allergic diseases (Kunz *et al.* 1991).

What might be causing these increases in incidence?

Environmental toxins, both airborne and in food, might be implicated in the rise in allergies. Japanese investigators searching for causes of the dramatic increase in pollen allergies in Japan since the 1950s, have shown that exposure to diesel exhaust exacerbates allergic responses to pollens (Miyamoto *et al.* 1988; Kunz *et al.* 1991). French researchers found that severe food allergies in France from 1984 to 1992 were most commonly caused by foods that are "not of a primary nutritional importance: celery, crustaceans, fish, peanuts, mango, mustard" but that are often "hidden allergens in commercial foods" (Andre *et al.* 1994).

In addition, we have some evidence of the onset of autoimmune diseases in a community that has recently begun to eat transported and processed food for the first time. Narjan-Mar, a town of 20,000 on the Barents Sea in Russia, has been very isolated until recently. Because the surrounding area is so boggy, Narjan-Mar's access to the outside has been possible only by boat and within the last decade by plane and helicopter. Until a decade ago, virtually all the food they consumed was produced locally. But in the last five to ten years, more and more of their food has been transported in from the outside. Concurrently, the medical staff of the local hospital has noticed an increasing number of allergies and "suppressed immune functioning." The medical staff thought the reason might be contact with outsiders or the poor quality of the food brought in from outside.[3] But the account we are about to give suggests quite a different explanation of why immune dysfunctions are increasing in places like Narjan-Mar and elsewhere, as well as how they may be linked in part to diet.

Immune disorders

What are the main types of immune disorders?

Allergies, such as hay fever and food allergies, occur when the immune system "overreacts" to airborne particles or components in food, treating benign or mildly toxic particles, such as ragweed pollen, as if they were highly toxic. The immune system expels these particles with such vigor that the immune reactions cause "bystander" damage to the lungs, gut, or other exposed tissue, and sometimes death by shock, dehydration, or suffocation. Autoimmune diseases occur when the immune system mistakenly attacks cells or tissues that are otherwise healthy "self"; in arthritis, the immune system attacks collagen or other tissues in the joints, in early-onset diabetes it attacks insulin-producing cells in the pancreas, and in multiple sclerosis it attacks nerve sheaths. Cancer can be considered a third type of immune disorder in that tumors grow only if the immune system fails to attack them, mistaking tumor cells for normal "self."

What are the roles of the immune system?

The immune system consists of multiple arrays of continuously interacting cells, many of which move around throughout the body. This "mobile brain," as the immune system is sometimes called, constantly monitors or observes not only all the tissues of the body, but also all the things in the environment that impinge upon the surfaces of the lungs, intestines, and other mucosal surfaces as well as the skin. Mobile arrays of immune cells are continuously learning and memorizing, and sometimes forgetting, what to attack, what to leave alone, and what to protect. Immune system cells can distinguish what is "self" from what is "non-self" and they can "keep house" in the body, ridding it of unwanted debris.

How does the immune system distinguish "self" from "non-self"?

For much of the past century, immunologists have focused on how the immune system learns to identify and attack pathogens, toxins, and other objects it recognizes as "foreign," such as parasites or tissue grafts, and how it learns to ignore cells it recognizes as "self." Interest in how the immune system distinguishes between "self and non-self" has led to major insights about how the immune system develops and matures. As each new immune cell begins to mature, if it reveals to its neighbors that it might later attack self, it is instructed to die before it matures (it is instructed to undergo "apoptosis," the dying process performed by normal cells at the, end of their appropriate life-span); only if a maturing immune cell demonstrates no proclivity for attacking self is it permitted to continue maturing. However, this step in self/non-self discrimination is merely a single step in cell maturation, and many subsequent interactions continuously help regulate all the activities of immune cells.

Who does the housework?

A major component of the immune system consists of phagocytic cells ("cell-eating" cells). In addition to attacking and eating invading pathogens, phagocytic cells of the immune system have another major role: macrophages ("big eaters") continuously explore around the body eating, digesting, and recycling the molecular subunits of dead cells and debris from the normal daily turnover of body tissues. Since the life-span of most cells in the body is a matter of days to weeks, phagocytosis of dead (apoptopic) cells is a major, though often ignored, activity of the immune system. Phagocytes spend *most* of their time eating, digesting, and recycling dead and dying "self"; encountering and eating a (foreign, "non-self") pathogen is a relatively *rare* event.

> *"Housekeeping" functions of the immune system have yet to become a major focus of interest in immunology – but I sometimes imagine what would happen if our phagocytes only chased after foreign invaders, but lost all interest in doing everyday housework, garbage removal, and recycling. We would literally clog up with our own garbage.*
>
> *(RAC)*

> *Like immunology, traditionally taught history highlighted the battles (men) fought, making maintenance activities (by women in the family and home) nearly invisible. Feminist accounts that attend to the importance of women's activities have revolutionized our understanding of history: it will be interesting to see whether a revolution in our understanding of the immune system could come about if the housekeeping activities of the lowly macrophage came to be regarded as more significant.*
>
> *(EM)*

What about the food we eat? Isn't it foreign?

Despite nearly a half-century of research on how the immune system distinguishes "self" from "non-self," surprisingly little attention has been directed at problems posed by this self/non-self perspective: phagocytes eat dying cells that are in every way "self"; how do phagocytes know when to start eating this "self" debris? The food we eat presents an even more challenging problem if viewed from the self/non-self perspective: food is "non-self," packed with foreign cells and foreign surfaces. But the immune system does not react against most of the food we eat. This clearly demonstrates that the immune system is *not* dedicated to attacking all that is foreign or "non-self." The immune system is more sophisticated than the seductively profound "self/non-self" dichotomy implies. If it attacked food as "non-self," we wouldn't survive. This is clearly (and fortunately only occasionally) illustrated by the dire results of eating a small amount of food to which one is allergic: salivation, nausea, vomiting, diarrhea, headache, and sometimes death. How is it that most food, all of which is "foreign," is "tolerated" by the immune system? Amongst all the foreign surfaces and molecules the immune system encounters, how does it distinguish food from foe? Or, in the terms suggested by Matzinger (1994), how does it distinguish between what is dangerous and what is not dangerous?

The immune system in the gut, which forms a major part of what is called the *mucosal immune system*, learns to recognize and accept ("tolerate") food, allowing it to be absorbed into the blood and lymph. It also learns to recognize dangerous pathogens and toxins ingested along with food and helps prevent them from being absorbed, in part by secreting antibodies (especially a type called secretory IgA) that trap the pathogens and toxins in mucus. Once trapped, this part of the immune system helps attack, eat, and otherwise detoxify them. Similarly, in the lungs, the mucosal immune system learns to recognize innocuous particles of foreign materials, such as house dust, and to distinguish them from toxic pollutants that must be immediately expelled by coughing and increased mucus flow. This allows us to breathe with ease even in the presence of multitudes of nontoxic foreign particles of dust (as revealed by a beam of sunlight), while making us sneeze, gag, or otherwise stop inhaling air when it contains too many toxic particles. By their speed and severity, allergic responses help us to identify the allergen and to avoid further contacts with it (see Profet 1991). In this way, our "mobile" brain can instruct our neural brain to alter our behavior.

I find it intriguing that immunologists have devoted far more attention to the systemic immune system, the system that monitors the blood and lymph, than to the mucosal immune system, the system that monitors the mucus on the surfaces of the gut, lungs, eyes, and reproductive tracts. It is the mucosal system that must distinguish between foreign substances that are food from foreign substances that are foe. Mucosal immunology has emerged as a separate discipline only recently, in part because it is easier to study immune activities in the blood than in mucus. It seems that studying the blood is somehow more noble or "important" than studying mucus. The research in my laboratory is aimed at developing better methods for preventing sexually transmitted diseases and unwanted pregnancy and as a result students must work with semen, cervical mucus, and other unmentionable secretions. They joke, somewhat defensively, about being "masters of mucus." The lack of interest in immune functions in mucous secretions contributes to our current lack of understanding of allergic responses. Immunologists are still at a loss for understanding why we have IgE, the class of antibodies that mediate allergic reactions. They have even proposed that we might be better off without any IgE and have investigated methods for entirely eliminating this arm of mucosal immune function.[4]

(RAC)

I can't believe it is an accident that mucosal immunology is relatively undeveloped. Much has been written by anthropologists like Mary

Douglas and Victor Turner about the deep and complex cultural meanings that often become attached to bodily substances like blood or mucus and bodily orifices like the mouth or anus. Especially strong and troubled significance seems to be attached to substances that are "betwixt and between" (neither solid nor liquid, for example, but a sticky glop like mucus).[5] Such substances arouse horror, but not because of "lack of cleanliness or health," rather because they "disturb identity, system, order: [They are] what does not respect borders, positions, rules. The in-between, the ambiguous, the composite" (Kristeva 1982: 4). In Kristeva's phenomenological account, horror is aroused by these substances because they attest to the impossible task of maintaining a clear bodily boundary between the self and the world: "the fragile border . . . where identities (subject/object, etc.) do not exist or only barely so – double, fuzzy, hetero-geneous, animal, metamorphosed, altered, abject" (p. 207).[6] Isn't it likely that scientists' disinclination to study mucus, and your lab members' joking about being "masters of mucus" would somehow be related to these cultural and phenomenological matters? Might not responses like Sartre's to "the viscous" come into play? "The slime is like a liquid seen in a nightmare, where all its properties are animated by a sort of life and turn back against me . . . the slimy offers a horrible image; it is horrible in itself for a consciousness to become slimy" (1981: 138, 140).

(EM)

How do the mucosal and systemic immune system interact with each other?

The mucosal immune system functions in partnership with the systemic immune system; each of the two systems performs markedly different func-tions, sometimes stimulating, sometimes opposing activities in the other system. Not only does the mucosal immune system learn to identify all the foreign substances in food as "food" (nontoxic, nonpathogenic), it also sends cellular messengers that can suppress systemic immune reactions against this food should it be encountered somewhere else in the body. This process is called "*oral tolerance,*" a somewhat cumbersome term used by immunolo-gists to mean "orally induced inhibition of systemic (not oral) immune reactions." In plain words, if you eat a nontoxic substance, your mucosal system can inhibit your systemic immune system from reacting against that substance. Thus the mucosal system, in the process of monitoring the diges-tion and absorption of food, learns what is nontoxic and "teaches" the systemic system to "tolerate" it, even though the substance is foreign.

If a food substance is combined with what immunologists call an "adju-vant," such as a toxin, a pathogen, or components of a pathogen, both the mucosal and systemic immune systems react *against* the substance, abro-gating oral tolerance to this substance. In short, if a toxin is attached to some food component, the mucosal immune system learns to treat that food component as dangerous and tells the systemic immune system to do the same. The details of how the presence of a toxin can switch oral tolerance (active immune suppression) to *"oral intolerance"* (active immune reaction) have yet to be clarified. Indeed, the potential abilities of toxins such as pesticides, pollutants, and food preservatives to switch oral tolerance to intolerance have yet to be investigated.

Oral tolerance was apparently discovered long ago: South American Indians are said to have fed their children poison ivy leaves to prevent the allergic skin reactions that otherwise occur if the skin contacts this plant prior to oral exposure (Dakin 1829). An early immunology experiment that demonstrated oral tolerance was reported in 1911 (Wells 1911): guinea pigs suffer a severe allergic response (sometimes fatal anaphylactic shock) if they are injected with chicken egg protein. However, guinea pigs can safely eat chicken egg protein, and if they are fed this protein for several weeks, they become tolerant to it. That is, they do not suffer a severe allergic response if it is injected into them. Oral exposure can thus produce systemic immune tolerance.

Can autoimmune disorders be treated by oral tolerance?

For much of the past century, oral tolerance has been viewed by most immunologists as merely a curiosity and given only passing mention in textbooks of immunology. Immunologic research has focused on systemic immune responses and on how to create vaccines that stimulate systemic immunity. Few immunologists have puzzled over how the immune system *learns* to tolerate that which is *not* dangerous, nor, until recently, have they focused on how it learns to distinguish between what is dangerous and what is not.[7] However, interest in autoimmune disorders has recently stimulated research on oral tolerance. Several clinical trials now in progress are testing whether oral tolerance can alleviate autoimmune diseases, such as arthritis and early-onset diabetes.

The question asked in these studies is remarkably simple: if you have arthritis, can you alleviate joint pain and swelling by eating collagen (the "antigen") to make your systemic immune system more "tolerant" of your own collagen? In a recent clinical trial, people with arthritis who ate collagen supplements derived from chicken breast bones experienced significant reductions in joint swelling and pain, and in some cases complete remission (Trentham et al. 1993). Similar trials are in progress in which patients with multiple sclerosis are eating nerve protein (myelin basic protein) from cow brain, patients with uveitis, an autoiminune degeneration of eye tissue that can lead to blindness, are eating a protein (S-antigen) obtained from cow eyes; and trials are being planned for treating juvenile and early-onset (type 1) diabetes by eating human insulin (Weiner 1994).

Diet, oral tolerance, and alternative health traditions

How can eating a substance cause oral tolerance? How might food processing, global marketing of food, and diet influence the incidence of allergies and immune dysfunctions?

Immunologists and anthropologists are only beginning to ask these questions, and before discussing what little they know we might learn more by considering alternative or folk dietary practices that relate to these questions.

Might oral tolerance play a role in alternative health traditions?

Consider first the claims made for the healing properties of honey. From the seventeenth century, honey has been described as a remedy for coughs, labored breathing, and sore throats (Mintz 1996: 6). A report from Bulgaria claims to have found that more than half of over 17,000 patients treated with honey for chronic bronchitis, asthmatic bronchitis, bronchial asthma, chronic rhinitis, allergic rhinitis, and sinusitis achieved complete remission of their symptoms (Brown 1993). Today honey is also widely believed to have anti-bacterial effects (effects that have been demonstrated in scientific studies [Subrahmanyam 1991; 1993]), anti-tumor effects as well as beneficial effects on the heart and the digestive system (Crane 1975: 260, 263; Challem 1995).

Popular contemporary sources that extol the healing properties of consuming honey abound in public libraries and health food stores (Nasi 1978; Jarvis 1960; Wade 1983). Jarvis, author of *Arthritis and Folk Medicine*, exclaims, "Honey taken every day is the body cell's best friend" (p. 120). Testimonial letters written to a company that sells raw honey, the "Really Raw Honey Company" indicate the degree of passion felt by people who get relief from allergies in such a simple way.[8] Word of mouth recipes and directions for using honey to alleviate the symptoms of allergy to airborne pollens are widespread, and news groups on the Internet, such as alt.med.allergy frequently describe how people try using honey in various ways.

> *Here is a selection from an e-mail message written to me after I responded to a message this person posted on the news group. She regularly eats a piece of honeycomb from a hive in a neighborhood adjacent to hers. She explains:*
>
> > *The honeycomb grown locally contains much if not all of the very allergens I'm allergic to. Ingesting these in small amounts is just what I'm doing with the injections [from her allergist], to increase my body's tolerance of them. The theory is, in time, your body hardly reacts to them at all. Now, [my neighbor] told me that honey*

harvested . . . in one season will have different allergens than what's collected in another season. So at that point I get confused, so I'm just operating now like, it can't HURT me. Do you know about any of that?

(EM)

Her allergist is injecting allergen to tolerize her immune system system-ically; meanwhile, she is trying to help her mucosal immune system do its normal job of causing systemic tolerance by exposing it to the allergen orally.

(RAC)

The virtues of eating honey can be understood as providing the mucosal immune system a way to learn which airborne particulates are harmless: in, the case of honey, the bees do the work of gathering up many of these parti-cles (pollen, dust, and other particles in the air) and concentrating them in honey. When we eat honey and the airborne particles it contains, the particles contact the mucosa of the mouth and the gut. In the process the mucosal immune system can learn to tolerate them and instruct the systemic immune system not to react to them as toxic.

Consider second, the health claims made for macrobiotics, a systematically devised program of diet and nutrition that stresses eating food that is local and seasonal. Macrobiotics was codified in its modern form in Japan by Sagen Ishizuka at the end of the nineteenth century (Kotzsch 1985: 28). Encouraged by his extensive study of traditional dietary practices around the world, as well as traditional Chinese and Japanese diet and medicine, Ishizuka also carried out systematic dietary experiments on himself and on patients he treated. One time he lived for a month on sweet potatoes alone to isolate their effect as a food. Since he was writing at a time of rising western influence in Japan, which some resented and resisted, it is important to note that Ishizuka in effect embraced a diet close to pre-western-influenced Japan, while at the same time proving its benefits through thoroughly western scientific experi-ments, theories, and record keeping. "He was above all a scientist in an age infatuated with science" (p. 27). In his two major books, Ishizuka sought to establish the "chemical and scientific" bases for his approach. One of Ishizuka's central tenets was that, for humans, health depends on a right rela-tionship with their natural environment. This includes eating both whole, unmilled grain and food of the immediate locality. "It provides those foods which allow him to function healthily and happily in that particular place and climate. Man should eat, then, those foods which occur naturally and abun-dantly where he lives" (p. 29).

In Japan, later scholars continued to develop Ishizuka's ideas, with a continued emphasis on eating whole and local foods (p. 44). One of these, George Oshawa, developed the idea that local food is healthiest in connection with nationalist sentiments that were running high in Japan in the late 1930s. "Oshawa urges that the government should encourage the consumption of local foods and should discourage by high taxes imported and luxury items such as sugar . . . the government . . . should stop promoting Western medicine. It should instead develop preventive programs and therapies based on traditional diet, on acupuncture, herbalism, and massage" (p. 71). Although his purpose was nationalistic, Oshawa brought vividly to light the connections between the world trade in foodstuffs and the threat to a diet based on local food.

Without a direct historical connection to Japanese thinkers, western health food advocates often came up with similar principles. For example, The Rev. Sylvester Graham (immortalized by Graham flour and the Graham cracker) advocated whole grains, fresh, local fruits and vegetables (p. 268). Henry Thoreau was influenced by Graham, and Graham's influence can be heard in this lament in *Walden* over the decline of local food in New England:

> Every New Englander might easily raise all his own breadstuffs in this land of rye and Indian corn, and not depend on distant and fluctuating markets for them. Yet so far are we from simplicity and independence that, in Concord, fresh and sweet meal is rarely sold in the shops and hominy and corn in a still coarser form are hardly used by any. For the most part the farmer gives to his cattle and hogs the grain of his own producing, and buys flour, which is at least no more wholesome, at a greater cost, at the store.
>
> (Thoreau 1930: 55; quoted in Kotzsch 1985: 268–269)

Thoreau, like Oshawa, draws a clear causal connection between distant food markets and the difficulty of obtaining local food, a connection we will explore in some detail later.

Graham also influenced the founders of the Seventh Day Adventists, whose ideas in turn were involved in the founding of the Battle Creek Sanitorium, the Kellogg diet, and the first Kellogg cereals, based on whole grains. "That the company they founded has become a giant manufacturer of products made with refined grains and white sugar is an ironic footnote" (Kotzsch 1985: 269). Regardless of the directions taken by the Kellogg company, contemporary advocates of the original principles of macrobiotics still explicitly stress eating whole and local foods (For example, see Kushi and Esko 1985: 2–9). In the United States, among those who adopt what they consider healthy and natural, eating practices, advocating eating the "whole food" is exceedingly common even without explicit adherence to macrobiotics: as it is often said, "if you eat it, eat the whole thing."

Three major postulates repeatedly emerge from these alternative health traditions: (1) eat whole food, not just refined, processed, or purified parts of animals or plants; (2) eat seasonal and local food that is minimally processed, stored, and transported; and (3) eating what you are allergic to can prevent the allergy (e.g. eat pollen in local honey to prevent hay fever).

The global food industry, dietary changes, and the immune system

Recent immunological findings and recent developments in our under-standing of the political economy of food production bear on all three of these postulates. Since changes in the organization of the food industry involving multinational firms and a global market have led to far more highly processed food being produced and consumed, food that is generally not obtained locally, eating according to any of these three postulates-becomes less and less a matter of course for most people in the world. Given the impact these changes in our diet may be having on health, understanding the interaction between the immune system and our diet has become extremely salient, and even urgent. We will discuss this interaction for each of the three postulates in turn.

I Eat whole food, not just refined, processed, or purified parts of animals or plants

Why might this make sense from the point of view of the immune system?

In addition to supplying vitamins and other diverse nutrients, eating whole, rather than refined or purified plant and animal foods, may broaden and enhance the efficacy of oral tolerance for suppressing autoimmune disorders. Recent research suggests there are at least two mechanisms by which food components can tolerize (suppress) systemic autoimmune responses (Weiner 1994). Mice can be experimentally induced to develop an autoimmune disorder that causes nerve degeneration. When such mice are fed low doses of a protein extracted from nerve tissue (myelin basic protein) they develop oral tolerance for this nerve protein, and suppress autoimmune activity against the entire surrounding nerve tissue (Miller *et al*. 1991), a form of "bystander protection." In addition, if such autoimmune mice are fed large doses of a protein (or "antigen"), they specifically suppress both antibody production and cellular immune responses against this protein. These and other experi-ments on autoimmune disorders in mice demonstrate that oral tolerance is best achieved by repeated feedings, and that a wide range of oral doses can induce oral tolerance. To date, immunologists have only tested the effects of feeding specific proteins, of "antigens," but the evidence now available suggests the broadest protection by oral tolerance might be obtained by eating the entire tissue being attacked in an immune disorder, not just one of its molecular components.

Animal tests of oral tolerance for treating autoimmune diseases have also demonstrated that molecular components obtained from many different species can stimulate protective oral tolerance. Thus, although molecules obtained from the same species may produce the strongest oral tolerance, it is not necessary to eat food components obtained from the same species (i.e. cannibalism is not required) (Miller *et al.* 1992). This illustrates a general principle in biology, that molecular structures are conserved across many species, with some molecules being nearly identical in structure in plants, yeast, bacteria, and animals. Thus, regardless of the plant or animal species from which a molecule or food component is obtained, it may stimulate oral tolerance for similar molecules or components in the body. Broad-spectrum oral tolerance is thus most likely to be achieved by eating whole plant and animal tissues, not just purified or refined components.[9]

Restated health postulate: eating a wide range of (whole) plant and animal food may create broad-spectrum oral tolerance for reducing autoimmunity and allergies

- Both plant and animal food may be useful since there is remarkable conservation of molecular structures across species. Hence diverse foods may present the broadest range of antigens and thereby suppress the largest array of potentially allergic and autoimmune cells.
- Although current immunological research has focused on molecular antigens, the results to date suggest that eating complete joint tissue, not just collagen, might be more protective against arthritis; eating whole pancreas, not just insulin, more protective against diabetes; and whole nerve or brain tissue, not just myelin basic protein, more protective against multiple sclerosis. By eating the entire tissue, clonal energy and active tolerance (immune suppression) is more likely to be generated for all the antigens in the tissue, not just for a single molecule or its nearby ("bystander") neighbors.
- Processed foods, such as refined sugar and flour from which most parts of the plant tissue have been removed, and meat products derived exclusively from skeletal muscle from which all other bodily organs have been removed, may not provide broad-spectrum oral tolerance.
- There may be no need to eat large amounts of the relevant tissue; indeed small amounts might provide the best "bystander" protection; chicken soup, or other broths made from whole animal tissue contain diverse arrays of antigens that might produce broad-spectrum oral tolerance. (On the other hand, extensive cooking, baking, and other processing either at home or in industrial kitchens may well diminish or alter the antigen-array of the fresh, unprocessed food.)

How the activities of the global food industry would make following this postulate difficult

The most obvious difficulty lies in the sheer growth in the proportion of processed food in contemporary diets, especially in developed countries. An obvious, but indirect measure of increased consumption of processed food is evidence by any number of different measures that the food processing industry has grown dramatically since the end of World War II (Connor 1988: 7–9). Processed food production, concentrated in a few countries, "account[s] for nearly two-thirds of total world food and agricultural trade" (Henderson and Handy 1994: 167). From the perspective of consumption, it is estimated that as of the mid-1990s, 80 percent of the food consumed in the developed countries is processed by the food industries (Würsch 1994: 758S). In the developed countries, although food comes to represent a smaller proportion of total expenditures, purchases of processed food make up the bulk of what is spent on food, with estimates reaching as high as 70 percent (Goodman and Redclift 1991: 30). Some of this change is because

> in most of Europe [and the United States], married women now make up a significant proportion of the total labour force. Families with two adults at work have less time to prepare meals, but two incomes provide the household with the means to purchase the relatively expensive animal products, convenience and/or high quality foods as well as to buy take-away meals or to eat in restaurants. The growth of the convenience food market indicates that consumers are prepared to pay the extra costs in order to reduce the amount of time and effort associated with home preparation of meals.
>
> (Frank and Wheelock 1988: 26)

Estimates of the dramatic growth in the amount of food eaten away from home, much of which would be processed, abound (Senauer *et al.* 1991: 32, Kinsey 1994: 47; Connor 1988: 15). In the United States "As incomes and the number of multiple-earner families rise, individuals eat out more often. The share of food expenditures away from home rose from 25 percent in 1954 to 46 percent in 1990. Most of this growth was in fast-food places" (Manchester 1995).

The amount of fresh fruit and vegetables in the American diet has been steadily decreasing in proportion to the amount of processed fruit and vegetables (Hadsell 1978: 137; Lebergott 1993: 83). Data from the US Department of Agriculture shows the nature of change between 1960 and 1981: per capita consumption of fresh potatoes declined by half, while frozen potatoes increased nearly sevenfold. Per capita consumption of fresh vegetables stayed constant, while frozen vegetables nearly doubled. Consumption of fresh fruit declined somewhat, while consumption of canned fruit juices, frozen citrus juices, and chilled citrus juice significantly increased (Prescott 1982; Food consumption 1968; 1977; *Food Consumption Supplement* 1968).

Changes in how much information the food processing industry discloses have made exact comparisons in some categories during the last few years difficult, but the rise in consumption of frozen potatoes, as well as processed fruits and vegetables continues through 1993 (Putnam 1994: 17, 43).

Not surprisingly, the impact of this increase in the amount of processed food consumed has had different effects on different ethnic and socio-economic groups.[10] Partly to express their ability to consume what is valued in the larger culture (see Decker *et al.*, this volume), low-income people do purchase processed foods: "finger foods, fun foods, snack foods, and fast and convenient foods" (Fitchen 1988: 323). But these foods have a different impact on the diets of the poor than on the affluent. An ethnographic study of poverty in the United States shows that the diets of low-income people nationwide "appear to be excessive in starches, fats, and sugars while being deficient in any or all of: meats and other proteins, vegetables and fruits, and milk products" (p. 318). "The well-to-do can afford both junk food and nutritious food; the poor can seldom afford both" (p. 324). In addition to the malnutrition that results from this diet, our argument suggests the preponderance of processed food eaten by low-income people might lead to a greater incidence of immune dysfunction (see Mann, this volume).

What exactly does food processing do to food? In the following glowing contemporary description from a report commissioned by a professional organization of food technologists, we can hear echoes of the faith that science could transform food and eating into good, rational products and processes, a faith that had first been so enthusiastically embraced in industrializing America (Brumberg 1989; Levenstein 1988):

> Food processing requires the application of a wide variety of production inputs to transform lower-valued food materials into higher-valued food products. Labor, machinery, energy, and knowledge are combined on factory floors to convert raw animal, vegetable, and marine materials into intermediate food-stuffs or finished edibles. In establishments employing one worker or thousands, farm and fishery products are slaughtered and sliced, milled and mixed, blended and bottled, fried and frozen, or subjected to any of dozens of other processes. The result is that relatively bulky, perishable, and often inedible farm products are converted into more refined; concentrated, shelf-stable, and palatable foods.
>
> (Connor 1988: 29)

Other analysts have different ways of describing what processing does to food. Richard Franke notes that transnational food firms, of which the 15 largest market most of the world's exported wheat, sugar, corn, pineapples, and bananas, "are in business to make a profit, and profits are maximized by two major factors: die cheapest possible land and labor and the maximum amount of processing" (1987: 463). For example, bananas, most of which are grown in Third World countries, return only 0.2 percent of the final price as gross margin to the producers. "The main profits go to packagers, insurance companies, shipping lines, and marketers, often owned by the same vertically integrated transnational" (pp. 463–464). Profits from pineapple, which is more processed than bananas, are increased by the processing itself, particularly when it occurs in the Third World. Profits from Dole pineapple in the Philippines are 17 times as high as in Hawaii (p. 463).

One result of increasing processing is what Magnus Pyke calls "the tendency towards *uniformity.*" Many categories of processed foods are to be found in largely similar form over widening geographic areas. Breakfast cereals, for example, are consumed over much of Europe, North America, and Australasia (1972).

> The style of 20th-century urban life, in which not only increasing numbers of people but also a steadily increasing proportion of the growing population are becoming involved, called for exactly the qualities that cornflakes provided: the cooking of maize in bulk in a factory rather than the domestic cooking of oatmeal in a thousand individual kitchens; service direct from the container rather than from a saucepan or serving bowl which would need subsequent cleaning; stability, allowing it to be put by in a cupboard without having to be covered or kept cool, thus allowing it to be taken out for a single individual living alone or eating alone separate from the rest of the household.
>
> (Pyke 1972: 77–78)

It seems paradoxical, but in addition to increased uniformity in its components, food processing now also involves increasing *product differentiation*: "the development of healthy foods for market 'niches,' often reflecting ethnic variety and traditions, but utilizing the full armoury of the food processing industry, and targeted to consumers willing to pay for high value-added products" (Goodman and Redclift 1991: 241; see also Kinsey 1994).[11] Some writers see the development of niche marketing of foods as an aspect of post-Fordist flexible accumulation which has supplanted homogeneous, industrially produced food (Goodman and Redclift 1991: 241). Others suggest a more complex phenomenon in which the same, uniform food components (soy powder, dried milk, wheat flour, sugar, flavorings, carrageen, etc.) are combined and recombined in ever more sophisticated ways to create a diverse array of final products. The supermarket aisles appear to be filled with a cornucopia of different things, but underneath the packaging and flavoring, they are all made up of the same things: "Heightened differentiation – veal oreganata, francese, milanese, pizzaiola, limonata, etc – is matched by the fact that any two packages of the same rare creation taste identical – and I mean *identical*" (Mintz 1986: 17). Mintz's astute account of the cultural context of food differentiation ties it, among other things, to the belief, common in late capitalist societies, that "consumption is by definition morally good, so that more consumption is morally better" (p. 19). "Increasing individual opportunities to consume . . . can be perceived as increasing individual freedom of choice" (p. 19).

One feature of food processing that has been on the increase since World War II is *disassembly*.

> Chickens and turkeys were originally sold as whole birds (that is, not disassembled), but since the early 1960s, more and more birds have been cut up, and some are further processed by the manufacturer. More than half of all poultry is now cut up by the manufacturer. Milk is now routinely disassembled into the butterfat and skim portions, and the latter is often further disassembled into a variety of products.
>
> (Manchester 1992: 124–125)

One cannot doubt the appeal of fast food, restaurant food, or, for the well-off, luxury items such as skinless chicken breasts or broccoli tips to time-pressed working people, especially parents. The food industry is able to profit from highly processed food in part because the work people do to survive demands the time savings it allows. Our effort is to identify how the skin, joints, inner organs, roots, peel, and leaves that are now being1 removed from our food might be altering the incidence of immune disorders so that at the very least we might learn whether what we are missing is important. In addition, highly processed foods require increased use of preservatives, which brings us to the second postulate.

2 Eat seasonal and local food that is minimally processed, stored, and transported

Why might this make sense from the point of view of the immune system?

Even though, to date, neither the food industry, nor immunologists, have addressed the effects of preservatives, food storage, and transport on immuno-logical functions, we would like to suggest that some of the pesticides and fungicides ubiquitous in contemporary agriculture, as well as some of the preservatives required for prolonged storage and transport, may play some role in the increasing incidence of immune dysfunctions. Such molecules, though demonstrated to be of relatively low acute toxicity for humans, may still be capable of occasionally triggering the mucosal immune system to switch from oral tolerance to intolerance. In addition, food handled and consumed in the presence of high levels of toxic substances in urban environments such as heavy metals (lead), solvents (gasoline), cigarette smoke, and other automobile and industrial exhaust products, must necessarily become contaminated with these toxic substances. Thus the array of pesticides, preservatives, and urban airborne toxins consumed with food may contribute to allergies and autoimmune diseases. This conjecture is based on the following immunological findings.

It has long been known that the end products of digestion, small soluble molecules, rarely if ever can stimulate immune responses – they are not effective "antigens" that generate antibodies. Most of the food we eat is in fact digested into small molecules; proteins are digested into amino acids, starches and carbohydrates into simple sugars. But some of the food we eat is only partially digested before it is absorbed into the blood and lymph. Indeed, some of the food molecules nursing mothers eat, remain incompletely digested after being secreted into their milk and even after being absorbed into the infant's blood. Thus, every time we eat a meal, despite all the digestive actions of the gut, our systemic immune systems are exposed to a vast array of foreign proteins, carbohydrates, and other incompletely digested cellular debris that is absorbed into the blood and lymph.[12]

Even though foreign molecules, oil drops, and other substances absorbed by the gut have not been fully digested, they usually do not stimulate the immune system to generate antibodies against them. Indeed, although they are foreign and obviously "non-self," most proteins are not "immunogenic"; only certain subsets carry "markers" of foreignness, like the molecules on bacterial cell walls called lipopolysaccharides (Janeway 1989).

Antibodies are likely to be generated only when "adjuvants" tell immune cells to attack the antigen. Adjuvants are sometimes called, even by immunologists, their "dirty secret." To "immunize" an animal against some molecule (the antigen), immunologists have found they must deliver the antigen together with an "adjuvant," typically Freund's adjuvant. Adjuvants are a sort of witch's brew containing toxins, pathogens, bacterial fragments, or other irritants of bacterial origin combined in a dispersion of microscopic drops of oil or other particles coated with the antigen; the process of making this oil/water dispersion is somewhat like making a toxic mayonnaise. Only if antigens are delivered in such an adjuvant do they usually stimulate strong immune reactions. Thus the toxic or pathogenic components of the adjuvant appear to instruct the immune system to recognize the antigen as "dangerous" and to generate antibodies against it and/or cellular responses that attack or expel it.

Adjuvants are such an important part of immunizing an animal against an antigen (and such a crude aspect of it) that immunologists have often forgotten to mention that they included an adjuvant in the process; they simply report that the animal was "immunized with the antigen" or "injected with the antigen," and fail to mention that the antigen was delivered in an adjuvant. This leads to difficulties in understanding since it obscures that the antigen generated immune reactions only when it was somehow labeled as dangerous. And just what labels an antigen as dangerous has yet to be investigated.

(RAC)

Some recent experiments in which a protein antigen was delivered with, and without, an adjuvant are especially revealing (Sun *et al.* 1994; Weiner 1994). In mice, if nerve sheath protein (myelin basic protein) is used as the antigen, and this antigen is combined with an adjuvant, in this case, cholera toxin, the combination acts like a vaccine,[13] a vaccine against nerve sheaths. Mice injected with this anti-nerve vaccine develop an autoimmune disease that attacks their nerves. However, as mentioned above, when these auto-immune mice are fed repeated doses of the nerve sheath antigen alone (no toxin or adjuvant the antigen induces oral tolerance that alleviates or cures their symptoms. In contrast, if a toxin is attached to the antigen, an oral exposure to this "oral vaccine" can abolish (abrogate) oral tolerance previously obtained by feeding the antigen alone, and generates both mucosal and systemic immune reactions against the antigen. In short, when an antigen is eaten without an adjuvant it is likely to stimulate the immune system to tolerate the antigen and suppress autoimmune reactions against tissues that display this antigen, oral tolerance. In contrast, if the antigen is combined with an adjuvant, it is likely to stimulate immune reactions that attack the antigen, and nearby cells, anywhere in the body that the antigen occurs, resulting in oral "intolerance."

When we eat food, most of the time the molecules we eat arrive in the *absence* of toxins, pathogens, or other things that act as adjuvants. Hence most of the time the immune system treats the food we eat as a "friend" and develops active tolerance that suppresses immune reactions against this food, as well as suppressing immune reactions against all the components in the body, or "self," that are closely similar to this food. In contrast, if a component of food is labeled with or attached to a toxin or a pathogen, the immune system treats it as "dangerous" and develops active immune reactions against it.

It is the potential "adjuvant-like" character of pesticides, preservatives, and toxic pollutants that suggests that local seasonal food that requires minimal storage and transport and requires minimal use of preservatives and exposure to pollutants may be least likely to stimulate immune disorders.

To avoid possible misunderstanding: we are not advocating any kind of simple valorization of "the local." We are only too aware that idealizations of localized communities and their cultures can play a role in nationalistic or ethnic movements with disturbing desires to achieve purity by expelling anyone who does not share the right "blood" or have a long enough historical link to local territory.[14] Since we know so little about how immuno-nutrition works, we can only speculate, but it may be that optimum conditions for the immune system do not require an unchanging locale. At either end of the class hierarchy, perhaps both itinerant farm workers and jet-setting businessmen would have fewer allergies if they were able to eat local food wherever they were: even though their locations might frequently change, their immune systems could benefit if, in each place, their guts could teach their noses not to sneeze.

Restated health postulate: eating local plant and animal food (and honey) may produce most effective oral tolerance against local airborne allergens

• Local plant and animal food, if produced and processed in ways that reduce the presence of pesticides, pollutants, and pathogens (to reduce adjuvant effects) may promote oral tolerance against airborne antigens from these same local plants and animals, and may help counteract the adjuvant effects of urban pollution. (See Profet 1991.)

How the activities of the global food industry would make following this postulate difficult

First of all we should note that the difficulty is recent. Only a little more than 100 years ago, most perishable food in Europe and America was bought at local markets. Dairy products, poultry, eggs, fruit, vegetables, meat, and fish were mainly produced locally and sold at nearby markets (Pyke 1972: 25). From almost all food passing through local markets 100 years ago, we have arrived at a situation today where almost none of it does (p. 25). Since the factors that contributed to this dramatic change are so many and complex, we can only briefly mention some of them here. They include the needs and demands of expanding industrial society to feed more workers more cheaply (Tannahill 1988: 306); the innovations of the Henry Ford of food supply, Thomas Lipton, who devised means of mass production in food processing, centralized production, and advertising for food; technological developments in transportation and preservation of food (railways, canning, and refrigeration to mention only a few) (Tannahill 1988: 306–313); and scientific innovations in hybrid seeds and fertilizer (Kloppenburg 1984: 303).

Emblematic of these changes is the situation of rural farm workers, who in a study done in Suffolk, England, in the early 1970s, "only rarely and infrequently consume[d] the food she or he produce[d] – and even then it [was] mainly in a fashion familiar to most suburban gardeners" (Newby 1983: 31). Using their deep freezer, ubiquitous among farm workers in this area, families could manage with infrequent trips to shops, located inconveniently far away. This purchased, non-local food, together with produce from their vegetable garden and gleanings from the fields after they had been harvested for Bird's Eye, made up their larder. "A deep freeze was a necessity, forced on such workers by changes in retailing and, more indirectly, by the special- ization of most farm production itself" (Goodman and Redclift 1991: 30). The people whose labor most directly produced food now purchased most of what they ate in the form of products that had gone through many stages of wholesaling, processing, packaging, retailing before it reached their hand (Newby 1983: 36).

To understand the increase in the amount of transported (not local) food consumed, we must first turn to the organization of the agricultural industry. Like many others, this industry has been marked by increasing concentration and internationalization. Indeed, in the United States, "average concentration is much higher in the food industry than in American manufacturing industry as a whole" (Leopold 1985: 320). Concentration into ever fewer and larger firms has characterized both the retail branch and the manufacturing branch of the food industry Manchester 1991: 3). For example, until recently food wholesaling was "typically a local business" (Manchester 1992: 41) because grocery wholesalers usually did not handle perishables. But in the 1950s and 1960s US wholesalers began to handle produce, frozen foods, and meat, and as they grew in size through mergers and acquisitions, distribution to retail outlets became more and more centralized. The retail source of food also became increasingly centralized with fewer stores (supermarkets) serving larger areas rather than more stores serving smaller local areas (Newby 1983: 42).

Data on the transportation of processed foods bears out the increasingly small role of consuming locally produced foods. In the United States some products are still marketed locally or regionally because of their perishability or high transportation costs: cottage cheese, fluid milk, ice cream, bread, soft drinks, and ice. But these are the only "industries where 80% of the value of shipments was delivered within 200 miles of manufacturing points" (Marion 1986: 210).[15] All other food industries are essentially "national in geographic scope: meat packing, most canned goods dried and frozen fruits and vege- tables, and beverages" (Marion 1986: 210). In other words, plants are located close to sources of major raw materials, and the finished products are distrib- uted from there around the whole country.

Rapid acceleration of the rate of internationalization of US food produc- tion may also bear on the decline of consumption of local foods. This internationalization is not just a matter of trade in food produced abroad, which would perforce not be local, it is a matter of firms themselves becoming multi-national.

When measured in terms of the value of sales, foreign operations of firms that have direct investment abroad are larger than direct trade in food and related goods by an order of several magnitudes. As a result of foreign investment and overseas operations, many firms have lost their national identities. For example, many Europeans are surprised to learn that the Kellogg Company is a US firm, and many Americans are equally surprised to learn that Pillsbury is a British firm.

(Henderson and Handy 1994: 166–167)

To achieve economies of scale across huge international markets, these firms are turning to such processes as "global ingredient procurement." For example, the New Zealand Milk Products company is owned by the multinational firm, New Zealand Dairy Board. All NZMP's raw material comes from New Zealand, and most of its dairy products are produced at its Hawera plant in New Zealand.

"You have to look at the economics of scale. It's better to supply global customers from one source," notes Patricia Boone, NZMP's vice president of sales and marketing. For instance, the Hawera plant can produce a milk protein for Kraft's specifications here in the US and with its 10 ton/hour spray dry capacity, can just as easily produce that same protein for Kraft's global operations.

(Mancini 1993: 101)

These firms also seek beneficial economic conditions within a global market. A spokesperson for Sysco, the giant distributor that supplies the "away-from-home-eating-market" in North America, explains how "economics" have led to importing from abroad many crops and products that could be obtained in the United States: seedless red bunch grapes from Chile, tomato paste from Hungary, and apricots from Spain. In some cases, to take advantage of low wage rates, California packing plants for quick frozen vegetables were "disassembled, put on barges, shipped down to the West Pacific Coast ports of Mexico and Central America, trucked into the interior and setup" (Woodhouse 1993: 208).[16]

The increase in the proportion of food that is now being stored and transported great distances suggests that the amount of preservatives consumed with this food is also increasing. Until careful research is performed to determine whether, or which, preservatives have adjuvant-like effects, the impact of increasing global food transport on immune disorders will remain unanswered.

3 Eating what you are allergic to can prevent the allergy

Does this make sense from the point of view of the immune system?

When people eat food produced in the place they usually live, the substances they ingest pass through, and are intimately monitored by, the mucosal immune system of the gut, giving it a chance to "learn" whether these substances are benign parts of the environment. When people eat food shipped across great distances, the substances eaten can be disjunct with local, airborne substances. In other words, if you eat local food (including particulate matter from the local air), your immune system may learn whether the pollen, dust, and other airborne particles you breathe are harmless. In urban environments with heavy burdens of airborne toxins, your immune system may also be more capable of distinguishing airborne toxins from benign airborne particulates.

As we discussed above, Wells demonstrated oral tolerance in 1911 by repeatedly feeding hen's egg protein to a guinea pig and thereby suppressing an otherwise fatal allergic response to an injection of this protein. More recently, an analogous process has been demonstrated in the laboratory: if mice are repeatedly fed extracts of ragweed pollen they suppress allergic reactions (production of IgE) against this allergen (Aramaki *et al.* 1994; see also Cooke and Wraith 1993; Hoyne *et al.* 1993; Metzler and Wraith 1993). These experiments in mice parallel, and help corroborate, the traditional use of honey to prevent hay fever, sinus headaches, and other human allergies.

Restated health postulate: eat the antigen (without an adjuvant) to prevent the allergy

How the global political economy of food makes this difficult

The proliferation of highly processed food in tandem with growth in the food processing industry means that food has become more and more alike. The food we buy has less and less of the local physical environment in which it was grown attached to it. Compare carrots bought from a local Farmer's Market with their roots and leaves intact and still dusty from the field to washed, frozen, diced, and peeled carrots processed by Bird's Eye in a plant far away. Food has become less and less likely to be eaten near its place of production, in tandem with the internationalization of the food industry and the growth of a global food market. All these factors mean that what we eat is often disjunct with local, airborne substances. Our immune systems are learning about one set of substances through the food we eat and another quite different set through the air we breathe. The mucosal immune system is given little chance to learn which local pollen, mold, and dust can be eaten without harm, and hence can also be breathed without harm.

Conclusions and future directions in immuno-nutrition

Immunological research now makes clear that if an antigen, such as an airborne particle or a food component, is delivered to a mucosal surface in the absence of a toxin or other adjuvant, the mucosal immune system is likely to learn to treat the antigen as a benign "friend" and actively suppress systemic immune reactions against this antigen, oral tolerance. To obtain oral tolerance, the antigens in food need not be identical to "self" antigens, they can be obtained from other species. Repeated feeding of antigens similar to a self-antigen in a tissue undergoing autoimmune attack may thus induce oral tolerance that can help alleviate or prevent autoimmune disease in that tissue. Similarly, oral doses of airborne antigens, delivered in the absence of toxins, pollutants, or other adjuvants, might alleviate allergies.

In contrast, if an antigen is combined with a toxin or other adjuvant and delivered to a mucosal surface, the mucosal immune system is likely to learn to treat the antigen as "dangerous," and stimulate both mucosal and systemic immune reactions against it. If the antigen is a self-antigen and it is delivered with an adjuvant, it can induce an autoimmune disease that attacks all cells displaying the self-antigen, and this autoimmune attack can spread to bystander cells as well, just as in allergic reactions.

Adjuvants, such as toxins and pollutants, can switch mucosal immune actions from tolerance to intolerance, or attack. Mucosal adjuvants have yet to be carefully studied or identified, but at present they are known to include toxins, such as cholera toxin, pathogenic bacteria including fragments of such bacteria, and probably smoke, solvents, and other industrial pollutants. It follows that reducing adjuvant loads, toxic air pollutants and toxins, pathogens, and other adjuvants in food may minimize the incidence of allergies and autoimmunity. Minimizing airborne toxins, such as diesel exhaust, gasoline and other solvents, lead and other heavy metals, may reduce the incidence of asthma and respiratory allergies (Profet 1991). Similarly, in food, reducing toxins, pathogens, and pesticides and preservatives with adjuvant-like activity, may minimize the likelihood of inducing food allergies and autoimmune reactions.

Pesticides play a major role in modern agriculture and food preservatives play a major role in reducing food spoilage and disease, but the potential role of pesticides and preservatives as adjuvants that might increase the incidence of immune disorders has yet to be investigated.

To achieve protective oral tolerance, optimum dose and frequency are important, yet virtually unexplored. As with vitamins and other nutrients, to develop and maintain oral tolerance, antigens need to be eaten repeatedly and in appropriate doses since the mucosal immune system is continuously learning, and forgetting, over time-spans of weeks to months. Optimal doses and frequencies for obtaining oral tolerance are still unknown.

The most protective antigens, and the most injurious adjuvants, have yet to be investigated or identified. For example, do vegetarian diets increase, or decrease, the risk of autoimmune diseases? Vegetarian diets might increase this risk by reducing oral tolerance toward self-antigens (all of which are of animal origin). On the other hand, a vegetarian diet might decrease the incidence of autoimmune disease by reducing the likelihood that animal anti-gens will be present in the gut whenever it becomes infected or irritated by toxins or other adjuvants.[17]

Conclusions and future questions in the political economy of food

Our argument links processes at very different levels: how the mucosal immune system operates, how the rate of allergy and autoimmunity is rising globally, and how both of these may be influenced by changes in the kinds of foods people have available to eat. Many elements in our argument are not demonstrable at the present time for lack of evidence. But unless the argu-ment is set forth, surely no one will bother to look! Our primary motivation in writing this paper is to stimulate studies that would investigate these links.

The ideal way to end the paper would be to discuss what is happening in a number of mediating sites, which would illustrate concretely whether and how the connections we describe are operating. The case of Narjan-Mar mentioned above, could, with the appropriate particulars, reveal how recent changes in diet, together with a high level of environmental toxins, have affected the rates of autoimmune problems. Or, if we had more information, we could discuss the extremely high rates of asthma in the south Bronx (hospitalization rates are eight times the national average): "asthma is so common that the pockets of men on street corners bulge with small breathing pumps the way they might bulge with cigars elsewhere" (Nossiter 1995: A1). These rates are already being investigated in relation to both indoor and outdoor pollution, but not in relation to recent increases in the proportion of processed and transported food (Nossiter 1995).[18]

In another place, Nogales, Arizona, rates of autoimmune diseases like lupus are extremely high (Walsh et al. 1993). For lupus alone, and considering only medically confirmed or probable cases, the rate is the highest-ever found (Cone 1996: A15).

> "To tell you the truth, it scares the hell out of me," said Anna Acuna, one of many longtime Nogales residents afflicted with lupus. "It frightens me when I see young people diagnosed, it frightens me when I see mothers incapacitated I think of us as being on the cutting edge of something that is happening all over the world."
>
> (Cone 1996: A14)

Scientists are now using new techniques to decide whether these high rates are connected to Nogales's high level of toxic contamination (mostly from industrial runoff produced by US-owned maquiladoras on the Mexican side of the town), but so far no one is looking at the additional role diet might play (pp. A14–15).

The reach and scope of the global forces now bearing on the food processing and transporting industries makes it plain there is no easy way to implement the lessons that can be learned about optimal health from immuno-nutrition. Unless the food industry's domination of food production and transport for the purpose of maximizing returns could be reduced or reversed (an unlikely prospect), diets made up of foods maximally processed and minimally local will continue to provide the path of least resistance for most, and, for the poor, the only possible path. Our hope might be overly optimistic, but one of our purposes in writing this chapter is to encourage directions in scientific research that, if communicated clearly and effectively to the general population, would, through consumer pressure, make some impact on food production and marketing. The food industry has responded many times – often led or forced by federal public health agencies – to new scientific discoveries about healthful diets and to consumer pressure to modify food accordingly. The stories of how vitamins, bran, calcium, or whole grains came to be added to foods would provide many examples.

It is quite possible that the outcome of such pressure might be a technological fix: remedy the faults of highly processed and transported food by further processing, such as close monitoring of the use of certain preservatives, or adding a "globally representative" cocktail of airborne particles. This would require careful evaluation! It is also possible that some consumers (if they were able) would react by withdrawing from the market, giving up their skinless chicken breasts or broccoli tips for homemade chicken stew or vegetable soup. Beyond these possibilities, there are many small ways people could at low risk experiment with variations in their diet without waiting for either the food industry or scientific research to catch up.

Revealing the operations of the powerful forces that bear on health in the interface between the body, diet, and the environment carries both encouraging benefits as well as frightening risks and we will end on this disquieting note. On the one hand, if the mucosal immune system could be harnessed to educate the body about what is and is not toxic, the incidence of auto-immune illness might be reduced. On the other hand, who will be in a position to say what the content of that education should be? For example, who will bear the costs if our bodies can be taught to "tolerate" higher levels of industrial pollution?

Notes

1 We would like to thank readers of earlier drafts of this paper for their insights and suggestions: Albert Bendelac, Lauren Berlant, Norma Field, Lorna Rhodes, Sharon Stephens, Adria Trowbridge, Rick Trowbridge, Martin Weigert, and Donna Haraway. We will answer for any faults that remain.
2 The conventions of biophysics about multiple authors generally place the senior author and head of the lab in the place of honor, last. The conventions of anthropology generally order multiple authors alphabetically. We are following the latter convention.

3 Thanks to Sharon Stephens for reporting this case to us after her trip to Narjan-Mar with a group from the University of Trondheim, Norway.
4 Janeway and Travers 1994.
5 See Mary Douglas (1980) and Victor Turner (1967) for the classic accounts in anthropology.
6 Grosz 1994: 192ff cogently discusses Kristeva, Douglas, and Sartre on the in-between and the viscous.
7 For an insightful discussion of this question, see Matzinger 1994.
8 Thanks to Mimi Roha at "Really Raw Honey Company" for showing me some of these letters and allowing me to use their extensive library of books and articles on honey.
9 Of considerable practical interest for treating autoimmune disorders, if certain nontoxic subunits of bacterial origin are coupled to the food component (e.g., lipopolysaccharide, subunit B of cholera toxin), they *enhance* oral tolerance, as if their bacterial origin acts as a recognition enhancer that, in the absence of a toxin, increases the vigor with which the mucosal immune system instructs the systemic immune system to tolerate the food component (Khoury *et al.* 1992; Sun *et al.* 1994).
10 Space limitations prevent us from dealing adequately with the enormously important cultural meanings attached to food and all aspects of its preparation. Exemplary works on this subject include Mintz 1985; Douglas 1984; Goody 1982; Levenstein 1988; Feeley-Harnik 1994.
11 Jerome notes the dramatic increase in the variety of foods carried in supermarkets in the United States from the 1920s to the 1970s (1975: 93).
12 One of the most striking examples of how undigested food enters the blood and lymph is the way undigested droplets of oils and fat ("chylomicrons"), along with any other food components adhering to their surfaces, are transported directly from the lumen of the gut to the lymph. Milk, like mayonnaise, is white in color because it is a suspension of fat droplets. After eating milk, or any meal high in fat content, the lymph vessels in the gut (the "lacteals") turn white as they collect all these transported drops of oil and fat.
13 *Ed. Robert Ader (Ader and Cohen 1991) has experimentally demonstrated the classical-conditionability of immune systems in rats. On classical conditioning, see Lyon, this volume.*
14 See Balibar 1991: 21 on culture, territory, and racism in Europe. See Holston and Appadurai 1966: 191 on exclusionary local movements across the globe.
    Ed. And see Martin 1990 and Sontag 1977–78 on the metaphorical rendering of foreigners as invading germs and the invocation of germ metaphors to frame immigration debates.
15 For lack of space we do not discuss it here, but the enormous growth in marketing and consumption of specialty water, "spring" water often shipped far from its place of origin, would be an interesting additional case to consider in comparison to foodstuffs.
16 Gretel and Pertti Pelto have coined the term "delocalization" to refer to processes in which "food varieties, production methods, and consumption patterns are disseminated throughout the world in an ever-increasing and intensifying network of socio-economic and political interdependency" (1983: 309). They argue that delocalization has improved the nutrition of people in industrialized nations through an increase in diversity of the diet, while it has deteriorated food diversity in less industrialized nations. Our argument would question whether there might be deleterious health effects from delocalization even when it leads to increased food diversity.

17 In all types of animals including insects, reduced food intake may contribute to increasing life-span. The mechanism by which reduced food intake has this virtually universal effect is not known, but it has been suggested that reduced food intake, especially reduced fat intake, may reduce the incidence of autoimmune diseases. Since fat and molecules associated with it are absorbed relatively undigested into the lymph and blood in the form of droplets (chylomicrons), and since many toxins are oil soluble, foods high in fats may be more likely to increase the incidence of immune disorders, especially in the presence of high burdens of toxins and pollutants.

18 Other studies that are investigating the impact of chemical toxins on the immune system include Germolec 1994 and Frolov *et al.* 1993.

References

Ader, R. and N. Cohen. 1991. The influence of conditioning on immune responses. In R. Ader, D. L. Felton, and N. Cohen (eds) *Psychoneuroimmunology* (2nd edn, pp. 653–670). San Diego: Academic Press.

Andre, F., C. Andre, L. Cacarace, F. Colin, and S. Cavagna. 1994. Role of new allergens and of allergens consumption in the increased incidence of food sensitizations in France. *Toxicology* 93(1): 77–83.

Aramaki, Y., Y. Fujii, H. Suda, I. Suzuki, T. Yadomae, and S. Tsuchiya. 1994. Induction of oral tolerance after feeding of ragweed pollen extract in mice. *Immunology Letters* 40(1): 21–25.

Brown, Royden. 1993. *Royden Brown's Bee Hive Product Bible*. Garden City Park, NY: Avery.

Brumberg, Joan Jacobs. 1989. Beyond meat and potatoes: a review essay. *Food and Foodways* 3(3): 271–281.

Centers for Disease Control and Prevention (CDC). 1994. *Vital and Health Statistics, National Ambulatory Medical Care Survey 1991 Summary*. DHHS Publication (No. PUS 94–1777). Washington, DC: US Department of Health and Human Services; Public Health Service; National Center for Health Statistics.

—— 1995. Asthma – United States. *Mortality and Morbidity Weekly Report* 43(51–52): 952–955.

Challem, Jack. 1995. Medical journals document value of bee propolis, honey, and royal jelly. *Natural Foods Merchandiser*.

Connor, John M. 1988. *Food processing: an industrial powerhouse in transition*. Lexington, MA: Lexington Books.

Cooke, A. and D. C. Wraith. 1993. Immunotherapy of autoimmune disease. *Current Opinion in Immunology* 5(6): 925–933.

Crane, Eva. 1975. *Honey: a comprehensive survey*. London: Heinemann.

Dakin, R. 1829. Remarks on a cutaneous affection produced by certain poisonous vegetables. *American Journal of Medical Science* 4: 98–100.

Douglas, Kate and Cathryn Prince. 1995. Eating away at disease? *New Scientist* 145 (1961): 36–40.

Douglas, Mary (ed.) 1984. *Food in the social order: studies of food and festivities in three American communities*. New York: Russell Sage Foundation.

Dressler, William M., Mauro Campos Balieiro, and Jose Ernesto Dos Santos. 1998. Culture, socioeconomic status, and physical and mental health in Brazil. *Medical Anthropology Quarterly* 12(4): 424–446.

Evans, R. 1992. Asthma among minority children: a growing problem. *Chest* 101(6): 368s–371s.

Farb, Peter and George Arinelagos. 1980. *Consuming passions: the anthropology of eating.* Boston: Houghton Mifflin.

Feeley-Harnik, Gillian. 1994. *The Lord's table: the meaning of food in early Judaism and Christianity.* Washington, DC: Smithsonian Institution Press.

Fitchen, Janet M. 1988. Hunger, malnutrition, and poverty in the contemporary United States: some observations on their social and cultural context. *Food and Foodways* 2: 309–333.

Food Consumption, Prices, Expenditures. 1968. Agricultural Economic Report (no. 138). Washington, DC: US Department of Agriculture, Economic Research Service.

—— 1977. Agricultural Economic Report (no. 138, 1977 supplement). Washington, DC: US Department of Agriculture; Economics, Statistics and Cooperatives Service.

Food Consumption, Prices, Expenditures Supplement for 1968. 1968. Supplement to Agricultural Economic Report (no. 138). Washington, DC: US Department of Agriculture, Economic Research Service.

Frank, Judith and Verner Wheelock. 1988. International trends in food consumption. *British Food Journal* 90(2): 22–29.

Franke, Richard W. 1987. The effects of colonialism and neocolonialism on the gastronomic patterns of the Third World. In M. Harris and E. B. Ross (eds), *Food and evolution: toward a theory of human food habits* (pp. 455–479). Philadelphia, PA: Temple University Press.

Gergen, P. J., P. C. Turkeltaub, and M. G. Kaovar. 1987. The prevalence of allergic skin reactivity to eight common allergies in the US population: results from the second National Health and Nutrition Examination Survey. *Journal of Allergy and Clinical Immunology* 80(5): 669–679.

Gofton, Leslie. 1989. Sociology and food consumption. *British Food Journal* 91(1): 25–31.

Goodman, David and Michael Redclift. *Refashioning nature: food, ecology, and culture.* London: Routledge.

Goody, Jack. 1982. *Cooking, cuisine, and class: a study of comparative sociology.* New York: Cambridge University Press.

Hadsell, Robert M. 1978. Food processing: search for growth. In J. Dye (ed.), *The feeding web* (pp. 131–140). Palo Alto, CA: Bull Publishing.

Henderson, Dennis R. and Charles R. Handy. 1994. International dimensions of the food marketing system. In L. P. Schertz and L. M. Daft (eds), *Food and agricultural markets: the quiet revolution* (pp. 166–195). Washington, DC: National Planning Association.

Horan, R. F., L. C. Schneider, and A. L. Scheffer. 1992. Allergic skin disorders and mastocytosis. *Journal of the American Medical Association* 268(20): 2858–2868.

Hoyne, G. F., R. E. O'Hehir, D. C. Wraith, W. R. Thomas, and J. R. Lamb. 1993. Inhibition of T cell and antibody responses to house dust mite allergen by inhalation of the dominant T cell epitope in naive and sensitized mice. *Journal of Experimental Medicine* 178(5): 1783–1788.

Janeway, C. A. 1989. Approaching the asymptote? Evolution and revolution in immunology. *Cold Spring Harbor Symposium in Quantitative Biology* 54: 1–13.

Janeway, Charles, and Paul Travers, 1994. *Immunobiology: the immune system in health and disease*. New York: Garland Publishing.

Jarvis, D. C. 1960. *Arthritis and folk medicine*. New York: Fawcett Crest.

Jerome, Norge W. 1975. On determining food patterns of urban dwellers in contemporary United States society. In M. L. Arnott (ed.), *Gastronomy: the anthropology of food habits* (pp. 91–110). The Hague: Mouton.

Khoury, S. J., W. W. Hancock, and H. L. Weiner. 1992. Oral tolerance to myelin basic protein and natural recovery from experimental autoimmune encephalomyelitis are associated with downregulation of inflammatory cytokines and differential upregulation of transforming growth factor beta, interleukin 4, and prostaglandin E expression in the brain. *Journal of Experimental Medicine* 176(5) 1355–1364.

Kinsey, Jean. 1994. Changes in food consumption from mass market to niche markets. In L. P. Schertz and L. M. Daft (eds), *Food and agricultural markets: the quiet revolution* (pp. 44–57). Washington, DC: National Planning Association, Report no. 270.

Kloppenburg, J. Jr. 1984. The social impacts of biogenetic technology in agriculture: past and future. In G. M. Berardi and C. C. Geisler (eds), *The social consequences and challenges of new agricultural technologies*. Boulder, CO: Westview Press.

Kotzsch, Ronald E. 1985. *Macrobiotics yesterday and today*. Tokyo: Japan Publications.

Kunz, B., J. Ring, and O. Braun-Falco. 1991. Are allergies really increasing? *Fortschritte der medizin* 109(17): 353–356.

Kushi, Aveline, and Wendy Esko. 1985. *The changing seasons macrobiotic cookbook*. Wayne, NJ: Avery Publishing Group.

Lebergott, Stanley. 1993. *Pursuing happiness: American consumers in the twentieth century*. Princeton, NJ: Princeton University Press.

Leopold, Marion. 1985. The transnational food companies and their global strategies. *International Social Science Journal* 37(3): 325–320.

Levenstein, Harvey. 1988. *Revolution at the table: the transformation of the American diet*. New York: Oxford University Press.

Malveaux, F J., D. Houlihan, and E. L. Diamond. 1993. Characteristics of asthma mortality and morbidity in African-Americans. *Journal of Asthma* 30(6): 431–437.

Manchester, Alden C. 1991. The food marketing revolution, 1950–90. *Agriculture Information Bulletin, Economic Research Service* (627): 1–8.

—— 1992. *Rearranging the economic landscape: the food marketing revolution, 1950–1991*. Agricultural Economic Report (660). Washington, DC: Economic Research Service, US Department of Agriculture.

Mancini, Leticia. 1993. The global ingredients supermarket. *Chilton's Food Engineering* 65: 95–101.

Marion, Bruce W. 1986. *The organization and performance of the US food system*. Lexington, MA: Lexington Books.

Martin, E. 1990. Toward an anthropology of immunology: the body as nation-state. *Medical Anthropology Quarterly* 4(4): 410–426.

—— 1993. Histories of immune systems. *Culture, Medicine, and Psychiatry* 17(1): 67–76.

Matzinger, P. 1994. Tolerance, danger, and the extended family. *Annual Review of Immunology* 12: 991–1045.

Metzler, B., and D. C. Wraith. 1993. Inhibition of experimental autoimmune encephalomyelitis by inhalation but not oral administration of the encephalitogenic peptide: influence of MHC binding affinity. *International Immunology* 5(9): 1159–1165.

Miller, A., O. Lider, and H. L. Weiner. 1991. Antigen-driven bystander suppression following oral administration of antigens. *Journal of Experimental Medicine* 174(4): 791–798.

Miller, A., O. Lider, A. al-Sabbagh, and H. L. Weiner. 1992. Suppression of experimental autoimmune encephalomyelitis by oral administration of myelin basic protein from different species. *Journal of Neuroimmunology* 39(3): 243–250.

Mintz, Sidney W. 1985. *Sweetness and power*. New York: Viking.

—— 1986. American eating habits and food choices: a preliminary essay. *Journal of Gastronomy* 2(3): 15–22.

—— 1996 The conquest of honey by sucrose: a psychotechnical achievement. In: Mintz, S. W. *Tasting food, tasting freedom: excursions into eating culture and the past* (pp. 50–66). Boston: Beacon.

Miyamoto, T., S. Takafuji, S. Suzuki, K. Tadokoro, and M. Muranaka. Environmental factors in the development of allergic reactions. In R. W. Estabrook (ed.), *Toxicological and immunological aspects of drug metabolism and environmental chemicals* (pp. 553–564). New York: F.K. Schattauer Verlag.

Moslehi, Javid. 1995. Asthma gene localized by Hopkins researchers. *Johns Hopkins Newsletter* (Baltimore, MD), A (Part 1): B1–11.

Nasi, Andrea. 1978. *The honey handbook*. New York: Everest House.

National Institute of Allergy and Infectious Diseases. 1995. *Asthma and allergy statistics*. Washington, DC: National Institutes of Health, Public Health Service.

Newby, Howard. 1983. Living from hand to mouth: the farmworker, food and agribusiness. In A. Murcott (ed.), *The sociology of food and eating* (pp. 31–44). Hants: Gower.

Paul, William E. (ed.) 1989. *Fundamental immunology*, 2nd edn. New York: Raven Press.

Pelto, Gretel H. and Pertti J. Pelto. 1983. Diet and delocalization: dietary changes since 1750. In R. I. Rotberg and T. K. Rabb (eds), *Hunger and history: the impact of changing food production and consumption patterns on society* (pp. 308–329). Cambridge: Cambridge University Press.

Prescott, Richard (compiler). 1982. *Food consumption, prices, and expenditures, 1960–80*. Statistical Bulletin (694). Washington, DC: Economic Research Service, US Department of Agriculture.

Profet, Margie. 1991. The function of allergy: immunological defense against toxins. *Quarterly Review of Biology* 66(1): 23–26.

Putnam, Judith Jones. 1994. Food consumption, prices, and expenditures, 1970–93. *Statistical Bulletin* (915). Washington, DC: Economic Research Service, US Department of Agriculture.

Pyke, Magnus. 1972. *Technological eating*. London: John Murray.

Randolph, Theron G. and Ralph W. Moss. 1989. *An alternative approach to allergies*. New York: Harper and Row.

Schertz, Lynn P. and Lynn M. Daft (eds). 1994. *Food and agricultural markets: the quiet revolution*. Washington, DC: National Planning Association, Report no. 270.

Schwartz, Robert S. and Syamal K. Datta. 1989. Autoimmunity and autoimmune diseases. In W. E. Paul (ed.), *Fundamental immunology*, 2nd edn (pp. 819–866). New York: Raven Press.

Senauer, Ben, Elaine Asp, and Jean Kinsey. 1991. *Food trends and the changing consumer*. St Paul, MN: Eagan Press.

Sharman, Anne. 1991. From generation to generation: resources, experience, and orientation in the dietary patterns of selected urban American households. In A. Sharman (ed.), *Diet and domestic life in society* (pp. 174–203). Philadelphia, PA: Temple University Press.

Sly, R. M. 1994. Changing asthma mortality. *Annals of Allergy* 73(3): 259–268.

Sontag, S. 1977–78. *Illness as metaphor*. New York: Farrar, Strauss, Giroux.

Subrahmanyam, M. 1991. Topical application of honey in treatment of burns. *British Journal of Surgery* 78(4): 497–498.

——— 1993. Honey impregnated gauze versus polyurethane film (OpSiter) in the treatment of burns – a prospective randomised study. *British Journal of Plastic Surgery* 46(4): 322–323.

Sun, J.-B., J. Holmgren, and C. Czerkinshy. 1994. Cholera toxin B subunit: an efficient transmucosal carrier-delivery system for induction of peripheral immunological tolerance. *Proceedings of the National Academy of Sciences USA* 91(28): 10795–10799.

Tannahill, Reay. 1988. *Food in history*. New York: Crown Publishers.

Taylor, W R. and P. W Newacheck. 1992. Impact of childhood asthma on health. *Pediatrics* 90(5): 657–662.

Thoreau, Henry David. 1930. *Walden*. London: J. M. Dent.

Trentham, D. E., R. A. Dynesius-Trentham, E. J. Orav, D. Combitchi, C. Lorenzo, K. L. Sewell, D. A. Hafler, and H. L. Weiner. 1993. Effects of oral administration of collagen on rheumatoid arthritis. *Science* 261: 1727–1730.

Wade, Carlson. 1983. *Propolis: nature's energizer: miracle healer from the beehive*. New Canaan, CT: Keats Publishing.

Weiner, Howard L. 1994. Oral tolerance. *Proceedings of the National Academy of Sciences USA* 91(23): 10762–10765.

Wells, H. 1911. Studies on the chemistry of anaphylaxis. III. Experiments with isolated proteins, especially those of hen's egg. *Journal of Infectious Diseases* 9: 147–251.

Woodhouse, John A. 1993. Sourcing fruits and vegetables in a global food system. In G. E. Gaull and R. A. Goldberg (eds), *The emerging global food system: public and private sector issues* (pp. 207–209). New York: John Wiley.

Würsch, Pierre. 1994. Carbohydrate foods with specific nutritional properties – a challenge to the food industry. *American Journal of Clinical Nutrition* 59 (suppl.): 758s–762s.

Yunginger, U. S., D. E. Reed, E. J. O'Connell, L. J. Melton, W M. O'Fallon, and M. D. Silverstein. 1992. A community-based study of the epidemiology of asthma: incidence rates, 1964–1983. *American Review of Respiratory Disease* 246(4): 888–894.

Further reading

Balibar, E. 1991. Is there a "neo-racism"? In E. Balibar, and I. Wallerstein (eds), *Race, nation, class: ambiguous identities* (pp. 17–28). London: Verso.

Cone, M. 1996. Human immune systems may be pollution victims. *Los Angeles Times*, May, pp. 1, A14–15.

Douglas, M. 1980. *Purity and danger: an analysis of the concepts of pollution and taboo.* London: Routledge and Kegan Paul.

Frolov, V M., N. A. Peresadin, V, Ya. Vitrishchak, and A. M. Petrunya. 1993. Assessment of immune status in employees of large chemical plants in Donbass. *Immunologiya* (5): 57–59.

Germolec, D. R. 1994. Immune alterations resulting from exposure to chemical mixtures. In R. S. H. Yang (ed.), *Toxicology of chemical mixtures: case studies, mechanisms and novel approaches.* San Diego, CA: Academic Press.

Grosz, E. 1994. *Volatile bodies: toward a corporeal feminism.* Bloomington: Indiana University Press.

Holston, J. and A. Appadurai. 1996. Cities and citizenship. *Public Culture* 8(2): 187–203.

Kristeva, J. 1982. *Powers of horror: an essay on abjection.* New York: Columbia University Press.

Nossiter, A. 1995. Asthma common and on rise in the crowded South Bronx. *New York Times*, September, pp. A1, B2 col. 3.

Sartre, J.-P. 1981. *Existential psychoanalysis.* New York: Philosophical Library.

Turner, V. 1967. *The forest of symbols.* Ithaca, NY: Cornell University Press.

Walsh, B. T., M. Reed, J. Emerson, E. P. Gall, L. Clark, and Living For Everyone Community Group (USA). 1993. A large cluster of systemic lupus erythematosus individuals in a Mexican-American border town in Arizona. *Arthritis and Rheumatism* 36(9 suppl.): S145.

Part IV

Critical retrospectives

Chapter 12: Editor's note

This chapter reflects on the chapters comprising this volume and proposes new ways of thinking about them together. David Napier, an anthropologist whose areas of expertise include metaphor, the arts, medicine and immunology, is the author of the forthcoming book, The Age of Immunology: Conceiving a Future in an Alienating World *(University of Chicago). Napier questions some of the assumptions underpinning much work in the psychobiology of stress and PNI. How can experience be studied via experiment, a different epistemological modality? Why should stress be so consistently considered harmful rather than transformative? What of the validity of immunology's claim that maintaining a self/nonself distinction is the central goal of the immune system? To such problems, Napier applies one of anthropology's most basic assertions – that meaning mediates the health impacts of events and that culture mediates all meaning – and asks about possibilities for such relativist perspectives in immunology. After critically reflecting on the philosophical foundations of immunology, Napier asserts the significance of this volume's arguments and findings for that discipline. In the end, he finds the authors' achievement in the way they have expanded the domain of inquiry, hoping that they have prompted a more honest inclusion of the social – not as a variable that can be reduced to a function of the autonomous individual psyche or soma but as a phenomenal field of its own.*

Stressful encounters of an immunological kind

The social dimensions of psychoneuroimmunology

David Napier

Whence experience?

In his study of how certain habits of thought influence the form and content of scientific systems of belief, Howard Margolis (1993) is careful to distinguish between "experience" (as a form of embodied knowledge) and "experiment" (as a domain of self-conscious contrivance). The point of the distinction is not only to show just how unlike the experience of living experimental contrivances actually are, but to emphasize how different – even antithetical – are their behavioral paradigms. Whereas experiments by definition seek to eliminate uncertainty and to limit novelty to a controlled domain of observation, experiences are assessed by the quality of a response to the unexpected. Experiments strive for replicability as a mode of validation, whereas being "experienced" is measured by the degree to which an event transcends what is commonplace. Experimental truths are predictably replicable, experiential ones are often extraordinary. The constrained novelty of laboratory life works, it may even be said, against the singular novelty that makes for meaning in the domain of experience.

Thus, experiences are important because they are unique, while experiments are so because they are easily repeated. Experiences depend upon novel responses to stress, while experiments catalogue predictable responses to stressors. At the level of stress, therefore, the two could not be more unalike, which, in a nutshell, is why the science of studying stress is always at odds with the social world of experience. While the unpredictability of daily living wreaks havoc on the controlled settings of scientific experimentation, the controlled nature of experimental contrivance is regularly a part of daily life. Games and rules are, as theorists well know, an excellent example of the infusion of testable regularity into the inchoate practice of living, to the extent that we have numerous settings in which the controlled domain of measurable stimuli – the basic building blocks of scientific experiment – depend deeply upon that which we commonly label as "social."

Though games are often perceived as a relief from daily toil, at times the chance meeting of these two domains – of uncontrolled social novelty and controlled experimental novelty – allows us to witness their differences dramatically. For me, such an event took place during a visit to a local shopping mall with my, then, twelve-year-old son. Like so many children of that age, the experience of visiting a games store (which today means a "video" games store) is as much of a ritual experience as is the experience of playing the games that are marketed by such establishments. But on that day, I became his unwitting accomplice, for on entering the establishment I was immediately taken aback by a frightening display of a new interactive game that invites one to engage in cellular warfare as an embodied microorganism. Players in this virtual battleground can project themselves into the very mitochondria that convert the energy provided by food into the energy that cells employ while engaging in their own versions of Armageddon.

My first reaction was the typical one of a wary parent in an altogether unhealthy place: what, I thought, could possibly be the benefit of my son's sitting in front of a television monitor moving his thumb and forefinger for hours on end while the rest of the muscles in his body cried out for what we Americans call quality time?

What's it like to play a video game in which one is able to assume the role of mitochondria or of protein envelopes? Will these experiences actually benefit our abilities to think creatively, or are they merely dulling experiences that make us duller still? All I could think about was the view I had so often heard expressed that this kind of activity was, in total, wholly unhealthy.

For sure, I would have probably never challenged this argument had the virtual spaces I witnessed been inhabited by the usual array of graphic war games, sports competitions, and science fiction. But the presence of those mitochondria drew to my attention an immediate irony: namely that these very kinds of battle images – the ones to which we attribute so many of the social ills of today – were precisely of the sort that, in psychoneuroimmunology (henceforth, PNI), had been touted as health-inducing stimulants for cancer sufferers. As Wilce and Price discuss herein, the idea of visualizing the defeat of pathogens has for some time now (e.g. Hall and O'Grady 1991, Rider and Weldin 1990, Rider et al. 1990) been promoted as a means of stimulating active immune responses. The idea that antibody production can be stimulated through visual imagery has, in fact, been enough acknowledged that at least one entire professional journal (*Journal of Mental Imagery*) was launched to publicize research on the relationship between mental imagery and well-being. Let children, for instance, engage in video warfare in which they can, say, reduce white blood cell counts, and promote in them a positive outlook on their potential for surviving cancer – or, at least, that is the working assumption.

So, what is ironic in this? Well, nothing really, if the victory one experiences produces a sense of success and well-being. Where the irony enters is in our common belief that stress, *in and of itself*, is unhealthy. How many heart attacks are attributed by families and friends to stress and to conscious stress in particular (see Mann, this volume)? How many meditation training courses are based upon the belief that relaxation promotes immunity? Indeed, how much research in psychoneuroimmunology (from Ader and Cohen onwards) is predicated on the assumption that stress is debilitating and that it is by definition harmful to immunity?

Yet, if stress is harmful to immune function, why do athletes remain healthy? Why do CEOs miss the fewest days of work on account of sickness? Why do so-called "invincible kids" transcend sometimes horrid familial circumstances to become productive members of society? Why do people attribute their most meaningful transformations in life to events that are often stressful? The answer, of course, is simple. It is because these all are instances in which the experience of stress produces a positive, empowering outcome. These are cases, in other words, where the results of a stress-induced transformation are positive rather than negative, and they are, all of them, mitigated by the ontological setting within which they unfold. Rats that display addictive behavior in a particular controlled environment will, as Peele has beautifully demonstrated (1985), elect for transcending their pathologies when that controlled space includes colorful objects and additional stimuli.

In short, it's the *context* and meaning of the stressful event, not merely one's response to a given stressor, that determines whether stress will be a catalyst for a beneficial transformation, or a harbinger of disaster. The former we see regularly in what are often called "religious experiences," the latter in so-called "illnesses." As structures of personal change, of course, the two are indistinguishable – both, that is, are profound forms of transformation, profound moments when individuals are brought to the threshold of a cathartic transformational change; but one turns out beautifully, the other, well, more often than not, abysmally. They seem opposite to us; yet, as the anthropological literature on rites of passage amply demonstrates, in form they are so alike. This unpredictability of stress is also precisely why evolution is not at all a theory in the sense of possessing rules that have predictive value – why evolutionary "challenges" are only recognized in retrospect as either destructive or enhancing. In fact, one might say that the goal of each of our lives is to orchestrate stressful events so that they have a productive, rather than a destructive, end. This may, indeed, be why life's struggles will always possess a deeply moral dimension.

Realizing the *ambivalence* of stress and its transformations is, of course, important – especially in the context of a book that examines the interaction between the social and what we call the exact sciences. First, it is important because the specificity of science (and especially its tendency to make fetishes of its quantitative measures) frequently devalues those repetitive social stressors whose effects are variable and cumulative. Second, the actual ambivalence of stress is important because all too often we look back upon events that have bad outcomes and only then label them as stressful. The ones that turn out well, on the other hand, get narratively reframed in ways that normalize them – that align them with paradigms of well-being that suppress their initial danger and uncertainty. That's why illness regularly is equated with chaos and disaster, while stressors that produce satisfying outcomes get absorbed in adaptive narratives of growth and health, if not of spirituality and religion. Stress, then, gets identified with changes that are largely negative, while happiness homogenizes potential disorder into stories that are at odds with the often unsettling nature of everyday life.

One of the major hurdles for PNI research (acknowledged centrally in this volume by the contribution of Flinn and England) is, then, to find ways in which the complex origins of illness outcomes – that is, the "algorithms" of stress – can be studied experimentally. In Indonesia, for instance, the *benefits* of destabilizing and paroxysmal trance states are contrasted to the awareness that repeated exposure to stressors that are experienced outside of trans-formative contexts – stressors that are not catalysts for growth – either over-stimulates a person, or wears him down. *Everything* here depends on the social context in which stressful experiences are carefully orchestrated. From a certain Southeast Asian perspective, for us to study stress as a specific stim-ulus to a measurable response is to fail to understand its meaning entirely.

Compare the Balinese view (as outlined in this volume by Wilce and Price) to the experimental method: now each time one introduces an addi-tional variable into one's research, each time one lets the lab animal wander around the neighborhood, one threatens to contaminate the controlled condi-tions of laboratory life, and, in so doing, to undermine the verifiable methods that are the basis of scientific truth. Indeed, one might even argue that the specificity that is characteristic of the experimental method in itself limits our ability to do justice to the social variables at work. An individual suffering the stress of a leg fractured while saving a child from an oncoming car has a much different view of the outcome of their stress than the individual who broke the exact same bone after plunging down a tenement staircase that a slumlord had failed to repair.

As so many of the contributors to this volume make clear, there is little or no attempt to account for social factors in the psychoneuroimmunology liter-ature, where, as Lyon points out, "lip service is given to action through such terms as 'behavior' and 'psychosocial factors.'" As a result of this neglect, explanations of a social nature are not only overlooked but also rarely, if ever, applied in the experimental study of biological response mechanisms. Sometimes, in fact, it is hard to resist the paranoid view that the field of PNI research was itself started as a means of limiting the authority of social explanations precisely at the moment when they seem most applicable – to reappropriate a domain that bench scientists felt to be slipping from their tightly controlled experimental grasp! So, the methods of scientific research themselves may, in part at least, be to blame for the limited impact of social explanations on scientific discourse. To create an experimental climate, then, where an event's effects on hormonal activity can be measured is not, in and of itself, to have quantified stress.

These observations seem so obvious and self-evident that, stepping back a bit from all of the media hype around stress and immunity, one is shocked by the absence of collections such as the present one. Where, one might ask, are all of the interdisciplinary collections in which the social and psychological dimensions of psychoneuroimmunology are attended to with the same degree of thoroughness as the many volumes of specious research in which the questionable belief that 'types' of people are cancer-prone not only goes unexamined, but is handsomely funded by our governments and universities?

Here, the domain of psychosomatic research, and, specifically, Mann's chapter on hypertension, seem especially applicable. In his work we see how the traditional view of psychosomatic conditioning – that perceived emotional distress repeatedly raises blood pressure and causes sustained hypertension – cannot be confirmed by research. Indeed, there appears to be at best a weak link between anger and/or anxiety and hypertension, and perhaps even an *inverse* relationship between perceived emotional distress and hypertension, despite popular belief and decades of research claiming that such a connection exists.

Setting aside for a moment the profound impact that his findings might have for, say, the therapeutic uses of biofeedback and meditation, Mann calls attention to a much more plausible connection between the *isolation* or *dissociation* of emotional states and severe hypertension. Survivors of severe trauma, for instance, who uniformly insisted that such experiences "had no lingering impact on them" are more frequent sufferers of severe and symptomatic paroxysmal hypertension. According to Mann, "recent studies have documented [for instance] that emotional support is more relevant to survival in the months and years following myocardial infarction than are any of the traditional risk factors such as cholesterol, blood pressure, or smoking." We've known for some time that anaesthetized patients undergoing surgical procedures have better outcomes when polite language is used in the operating room, and that, conversely, individuals experiencing shock will have poorer outcomes when family members mourn their suffering.[1] Why not, then, step out of the lab for a moment to discover how the actual living of life does, indeed, influence the effects of stress on each of us?

Recognition of these relationships goes back to Cannon's days (1942) and beyond. This long history, however, seems to have done little to promote a serious attending to the beneficial and detrimental influences that the social has upon the physical, especially as the social relates not only to pathology and morbidity, but to health and well-being also. Perhaps it may yet become wholly obvious why we need to face the individual and social powers of placebos – where the care and the giving mean as much as what is given. Perhaps we may even finally accept how, as Moerman so cogently puts it, "meaning is the inescapable complementary medical treatment" (this volume).

The incision quest

So, two people playing the same video game of cellular war may have totally different responses to their respective visceral projections. For one person it might be a dulling, mechanically repetitive activity that is actually numbing, while for another, or for that same person in another setting, that stimulus might be the precise vehicle for inducing a positive transformation. We've seen both arguments convincingly made – which, in itself, ought to alert us to the fact that something much deeper is going on when we examine stress. In the face of the laboratory conditions that gave rise to Ader and Cohen's landmark work, we must, then, place Peele's equally provocative finding that an addictive stimulus can have a radically different outcome once we modify the social setting in which that stimulus is experienced (1985, 79 ff.). In West Africa, female circumcision may have deep cultural meaning, while to some American activists it is nothing more than genital mutilation. For the Sioux Indian, a vision quest makes enlightenment possible through imposed hardship; for that Indian's psychiatrist, the patient is merely a troubled masochist.

So, going through the motions without the right "spirit" quickly changes the meaning of a creative activity into something less encouraging. The difficulty for illness experiences is that the odds of manipulating the experience of ill-health into a life-giving kind of change seem, and so often are, overwhelming. Though illness is, almost by definition, wholly undesirable, it shares with love its transformative power.

What is lost in seeing illness monolithically (as only a saddening moment in an otherwise happy life) is the reality of change – that, in fact, transcending hardship can be a hugely fulfilling experience in even the dullest moments of daily living. Why, then, not look at illness more positively? Well, first of all because our images and metaphors for illness are also monolithically appalling: body warfare, loss of self-control, giving up one's body to the invader – i.e. our dominant images are defeating us from the outset. And second, because illness is, well, sickening: it is simply naïve to promote in the face of genuine suffering a "don't-worry-be-happy" message, such as one may readily find in all of the self-help and recovery books that say "feel good and you'll get better."

Let's face it; serious illnesses are mostly not transcended. For every Lance Armstrong who turns cancer into a catalyst for winning the Tour de France, there are millions who succumb. But who is to say who is the nobler, though we rush to make heroes of those who "win out" over their illnesses? And in our efforts to make the Lance Armstrongs of the world more than mortal, we cover up the fact that something happened *within the illness experience itself* that allowed him to love who he was – that made it possible for him to see the beauty in the video game he had crawled into. He *wanted* to discover some new dimension of experience and he was lucky enough to discover it, or believed strongly enough to see the discovery of it when he found its door unlocked.

Why, then, do we appear so culturally unaware of the ambivalent nature of stressful encounters? Why, at the molecular level, do we suppress our knowledge of the true sympathy between antigen and antibody that is necessary for their induced binding? In immunology, I suspect, this suppression occurs primarily because our culturally preferred ways of describing transformational encounters leave no room for ambivalence, real though its transformational role may be. We see warfare and hatred everywhere, even if the facts of molecular induction prove that metaphors of vaccinology (the assimilation of difference rather than its elimination) fit what can be observed much better than do the self/nonself models of immunology.

Thus, recognizing the limited accuracy of immunological models of cell–cell relations in no way helps us to understand why culturally we think of pathogenic encounters as *only* sickening. So, the moment a Lance Armstrong surfaces, all we know how to do is make a hero of him even though his illness may be as conditioning as it is punishing; we suppress, in the end, the awareness that his pathogens actually had a highly *creative* impact upon his well-being. Our views of stressful events, in other words, change just as much as we ourselves are changed by them – so much so, in fact, that *time* itself becomes an essential ingredient in the codification of a stressful event's meaning.

Indeed, once we begin to look at a particular form of stress as a catalyst (positive or negative) for social transformation, we also begin to recognize that the meaning of a stressful event not only changes over time, but changes quite variably from one individual to the next. This fact became quite apparent to me while working over many years with undergraduate students who had agreed to volunteer at a shelter for the homeless. Initial responses from students immediately following a one-month hospital residency included feelings of uncertainty, and a desire for more "structure" within a hospital setting that did not necessarily shelter them from the aggressive and often hostile abuses they daily had to endure. Interviews with the same twenty-five students six months after their internships illustrated an absence of concerns about guidance within the program, and a heightened awareness of the potential benefits of what was initially a quite destabilizing period in their lives. Two years following the internships, nearly every student stated that the experience had been one of the most meaningful events of their lives, describing the time they spent, to the person, as "worthwhile."

Likewise, research I have conducted over ten years with some two hundred and fifty primary-care doctors has demonstrated repeatedly that success as a primary caregiver (especially in remote areas where self-sufficiency has real advantages) can be directly correlated to having had an unsettling, sensitizing experience before the age of eighteen. Even when interviewees had not decided to become doctors until they were thirty or even forty years of age, they uniformly recalled early experiences when asked to identify the most important event that allowed them to make an informed professional decision.

Why, then, are we spending so much money trying to humanize medical school students, rather than spending those funds on providing informative experiences for our youth? Because that young family member or hospital volunteer standing stressfully in an emergency room watching a procedure he or she cannot influence will come back again and again to that moment. Yes, it may put them over the top, but it can also be the very event that galvanizes them *over time* to commit themselves – even against all odds – to a career in primary care. What we are witnessing, in other words, is a transformation, a rite of passage, but one that in a contemporary setting may take years to unfold. So, why DON'T we spend money on it? In part because the benefits take so long to unfold that they are no longer linked – especially on a policy level – with the stimulus; but also because we have conditioned ourselves as a society to think of stress primarily in debilitating terms.

The outcome of stress, then, has as much to do with our sense of what its experience might give way to – our feelings about it (meta-emotions and metasentiments, [see Wilce and Price in this volume]) over quite variable lengths of time – as it does to the immediate influence it may have upon us in a controlled setting. And what else, besides the way we place in context a specific experience, can account for how we ascribe to that experience a particular meaning? As Hampshire, the empirical philosopher, once put it: "How can you say what a man is trying to do, unless you know what he expects to happen?" Therein lies the case for a true need for recognizing the role of anthropology – indeed, for the social sciences in general – in psychoneuroimmunology.

"That art thou"

To varying degrees, every contribution to this volume acknowledges the deep role of the social sciences in achieving a better understanding of immunology. Indeed, for some, building this bridge is a primary goal. As Lyon describes it, the original mission of PNI was to understand how immune function, as a process, could be "conceptualized as *emergent in the context of ongoing social and bodily relations,*" to move, in other words, "beyond the limited conception of the immune system as autonomous and self-regulating." But, as she rightly argues, the fundamental question remains: "How are we to understand and represent the linking of body and behavior in a way that goes beyond the measurement of simple correlations in the two domains" – especially when "there is little attempt in the PNI literature to deal with the question of social action, even though lip service is given to it through such terms as 'behavior' and 'psychological factors'"?

Well, the long and the short of it is that, for immunology (if not for all of medical science), one can't and, indeed, may never so do within the current Cartesian construct of autonomous individuals confronted with social stimuli (ten Have 1987). It may even be the case that social explanations will never be brought fully to bear on biological mechanisms so long as the body is understood as a wholly autonomous agent. At the same time, however, the Cartesian nature of how we see ourselves does not keep us from recognizing how a broader view of emotion might, as Lyon says, provide "a very different framework for the examination of how social and biological being are intertwined and emergent in the context of social life."

Examining the concepts of "conditioning" and "mimesis" (and, to a lesser extent, of "habit" and "emotional contagion"), Lyon argues that emotion is "a crucial concept in any understanding of the dialectic between social and bodily life," illness and health and thus (by implication) immune function. "Whereas behaviorist forms of explanation imply that persons or animals are conditioned, in fact it is always a particular aspect of [a person's] behavior in a particular context which is subject to the conditional influence *not the person*" per se. Mimesis, in other words, makes possible a kind of Maussian contagion in which the relationship between self and world need not take on a conceptual or a verbal form. For Lyon (following Taussig), mimesis provides the medium for linking self and other because of its emphasis "on visceral involvement and on movement and intention."

The focus here is on how people construct and "construe themselves in terms of their interrelatedness," embryologically, as it were, rather than specifically. Contagion, conditioning, habit, and mimesis all involve "a drive toward association, attunement, attachment, becoming," and emotion is the movement of *being* across these social and physical processes. This is where the work of Wilce and Price makes its contribution. While Lyon (again following Taussig) calls for some assessment of the visceral involvement of individuals as a way of understanding contagious action across domains of self and other (where the self is both the subject of conditioning and also the agent linking different events), Wilce and Price claim that "cultures help to shape actual bodies, partly by means of widely held models, images, and metaphors." Extending Kirmayer's notion that metaphors have psychophysiological components, they ask, if this is the case, whether or not culturally-valued images themselves can change somatic processes to the degree that we might accord the body "first priority" as a "sign and determiner . . . of the social realm." To this relationship they apply the term "somatosocial," by which they mean that collectivities of human beings not only create social worlds, but that social worlds literally define and limit what bodies become. Examples of this sociocultural defining are everywhere in this collection, but most notably of consequence in the three chapters constituting "PNI in the wild," namely, the contributions of Decker *et al.* (for Dominican men), Flinn and England (for Dominican children), and McDade (for Samoan adolescents).

What makes the concept of the somatosocial so extraordinary is, as one might guess, its potential to reorient, and even to overturn, science's preference for experimental facts in favor of social ones; because the obvious consequence of there being a link between embodiment and metaphor is that "culturally variable images of body and healing are variably embodied within and across societies." This is a case that I have, for example, tried to make for the creative endeavors of the great Baroque sculptor, Bernini (Napier 1992, 112–38) – where spiritual exercise and realized artistic images actually make possible forms of embodiment that are all but inaccessible to us today.[2] It is also an argument that many of us have made for the visceral transformations that accompany various so-called trance states.

But the question remains as to how – if these relations are culturally produced – one might actually appreciate the uniqueness of such productions in *another cultural setting*. In other words, unless we can consciously experience the cultural dimensions of our own transformations, how can we know that these transformations are so culturally influenced? Furthermore, if in the end we do accept that culture has the ability to offer particular kinds of somatic possibilities, how do we keep from falling into a kind of Social Darwinism within which the establishment of a hierarchy of such relational possibilities becomes, in itself, oppressive?[3]

The answer to the first question must, of course, ultimately come through some demonstration of how cultural models are embodied – not only in others, but in each of us as we assimilate – agree with or contest – the very arguments made within this volume. And the answer to the second question comes, as it only can, through experiencing how variably the influences of culture are embodied by each of us – how, for one person, the same so-called "stressor" can have, as Wilce and Price point out of cancer imagery, quite variable outcomes among members of the same culture. The need for an understanding of diversity and social variability is, in other words, much more relevant even to the most extreme Social Darwinist than a simple hierarchy of cultural "sensitivities" would admit. If, that is, the Social Darwinist keeps insisting that different cultures will look at the world differently (and that, therefore, one will be better suited to a certain task than another), all he or she need do is examine that cultural variability at the social level to see that the central tropes of every culture will have their users, their abusers, their ignorers, and their transformers.

Indeed, while the reaction to outside stress may vary from individual to individual and across cultures, the use of a perceived outside stressor as a guide for defining the self means that the relationship between an individual and his or her environment may be far more reciprocal and dynamic than our Cartesian notions of the self would permit. Any simple simulation of a "cultural factor" in a controlled experimental setting can, then, provide a possible or hypothetical response, but not a paradigmatic one; for "experience" will always creatively transcend the uncreative certitude of the experimental method. And any notion of a self that defines a person as exclusive of his or her social meaning will, likewise, lack the dynamism by which an individual shapes and is shaped by experience. In immunology, as Booth and Davison discover, the need for a perceived adversary in defining the self means that "as people re-invent themselves by integrating traumatic issues through emotional disclosure, their immune self/non-self processes are also modulated." Here, the boundaries of the self are continuously adjusted by one's environmental and social outside, so much so that knowing how a "self" is culturally manifested may be altogether impossible without a complex sense of the etiology of stress in its social setting.

As one thinks about the many ways in which the relationship between anthropology and immunology are reflected in this volume, the possibility that one might summarize all of them by reference to a few simple themes appears increasingly remote. Still, the time when these fertile relations generate new hypotheses seems increasingly imminent. Perhaps the most extraordinary example of this is represented by the contribution of Cone and Martin. Here the knowledge of the importance of mucosal immunity in the body's responses to local allergens is combined with social research on food production and distribution of processed foods to argue for a possible social origin for the alarming rise in specific autoimmune disorders.

Feeding the body discrete amounts of the very cause of one's disorder is the theoretical basis of homeopathy, of certain Ayurvedic practices and, of course, of vaccinology itself. But to recognize that mucosal immunity enables the body to distinguish food from irritating foreign substances, and to place this idea in the context of commercial trading practices that limit the body's ability to be mucosaly stimulated, is to raise a truly novel theory about autoimmunity that could only be suggested through interdisciplinary work. It may be that the social shaping of immunological knowledge, combined with the inability of the experimental world to account for the functioning of stress, require not only that we attend to the social dimensions of PNI, but that we take its basic questions out of the hands of immunologists and experimental psychologists.[4] Whether the hypothesis ultimately holds up is, in some sense at least, less crucial than the argument it makes for expanding the ambient domain of research to reflect more honestly the various social settings within which illness unfolds and flourishes. That is exactly what makes this collection so exciting.

Notes

1   *Ed. This empirical finding resonates in a quirky way with the widespread cultural belief that mourning the dead – in a loud, violent, but especially prolonged way – hinders the journey into the beyond.*
2   *Ed. That "embodiment" (Csordas 1990) is the result of a cultural process, and that such cultural processes and embodied products vary across history, is the theme of much of Michel Foucault's work, e.g. Foucault 1990.*
3   *Ed. This is precisely what Susan DiGiacomo warned against (1992).*
4   *Ed. Among psychoimmunologists raising philosophical questions about self–other processes is Steven A. Hoffman at Arizona State University (personal communication, 2002).*

References

Cannon, W. B. (1942). "Voodoo" death. *American Anthropologist*, *44*, 169–181.

Csordas, T. (1990 [1988]). Stirling award essay: embodiment as a paradigm for anthropology. *Ethos*, *18*(1), 5–47.

DiGiacomo, S. M. (1992). Metaphor as illness: postmodern dilemmas in the representation of body, mind and disorder. *Medical Anthropology*, *14*(1), 209–247.

Foucault, M. (1990 [1978]). *The history of sexuality: an introduction* (R. Hurley, trans.), vol. 1. New York: Vintage.

Hall, N. R. S. and O'Grady, M. P. (1991). Psychosocial interventions and immune function. In R. Ader, D. L. Felten, and N. Cohen (eds), *Psychoneuroimmunology* (2nd edn, pp. 1067–1080). San Diego: Academic Press.

Margolis, H. (1993). *Paradigms and barriers: how habits of mind govern scientific beliefs*. Chicago: University of Chicago Press.

Napier, A. D. (1992). *Foreign bodies: performance, art, and symbolic anthropology*. Berkeley: University of California Press.

Peele, S. (1985). *The meaning of addiction: compulsive experience and its interpretation*. Lexington, MA: D. C. Heath.

Rider, M. S. and Weldin, C. (1990). Imagery, improvisation, and immunity. *Arts in Psychotherapy*, *17*(3), 211–216.

Rider, M. S. Achterberg, J., Lawlis, G. F., Govens, A., Toledo, R., and Butler, J. R. (1990). Effect on immune system imagery on secretory IgA. *Biofeedback and Self-regulation*, *15*(4), 317–333.

ten Have, H. (1987). Medicine and the Cartesian image of man. *Theoretical Medicine*, *8*(2), 235–246.

Chapter 13: Editor's note

For many years, cultural psychiatrist Laurence Kirmayer has argued for an approach to the body that is sensitive to sociocultural processes and to the role of metaphor in imagination and cognition. He pursues those themes here with clarity and particular relevance to PNI.

Kirmayer's essay, like Napier's, offers commentary on other chapters. Kirmayer sees some value in metaphors of the immune system as self and agent, yet his vision of the immune system's agentive selfhood is full of nuances and complexities. In Kirmayer's "interactional view of embodied cognition," human immune functions constitute a cognitive system. For Kirmayer, metaphor theory sheds light on PNI at many levels because, rather than defining metaphor as a strictly linguistic phenomenon, he sees it as a fundamental function of mind/imagination that enables actors (even immune systems?) to map one sort of knowledge onto another. If, as many contributors to this volume agree, biomedicine and its immunological branch constantly face the danger of reductionism, Kirmayer prescribes "a new medicine of the imagination."

Recognizing embodiment as a complex phenomenon composed at least of phenomenological, biological, and political dimensions, Kirmayer finds this volume contributing to three disciplinary languages necessary to address it. Those are psychophysiology, sociophysiology, and an ethnography of those discursive practices whose power helps constitute shared notions of immune systems. In short, Kirmayer's chapter serves several functions with excellence, adding critical perspectives on what these chapters do and do not accomplish, providing an encompassing framework in which to understand them, and thus being a capstone for the book.

Chapter 13

Reflections on embodiment

Laurence J. Kirmayer[1]

Introduction

> Suppose that a medical journal carried two articles reporting two different cures for scrofula: one by ingestion of chicken soup and the other by a king's touch. Even if the statistical evidence presented for these two cures had equal weight, I think that the medical community (and everyone else) would have very different reactions to the two articles. Regarding chicken soup I think that most people would keep an open mind, reserving judgment until the cure could be confirmed by independent tests. Chicken soup is a complicated mixture of good things, and who knows what effect its contents might have on the mycobacteria that cause scrofula? On the other hand whatever statistical evidence were offered to show that a king's touch helps to cure scrofula, readers would tend to be very skeptical, suspecting a hoax or a meaningless coincidence, because they would see no way that such a cure could ever be explained reductively. How could it matter to a mycobacterium whether the person touching its host was properly crowned and anointed or the eldest son of the previous monarch?
>
> (Weinberg, 1992, 63)

Why is chicken soup a more plausible healing agent than the King's touch? This passage by a Nobel laureate physicist reveals a common reductionist bias in explanations of the causes of disease: the chemistry of chicken soup has more obvious links to the tubercle bacillus than does the symbolic gesture of the touch of a specific human being. But why shouldn't a king's touch be even more antibacterial than chicken soup – at least in a feudal society where its symbolic power can inspire, ennoble and empower the peasant who receives that favored touch (Bloch, 1989)?

In his scenario, Weinberg misplaces the causal action in infectious disease, privileging the mycobacterium as the locus of infection and healing. But the proximate "cause" of a disease is not simply the virulence of bacteria – it includes the host organism's immune response. On most occasions, bacteria and viruses are successfully fought off by the body's immunologic lines of defense. Only when the immune system faces an overwhelming challenge or is compromised in some way does an infectious agent take hold and cause disease.

The King's touch, then, need not act directly on the mycobacterium to have antibacterial effect: it can act on the thoughts and feelings of the person who is touched, mediated by the central nervous system, which in turn modulates the immune system. Although touch may have physiological effects in infants that do not depend entirely on cognition, the meaning of touch is crucial to its impact on adults. A touch by oneself is not the same as the touch of an other – which may sooth, tickle, irritate or excite. The meanings of touch involve cognitive processes of attribution and interpretation that give rise to distinction: *a* king's touch is not at all the same as *the* King's touch.

Beyond these culturally mediated psychological processes, touch may have social meanings that alter the behavior of others toward the person who is touched. The King's touch may confer higher social status, prestige or protection on the person so marked. Such changes in social status and position may have direct effects on emotional well-being and immune status as well as indirect effects – if the King's touch results in increased wealth, or other material advantage. The effectiveness of the King's touch depends on its social and personal meaning.

Given all these potential effects of the King's touch, Weinberg's conviction that chicken soup is a more plausible antibiotic agent than a human touch, must reflect a pervasive prejudice in our culture. We have dematerialized social symbols and relationships – which are in fact quite solidly material in their manifestations and consequences.[2] The essays in this volume serve to re-materialize the social and symbolic world, to begin to fill in the over-arching interactional patterns that influence our vulnerability to illness and our resilience.

Embodiment, agency, and identity

The interaction of body, self, and society requires multiple languages of description that are not reducible to a single level or aspect. In medical anthropology, talk of the body has come to stand for several distinct (though interacting) domains: (1) the fact that we are physical beings, with a biology or physiology, and a wide range of responses to physical and social circumstances that do not depend exclusively on our symbolic constructions (the physiological body); (2) the bodily or sensory and affective dimensions of experience (the phenomenological body); and (3) the material and political economic reality of bodies as objects and agents of power and value (the body politic) (Lock, 1993; Scheper-Hughes and Lock, 1987). The notion of embodiment recognizes that these "three bodies" live and interact in one body so that we bear the effects of culture and social structure in our physiology, bodily habitus, and experience (Bourdieu, 1977; Csordas, 1990, 1994; Radley, 1984; Yardley, 1997).

Sometimes these domains are conflated in the notion that our bodies have lives of their own, so that we speak of bodies (rather than persons) as agents and even subpersonal components of the body, like the immune system, as having a distinct agency (Csordas, 1999; Lock, 1993). This is contentious not only because of the likelihood that we are drastically over-extending the metaphor of agency to subpersonal systems, but also because it implies that human agency itself is limited and exists only in the interstices or at the behest of bodies which have their own agendas.[3] This invocation of bodies as subjects and agents is intended in the anthropological literature not as a claim about selfish genes (or phenotypes) but in a Foucaldian sense, in which bodies have both their subjectivity and power created by discursive practices that in some way precede (at least some aspects of) the selves that we take for granted. But in what sense can we speak of the body's subjectivity (rather than the person's) and, to address the specific concerns of this volume, in what sense do immune systems have their own cognitive properties, subjectivity and agency?

Blalock (1989) suggested that the immune system is a chemical sense organ, using molecular receptor site recognition much like olfaction or taste. The immune system provides the organism with information about the microscopic environment. From this, and the recognition that the immune system constitutes a network capable of information processing or computation, it is a short step to understanding the immune system as a cognizing agent with its own "sense of self." As Booth and Davison put it in their chapter, "the immune system . . . shares with the neurological and psychological domains the common goal of establishing and maintaining self-identity."

Darwinian theory leads to a notion of the organism not as a given but as adapting and changing over generations. It follows that "identity is an evolving and dialectical process of an organism engaged in challenges from both its internal and external environments. The model most closely approximating that activity is our own behavior – both in our encounters with the world and in our own personal inner space" (Tauber, 1997, p. 5). It is no accident then, that metaphors of the self – drawn from everyday experience and contemporary philosophy – have guided immunological theory and research. The explicit notion of the immune system discriminating between self and non-self has been the dominant metaphor in immunology since Macfarlane Burnet's seminal work in 1949 (Tauber, 1997). The continuous process of immune system interaction with the environment has been hypostatised or personified as the immune self.[4]

Current immunology views the immune system as an actively cognizing agent (Varela and Coutinko, 1991; Varela et al., 1988). Cognitive science, in turn, has come to understand natural cognition as occurring not just within the computational networks of neurons, but through the feedback loops of a body interacting with a physical environment (Clark, 1997). This interactional view of embodied cognition is readily extended to the active engagement of individuals with the social world (Henningsen and Kirmayer, 2000). The implications of this social embodiment of cognition are just beginning to be explored within cognitive neuroscience and have hardly been considered in immunology.

The anthropological use of the metaphor of embodiment serves to maintain a place for the richness of bodily experience and significance of bodies as agents and arenas of action. Embodiment works against the tendency to treat bodies simply as property (my body and yours) or as vehicles entirely subordinate to our will. The essential insight of embodiment is that the body has a life of its own and that social worlds become inscribed on, or sedimented in, bodily physiology, habitus, and experience. Through its sensory apparatus, mobility, and affective responses, the body presents the natural metaphoricity of symbolic stimuli (Johnson, 1987; Lakoff and Johnson, 1999). Red pills are hot and activating, while blue pills are calming, soporific, or depressant. As a result of this natural metaphoricity, there is a tendency to conflate levels in explanation based on analogical reasoning or metaphor. Thus, angry thoughts meet their match in an aggressive cancer that eats the body alive. Depressed mood depletes and depresses the immune system, resulting in chronic fatigue, weakness, and vulnerability to illness. Many traditional systems of medicine rely on such metaphorical systems of correspondences to explain, diagnose, and treat illness. Similar analogies sometimes pass for causal explanation in lay thinking about disease.

This sort of metaphorical reasoning was revealed in Booth and Davison's study (this volume) correlating mood variables with perceived immune status. They found that college students made a metaphorical equation between subjective vitality and the level of functioning of the immune system. In this equation, vigor = health = activity = specific activity of the immune system. Further comparative cross-cultural work could establish whether these equivalences reflect popular theories of the immune system (i.e. explanatory models) or are based on the natural metaphoricity of the body (e.g. energy = up = greater activity, etc.), without any elaborate conceptual model.

The effortless jumping of levels of explanation by analogy obscures the fact that the hierarchical levels of organization in a biological system involve different dynamics for which words like activity, depression, suppression, or depletion have quite different meanings. Activation at one level may be due to suppression at another. The link between levels cannot be captured by a single metaphor, it must be systematically investigated and explicated – and we should expect surprises along the way.

Placebo effects: inscribing the social world on the body

Placebo effects provide a dramatic instance of the inscription of the social world on the body. In his chapter, Moerman defines placebo effects broadly as "desirable psychological and physiological effects of meaning in the treatment of illness." Placebo effects cover a wide range of psychophysiological responses to a perceived treatment. There are many (perhaps limitless) placebo effects based on the specific expectation (Lyon, this volume) or symbolic meaning of a treatment and the pattern of endogenous control systems or physiological processes that are activated (Harrington, 1997; Price et al., 1999; White et al., 1985). Thus, it is misleading to speak of "the" placebo effect and to imply that placebo effects are somehow "nonspecific." They are nonspecific only in the sense that many different symbolic stimuli can elicit them in different people. There are distinct placebo effects involving different physiological systems and every treatment intervention or situation may elicit a variety of interacting placebo responses.

In clinical trials, placebo effects usually are treated as a nuisance factor, as "noise" or variance in the system that must be controlled in order to identify and measure the therapeutic effect of specific treatments. Many clinical trials include a placebo control group so that any evidence for a better outcome in the group exposed to a treatment compared to a similar group given only placebo can be attributed to the impact of the "active" treatment. These experiments are not studies of placebos but are explicitly designed to cancel out placebo effects along with many other non-treatment factors in order to isolate the effect of a treatment or exposure. This point is crucial to appreciate some limitations of Moerman's study presented in this volume.

Moerman reviews placebo-controlled studies on the effectiveness of histamine (H_2) receptor blockers for the treatment of peptic ulcer disease in several different countries. He finds wide variation in the reported rates of improvement for the placebo-treated group. He suggests that this may reflect cross-national or cross-cultural variation in the rate of placebo responding. However, placebo-controlled clinical trials are not designed to study the placebo effect per se. The rate of improvement in the placebo arm of a clinical trial reflects many factors other than the impact of placebo including differences in the clinical population enrolled in the study, the local biology of the disease, and the larger environmental, social, and cultural context.

The population from which samples of patients are drawn for studies in different countries may vary in sociodemographic composition, general health, diet, nutrition, use of tobacco, alcohol or other substances, physical activity, social stressors, exposure to pollutants, previous medication use, and so on – all of which can affect the disease process, host resistance, and treatment response. Patients in different countries have different histories of illness experience and access to care. Differential access to care and patterns of health care utilization will affect the subpopulation of all those affected who are enrolled in clinical trials as well as their subsequent illness behavior (adherence to treatment, use of alternative care, expectations for recovery). A major variable in cross-national comparisons, even where concomitant medical care is controlled as part of a clinical trial, concerns the use of complementary medicine and home remedies.

Despite a common diagnosis made by standardized criteria, patients at different sites may differ in the nature and severity of their illness. There may be differences in the prevalence of causal or aggravating factors. For example, in the case of peptic ulcer disease, there may be differences in the prevalence of infection with *Helicobacter pylori*, the bacterium that contributes to many cases of peptic ulcer disease (Axon, 1991).[5] Even where there is a similar prevalence of *H. pylori*, there may be differences in the virulence of specific strains.

All of these variables may influence the course of peptic ulcer disease and result in variations in outcome in the placebo arm of a clinical trial. Of course, they will also affect the treatment arm. As a result, the only way to identify a specific placebo response is to have a "non-placebo, non-treatment" control group (Ernst and Resch, 1995). This may be difficult, since any group that is scrutinized may experience some form of placebo effect, but it can be approached and approximated.

Although Moerman acknowledges this problem in his essay, he goes on to claim that "it is also possible to infer the existence of a placebo effect in many controlled trials where placebo groups but no 'natural history' groups are utilized." With the data Moerman presents, however, there is simply no way to partial out how much of the variation is due to placebo and how much to unspecified aspects of natural history that also vary geographically or cross-culturally. Without special experimental designs, the placebo effect cannot be disentangled from these other environmental or regional effects. In medical textbooks, the course of illness in an untreated population is often called "the natural history" of the disease. However, the laundry list of social and environment factors potentially modifying the course of illness makes it clear that there is no unique "natural history" of disease, as Moerman points out, only a multitude of different social histories that depend on the particularities of the local physical, social, economic, and political world. Peptic ulcer disease in Brazil is not the same entity as PUD in Germany, because of a myriad of different social and biological factors. Any or all of these factors may interact with the psychophysiological processes that underlie placebo responses. The challenge for social sciences is to identify and describe regularities in placebo responding shared by individuals living in some region or group that can be attributed to social factors. To do this, the local ecology of disease vectors and modulating factors must be taken into consideration.

This variation in the biology of disease is compounded by tremendous individual variation in placebo responding that reflects each person's idiosyncratic history of experiences of illness and healing. This idiosyncrasy affects not only networks of associations but extends to the physiological effects of symbols. Moerman has raised the distinct possibility of cross-national differences in placebo effects. Yet, we are left with the problem of specifying what is shared or "cultural," and what is personal or biographical, in the bodily response of any individual (or population) to symbolic stimuli. This requires a theory of sociophysiology.

From psychosomatics to sociophysiology

Several of the chapters in this volume are contributions to a sociophysiology of the immune system, one that steps outside the laboratory to consider the social ecology of disease vulnerability. An ethnographically informed sociophysiology could address many basic questions left unexamined in current psychoneuroimmunology. Anthropological research can: (1) identify ecologically meaningful events and experiences that have salience for psychophysiological responses; (2) explore the social origins and physiological significance of the unequal distribution of these events and experiences; (3) reveal the ways in which different psychophysiological processes are yoked together by social contexts and interactions that result in trade-offs between conflicting goals; and (4) examine the temporal dynamics of socio-physiological responses on the scales of individual biography and larger historical changes in the life of cultures and communities.

Flinn and Decker present results from a unique project that tracks the health status of interacting members of a small community in Dominica. This exemplary study combines sophisticated biological field methods, multi-variate statistical analysis, and ethnographically informed interpretation of longitudinal data. It clearly shows the links between socially significant relationships and neuroendocrine and immune functioning. Social status and relationships clearly involve many trade-offs. As McDade notes in his chapter, referring to another small-scale society, "in cultures with extended kin-based networks of interaction and exchange, social relationships can entail considerable expectation and obligation." Thus, higher social status can be a burden as well as a buffer and so, may be associated with depressed immune function. Indeed, cross-cultural variation in notions of status may mean that no universal measure is possible and that physiological effects will differ. At the very least, we must follow Decker in distinguishing between various forms of status – in particular, recognizing the different physiological consequences of affiliative/cooperative modes of achieving status as distinct from the social structural constraints of socioeconomic status.

Cultural and biological processes are usually linked through processes of constructing meaning. But the term "meaning" covers a complex set of relational processes through which the cultural world is engaged by active cognizing agents. There are many ways to unpack the meanings of meaning and it is unclear which theories of semantics, semiotics, and pragmatics will best serve the development of sociophysiological theory.

In previous work, I have suggested that metaphor theory provides a useful way to approach the problem of psychosomatic and sociosomatic mediation (Kirmayer, 1992, 1993, 1994). Lyon critiques metaphor as primarily a linguistic phenomenon that fails to capture the essentially affective processes that translate social experience into bodily responses. Conceptual metaphor, however, is not simply a linguistic trope but a basic set of cognitive processes for mapping one domain of knowledge (encoded as story, image, or other type of cognitive model) onto another (Fauconnier, 1997; Gibbs, 1994; Turner, 1996). As such, metaphor theory provides models for the coordination of different levels in representational and action systems. Prominent among these action systems are those basic stances or dispositions to act, that we call emotion. Metaphor theory shows how thought is under-girded by affective meaning, which has both universal and culturally specific dimensions (Kirmayer, 1992).

In place of metaphor, Lyon proposes the esthetic notion of mimesis, the "movement of approximation between things and people." She admits that "mimesis is analytically vague"; but joins Benjamin and others to speak of the "mimetic faculty." To advance sociophysiology, the notion of a mimetic faculty must be unpacked into its many disparate processes, including imag-inative reconstruction, empathy, and bodily mirroring or synchrony. What all of these have in common is some similarity or parallelism in representation or experience. At the most basic level, similarity involves cross-modal sensory comparisons and may be innate (for example, a loud noise and bright light are similar in their intensity). But recognizing similarity in more complex experiences and events involves specific cognitive processes. Indeed, there is no way to recognize similarity between complex objects or events except through analogical transformations – and metaphor is the term we use for those analogies that link disparate domains or representational spaces.[6] Unpacking mimesis, then, reveals the conceptual machinery of metaphor at its core.

Metaphor theory can help us to understand how complex interpersonal communications are transduced to lower level bodily experiences and, ulti-mately, to physiological processes. Language and concepts that are learned in and through bodily responses and practices may use the same sensory and action systems of the brain. As a result, the effects of images and actions remain accessible to, and readily evoked by, metaphor and imagistic language.

Lyon points to emotion as the mediator between the social world and physiology. She suggests that a focus on emotion will lead to concepts that can encompass both the experiential or lived body and larger social struc-tures. As examples of mediating concepts derived from the study of emotion she considers notions of expectation, conditioning, empathy, and emotional contagion. The study of metaphor can help us understand the cognitive, social, and physiological dynamics of these processes.

Most complex emotion terms are not names for bodily or experiential states but for configurations of social relations unfolding over time. As such, complex emotions not only govern (or rationalize) one's interpersonal actions, but also carry expectations about how others will react (or should have reacted) to one's actions.[7] However, not all emotions are future oriented or involve expectations; instead, they speak to a stretch of social interaction including specific antecedents, behaviors, and larger social consequences. Emotions have their own time horizons and may refer to the past (and be situated there as in nostalgia, grief, or shame) or to the future (as in anticipatory joy, fear, or anger). This temporal structure is shaped by metaphors grounded in bodily experiences involving posture, spatial disposition, and movement (Alverson, 1994), as well as in the functioning of sensory systems like olfaction, which has strong links to memory and emotion (Ibarretxe-Antuñano, 1999).

Empathy is not a specific feeling but a stance toward another's experience – a metaphoric "as if" or "feeling with" that involves imaginative reconstruction of the other's situation, and a willingness to dwell in similar feelings or surroundings. There are forms of empathic understanding that are not centered on emotion per se but on tracing the ramifications of a person's social predicament. This understanding is based on the ability of story, parable, and image to evoke a world in the theater of the mind.

Emotional contagion is empathy writ large: emotional arousal (usually anxiety) and specific beliefs that fit with pre-existing systems of meaning and concerns give rise to similar feelings and convictions in others (Hatfield *et al.*, 1994). The classical example is *koro*, seen in epidemic form in Southeast Asia and China, in which fears that one's penis is shrinking and that death is imminent may spread rapidly through a population affecting many individuals (Bartholomew, 1998). Other forms of emotional contagion are common in industrialized societies where plausible fears involve toxins, viruses, or work-related environmental conditions like poor air quality or occupational injury (Bartholomew and Sirois, 2001). Such prevalent fears and concerns may contribute to epidemics of syndromes like sick building, repetitive strain injury, and chronic fatigue, which are often viewed as "psychosomatic" conditions, with or without clear justification (Reid and Reynolds, 1990; Ware, 1992).

The basic premise of psychosomatic medicine is that the meaning of events influences the regulation of physiological systems to give rise to disease and modulate the course of illness and response to treatment. Meaning may be cognitive (involving dissonance reduction, causal explanation, completeness, coherence, reference to core values and beliefs, tacit assumptions, and creative efficacy), affective (related to strongly held or felt emotions); and social performative (resulting in rhetorical force, social value, interpersonal effectiveness, social positioning). This broad view of meaning leads to a sociosomatic perspective in which there may be links between psychosocial events and immune functioning involving feedback loops at multiple levels:

1   There are unconditioned effects of certain types of stimuli on the immune system. For example, the loss of someone we are attached to can lead to prolonged and profound immune suppression (Bartrop et al., 1977). Marital conflict is an especially powerful immune suppressant (Kiecolt-Glaser and Glaser, 1995; Uchino et al., 1996). Although the sensitivity of immune regulation to disruption of interpersonal bonds is probably "hard-wired," the identification of who and what constitutes a significant relationship is culturally mediated.

2   There are conditioned effects of stimuli on the immune system that build on unconditioned responses through the individual's history of exposures and experiences (Ader et al., 1995). The phenomenon of classical conditioning of the immune system implies that such bodily responses to context and contingencies need not be mediated by conscious awareness or complex cognition. Classical conditioning provides a model of how personal history or biography and larger political economic formations are inscribed on the body. Exposure to environment events and social contingencies is not random and idiosyncratic but socially and economically patterned (e.g. poverty is racialized). Thus, there are predictable regularities or biases in conditioning history.

3   There are learned effects regarding the meaning of situations that have indirect effects on the immune system through changes in morale, emotional state, or level of well-being. Mood disorders, such as depression, impair immune functioning (Miller et al., 1999). And depression, in turn, may result from evaluating a social situation as one of symbolic loss, defeat, and powerlessness.

4   The immune system itself has effects on mood and thinking. The feelings of fatigue and malaise that accompany most illness are largely due to the effects of cytokines on the central nervous system (Maier and Watkins, 1998).

5   Our own notions of the immune system affect behavior, which in turn has effects on immune responsiveness. The immune system, as a symbolic object, becomes something that influences its own functioning. This is an instance of what Ian Hacking has called "the looping effect of human kinds" (Hacking, 1995, 1999). In fact, there are multiple such loops that may affect the immune system.

For example, although the immune system is usually silent, it may signal its presence through allergic reactions that cause us to be wary of certain substances, places, or people. This may generalize to a sense of one's self as "allergic" to life, as in total allergy syndrome in which the ambiguity of symptoms, and the ubiquity of the novel and foreign, supports an intense sense of personal vulnerability.

Based on these different levels of sociosomatic interaction, we might develop a typology of meanings, framed in sufficiently abstract terms that they are universal (e.g. loss, threat, positive expectancy), to explore whether there are generic biological responses to these meanings across cultures. This might allow us to make cross-cultural comparisons both of the magnitude of sociophysiological responses and their specific symbolic mediation. This is important not only for more complete theoretical models but because clinical interventions based on specific psychosomatic notions are widely exported and employed with little regard for their fit with local social ecology and systems of meaning.

Psychotherapy as sociosomatic praxis

Psychosomatic theory has given a prominent place to the notion that failure to regulate strong emotion can lead to physical illness (Taylor *et al.*, 1997). This regulation may occur through symbolic expression in dreams, fantasy, and conversation with others; hence, an inability to articulate distress may contribute to disease.

Consistent with this viewpoint, Mann describes a patient with "post-traumatic" hypertension and implies that the continuous effort to repress emotional conflict results in illness. He posits a similar mechanism for many other types of unexplained illness.[8] Mann speaks of emotions that are hidden from awareness. Lack of awareness of emotions is a complex process and the various terms Mann lists (denial, dissociation, repression, alexithymia, isolation of affect) are not all equivalent: some are states, others traits, some are conscious strategies, others more or less automatic, all involve interactions between cognition, emotion, and interpersonal behavior.[9] In general, theories of emotional control do not sufficiently incorporate the interpersonal, social, and cultural dimensions that make such control important.

The notion that there is a cost associated with hiding or suppressing emotions and, on the contrary, a beneficial or therapeutic effect associated with disclosing and re-narrating traumatic events has been a key assumption of many forms of psychotherapy. Part of the popularity of this notion may be its fit with American values of expressive individualism (Bellah *et al.*, 1985). The work of James Pennebaker, summarized in this volume, has also lent considerable support to this theory.

Pennebaker's experimental paradigm involves having subjects write repeatedly about their deepest thoughts and feelings about a past traumatic experience. Confronting traumatic experiences in this way has a salutary effect on health, reducing help-seeking in most studies, as well as improving some actual indices of physical health. Pennebaker finds that expressing moderate amounts of negative or positive emotion are both associated with good outcomes. Both very low levels of expression of negative emotion (characteristic of individuals termed "repressors" in psychophysiological research) and very high expression of negative emotion (characteristic of individuals high on the personality trait of neuroticism) are associated with poor outcome. Narrating past traumas may not benefit patients with post-traumatic stress disorder (PTSD) whose distress is too severe (Gidron et al., 1996).

The precise mechanisms that underlie the beneficial effects of disclosure and re-narration are unclear and might include: the relief of negative effects of emotion suppression or some direct effect of emotional expression; the ability of re-narration to organize memory and experience in ways that may allow the individual to forget trauma more efficiently; and the possibility that talk about past trauma and distress increases health consciousness with consequent modification of health behaviors (Kemeny and Miller, 1999).

The effectiveness of writing appears to depend on the coherence of the story reconstructed. Good outcome is associated with increasing use of causal and insight words in successive re-narrations. Those who start out with a coherent story from the past do not experience the same benefits from the writing exercise. The story can be autobiographical or in the third person and still have similar organizing effects. Even narrating fictitious traumatic events may help. One study showed that writing about imaginary trauma also helped people who had been previously traumatized (Greenberg et al., 1996).

Based on this work, Pennebaker proposes two putative cultural universals: (1) All human groups use language to create stories. The purpose of narrative is to structure experience and find meaning in complex, unpredictable events. (2) "The act of translating upsetting experiences into words is associated with physical and mental health under some circumstances in virtually all societies." This might arise because most individuals must actively conceal important information from some others in their social network and the act of concealment is inherently stressful.

Although the therapeutic effect of writing about trauma has been confirmed across social classes and major ethnoracial groups in the US, as well as students or other populations in Mexico City, New Zealand, Belgium, and the Netherlands, there is a paucity of studies from non-Western cultures. Nevertheless, psychological debriefing interventions based in part on this paradigm have been widely promoted in settings of natural disasters, war-related trauma, and political violence (Solomon, 1999).[10]

To what extent does coherence relate to specific cultural templates for a good narrative? Linguistic coherence involves structure, use of causal explanation, repetition of themes, appreciation of listener's perspective, and conventional order (temporal, causal, or other) (Clark, 1993). Narrative coherence is dependent on content as well as form and varies cross-culturally in ways that are likely to affect psychosomatic process. For example, in their chapter, Booth and Davison compare heterogeneous ethnocultural groups ("Caucasians," "Polynesians," and "Asians") and find differences in the style of narration using Pennebaker's method of content analysis. In fact, the categories of words that correlated most strongly with immune function were those that varied most cross-culturally, notably: self, positive feelings, anger, friends, community, time, and religion. This suggests that cross-cultural comparisons of the health effects of narration may require different measures of coherence and thematic content and that there may be differences in outcome as well.[11]

Narratives are not just used to create internal psychological coherence, they also have social meaning as acts of positioning, defining roles, rules and relationships, and influencing others. Cultural differences in social norms for self-presentation and in the meaning of emotions may affect the impact of disclosure and re-narration of trauma and distress. For example the Cambodian Buddhist who narrates personal loss or trauma may be placing undue emphasis on his personal tragedy, undermining his own efforts to seek equanimity through acceptance, and failing to protect others from the damaging effects of ignorance and aggression (Silove *et al.*, 1995). On the contrary, in some Mediterranean Catholic communities, talk of one's suffering imbues the self with positive social value (Gaines and Farmer, 1986). Again, in Jewish culture, talk of suffering may affirm one's communal solidarity and worldliness and lead to a renewed commitment to social justice (Sacks, 1997; Steiner, 1997; Wilce and Price, this volume). Although Pennebaker claims that "the effects of the writing are not related to the presumed audience" – based on studies that involved writing in diaries that are never read – this is hard to credit. There is always a virtual audience for our diary, monologue, or reverie. The potential response of this audience is usually of vital importance. In situations like political rape, for example, talk of one's past trauma may be perceived as carrying out the attacker's intention to destroy the bonds of community and collective identity.[12] The mere creation or existence of a written record may be threatening. Clearly, the trade-offs involved with presenting one's suffering to specific audiences may be so important that the potential positive effect of narration is entirely vitiated.

We can view emotion talk as action rather than expression (presentation rather than representation). This leads to different models of the interaction of mind, body, and society. This broader framework allows us to consider the social context of narration and the likelihood that talking about strong emotion, trauma, and distress is not simply good or bad for one's health but involves trade-offs between bodily, intrapsychic and interpersonal effects. Rather than the suppression or repression of "bad" or strong emotions, we must understand their social management.

Thus, the beneficial effects of emotional disclosure and re-narration through writing may be modulated by social and cultural factors. Culture provides norms and standards by which people are judged (and judge themselves), giving rise to moral emotions like guilt, shame, and anger, which have health consequences. Culture also provides materials for improvising a new self and novel life story. Booth and Davison state "people re-invent themselves by integrating traumatic issues through emotional disclosure." We might ask, though, whether this is truly re-invention or simply conformity to a dominant – even hegemonic – ideology of the person and template for the self.

Conclusion: toward a medicine of imagination

The essays in this volume traverse notions of the body as the ground of experience (the phenomenological body), the structure underlying physiological processes (the biological body) and the discursive object of medical power and knowledge (the body politic). To weave these forms of embodiment together we need the languages of psychophysiology, sociophysiology, and discursive practices. The cognitive processes that join these languages are fundamentally metaphoric.

Metaphors for the immune system are drawn from psychological and social domains and imbue it with a real presence in our social lives. The immune system is a "mobile brain," a "cognizing agent," a "self," even a society. Interactions with the central nervous system justify a view of the immune system as a sensorimotor system that both receives information from and acts on, the environment. The discipline of immunology has drawn from social and neural metaphors to create a portrait of the immune system as a coordinated, "intelligent" network of microscopic agents responding to incursions of the other into the body with powerful, sometimes catastrophic, effects. This notion of agency borrows from, but cannot be conflated with, human agency.

We need to attend carefully to the work of the metaphors of agency and intelligence in talking about the immune system. Not all action is agentic and not all agency is expressed through action. Ascriptions of agency have important implications both for how we theorize the immune system and how we think about others in everyday life. The language of agency and volition goes beyond the teleology of goal-directed systems to imply a hierarchy of aims and values that may conflict with those of persons and institutions.

Ordinarily silent and invisible, the immune system enters awareness through its derangement or failures to protect us from disease. Biotechnology can make the immune system visible even when it is silent, so that the immune system becomes a discursive object as well as a biological fact. Anthropological accounts of the social construction of our notions of immunology must be placed beside the material-discursive aspects of immune function and failure (that is to say, the ways in which discourses are grounded in the physical particulars of local worlds, which include bodies and their physiologies, as well as interpersonal relationships and social institutions with their several forms of power. This suggests three basic questions for future anthropological research and interdisciplinary collaboration: (1) How does the social landscape look to the immune system? That is, what features of the social world are salient from the perspective of immune functioning? (2) How do personal and collective history shape the immune system's modes of recognition and response? And, (3) how does the immune system, in turn, shape our social world?

The immune system contributes its own mapping of the social world to our constructions of self and other. Like infrared goggles, this view may reveal things hidden from ordinary vision while obscuring others. Salient features of the social landscape for the immune system include perceived social status, threat, loss, social support, and other dimensions that may have universal significance for evolutionary or existential reasons. These are not independent factors, however; they form part of an interactive web, system or social fabric that must be studied as such to identify the role of any specific factor (Berkman et al., 2000).

In turn, we can ask how social factors shape our metaphors of the body and the immune system. The politics of metaphor inhere in the rhetorical use of language to manipulate our views of the social world and shape our commitments and allegiances. For example, the word "natural" is used to sell us processed foods and other products of dubious value, which are imbued with an aura of health, safety, and vitality by this metaphorical sleight of hand.

This politics reaches into the body. In their provocative essay, Cone and Martin show how the global economy in processed food, and other consequences of consumer capitalism, may impact directly on the immune system resulting in an increase in allergies in urban centers of industrialized societies. The unprecedented diversity in foodstuffs, information, and lifestyles brought about by globalization makes novelty itself a health problem, both for immune functioning and psychological equilibrium.[13]

Consumer capitalism drives the structure and content of health care systems in developed countries. Psychoneuroimmunology has become part of holistic health packages in the US and is increasingly accepted as a facet of standard health care. For example, the Cancer Treatment Centers of America offers a "Mind-Body Connections Program" as part of a comprehensive range of treatment modalities. Here is how they describe the program:

> The mind-body connections program is based on a relatively new area of care called psychoneuroimmunology (PNI). "Psycho" refers to thinking, emotions and mood states. "Neuro" refers to the neurological and endocrine systems. And "immunology" refers to cellular structures and the immune system. PNI explores the influence of the mind on the body and the immune system. Using a variety of techniques, the Mind-Body Connections Program helps people with cancer direct their energies toward healing and health.[14]

The specific interventions offered include: stress management, relaxation and imagery training,[15] spiritual meditation, support groups for patients, women and families, individual, couple and family counseling, psychoeducational groups, educational resources, and humor therapy. The appeal of this "cutting edge" program owes as much to popular rhetoric as it does to any compelling evidence for the therapeutic effects of psychosocial interventions on immune function (Kemeny and Miller, 1999).

The contributions to this volume make it clear that the immune system is both a biological and a cultural presence. Wilce and Price offer a model of culture as multistory, metalevel phenomenon that allows for contradiction, negotiation, and complex trade-offs between individual and collective strategies for adaptation. Against the romantic assumption of cultural homeostasis, it is important to appreciate that there is no reason why cultures have to be functional for individuals or for immune systems per se. We need to rethink our concepts of culture in terms of symbolic and social interactional processes that may engender disease or promote healing. The essays in this volume are a good start on this larger project.

As Wilce and Price point out, cultures are resources for the imagination. Though the term has become debased or trivialized in our time, in renaissance philosophy imagination held a place equal to reason among the human faculties (Jackson, 1990). The study of metaphor helps us to understand imagination both as a cognitive faculty and as a bodily disposition, mode of enactment, or way of being in the world. Cognitive science, psychophysiology, political economy and sociosomatics all reveal processes that underlie the embodiment of metaphor. Metaphor theory, in turn, can contribute to the development of a new medicine of the imagination.

Notes

1 Division of Social and Transcultural Psychiatry, McGill University, Institute of Community and Family Psychiatry, 4333 Cote Ste Catherine Rd., Montreal, Quebec H3T 1E4.
2 I cannot resist pointing to another obvious cultural aspect to Weinberg's example. As a mainstay of Jewish home-cooking, chicken soup represents the sort of remedy available to the marginalized peasant, not allowed access to the King. It is explicitly within the ironic, hierarchy disdaining culture of Eastern European Jewry that Bubbie's (Yiddish for "grandma's") soup is valued as more powerful than the King's touch. Indeed, it is Bubbie's special touch in preparing the soup that makes it so effective. So we really have one relationship set against another.
3 Indeed, the reluctance to give much weight to classical conditioning in contemporary social science has to do with the valorization of agency and consciousness and discomfort acknowledging the automatic or habitual nature of many aspects of human life – such automaticity is tantamount to powerlessness.
4 There is an interesting connection between the immune self and our psychological individuality and recognition of others (Eggert and Ferstl, 1999). Proteins associated with the major histocompatibility complex (MHC) (which provides an immunologic signature of the individual) are expressed in saliva, sweat, urine, and other secretions where they are broken down by bacteria into smaller fragments. These give rise to a distinctive odor by which animals may recognize

others who are more or less genetically similar. This information may influence sexual attraction and altruistic behavior. There is thus a potential link between the immune system's way of identifying self and social interactional processes of affiliation mediated by olfaction, which has close anatomical connections to emotional processing in the limbic system of the brain.

   Ed. Limbic mediation must be seen as just as important to the socioemotional processes Lyon describes (this volume) as to the immune-relevant processing of olfaction.

5 It is misleading to state that *H. pylori* causes peptic ulcer since only 5–20 percent of people with *H. pylori* infection have peptic ulcer disease (and in many of these cases it is asymptomatic) (Vaira *et al.*, 1994). Clearly, other factors are at work in determining who gets the disease and who entirely resists the infection, carries a chronic low-grade infection, or suffers only mild, sub-clinical symptoms.

6 The notion of mimesis in esthetic theory has to do with the creation of the semblance of reality in literature, painting, or other media through imagery and narrative conventions (Auerbach, 1953). Through mimesis a story becomes a mirror of our own world or a window onto another that, however fabulous, seems real. Turner (1996) argues that our ability to extend and blend imaginary worlds through stories is at the heart of metaphor.

   Ed. Students of the philosopher and semiotician Charles Peirce argue that iconicity is the mode of semiosis underlying metaphor and *mimesis – see Wilce and Price (this volume).*

7 In this sense, expectation (which Lyon names as an emotion) is not so much a specific emotion as a label for the temporal stance of all future-oriented emotions or cognitive evaluations. We may have positive or negative expectations, fearful apprehensions or pleasurable anticipation – all of which function as different types of expectancy that may have corresponding "placebo" effects. Expectation may be best described, following Wilce and Price (this volume), as a metalevel phenomenon in the hierarchy of semiotic levels they describe as relevant to emotion.

8 Mann's list of medically unexplained symptoms "believed to be at least partly emotion-related," which includes "colitis," obesity," rheumatoid arthritis, and irritable bowel syndrome, reflects an old-fashioned way of thinking about psychosomatics. Clearly, medically unexplained does not equal emotionally explained; this is a common but tendentious move in psychosomatic medicine and psychiatry (Kirmayer, 1988, 1999, 2000). Every illness is potentially related to emotional distress, if not as a causal contributor then as an exacerbating factor. There is little evidence that the disorders that Mann singles out are more closely related to emotional distress than are other illnesses. However, there is a common tendency among psychologically minded clinicians to assume that the lack of a medical or physiological explanation is prima facie evidence of a psychological cause. This may be deeply distressing for patients who seek to have the medical legitimacy of their symptoms confirmed (Kirmayer, 1999, 2000).

9 There are serious epistemological and methodological problems posed by the notion of unexperienced emotion. Emotions may be ascribed to people because we think they ought to have them, given their social predicaments, past experiences or future likelihood. But not everyone reports the same feelings in the same situation, whether because of differences in temperament, coping style, or cognitive evaluation of the situation and their larger social position. An overarching ethical or spiritual commitment can radically transform the emotional impact of events. When someone eventually expresses an emotion like anger or fear that was expected by others we may be tempted to say that the emotion was there all along (but was "unconscious," that is, suppressed, repressed, dissociated, or

incompletely cognized) and that it is now finally expressed. But this could simply be a *post hoc* retrodiction or rewriting of purely hypothetical subterranean processes. Most commonly, an emotion is created *de novo*, along with the reconstruction of events in memory – as when we feel shame for the first time recollecting a situation and realizing that we said something embarrassing. Even if some sort of emotional process or stance is possible without awareness, we must recognize that they are likely to be different from ordinary emotions simply by virtue of their occurring outside awareness. Certainly, if we wish to allow for such proto-emotional processes, we must consider that they are either not experiential (that is, they modify cognitive processing, bodily habitus, and physiology outside of conscious experience) or they have an experiential dimension quite distinct from that of the fully expressed emotion they are said to be part of.

10 Anglo-American mental health practitioners and researchers are part of an active industry exporting models of psychological intervention and, indeed, notions of psychological health itself. For example, in Japan, in the wake of the Hanshin earthquake, psychological debriefing for trauma relief was rapidly deployed by American and other Western teams, and Japanese practitioners were trained in Los Angeles (Breslau, 2000). This wide dissemination has occurred despite questions about the efficacy of psychological debriefing and the cross-cultural applicability of existing intervention models (Solomon, 1999; Summerfield, 1999).

11 The constraints of memory on narrative may be different than those that confer social efficacy. There is a basic tension between efficient recollection of events, which requires simplification and encapsulation, and acknowledging the complexity and multivocality of events, which keeps recall open, multiple, and deferred. This is one reason why philosophers and artists are melancholy: they strive to hold the complexity of social situations, emotions, human tragedy, close, and even open it up and amplify it rather than create a mummified and compressed version to be put in the vault or deep freeze.

12 This may well underlie the Punjabi metaphor supporting silence after intercommunal violence and rape during the Partition of India and Pakistan (discussed by Wilce and Price, this volume).

13 Bubbie's chicken soup, with its memories of home, may provide an antidote to the unhealthy geographic dislocations created by the mass market and consumer capitalism. Cone and Martin discuss the value of ingesting different parts of animal tissue to promote immunologic tolerance: "There may be no need to eat large amounts of the relevant tissue; indeed small amounts might provide the best 'bystander' protection; chicken soup, or other broths made from whole animal tissue contain diverse arrays of antigens that might produce broad-spectrum oral tolerance" (p. 246). This puts an interesting spin on Weinberg's chicken soup story.

14 www.cancercenter.com/home/2/39/55; accessed 8/12/2000

15 On imagery interventions, see Napier and Wilce and Price, this volume.

References

Ader, R., Cohen, N., and Felten, D. (1995). Psychoneuroimmunology: interactions between the nervous system and the immune system. *The Lancet*, *345*(8942), 99–103.

Alverson, H. (1994). *Semantics and experience: universal metaphors of time in English, Mandarin, Hindi, and Sesotho*. Baltimore: The Johns Hopkins University Press.

Auerbach, E. (1953). *Mimesis: the representation of reality in Western literature*. Princeton, NJ: Princeton University Press.

Axon, A. T. R. (1991). Duodenal ulcers: the villain unmasked? *British Medical Journal, 302*, 919–921.

Bartholomew, R. E. (1998). The medicalization of exotic deviance: a sociological perspective on epidemic koro. *Transcultural Psychiatry, 35*(1), 5–38.

—— and Sirois, F. (2001). Occupational mass psychogenic illness: a transcultural perspective. *Transcultural Psychiatry, 38*(1), 495–524.

Bartrop, R. W., Luckhurst, E., Lazarus, L., Kiloh, L. G., and Penny, R. (1977). Depressed lymphocyte function after bereavement. *The Lancet*, (8016) 834–836.

Bellah, R. N., Madsen, R., Sullivan, W. M., Swidler, A., and Tipton, S. M. (1985). *Habits of the heart: individualism and commitment in American life*. Berkeley: University of California Press.

Berkman, L. F., Glass, T., Brissette, I., and Seeman, T. E. (2000). From social integration to health: Durkheim in the new millennium. *Social Science and Medicine, 51*(6), 843–857.

Blalock, J. E. (1989). A molecular basis for bidirectional communication between the immune and endocrine systems. *Physiological Review, 69*(1), 1–32.

Bloch, M. (1989). *The royal touch: monarchy and miracles in medieval France and England* (trans. J. E. Anderson). New York: Dorset Press.

Bourdieu, P. (1977). *Outline of a theory of practice*. Cambridge: Cambridge University Press.

Breslau, J. (2000). Globalizing disaster trauma: psychiatry, science, and culture after the Kobe earthquake. *Ethos, 28*(2), 174–197.

Clark, A. (1997). *Being there: putting brain, body, and world together again*. Cambridge: MIT Press.

Clark, L. F. (1993). Stress and the cognitive-conversational benefits of social interaction. *Journal of Social and Clinical Psychology, 12*(1), 25–55.

Csordas, T. J. (1990). Embodiment as a paradigm for anthropology. *Ethos 18*(2), 5–47

—— (ed.). (1994). *Embodiment and experience: the existential ground of culture and self*. Cambridge: Cambridge University Press.

Csordas, T. S. (1999). The body's career in anthropology. In H. L. Moore (ed.), *Anthropological theory today* (pp. 172–205). Cambridge: Polity Press.

Eggert, F. and Ferstl, R. (1999). Functional relationship between the olfactory and immune systems. In M. Schedlowski and U. Tewes (eds), *Psychoneuroimmunology: an interdisciplinary introduction* (pp. 443–452). New York: Kluwer.

Ernst, E. and Resch, K. L. (1995). Concept of true and perceived placebo effects. *British Medical Journal, 311*(7004), 551–553.

Fauconnier, G. (1997). *Mappings in thought and language*. Cambridge: Cambridge University Press.

Gaines, A. D. and Farmer, P. E. (1986). Visible saints: social cynosures and dysphoria in the Mediterrean tradition. *Culture, Medicine and Psychiatry, 10*(1), 295–330.

Gibbs, R. W. (1994). *The poetics of mind: figurative thought, language and understanding*. New York: Cambridge University Press.

Gidron, Y., Peri, T., Conolly, J. F., and Shalev, A. Y. (1996). Written disclosure in posttraumatic stress disorder: is it beneficial for the patient? *Journal of Nervous and Mental Disease, 184*(8), 505–507.

Greenberg, M. A., Stone, A. A., and Wortman, C. B. (1996). Health and psychological effects of emotional disclosure: a test of the inhibition-confrontation approach. *Journal of Personality and Social Psychology, 71*, 588–602.

Hacking, I. (1995). The looping effect of human kinds. In D. Sperber, D. Premack, and A. J. Premack (eds), *Causal cognition: a multidisciplinary debate* (pp. 351–383). Oxford: Oxford University Press.

—— (1999). *The social construction of what?* Cambridge, MA: Harvard University Press.

Harrington, A. (ed.). (1997). *The placebo effect: an interdisciplinary exploration.* Cambridge, MA: Harvard University Press.

Hatfield, E., Cacioppo, J. T., and Rapson, R. L. (1994). *Emotional contagion.* Cambridge: Cambridge University Press.

Henningsen, P. and Kirmayer, L. J. (2000). Mind beyond the net: implications of cognitive neuroscience for cultural psychiatry. *Transcultural Psychiatry*, *37*(4), 467–494.

Ibarretxe-Antuñano, I. (1999). Metaphorical mappings in the sense of smell. In R. W. Gibbs Jr, and G. J. Steen (eds), *Metaphor in cognitive linguistics* (pp. 29–45). Amsterdam: John Benjamins.

Jackson, S. W. (1990). The imagination and psychological healing. *Journal of the History of the Behavioral Sciences*, *26*(4), 345–358.

Johnson, M. (1987). *The body in the mind: the bodily basis of meaning, imagination, and reason.* Chicago: University of Chicago Press.

Kemeny, M. E. and Miller, G. (1999). Effects of psychosocial interventions on the immune system. In M. Schedlowski and U. Tewes (eds), *Psychoneuroimmunology: an interdisciplinary introduction* (pp. 373–415). New York: Kluwer.

Kiecolt-Glaser, J. K. and Glaser, R. (1995). Psychoneuroimmunology and health consequences: data and shared mechanisms. *Psychosomatic Medicine*, *57*(3), 269–274.

Kirmayer, L. J. (1988). Mind and body as metaphors: hidden values in biomedicine. In M. Lock and D. Gordon (eds), *Biomedicine examined* (pp. 57–92). Dordrecht: Kluwer.

—— (1992). The body's insistence on meaning: metaphor as presentation and representation in illness experience. *Medical Anthropology Quarterly*, *6*(4), 323–346.

—— (1993). Healing and the invention of metaphor: the effectiveness of symbols revisited. *Culture, Medicine and Psychiatry*, *17*(2), 161–195.

—— (1994). Improvisation and authority in illness meaning. *Culture, Medicine and Psychiatry*, *18*(2), 183–214.

—— (1999). Rhetorics of the body: medically unexplained symptoms in sociocultural perspective. In Y. Ono, A. Janca, M. Asai, and N. Sartorius (eds), *Somatoform disorders – a worldwide perspective* (pp. 271–286). Tokyo: Springer-Verlag.

—— (2000). Broken narratives: clinical encounters and the poetics of illness experience. In C. Mattingly and L. Garro (eds), *Narrative and the cultural construction of illness and healing* (pp. 153–180). Berkeley: University of California Press.

Lakoff, G. and Johnson, M. (1999). *Philosophy in the flesh: the embodied mind and its challenge to western thought.* New York: Basic Books.

Lock, M. (1993). Cultivating the body: anthropology and epistemologies of bodily practice and knowledge. *Annual Review of Anthropology*, *22*, 133–135.

Maier, S. F. and Watkins, L. R. (1998). Cytokines for psychologists: implications of bidirectional immune-to-brain communication for understanding behavior, mood, and cognition. *Psychological Review*, *105*(1), 83–107.

Miller, G. E., Cohen, S., and Herbert, T. B. (1999). Pathways linking major depression and immunity in ambulatory female patients. *Psychosomatic Medicine*, *61*(6), 850–860.

Price, D. D., Milling, L. S., Kirsch, I., Duff, A., Montgomery, G. H., and Nicholls, S. S. (1999). An analysis of factors that contribute to the magnitude of placebo analgesia in an experimental paradigm. *Pain*, *83*(2), 147–156.

Radley, A. R. (1984). The embodiment of social relations in coronary heart disease. *Social Science and Medicine*, *19*(11), 1227.

Reid, J. and Reynolds, L. (1990). Requiem for RSI: the explanation and control of an occupational epidemic. *Medical Anthropology Quarterly*, *4*(2), 162–190.

Sacks, J. (1997). *The politics of hope*. London: Jonathan Cape.

Scheper-Hughes, N. and Lock, M. (1987). The mindful body: a prolegomenon to future work in medical anthropology. *Medical Anthropology Quarterly*, (n.s.) *1*(1), 6–41.

Silove, D., Chang, R., and Manicavasagar, V. (1995). Impact of recounting trauma stories on the emotional state of Cambodian refugees. *Psychiatric Services*, *46*(12), 1287–1288.

Solomon, S. D. (1999). Interventions for acute trauma response. *Current Opinion in Psychiatry*, *12*, 175–180.

Steiner, G. (1997). *Errata: an examined life*. London: Weidenfeld & Nicolson.

Summerfield, D. (1999). A critique of seven assumptions behind psychological trauma programmes in war affected areas. *Social Science and Medicine*, *48*(10), 1449–1462.

Tauber, A. I. (1997). *The immune self: theory or metaphor?* Cambridge: Cambridge University Press.

Taylor, G. J., Bagby, R. M., and Parker, J. D. A. (1997). *Disorders of affect regulation: alexithymia in medical and psychiatric illness*. Cambridge: Cambridge University Press.

Turner, M. (1996). *The literary mind*. New York: Oxford University Press.

Uchino, B. N., Caioppo, J. T., and Kiecolt-Glaser, J. (1996). The relationship between social support and physiological processes: a review with emphasis on underlying mechanisms and implications for health. *Psychological Bulletin*, *119*(3), 488–531.

Vaira, D., Miglioli, M., Mule, P., Holton, J., Menegatti, M., Vergura, M., Biasco, G., Conte, R., Logan, R. P., and Brabara, L. (1994). Prevalence of peptic ulcer disease in *Helicobacter pylori* positive blood donors. *Gut*, *35*, 309–312.

Varela, F. J. and Coutinko, A. (1991). Second generation immune networks. *Immunology Today*, *12*, 159–166.

——, ——, Dupire, B., and Vaz, N. N. (1988). Cognition and networks: immune neural, and otherwise. In A. S. Perelson (ed.), *Theoretical immunology* (vol. 2, pp. 359–375). Reading, MA: Addison-Wesley.

Ware, N. (1992). Suffering and the social construction of illness: the delegitimation of illness experience in chronic fatigue syndrome. *Medical Anthropology Quarterly*, *6*(4), 347–361.

Weinberg, S. (1992). *Dreams of a final theory: the search for the fundamental laws of nature*. New York: Pantheon Books.

White, L., Tursky, B., and Schwartz, G. E. (eds). (1985). *Placebo: theory, research, and mechanisms*. New York: Guilford Press.

Yardley, L. (ed.). (1997). *Material discourses of health and illness*. London: Routledge.

Index

Page numbers in *italic* indicate figures, tables, and plates; those in **bold** indicate major discussions.